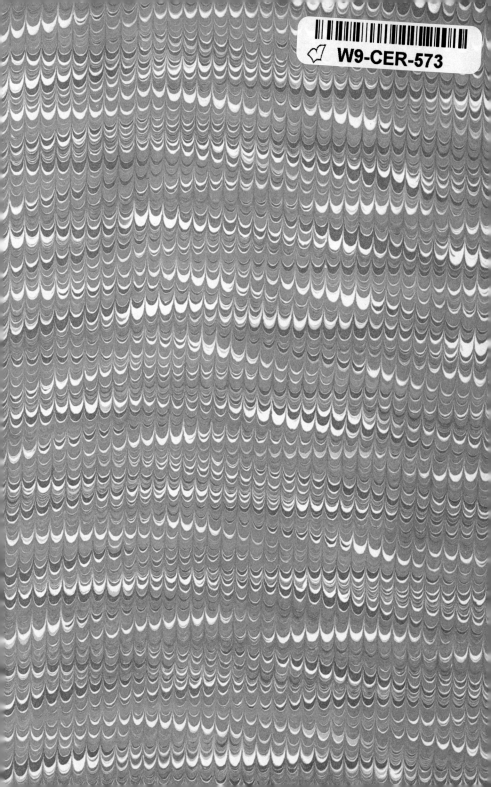

Reprinted 1984 from the 1906 edition.
Cover design © 1981 Time-Life Books Inc.
Library of Congress CIP data following page 480.

This volume is bound in leather.

CONFEDERATE OPERATIONS IN CANADA AND NEW YORK

JOHN W. HEADLEY
1900

Confederate Operations In Canada and New York

BY

JOHN W. HEADLEY

Illustrated by Portraits

NEW YORK AND WASHINGTON
THE NEALE PUBLISHING COMPANY
1906

TO THE MEMORY

OF THE

DEFENSELESS NON-COMBATANT PEOPLE OF THE
SOUTH WHO SUFFERED THE UNTOLD HORRORS OF
MERCILESS WARFARE—DESOLATION, DESTITUTION,
IMPRISONMENT OR DEATH; OF THE PERSECUTED
PEOPLE OF THE NORTH WHOSE SENSE OF JUSTICE
AND HUMANITY REVOLTED AT A CRUSADE FOR THE
CAUSE OF JOHN BROWN, AND OF HORACE GREELEY,
GERRIT SMITH AND CORNELIUS VANDERBILT,
THIS VOLUME IS REVERENTLY DEDICATED BY THE
AUTHOR.

ILLUSTRATIONS

CONTENTS

Chapter VIII

Chapter IX

Chapter X

Chapter XI

Chapter XII

Chapter XIII

Chapter XIV

Chapter XXII

Chapter XXIII

Chapter XXIV

Chapter XXV

Chapter XXVI

Chapter XXVII

Chapter XXVIII

Chapter XXIX

Chapter XXX

Chapter XXXI

Chapter XXXII

Chapter XXXIII

Chapter XXXIV

Chapter XXXV

Chapter XXXVI

Chapter XXXVII

Chapter XXXVIII

Chapter XXXIX

Chapter XL

Chapter XLI

Chapter XLII

Chapter XLIII

Chapter XLIV

Chapter XLV

Chapter XLVI

Chapter XLVII

INTRODUCTION

There is little consolation in relating the particulars of the hostile operations along the northern borders of the United States, by Confederate soldiers from Canada, who were assigned to this service by the authorities of the Confederate States in 1864.

And yet the authentic narrative of this desperate warfare which recalls and includes the cruel phases of the deplorable conflict may be due to the survivors and the dead of the North and the South who were military foes, and may serve as a lesson and a guide to the present and future generations of our reunited country in determining the price of peace and the pretexts for war.

All references that pertain to the conduct of the Federal Government and soldiers toward non-combatants are derived entirely from verified authority and the official records of the War Department of the United States. But little account of the engagements between the great armies is attempted. And it is deemed sufficient to submit the summaries of Generals Buell and Grant, the commanders of the two Federal armies at the battle of Shiloh, concerning the results of battles, the forces engaged, the morale of soldiers, and the cause of the war.

The military operations in the Department of Tennessee are noted partially from personal knowledge, but those west of the Mississippi River, being of like character under like conditions, are omitted. And besides, the commanders in both these Departments of the Confederacy appear to have missed opportunities alike at the critical period—1862-3, whilst Gen. Robert E. Lee was never driven, by generalship or numbers, from Virginia, but upon her bosom ended his struggle and breathed his last sigh as a soldier of the Southern Confederacy.

JOHN W. HEADLEY.

Louisville, Kentucky, 1906.

CONFEDERATE OPERATIONS IN CANADA AND NEW YORK

CHAPTER I

Election of Abraham Lincoln precipitates secession—Southern
Confederacy organized, Jefferson Davis chosen President
—Mr. Lincoln inaugurated—Attempt to reinforce Fort
Sumter—Fall of Fort Sumter—Beginning of the war—
Situation in Missouri, Maryland and Kentucky—President
Lincoln declares martial law.

The sectional animosities engendered by the agitation in
the Northern States for the abolition of African slavery
reached a climax upon the election of Abraham Lincoln to
the Presidency of the United States in November, 1860.
The Southern people construed this event to mean the freedom of their negroes. Indeed, the passions of the triumph-
ant party in the Northern States and their purposes were
no longer concealed.

The period of reason appeared to have passed and the
question was at once agitated in the South of withdrawing
from the Union and of organizing a new government on
the same basis as that of the United States, and accordingly
South Carolina initiated the movement by an Act of Secession from the Union, December 14, 1860. Other States
followed, and a provisional new government was formed
by delegates from South Carolina, Georgia, Florida, Alabama, Mississippi, Louisiana, and Texas, who assembled in
convention at Montgomery, Alabama. Jefferson Davis was
chosen President, and Alexander H. Stephens, of Georgia,
Vice-President, on the 9th of February, 1861.

In his inaugural address, February 18, 1861, Mr. Davis set forth the objects and purposes of the new General Government, which was called "The Confederate States of America." In part he said:

*   *   *   *   *   *   *

Our present condition, achieved in a manner unprecedented in the history of nations, illustrates the American idea that governments rest upon the consent of the governed, and that it is the right of the people to alter or abolish governments whenever they become destructive of the ends for which they were established.

Through many years of controversy with our late associates, the Northern States, we have vainly endeavored to secure tranquillity, and to obtain respect for the rights to which we were entitled. As a necessity, not a choice, we have resorted to the remedy of separation; and henceforth our energies must be directed to the conduct of our own affairs, and the perpetuity of the Confederacy which we have formed.

If a just perception of mutual interest shall permit us peaceably to pursue our separate career, my most earnest desire will have been fulfilled; but if this is denied us, and the integrity of our territory and jurisdiction be assailed, it will but remain for us, with firm resolve, to appeal to arms, and invoke the blessings of Providence on a just cause.

*   *   *   *   *   *   *

We have changed the constituent parts, but not the system of our Government. The Constitution formed by our fathers is that of these Confederate States, in their exposition of it; and, in the judicial construction it has received, we have a light which reveals its true meaning.

President Lincoln, in his inaugural address on March 4, 1861, said:

Apprehension seems to exist among the people of the Southern States that, by the accession of a Republican Administration, their property and their peace and personal security are to be endangered. There has never been any cause for such apprehensions.

Indeed, the most ample evidence to the contrary has all the while existed and been open to their inspection. It is found in nearly all the public speeches of him who addresses you. I do but quote from one of those speeches when I declare that I have no purpose, directly or indirectly, to interfere with the institution of slavery in the States where it exists. I believe I have no lawful right to do so, and I have no inclination to do so. Those who nominated and elected me did so with full knowledge that I had made this and many similar declarations, and had never recanted them. And more than this, they placed in the platform for my acceptance, and as a law to themselves and to me, the clear and emphatic resolution which I now read:

"*Resolved,* That the maintenance inviolate of the rights of the States, and especially the right of each State to order and control its own domestic institutions according to its own judgment exclusively, is essential to that balance of power on which the perfection and endurance of our political fabric depend, and we denounce the lawless invasion by armed force of the soil of any State or Territory, no matter under what pretext, as among the gravest crimes."

* * * * * * *

However, President Lincoln at once began the preparations for reinforcing Fort Sumter. Eleven vessels were fitted up and loaded with several thousand troops, arms, and supplies. They were instructed to reinforce Major Anderson at Fort Sumter, peaceably if they could, but by force if they must. Just before they arrived, General Beauregard, in command at Charleston, reduced the Fort, and the garrison surrendered, upon honorable terms, April 13, 1861, without the loss of life on either side.

On the 15th of April, 1861, two days after the fall of Fort Sumter, President Lincoln issued a proclamation, calling for seventy-five thousand troops, in which he said:

I appeal to all loyal citizens to favor, facilitate and aid this effort to maintain the honor, the integrity, and the existence of our National Union, and the perpetuity of popular government, and to redress *wrongs already long endured.*

* * * * * * *

And I hereby command the persons composing the combinations aforesaid to disperse and retire peaceably to their respective abodes within twenty days from this date.

The States of Virginia, Tennessee, Arkansas and North Carolina at once proceeded to enter the Confederacy.

The Provisional Government organized at Montgomery was merged into a permanent Government, with no special changes except the removal of the capital to Richmond, Virginia.

It was with rivalry that the volunteers in the Southern States were organized and rushed into the conflict. And likewise in the Northern States. Indeed, active preparations were being made from the day of the inauguration of the new Presidents.

Gen. John C. Fremont was one of the first generals appointed by President Lincoln, and was assigned to the command of the Department of the West, in which Ohio and Kentucky were included. His headquarters was established at St. Louis.

The State Administration, including the militia, was openly arrayed against the Union in Missouri. General Fremont was confronted from the start by a condition of revolt against his authority, and his military jurisdiction in the State was practically limited to St. Louis for some time.

General Fremont says when he parted from the President in Washington to assume his command in the West that Mr. Lincoln said:

I have given you carte blanche. You must use your own judgment and do the best you can. I doubt if the States will ever come back.

General Fremont, therefore, within a few months deemed it advisable to issue a proclamation declaring martial law, from which the following extracts are quoted:

St. Louis, August 30, 1861.

* * * * * * *

All persons who shall be taken with arms in their hands within these lines shall be tried by court-martial, and if found guilty will be shot.

The property, real and personal, of all persons, in the State of Missouri, who shall take up arms against the United States, or who shall be directly proven to have taken an active part with their enemies in the field, is declared confiscated to the public use, and their slaves, if they have any, are hereby declared free men.

All persons who shall be proven to have destroyed, after the publication of this order, railroad tracks, bridges, or telegraphs, shall suffer the extreme penalty of the law.

All persons engaged in treasonable correspondence, in giving or procuring aid to the enemies of the United States, in fomenting tumults, in disturbing the public tranquillity by creating and circulating false reports or incendiary documents, are in their own interest warned that they are exposing themselves to sudden and severe punishment.

All persons who have been led away from their allegiance, are required to return to their homes forthwith; any such absence, without sufficient cause, will be held to be presumptive evidence against them.

The object of this declaration is to place in the hands of the military authorities the power to give instantaneous effect to existing laws, and to supply such deficiencies as the conditions of war demand.

* * * * * * *

Gen. Jeff. Thompson, then in command of the Missouri militia forces about St. Louis, at once issued the following proclamation of retaliation:

HEADQUARTERS FIRST MILITARY DISTRICT MO.

ST. LOUIS, August 31, 1861.

To All Whom It May Concern:

Whereas, Maj.-Gen. John C. Fremont, commanding the minions of Abraham Lincoln in the State of Missouri, has seen fit to declare martial law throughout the whole State, and has threatened to shoot any citizen-soldier found in arms within certain limits; also, to confiscate the property and free the negroes belonging to the members of the Missouri State Guard:

Therefore, know ye, that I, M. Jeff. Thompson, Brigadier-General of the First Military District of Missouri, having not only the military authority of brigadier-general, but certain police powers granted by Acting-Governor Thomas C. Reynolds, and confirmed afterward by Governor Jackson, do most solemnly promise that for every member of the Missouri State

Guard, or soldier of our allies, the armies of the Confederate States, who shall be put to death in pursuance of the said order of General Fremont, I will hang, draw, and quarter a minion of said Abraham Lincoln.

While I am anxious that this unfortunate war shall be conducted, if possible, upon the most liberal principles of civilized warfare, and every order that I have issued has been with that object—yet, if this rule is to be adopted (and it must first be done by our enemies), I intend to exceed General Fremont in his excesses, and will make all tories that come within my reach rue the day that a different policy was adopted by their leaders.

Already mills, barns, warehouses, and other private property have been wastefully and wantonly destroyed by the enemy in this district, while we have taken nothing except articles contraband or absolutely necessary. Should these things be repeated, I will retaliate ten-fold, so help me God.

M. Jeff. Thompson,
Brigadier-General Commanding.

President Lincoln wrote:

(private).

Washington, D. C., September 2, 1861.

My Dear Sir: Two points in your proclamation of August 30th give me some anxiety:

First. Should you shoot a man according to the proclamation, the Confederates would very certainly shoot our best man in their hands, in retaliation; and so, man for man, indefinitely. It is, therefore, my order that you allow no man to be shot under the proclamation without first having my approbation or consent.

Second. I think there is great danger that the closing paragraph, in relation to the confiscation of property, and the liberating of slaves of traitorous owners, will alarm our Southern Union friends, and turn them against us; perhaps ruin our rather fair prospect for Kentucky.

Allow me, therefore, to ask that you will, as of your own motion, modify that paragraph so as to conform to the first and fourth sections of the Act of Congress entitled, "An Act to Confiscate Property Used for Insurrectionary Purposes," approved August 6, 1861, a copy of which Act I herewith send you.

This letter is written in a *spirit of caution, and not of censure.* I send it by a special messenger, so that it may certainly and speedily reach you.

Yours very truly,
A. LINCOLN.

Major-General FREMONT.

General Fremont replied to President Lincoln's suggestions, in a long letter, from which I make extracts:

HEADQUARTERS WESTERN DEPARTMENT.

ST. LOUIS, September 8, 1861.

MY DEAR SIR: Your letter of the second, by special messenger, I know to have been written before you had received my letter, and before my telegraphic dispatches and rapid developments of critical conditions here had informed you of affairs in this quarter.

* * * * * * *

This is as much a movement in the war, as a battle, and, in going into these, I shall have to act according to my judgment of the ground before me, as I did on this occasion.

* * * * * * *

If I were to retract of my own accord, it would imply that I myself thought it wrong, and that I had acted without the reflection which the gravity of the point demanded. But I did not. I acted with full deliberation, and upon the certain conviction that it was a measure right and necessary, and I think so still.

In regard to the other point of the proclamation to which you refer, I desire to say that I do not think the enemy can either misconstrue or urge anything against it, or undertake to make unusual retaliation. The shooting of men who shall rise in arms against an army in the military occupation of a country, is merely a necessary measure of defense, and entirely according to the usages of civilized warfare. The article does not at all refer to prisoners of war and certainly our enemies have no grounds for requiring that we should waive in their benefit any of the ordinary advantages which the usages of war allow us.

As promptitude is itself an advantage in war, I have also to ask that you will permit me to carry out upon the spot the provisions of the proclamation in this respect.

I am, with respect and regard,

Very truly yours,
J. C. FREMONT.

THE PRESIDENT.

President Lincoln rejoined, as follows:

WASHINGTON, September 11, 1861.

SIR: Yours of the 8th, in answer to mine of the 2nd instant, is just received. Assuming that you, upon the ground, could better judge of the necessities of your position than I could at this distance, on *seeing your proclamation of August 30th, I perceived no general objection to it.*

The particular clause, however, in relation to the confiscation of property and the liberation of slaves, appeared to me to be objectionable in its non-conformity to the Act of Congress, passed the 6th of last August, upon the same subjects; and hence I wrote you expressing my wish that that clause should be modified accordingly.

Your answer, just received, expresses the preference, on your part, that I should make an open order for the modification, which I very cheerfully do.

It is therefore ordered, that the said clause of said proclamation be so modified, held and construed to conform to, and not to transcend, the provisions on the same subject contained in the Act of Congress entitled, "An Act to Confiscate Property Used for Insurrectionary Purposes," approved August 6th, 1861, and that said Act be published at length with this order.

Your obedient servant,

A. LINCOLN.

Major-General JOHN C. FREMONT.

Practically the same conditions existed in Maryland and Kentucky.

The legislatures of both States were assembled to consider the Act of Secession. In Maryland there was little doubt that the Act would be passed.

On the same day that Mr. Lincoln wrote to General Fremont, the following order was issued to Gen. Nathaniel P. Banks:

WAR DEPARTMENT, September 11, 1861.

GENERAL: The passage of an Act of Secession by the Legislature of Maryland must be prevented. If necessary, all or any part of the members must be arrested. Exercise your own judgment as to the time and manner but do the work effectually.

Very respectfully your obedient servant,

SIMON CAMERON,

Secretary of War.

The General Assembly of Kentucky had adopted a resolution declaring "that Kentucky should maintain a strict neutrality during the contest between the North and the South." This was the position of the Union men of the Legislature. A Union mass meeting, held in Louisville and attended by persons from all parts of the State, issued an address affirming the same position.

A regiment of infantry recruited, armed, and equipped at Louisville by Col. Blanton Duncan, with Thomas H. Taylor, lieutenant-colonel, had already volunteered and enlisted under General Beauregard in Virginia.

Meantime, President Lincoln had issued his proclamation declaring martial law, and citizens were arrested for disloyalty in all the border States. They were requested to take an oath of allegiance to the United States or were committed to prison.

CHAPTER II

Battle of Bull Run—Armies invade Kentucky—Author enlists—Military operations in Kentucky.

During this period the ports of the Confederacy had been blockaded by the warships of the United States. The Confederate States had been recognized as belligerents by the Governments of Great Britain and France, and the hostile armies had been engaged in actual warfare in Virginia and Missouri. But the army of the Confederacy was at Manassas under General Beauregard and in the Shenandoah Valley under Gen. Joseph E. Johnston. General McDowell advanced his army from Washington and on the 21st of July attacked Beauregard. General Johnston arrived on the field with his troops in the afternoon, when the battle resulted in the defeat and rout of McDowell's army. The stampede continued to Washington City without pursuit by the Confederates. General McDowell reported to the War Department as follows:

FAIRFAX COURT HOUSE, July 21, 1861.
The men have thrown away their haversacks in the battle and left them behind; they are without food, have eaten nothing since breakfast. We are without artillery ammunition. The larger part of the men are a confused mob—entirely demoralized. It was the opinion of all the commanders that no stand could be made this side of the Potomac. We will, however, make the attempt at Fairfax Court House. From a prisoner we learned that 20,000 from Johnston joined last night and they march on us to-night.

IRWIN McDOWELL.

Again General McDowell dispatches:

FAIRFAX COURT HOUSE, July 22, 1861.
Many of the volunteers did not wait for authority to proceed to the Potomac, but left on their own decision. They are now

pouring through this place in a state of utter disorganization. They could not be prepared for action by to-morrow morning even if they were willing. I learn from prisoners that we are to be pressed here to-night and to-morrow morning, as the enemy's force is very large and they are elated. I think we heard cannon on our rear-guard. I think now, as all my commanders thought at Centerville, there is no alternative but to fall back to the Potomac, and I shall proceed to do so with as much regularity as possible.

IRWIN McDOWELL.

This event electrified the heart of the South and aroused the war spirit in the border States to such a degree that the drastic measures of the Federal authorities recorded in the preceding chapter were doubtless deemed essential to prevent the regular secession of Missouri, Maryland and Kentucky. Meanwhile, there had been organization on the northern and southern borders of Kentucky, and volunteers were enlisting on both sides.

Finally the Union army moved into Kentucky and advanced to Munfordsville under Brig.-Gen. W. T. Sherman, with Brig.-Gen. George H. Thomas on the left at Lebanon and Columbia, while on the right, posts were established at Owensboro, Calhoun, Henderson and Paducah, and also at Cairo, Illinois, under Brig.-Gen. U. S. Grant—the whole under Gen. Henry W. Halleck at St. Louis, he having succeeded General Fremont.

The Confederate army under command of Gen. Albert Sidney Johnston promptly advanced from Nashville to Bowling Green with Brig.-Gen. Felix Zollicoffer on the right toward Cumberland Gap, while on the left, troops were posted at Hopkinsville, Fort Henry and Fort Donelson, Tennessee, and also at Columbus, Kentucky, under Brig.-Gen. Leonidas Polk.

It will be observed that these opposing forces extended along a line from the Mississippi River to Cumberland Gap, a distance of perhaps 300 miles.

The presence of both armies created intense excitement in Kentucky. Neighbors and members of the same families became aroused against each other. Volunteers singly or in squads from every neighborhood rushed to both armies, and were soon organized into companies, regiments and brigades.

At this juncture I left my home in Hopkins County to join the Confederates at Hopkinsville. I found Brig.-Gen. James L. Alcorn of Mississippi in command. The First Mississippi Infantry was here under Col. John T. Simonton and Lieutenant-Colonel Davidson. There were two companies of cavalry under Capt. Ned Merriweather and Capt. Gowan Bell, nearly all the men recruited from Christian County. But in another camp were about one hundred cavalry under Capt. James K. Huey of Smithland.

Most of these men were from Hopkins and Webster counties, and many of them my neighbors, some being relations, and I located with them at once. The company was sworn in under Captain Huey by General Alcorn on October 21, 1861, for one year.

I had been restless all the summer because I could not conveniently leave to volunteer, having been detained on account of my father's business, being his reliance in a store at Nebo, his home being four miles distant, on a farm. I had been afraid the independence of the Confederacy would be acknowledged and the war ended before I could get in it. I was now satisfied at last.

About this time an encampment was located at Saratoga Springs in Lyon County, where W. D. Wilcox and Benjamin D. Terry had recruited about 150 cavalry for the Confederacy, with a good prospect of a battalion or regiment.

But a transport, accompanied by a gunboat, came up the Cumberland River from Smithland with a command of Federals under Major Phillips. They were landed after midnight within five miles of Saratoga Springs. At daybreak they attacked the encampment. The sleeping men were not only surprised but unarmed, excepting a few who had double-barreled shotguns and some with pistols. There was consternation for a few moments after the first volley of the enemy was fired, but a dash was instantly made to escape, led by

Captains Terry and Wilcox. The casualties of the Southerners were three killed and eight wounded. The remainder and a number of horses were captured. Captain Wilcox was wounded, but he and Captain Terry reached Hopkinsville safely with a hundred of the men. I saw them on their arrival, and though fatigued they were in the best of spirits. The command was at once enlisted for three years, or the war, and organized in one company. W. D. Wilcox was elected captain and Benjamin D. Terry first lieutenant. This was perhaps the first hostile encounter and the first loss of life in Kentucky.

The members of all these cavalry companies furnished their own horses and generally their own shotguns and other equipments.

Early in November a battalion of cavalry arrived from Fort Henry under command of Lieut.-Col. N. B. Forrest and Maj. D. C. Kelly, and encamped on the other side of the town.

A short while after the arrival of Forrest at Hopkinsville he started with about three hundred men toward Henderson, Lieutenant Wallace with some twenty of Huey's company being of the number. At Marion Forrest learned that a prominent friend of the South had been arrested and sent away to prison on the information of Jonathan Belt, an enthusiastic Union man. With a detachment, Forrest went to arrest Belt and hold him as a hostage. As they proceeded on the way, Forrest and Dr. Van Wyck, surgeon of the regiment, rode in front. When they reached Belt's house he was inside, and, firing upon the advance, he killed Dr. Van Wyck. Belt then ran out through the back of his premises and escaped.

There was now a quiet time for several weeks at Hopkinsville, when all the troops went into winter quarters. This, however, was a monotonous existence for the class of men composing our company. Perhaps half of them had left a wife and children behind and all of them comfortable homes. Some were wealthy for that country, but in the enthusiasm of the moment had rushed into the war for Southern independence.

The regiment of Colonel Forrest had now been joined by two additional companies from Alabama, commanded by Captains Davis and McDonald, and one company from Tennessee, commanded by Captain Starnes. It was now composed of ten companies, with a total strength of eight hundred men.

Early in Christmas week Colonel Forrest was sent with about three hundred men, including thirty men from the company of Captain Merriweather, in the direction of Calhoun. In Muhlenburg County, Forrest heard a cavalry command of the enemy, estimated at four hundred, was on the road between Greenville and Sacramento. He overtook them near the latter place and found them formed across the road in line of battle. Forrest now halted and prepared for action. He sent Captain Starnes with about forty men to the left and Major Kelly with a similar number to the right to attack both flanks. At the same moment Forrest moved his main line forward with sabers drawn, and charged the enemy's front. The attack was simultaneous and the enemy did not wait to meet the assault. Their line broke up in confusion and stampeded through the town of Sacramento, with the Confederates yelling and pressing the pursuit, Forrest, Merriweather and Starnes being in the lead. They soon began to overtake and slay those in the rear who did not surrender.

Some two miles beyond Sacramento the Federal commander rallied a portion of his command, after passing through a lane that ran over a ridge that crossed a farm. As Forrest and his followers reached the top of the ridge in the lane and found the enemy forming some two hundred yards distant, at the end of the lane, they did not halt or wait for all the command to come up, but Forrest dashed forward at the head of his foremost men, formed in column of fours, and went headlong into the enemy with sabers and pistols, forcing a hand-to-hand combat. Captain Merriweather at Forrest's side fell dead with a ball through the head. Forrest being surrounded by his desperate foes, slew Captain Bacon with his saber, who fell from his horse. But Forrest's men rushed to his aid, and one named Terry fell dead at the hands of Captain Davis of the Federal force. Forrest dashed at the Captain with such force that their horses collided and both went down. Davis was disabled and surrendered. Forrest was up and remounted instantly. But there was nothing more to do. Captain Starnes and others who composed the advance had made common cause with Forrest.

All who rallied around Bacon and Davis for this desperate struggle with Forrest and his men had been killed, wounded or captured. And here the conflict ended. The Confederates had three men wounded. The struggle had not lasted over fifteen minutes. Though an insignificant affair it was regarded at the time as the most sensational and romantic fight of the war, and the daring and intrepidity of Forrest in this, his first battle, brought him instant fame.

Early in January, 1862, Gen. George B. Crittenden succeeded Gen. Felix Zollicoffer in command of the little army on the Upper Cumberland encamped at Mill Spring.

Gen. George H. Thomas advanced his column from Lebanon and through Columbia to a point within ten miles of Crittenden. Crittenden moved forward and attacked. A desperate engagement ensued, which finally resulted in the defeat of Crittenden, who retreated to his entrenched camp at Mill Spring. But upon the approach of Thomas with a superior force the Confederates evacuated their position and their retreat became a rout. General Zollicoffer was among the killed. The Confederate command was practically scattered for the time being, leaving the Federals in possession of that part of Kentucky.

During this period General Alcorn was relieved and was succeeded at Hopkinsville by Gen. Charles Clark of Mississippi. General Sherman had been relieved of his command in Kentucky and succeeded by Gen. Don Carlos Buell.

The other operations in this section during the past three months had not been of great importance excepting the battle of Belmont, Missouri, on the Mississippi River. Brig.-Gen. U. S. Grant, in command at Cairo, Illinois, had conveyed his forces on steamboats down the river and disembarked on the Missouri side several miles above Columbus, Kentucky. He then moved down to make a demonstration against the Confederate position across the river, but Maj.-Gen. Leonidas Polk managed to get his forces ferried over and attacked Grant at Belmont. After a spirited battle Grant retreated to his boats and returned to Cairo.

CHAPTER III

Battle and surrender of Fort Donelson—Grant absent during the battle—Forrest refuses to surrender and escapes and is followed by over half his regiment.

We were surprised by the announcement that General Grant in command of an expedition up the Tennessee River had surrounded and captured Gen. Lloyd Tilghman and one hundred men at Fort Henry on the 6th of February, 1862. The only comfort we got out of the disaster was the escape of the greater part of the garrison. We realized that the Federal army was seventy-five miles in our rear. The fall of Fort Henry opened the way for the Federals up the river to Mississippi and Alabama. The next morning early we marched through Hopkinsville and out the turnpike leading to Clarksville, Tennessee. The company was disbanded to go in squads through the country to find accommodations and report next morning at Clarksville. We learned at Clarksville that a Confederate army was assembling at Dover to defend Fort Donelson, which was located two miles below the town on the Cumberland River. We arrived at the ferry landing opposite Dover about an hour before night. It was after dark when we got across and went into camp with Forrest.

Colonel Forrest went out the Fort Henry road the next afternoon to reconnoiter. After going about three miles we were marching through a short lane, when a single shot was fired. The head of the command pushed forward and the order was passed back down the line to form fours and close up ranks. The regiment rode in a gallop for half a mile or more. The whole command in front seemed to be breaking ranks in some confusion and when we got up it was found that a Federal cavalryman had been captured by Wm. Davis, of our company, and he too had fired the first shot, being at the head of the advance guard when it met the Federal scouts. We went out again the next morning on the Fort Henry road and had gone about a mile when there were several shots at the head of the column and a halt. Colonel Forrest hurried from the right along the front of the line, and as he halted at our company on the left and was talking to Captain Huey, Major Kelly galloped up and reported something to Forrest. I was designated to take six men and go forward. Forrest directed me to deploy the men fifty yards apart, going in the center myself along the road, with three men off in the woods on each side, and when we came upon the enemy to fire and fall back after observing closely all the troops in sight. We proceeded for half a mile without seeing or hearing of the enemy, when we were called back.

Forrest seemed very busy along the line, and in a few minutes dismounted a part of it. He then galloped to Captain Huey and ordered him to follow with his company. We filed around to the right through the woods and went a hundred yards, halting and forming a line fronting a little hill. Forrest went back to the regiment but returned presently with Major Kelly and two companions. They hurried by, passing in the rear of our line, halting about a hundred yards to our right on higher ground, and began to form in line. Forrest then came back, ordered Captain Huey to take the hill in front of us, and galloped on to the other part of the regiment he had left in the original position.

Captain Huey had about got ready, when suddenly a volley was poured from the hill, about seventy-five yards distant, into our ranks. I heard something strike with a dull spat on my left. Tiller Younger was next to me, and said he was shot through the left arm. When I turned and looked up, I saw that the whole company had given way in some confusion. I called to the men to come up in line and they rallied quick as a flash, every man to his place. The confusion had all been caused by the frightened horses. Captain

Huey had just got the line dressed, when Major Kelly charged the hill with his two companies and went within fifty yards of the Federals, who fired two volleys into his ranks and then opened on him with a piece of artillery, when he fell back in disorder, but quickly rallied and maintained his position. His charge saved our company from the same experience. A number of his men were wounded and several horses killed. Before our company did anything Forrest withdrew the whole command, which marched back within our lines.

The Federals brought several pieces of artillery in sight, half a mile from our trenches, and began to throw shells into our works. It was a straggling fire, however, and met with no response from our artillery. But the booming of the enemy's cannon served to rouse all our forces.

It was now settled that Grant's army was arriving and taking position in our front. Next morning, the 13th, we expected a battle in earnest. The enemy opened with artillery early and continued a desultory cannonade. Several feeble attempts were made by infantry on our works, and one by at least a brigade, which was repulsed after renewed assaults, with considerable loss to the enemy and some in our trenches.

On the 14th the armies remained quiet. The enemy's fleet of gunboats, however, attacked the Fort in the afternoon, but was badly crippled and retired down the river.

It appears that General Grant left his army about daylight on the 15th to visit Commander Foote (who was wounded and desired a conference) on his gunboat about seven miles below and did not return until about three o'clock in the afternoon.

Meanwhile, Gen. Gideon S. Pillow moved our army out of our works from the right center all round on the left and attacked Grant's right wing. Captain Huey's company was detailed as an escort for Gen. John B. Floyd, who was in chief command, but we viewed the battle from a safe position. It was an exciting scene to witness the contest for hours not more than half a mile away.

About two o'clock in the afternoon the enemy retreated toward the Tennessee River, according to our information on the field, and our army returned to the trenches. Late in the afternoon the enemy, by an assault with a division, gained a foothold on Fort Donelson hill, but was checked and partially dislodged by General Buckner. Colonel Forrest and all the cavalry except Captain Huey's company had been in the thickest of the battle.

General Grant says:

After these mishaps to the fleet I concluded to make the investment of Fort Donelson as perfect as possible, and partially fortify, and await repairs to the gunboats.

$$* \quad * \quad * \quad * \quad * \quad * \quad *$$

On the morning of the 15th, before it was yet broad day, a messenger from Flag-officer Foote handed me a note, expressing a desire to see me on the flag-ship, and saying that he had been injured the day before so much that he could not come himself to me. I at once made my preparations for starting.

When I reached the fleet I found the flag-ship was anchored out in the stream. A small boat, however, awaited my arrival and I was soon on board with the flag-officer.

I saw the absolute necessity of his gunboats going into hospital and did not know but I should be forced to the alternative of going through a siege. But the enemy relieved me from this necessity.

When I left the National line to visit Flag-officer Foote I had no idea that there would be an engagement on land unless I brought it on myself.

From the 12th to the 14th we had but 15,000 men of all arms and no gunboats. Now we had been reinforced by a fleet of six naval vessels, a large division of troops under Gen. L. Wallace, and 2,500 men brought over from Fort Henry belonging to the division of C. F. Smith. The enemy, however, had taken the initiative. Just as I landed I met Captain Hillyer, of my staff, white with fear, not for his personal safety, but for the safety of the National troops. He said the enemy had come out of his lines in full force and attacked and scattered McClernand's division, which was in full retreat.

The attack had been made on the National right. I was some four or five miles north of our left. The line was about three miles long.

The enemy had come out in full force to cut his way out and make his escape. McClernand's division had to bear the brunt of the attack of this combined force.

The division broke and a portion fled, but most of the men, as they were not pursued, only fell back out of the range of the fire of the enemy.

At all events, the enemy fell back within his entrenchments and was there when I got on the field. I saw men standing in knots talking in the most excited manner. No officer seemed to be giving any directions. The soldiers had their muskets, but no ammunition, while there were tons of it close at hand.

I was awakened in the night by confusion in our tent and horses tramping the frozen snow outside. I was told that Floyd, Pillow, and Buckner were going to surrender the army at sunrise next morning. It was said that Forrest was sent for and told that an overwhelming force had been extended on the line from the river above Dover, around to Hickman Creek, below Fort Donelson, and no alternative remained but a surrender. Forrest notified them that he would take his men and cut through Grant's lines. He had notified all the captains of the companies that every member of the regiment could remain and surrender or follow him and take the chances of escape. When I got outside and saddled my horse all were gone.

I rode in the dark to find the company. There was so much talking and calling in all directions, I wandered around for several minutes before I could locate it. I hurried on and heard the voice of Captain Huey, but before I got to him I observed a column of cavalry approaching, and rode to see where it was going. Forrest was at the head. I asked him if it was true that he was going out. "I am going to try," he said. "When will you start, Colonel?" I asked. "I am going now," he answered. I hurried to find the company. I met several and told them I was going with Forrest. I found the company breaking ranks in confusion. Forrest's column had passed on. It was a little cloudy and so dark we must get with him then or get left. I got Isaac M. Bowers, who said he roused me as he left the tent. We caught up with Forrest at once.

After we had gone about a mile there was a halt. An order was whispered along down the line that there must be absolute quiet and to close up ranks. We rested here a little while and again moved forward slowly. No lights were in view anywhere in the direction of the enemy and yet I judged we must be nearing their line, from the distance we had come, and besides we seemed to be moving very cautiously. Presently there was a strange noise toward the head of the column. It could soon be understood that the horses in front were in water, and it was not long till we came to it. It was in woods and dark as pitch, but in we went, following the noise ahead of us. The deepest place I struck was about half way up my saddle skirts. When we reached the other side the command was going forward in a trot and we closed up promptly. Day was just breaking. I observed Major Kelly and a citizen on the roadside after we came out of the water, at a little distance on the right. They had halted at the intersection of the road from Cumberland City to Dover. There were only forty-two of our company, including Captain Huey, that had followed Forrest. Forrest had only about half of his regiment.

Colonel Forrest tells the true story of the battle and his opinion of the surrender was the opinion of the soldiers. He says in his official report:

During the night I was called into council with the generals commanding, when it was determined to bring on the attack the next day by again passing our entrenchments and attacking the enemy's right.

In the early gray of the morning I moved to the attack, the cavalry on the left and in the advance. I found the enemy prepared to receive us, and were again engaged with the sharp-shooters till our infantry were formed for the attack, the first gun from the enemy killing a horse in my regiment. General B. R. Johnson, commanding the left, which now moved to the front. An obstinate fight of two hours ended in the retreat of the enemy. The undergrowth was so thick I could scarcely press my horse through it. Finding that the flank of the enemy in retreat was exposed across an open field to my front and left, I immediately led my cavalry to the field, but found the ground a marsh, and we were unable to pass it.

The enemy formed in the edge of a second field to our front and right, and flanking the left of our advancing line of infantry. We could not move to flank them, but by maneuvering to their front and right doubtless prevented their attempting a flank movement on our infantry. Finding that our advancing line of infantry would cut them off, while the cavalry prevented their flanking us, they commenced a retreat, accompanied by their cavalry, which we could now see in the distance, but not participating during the day in the fight. Our infantry had now driven them near a mile, they doggedly disputing the whole ground, leaving dead and wounded scattered through the woods and fields up to the ravine. The enemy, leaving their third position for the first time, retreated in great haste, advancing by a road through a ravine. I here passed our line of infantry with my command moving in the center.

I charged the enemy's battery of six guns, which had kept several of our regiments in check for several hours, killing and slaughtering a great many of our men. I captured the battery, killing most of the men and horses. I then immediately moved on the flank of the enemy, obstinately maintaining their position. They finally gave way, our infantry and cavalry both charging them at the same time, committing great slaughter. Moving still farther to our right, I found a regiment of our infantry in confusion, which I relieved by charging the enemy to their front. Here sixty-four of the enemy were found in forty yards square. General Pillow, coming up, ordered me to charge the enemy in a ravine. I charged by squadrons, filing the first company of each squadron to the right, and the second to the left, on reaching the ravine, firing and falling in the rear of the third squadron until the three squadrons had charged. We here completely routed the enemy, leaving some two hundred dead in the hollow, accomplishing what three different regiments had failed to do. Seeing the enemy's battery to our right about to turn on us, I now ordered a charge on this battery, from which we drove the enemy, capturing two guns. Following down the ravine, captured the third, which they were endeavoring to carry off, gunners and drivers retreating up the hill. In this charge I killed about fifty sharpshooters, who were supporting the guns. I ordered forward a number of scouts, who, returning, informed me that the enemy, with three guns and three regiments of infantry, were moving up by the road from Fort Henry. We had driven the enemy back without a reverse from the left of our entrenchments in the center, having opened three different roads by which we might have retired if the generals had, as was deemed best in the council the night before, ordered the retreat of the army. Informing General Pillow of the position the enemy had taken, he ordered two new regiments and one of the regiments in the field, with one piece of artillery, to attack the enemy.

The fight here ended about 2.30 p. m. without any change in our relative positions. We were employed the remainder of the evening in gathering up arms, and assisting in getting off the wounded. I was three times over the battlefield, and late in the evening was two miles up the river on the road to the ford. There were none of the enemy in sight when dark came on. SATURDAY NIGHT OUR TROOPS SLEPT, FLUSHED WITH VICTORY, AND CONFIDENT THEY COULD DRIVE THE ENEMY TO THE TENNESSEE RIVER THE NEXT MORNING.

About 12 o'clock at night I was called in council with the generals, who had under discussion the surrender of the fort. They reported that the enemy had received 11,000 reinforcements since the fight. They supposed the enemy had returned to the positions they had occupied the day before.

I returned to my quarters and sent out two men, who, going by a road up the bank of the river, returned without seeing any of the enemy, *only fires, which I believed to be the old camp-fires, and so stated to the generals; the wind, being very high, had fanned them into a blaze.*

When I returned General Buckner stated he could not hold his position. Generals Floyd and Pillow gave up the responsibility of the command to him, and I told them that I neither could nor would surrender my command. General Pillow then said I could cut my way out if I chose to do so, and he and General Floyd agreed to come out with me. I got my command ready and reported at headquarters. General Floyd informed me that General Pillow had left, and that he would go by boat.

I moved out by the road we had gone out the morning before. When about a mile out crossed a deep slough from the river, saddle-skirt deep, and filed into the sand road to Cumberland Iron Works. I ordered Major Kelly and Adjutant Schuyler to remain at the point where we entered this road with one company, where the enemy's cavalry would attack if they attempted to follow us. They remained until day was dawning.

Over 500 cavalry had passed, a company of artillery horses had followed, and a number of men from different regiments, passing over hard frozen ground. More than two hours had been occupied in passing. Not a gun had been fired at us. No enemy had been seen or heard.

The enemy could not have reinvested their former position without traveling a considerable distance and camped upon the dead and dying, as there had been great slaughter upon that portion of the field, and I am clearly of the opinion that two-thirds of our army could have marched out without loss, and that, had we continued the fight the next day, we should have gained a glorious victory, as our troops were in fine spirits, believing we had whipped them, and the roads through which we came were open as late as 8 o'clock Sunday morning, as many of my men, who came out afterwards, report.

* * * * * * *

N. B. FORREST,
Colonel, Commanding Forrest's Regiment of Cavalry.

CHAPTER IV

Evacuation of Tennessee by Confederates—Battle of Shiloh—
Campaign in Virginia—Buell in North Alabama—Bragg at
Chattanooga—Forrest and Morgan in Buell's rear—Bragg
and Kirby Smith invade Kentucky.

At Nashville there was confusion and demoralization.
Gen. Albert Sidney Johnston was here and his army was
arriving from Bowling Green. The soldiers were indignant
and somewhat disheartened on account of the ridiculous surrender of the sleeping army at Fort Donelson. Forrest and
the 500 who followed him, to cut through Grant's lines if
necessary, were the heroes of the hour. Everybody wanted
to see Forrest. I saw Floyd and Pillow here and they looked
"pretty cheap."

The next morning Captain Huey moved our company out
the Murfreesboro pike a few miles. The roll call showed
42 present. Our lieutenants had been left at Fort Donelson
and Captain Huey held an election. I was elected first lieutenant. The company being without baggage and camping
utensils was disbanded to secure accommodations and report
at Huntsville, Alabama, on the 25th.

At Huntsville we met Captain Huey, and going down the
valley were attached permanently to the First Kentucky
Cavalry. Col. Ben Hardin Helm and Lieut-Col. Thomas G.
Woodward were the commanders. Col. Helm's wife was a
sister of Mrs. Abraham Lincoln.

The regiment was encamped near Tuscumbia, guarding
the railroad bridge at Florence and watching the advance
of Buell from Nashville. Meanwhile, the army of General
Johnston had concentrated at Corinth, confronting General
Grant's main body of troops at Pittsburg Landing.

There was great excitement in the regiment when the news was received that Johnston's army had started from Corinth to attack Grant. By going to the water's edge at Tuscumbia Landing, not far from camp, we could distinctly hear the cannonade during the battle, which was sixty miles distant by the river. The news of the victory of our army the first day caused great rejoicing throughout the regiment, and an eagerness to go to the field. But it looked as if we were fated to disappointment in our anxiety for actual experience in battle. The result of the second day's conflict and the retreat of Beauregard, together with the death of General Johnston, were dispiriting, and yet we felt that our army got the best of the battle and was safe.

Buell had arrived with thirty thousand troops after the close of the first day's engagement and saved Grant's army.

The army of General Beauregard finally abandoned Corinth, and was recuperated and reorganized just south of Tupelo, Mississippi, where it remained until June. In the mean time, Colonel Helm had the Florence bridge burned and broke camp, marching down the valley to Buzzard Roost. All the regiment left with Helm except Captain Huey's company. It was detailed for outpost duty below Tuscumbia, the enemy being at Decatur.

Finally, in May, Brig.-Gen. John Adams came up the valley with a regiment of Texas Rangers commanded by Col. John A. Wharton, and with the First Kentucky Cavalry just in the rear. He crossed the Tennessee River at Lamb's Ferry, and proceeding across the country attacked a garrison stationed at Hughey's Bridge on the Nashville and Decatur Railroad. Here Huey's company had its first fight.

The enemy was barricaded in a large log barn or stable, near the bridge, which was inclosed by a rail fence with stakes and riders. The command dismounted and surrounded the enemy. This was a bloody fight for more than an hour. Finally we charged the barn on three sides. As I straddled the top rail of the fence going over, Ida Younger, at my side, was shot in the forehead and fell outside, dead. At this moment the First Kentucky arrived at full speed, and Captain Noel at the head of his company, mounted, came through the gate. They at once received the enemy's fire and Captain Noel was among the killed. The garrison now surrendered when we were within a few steps of the barn.

Adams returned now to the Tennessee River, but found the way blocked by the enemy's infantry and artillery. He then turned and ran the gauntlet of the garrisons and went into camp at the foot of the mountains beyond Decherd. But the second day the enemy approached in pursuit. We made an all-night ride across the mountains to Swedens Cove, but to our surprise at about 10 o'clock in the forenoon we discovered that we were nearly surrounded. Adams and his staff were cut off, but escaped by a mountain path. The command was stampeded for several miles and then leisurely proceeded across the Sequatchie Valley ten miles, and continuing across the mountain arrived before morning at Chattanooga.

It occurred to Captain Huey's company that we now had some actual experience in the war. We had been in a hot fight at close range; we had been marched without sleep to the point of starvation, and had been surprised and stampeded, disgracefully, and all this within five days' time. But we were not discouraged. We enjoyed everything that happened.

Our encampment above Chattanooga, a few miles, was comfortable and prolonged, but without noteworthy incident. We had nothing to do but think of the war. It was a bitter memory to recall the action of the generals in command at Fort Donelson and the death of Albert Sidney Johnston. And all the news from Middle Tennessee and Kentucky was distressing.

But having communication with Knoxville and Atlanta we were still rejoicing over the news from Stonewall Jackson in the Shenandoah Valley.

Since this campaign of Jackson is omitted (along with the first and second battles of Manassas) from the "summary" of the battles of the war by General Buell which is quoted in Chapter 49, it may be pardonable to sketch it here.

The operations of the armies in Virginia under Stonewall Jackson, Robert E. Lee and Joseph E. Johnston had been active and had defeated several armies since the first great victory of Bull Run.

In March, 1862, Stonewall Jackson was near Winchester, with about 5,000 men of all arms to hold the enemy in that section. General Shields with over 8,000 men attacked Jackson a few miles south of Winchester at Kernstown. After a sanguinary battle which lasted till night, Jackson retreated up the Valley. General Ewell's division was sent to reinforce Jackson, which increased the force to about 15,000 of all arms before the first of May.

At this time General Fremont on the west was concentrating about 30,000 men at Franklin. He had advanced General Milroy with about 5,000 men to a point within forty miles of Staunton, which was Jackson's base. General Banks with 20,000 men, including the force of Shields, had established his base at Strasburg, seventy miles down the Valley from Staunton. General McDowell with about 35,000 men occupied points immediately east of the Blue Ridge, where he was in position to enter the Valley by any of the gaps and march upon Staunton or could march to the assistance of McClellan on the Chickahominy.

Jackson with his 15,000 men, located at Port Republic in the early part of May, was thus confronted by three armies aggregating over 80,000 men. Johnston had concentrated about 70,000 men in front of Richmond to contest the advance of McClellan's army of over 100,000 men.

Jackson suddenly marched through a gap of the Blue Ridge, and loading his army on the cars went to Staunton. He immediately marched northwest and fell upon Milroy and Schenck, within twenty-five miles of Staunton, whom he defeated and sent flying back on Fremont at Franklin, forty miles west. Meanwhile, Jackson had left Gen. Turner Ashby with his cavalry to annoy the enemy in the Valley. Jackson now fell back toward Harrisonburg in the Valley. He reached New Market within three days.

He promptly moved, May 23d, upon the forces of General Banks at Front Royal, which he surprised and routed. This placed Jackson in the rear of Banks, at Strasburg, who did not wait, but began at once a retreat to Winchester. Jackson struck his flank at Newtown, May 24th, routing the forces and capturing a large number of prisoners, 9,000 stands of arms, camp equipage, and a great quantity of provisions, ammunition and other army supplies. Jackson chased Banks through Winchester, where there was an engagement, but Banks went on and crossed the Potomac into Maryland. A Federal force of 7,000 or 8,000 were fortified at Harper's Ferry, and Jackson threatened it with assault long enough for the property captured at Winchester and Newtown to be removed to Staunton.

Fremont was now marching with about 15,000 men toward Harrisonburg, seventy miles in Jackson's rear, on the Valley road to Staunton. Jackson sent Gen. John D. Imboden with Ashby's cavalry and some artillery to block the gap and hold Fremont back. It forced Fremont around to another gap, but when he got into the Valley and reached Strasburg, Jackson had just passed, and went on to Harrisonburg, closely pursued by Fremont. On May 31st Johnston moved out and attacked McClellan's advance, and the two days' battle of Seven Pines or Fair Oaks was fought, in which General Johnston was wounded, though achieving success. Meanwhile, the Washington authorities were in a state of terror, and General Shields was sent by McDowell with a large force to the assistance of Fremont. Jackson now sent cavalry detachments, which burned all the bridges on the Shenandoah River, below Port Republic, to prevent Shields from crossing. The water was now too deep to ford. He then retreated toward Port Republic with Fremont at his heels.

At Cross Keys, six miles from Harrisonburg, Jackson turned suddenly and gave battle, defeating Fremont, who retreated. Jackson left Ewell here, on the battlefield, with a force to confront Fremont if he returned. Gen. Turner Ashby was killed in this battle, June 8th. Jackson summoned Imboden with his force of artillery and cavalry to Port Republic and marched his force to that place. The enemy, from McDowell's army, had approached from the east and was encamped near the town on the Lewis farm. Early next morning Jackson met them at the bridge and drove the advance back to the encampment. The battle was at once opened and resulted in a victory for Jackson. The routed enemy was pursued beyond the defile in the mountain by forces under General Imboden. Fremont had heard the noise of the battle and hurried forward from Harrisonburg, but Ewell falling back had rejoined Jackson and burned the bridge over the river behind him. When Fremont arrived on the other side the victory had already been won by Jackson and the river could not be crossed.

The battle of Port Republic was fought on the 9th of June. Thus, beginning with Milroy on the 8th of May, Jackson had within one month defeated and scattered all the forces sent against him.

Fremont did not advance, and Jackson, on June 17th, leaving Generals Imboden and Robertson with a small force and a battery, passed from the Valley with his troops, and marching steadily he reached Ashland on the 25th.

On the next morning, June 26th, General Lee's army, with Jackson's troops composing his left wing, moved against McClellan and opened the Seven Days' battles, resulting in the discomfiture and retreat of McClellan's army to Harrison's Landing on the James River. Meanwhile, just before these engagements began, Gen. J. E. B. Stuart, the peer of Forrest and Morgan, with his division of cavalry, had passed around the right flank of McClellan and scattered everything in his path until he made the complete circuit of McClellan's army, crossing the Chickahominy below and reaching Lee's army in safety. It was upon the strength of Stuart's observations that Lee decided to attack immediately.

There was little occurring in Mississippi, though we understood our army was being reorganized and strengthened under Gen. Braxton Bragg.

The information was received that General Buell was advancing from Corinth up the Tennessee River in June. And to our relief the troops from Mississippi began to arrive by railroad at Chattanooga, and in fact an army was formed here under General Bragg.

I was sent across the river with fifteen men to establish a picket post at Suck Creek, five miles from Chattanooga. There was just room here for the big road between the river and the foot of the mountain. Just a little distance beyond the creek the road ascended the mountain. It was twenty miles across to the Sequatchie Valley, where Buell's advance was now reported. Soon after I located at Suck Creek to send scouts daily across the mountain, Colonel Forrest arrived at Chattanooga with his escort company under Captain Bill Forrest. He at once organized a brigade composed as follows: Colonel Wharton's Texas Rangers, Colonel Woodward's First Kentucky, a Georgia regiment under Colonel Lawton, and a Georgia battalion under Colonel Morrison.

About the 10th of July General Bragg sent Forrest to Middle Tennessee to attack Buell's line of communications. At McMinnville Major Smith, with two companies under Captains Taylor and Waltham, joined Forrest, and his force now numbered fifteen hundred men. On the 12th, without artillery, Forrest marched from McMinnville, and at daybreak on the 13th he captured the outposts without firing a gun and entered Murfreesboro. A superior force under Gen. T. T. Crittenden was assailed in detail and captured, Crittenden being taken at a hotel. The official report says Forrest captured "two brigadier-generals, staff and field officers; burned $200,000 worth of stores; captured sufficient stores with those burned to amount to $500,000; 60 wagons, 300 mules, 150 to 200 horses, and a field battery of four pieces." He then returned to McMinnville on account of the large number of prisoners to be guarded.

About the same time Col. John H. Morgan, who now had a regiment, left Knoxville and crossed the mountains to Sparta, then crossed the Cumberland River and began at Tompkinsville, Kentucky, to capture garrisons. He rode all over central Kentucky, reaching within sixty miles of Ohio. He drew after him in pursuit 8,000 to 10,000 of the enemy's cavalry gathered from all parts of Kentucky.

In his official report Colonel Morgan says:

I left Knoxville on the 4th day of this month (July) with about nine hundred men and returned to Livingston (Tenn.) on the 28th with nearly twelve hundred, having been absent just twenty-four days, during which time I have traveled over a thousand miles, captured seventeen towns, destroyed all the government supplies and arms in them, dispersed about fifteen hundred home guards, and paroled nearly twelve hundred regular troops. I lost in killed, wounded, and missing of the number that I carried into Kentucky about ninety.

It is important to observe the effect of the operations of Forrest and Morgan upon the situation of Buell's army. It is well stated by General Buell himself as follows:

HEADQUARTERS, ARMY OF THE OHIO.
In Camp, Huntsville, Ala., July 21st, 1862.
GENERAL ORDERS, NO. 32:

On the 13th inst. the army at Murfreesboro, under command of Brig.-Gen. T. T. Crittenden, late colonel of the Sixth Indiana Regiment, * * * was captured at that place by a force of the enemy's cavalry variously estimated from 1,800 to 3,500. It appears from the best information that can be obtained, that Brig.-Gen. Crittenden and Colonel Duffield, of the Ninth Michigan, with the six companies of that regiment and all of the cavalry, were surprised and captured early in the morning in the houses and streets of the town, or in their camp near by, with but slight resistance and without any timely warning of the presence of the enemy. The rest of the force, consisting of the Third Minnesota and the artillery under Colonel Lester, left its camp and took another position, which it maintained with but few casualties against the feeble attacks of the enemy until about three o'clock, when it was surrendered and marched into captivity.

Take it in all its features, few more disgraceful examples of neglect of duty and lack of good conduct can be found in the history of wars. It fully merits the extreme penalty which the law provides for such misconduct. The force was more than sufficient to repel the attack effectually. The mortification which the army will feel at the result is poorly compensated by the exertion made by some—perhaps many—of the officers to retrieve the disgrace of the surprise. The action fit to be adopted with reference to those who are blamable, especially the officers highest in command, cannot be determined without further investigation.

*   *   *   *   *   *   *

James B. Fry,
Colonel and Chief of Staff.

By command of Maj.-Gen. Buell.

General Buell says further:

The road from Nashville to Stevenson was completed on the 12th of July, and a train was started the next morning with supplies for the depot at Stevenson. My attention had been attracted to the importance of McMinnville as an outpost. It was at the foot of the mountain on the direct mountain road between Nashville and Chattanooga, and was the terminus of a branch railroad, twenty miles east of the Nashville and Chattanooga Railroad. I had just organized a new brigade at Murfreesboro to occupy McMinnville. On the morning of the 13th, Forrest, with a large body of cavalry, surprised the brigade, killed and wounded some and captured the rest, damaged the railroad seriously, and produced alarm in Nashville where the force was not large.

*   *   *   *   *   *   *

This was the first appearance of any large body of the enemy in our rear south of the Cumberland, though Morgan was at the same time engaged in a formidable raid in Kentucky. Nelson was immediately ordered to occupy Murfreesboro and McMinnville with his division, himself and one brigade going by railroad. He had just reached Murfreesboro with a portion of his troops when Forrest, on the 18th, appeared again on the railroad between him and Nashville, captured guards, and destroyed two more bridges.

* * * * * * *

Our communications south of the Cumberland had been made secure by the distribution of the troops, but to the north the depredations were prosecuted with increased vigor. Our cavalry was totally insufficient to cope with these incursions, which, it must be said, were seldom resisted by the infantry guards with vigilance and resolution. On the 10th of August, Morgan again appeared on the railroad north of Nashville, captured the guard of about 150 men at Gallatin, effectually disabled the tunnel north of that place, and destroyed several bridges toward Nashville. Our communication with Louisville, on which we were dependent for supplies, was thus, for the present, effectually severed. Work was immediately commenced to repair the damage, but the constantly recurring presence of the enemy's cavalry interfered so effectually as to require a large increase of force from the front or the rear for the defense.

On the 18th a guard of a regiment belonging to Grant's command was captured without a show of resistance at Clarksville,* where a considerable quantity of supplies had been deposited for transshipment in consequence of suspension of navigation by low water in the Cumberland.

Upon hearing of Morgan's appearance again on the Cumberland, north of Nashville, General R. W. Johnson, a spirited cavalry officer, under whose command I had assembled all the cavalry that was available, moved promptly in pursuit, and with his inferior force attacked Morgan vigorously near Hartsville. Johnson was defeated with a loss of 80 killed and wounded and 75 prisoners, himself among the latter. The rest escaped and made their way as stragglers or in small bodies to Nashville.

* * * * * * *

We were now reduced to ten days' rations. Our railroad communication north of Nashville had been broken for twenty days, and no effort was being made at Louisville to reopen it.

The last week in August Major Clare, of General Hardee's staff, came over from Chattanooga to my post. He directed me to break up camp and accompany him across the mountain to find out if Buell's army was still at Battle Creek and

---

*Captured by Col. Adam R. Johnson.

Jasper. We reached the Sequatchie Valley about sunset and learned positively that no change had occurred in the position of the enemy. Major Clare left me here with Rolla Humphrey to remain another day, while he returned with the rest of my men.

I secured all the information possible the next day, and starting about dark across the mountain, reached Chattanooga at sunrise. Here to my surprise I found that Bragg's army, about 28,000 troops, had crossed the river and marched over the Walden Ridge toward Nashville, and that Kirby Smith had already entered Kentucky from Knoxville with about 20,000 men. Bragg had finished crossing on the 30th.

I at once started on the trail of Bragg's army. I was joined by Dr. J. B. Cowan, medical director on Forrest's staff. He had been left in Mississippi. We traveled together to Burkesville, Kentucky, where he stopped to go another route. I found the army at Bardstown and rejoined my company. Captain Huey had not lost a man on the expedition.

Bragg had taken Forrest's brigade and Wheeler was now in command of all the cavalry.

CHAPTER V

Battle of Perryville—Bragg and Smith evacuate Kentucky.

General Wheeler had guarded the front during the expedition and now reported the advance of Buell's army from Louisville.

On the 2d of October the army began to move and marched on the Springfield pike at an early hour in the morning. We passed through Springfield and on to Perryville, where we camped. After some delay here next day we took the pike to Harrodsburg and went into camp just beyond in a large woodland along a small creek. We were now going directly toward Lexington from Perryville and the army was happy. It was rumored in camp that Bragg and Kirby Smith would unite their forces and a great battle would follow.

I moved around among the infantry awhile to talk with some of those who had fought at Shiloh. I happened upon a mess composed of several officers and privates from Louisiana. Maj. J. E. Austin was in the party. He told me he commanded the 14th Louisiana battalion of sharpshooters. The interview was cut short, however. An order came to get ready to march. It was then 10 o'clock at night. I hurried back to my own company.

We passed through Harrodsburg about 12 or 1 o'clock, and to my surprise were in sight of Perryville again by sun-up. We halted and our company dismounted and rested on the roadside while eating a lunch and napping. I learned that our cavalry, under Colonel Wheeler, had been fighting the enemy beyond Perryville on the Springfield road in the afternoon before. And this morning there was more or less firing in that direction. It was obvious that our infantry was being formed over on the right of the pike in line of battle. The artillery was also leaving the pike on that side. Captain Huey came up the pike from the direction of Perryville and notified the company that we had been detailed as an escort for Gen. Patton Anderson, who was commanding a division, and that a battle was imminent. There was disgust in the company over the arrangement.

I went to Captain Huey and told him that I wanted to go and get with Major Austin's sharpshooters and go into the battle. He objected until I insisted that I did not want it said that I had been in the army a year without having fought in a battle. I reminded him that our one year expired in two weeks. I dropped in the rear as the company moved off toward Perryville. I then worked along, through different commands, inquiring for the headquarters of Gen. Dan W. Adams. When I found him he pointed out the locality where I would find Major Austin. The Major was delighted to see me. I told him the circumstances that caused me to come to him. I proposed that he ride my horse and let me go as a sharpshooter. He promptly installed me in his mess. I was furnished with the rifle and ammunition of one of his men who was too ill for duty.

About noon General Adams sent for Major Austin. On his return the battalion was ordered under arms and in line. I surveyed the surrounding commands and saw there was a general formation. I could not see any of the enemy in sight, and a sharp firing to the left was the only indication that any was near. The battalion was soon ready and Major Austin mounted my horse and marched forward two or three hundred yards through a timbered pasture in which there was considerable brush and a good many stumps. We were then halted. I also observed other battalions or parts of regiments were going forward like ours. We were deployed about twenty yards apart so that our line covered the front of General Adams's brigade. Major Austin ordered the line forward. In a few minutes the enemy's cannon opened up and was soon firing all along the line.

We were now getting close enough to see that the Federal line extended away to the right with a gap to the left. When we were within about four hundred yards of their line of battle, the enemy's sharpshooters opened fire on us from behind trees and stumps, and all along the front of their line, which was a long distance in both directions, but we moved on as though nothing had happened. The sharpshooters of the enemy continued their fire while we were halted, but our line was close behind us now, and suddenly the brass bands broke loose and filled the woods full of music, the troops began to cheer and the enemy's artillery began to roar. Major Austin ordered our line to move and with a yell we went forward. The sharpshooters fired at us once more and then ran. We were halted to fire, and after one shot the battalion was formed in line within a hundred yards of the creek. The fight was already raging to the right and away to the left and the whole army was cheering. We then went forward. As we neared the creek the enemy's infantry line opened fire on us. Major Austin ordered us to go double-quick to a rock fence. The creek had some water in it but was easily crossed and we went to the fence under fire. A perfect storm of bullets was rained on us, or rather on the fence.

Our own artillery was now pouring a continuous storm of shot and shell on the enemy's infantry line and the battle was hot from end to end. Major Austin, galloping to our left, ordered us to double-quick straight down to the left and right-face to the enemy. Then he yelled "Charge!" It was a clean spot of ground outside of the farm between the creek and the enemy. We went yelling about half way, aiming to flank the enemy at a large barn. Major Austin was right along on my horse. I did not see how he escaped. The fire in front of us and from both flanks was too hot and Major Austin ordered us back behind the rock fence. A number of our men fell in the five minutes we were out there. But in a moment General Adams, with

four regiments, crossed the creek to the left, and we were
ordered to go out to the same spot again, and did, when
Adams brought his line even with us.

Meanwhile, the large barn across the orchard had been
set on fire by the shells from our cannon. We went forward in Adams's line, all walking and firing as we went.
The enemy broke on the left of the barn from us and General
Adams pushed his men forward. We pressed the enemy
back. Their line was still standing from the barn on to the
dwelling-house, but our whole line was right up against
them. Major Austin turned us to the right, in the rear of
the line behind the orchard, and the enemy gave way in a
disorderly retreat, as did the line down to our left. We
were in a cornfield, but the cornstalks were cut and shocked.
A ridge ran about the middle, parallel with the creek or
front. There was about the same slope from the crest of
the ridge to the rear as to the creek. We got to the top
of the ridge about the time the enemy got over the back
fence of the field and squatted behind it. Many of them
went on that the officers could not rally. We were about
seventy-five yards from the fence in the open, General
Adams's whole brigade being in line. We had been firing
all the time at thirty to fifty yards' range, but the losses were
all on their side after we passed the barn.

General Adams now ordered us to lie down and shoot.
He and Major Austin were riding up and down our line
while we exchanged volley after volley with the enemy.
But our whole army was driving the enemy to the right and
left and General Adams ordered a charge. Austin rode
with us bareheaded and waving his hat. He was a charmed
target. The enemy gave way in disorder, going down
for fifty yards and then up a hill in a clean woods pasture. They were in a drove now like a flock of sheep, and
we could not miss such a dense crowd. The poor fellows
fell like leaves from trees in the fall of the year. It seemed
to me that half of them were left on the ground in that pasture. We were now veered to the right and helped drive a

force posted behind a fence. This ended in our favor, and as we pressed forward the right of our battalion rested on a lane. I with others went along this lane in line, but now everything in front of us seemed to be routed. Reinforcements came up on the other side and we ran into another fight in a skirt of woods. Here we won again, capturing a lot of cannon and some prisoners.

The battle, in the mean while, was a perfect storm, the sound of musketry never ceasing and the roar of cannon rolling without a break. And the yelling was continuous along the line of our army. We had passed through camps and over the dead and dying. Loose horses were running in all directions and wounded men were crying for help. There were halts and moves forward, but not as hard or hot fighting, except near another house on the lane, after the first two hours, as the enemy continued to give way, leaving a waste of everything behind that a soldier carries in battle. The sun had gone down and there was a lull all along the line. Our battalion had got somewhat mixed with other men in crossing or going around lots and I got separated from the main part, but six or eight were with me. When the order came to fall back we were in rather thick woods and I could not see Major Austin anywhere. We went on back with the line, which began to straggle along. Every one was hungry and thirsty. It must have been a mile or more, over the horrible battlefield, to the creek.

It was understood that the battle would be renewed the following morning. Major Austin waked me late in the night and told me we were ordered to march. We reached the Harrodsburg turnpike, a mile from Perryville, soon after daylight. There was considerable skirmishing beyond Perryville some distance toward Springfield and Danville.

The formation of brigades and divisions began to indicate a battle on different ground. However, we broke ranks later in the day and resumed the march to Harrodsburg. Taking leave of Major Austin and his friends I mounted my horse and made my way along the pike to rejoin my company.

I camped along with different commands where I could get forage for my horse, and did not overtake Captain Huey's company for several days. We retreated through Lancaster, Crab Orchard, Mt. Vernon, London, Barboursville and Pineville. There was a pause for battle at Crab Orchard, but the retreat was continued without anything of special interest, moving leisurely along over the mountain at Cumberland Gap. The troops were weary and disappointed, and there was no cheering when generals passed along the column. They could not understand why Bragg and Smith with about 50,000 men had marched into Kentucky and were marching out again.

CHAPTER VI

Breckinridge at Murfreesboro—Forrest at Franklin—Johnson and Martin in western Kentucky—John W. Foster levies on citizens to reimburse Union men.

We were in camp at Knoxville two days before the arrangement was made to muster the company of Captain Huey out of the service. There were none who wanted to reorganize and reenlist to continue the experience of the past year. All wanted to get with Morgan.

Our exalted ideas in the beginning, of generals commanding armies, had changed. The commanders at Fort Donelson, Beauregard at Shiloh, and Bragg and Smith in Kentucky had taxed our patience. Forrest and Morgan had been the campaigners. Morgan had been the first man in history to raid far in the rear of the enemy's great armies and successfully defy overwhelming numbers.

The infantry soldiers felt that they had never gotten the worst of a battle and could not understand how Buell with 60,000, including fresh drafted men, could frighten Bragg and Smith out of Kentucky when they had nearly 50,000 men.

I agreed with both soldiers and citizens at this time, that our cause was lost, by poor generalship in the West, unless the independence of the Confederate States should be acknowledged by England and France.

I started from Knoxville with Isaac M. Bowers as my companion. We had agreed to go through to our homes in western Kentucky for a new outfit, see our families, and then get with Adam Johnson's regiment or go to Morgan.

We found Gen. John C. Breckinridge with a division at Murfreesboro. At Franklin we found Forrest with a bri-

gade of cavalry. At Charlotte we reached the danger line.
We proceeded to the home of Mrs. Batson on Barton's Creek
and got a guide to go through the "coalings" for miles, to
reach Palmyra, where we crossed the Cumberland. It was
necessary now to travel paths and wagon-ways to avoid the
cavalry of the enemy which scouted from the county-seats.
But we reached our homes in safety. Our parents lived
six miles apart in Hopkins County. However, the family
could not keep my return a secret, on which I depended for
safety. The citizens of this whole county were divided into
friends and enemies, and the feeling was bitter. Every man
and woman was either "Secesh" or "Lincolnite." There had
been exciting times in all this section since early spring until
October.

Adam R. Johnson and Robert M. Martin, two scouts,
for General Floyd at Fort Donelson, and for General
Breckinridge at Shiloh, came into this section and began to
recruit soldiers and organize a command. Martin was a
young merchant at Carlow, four miles from Dixon, the
county-seat of Webster County, on the road from Dixon to
Henderson. Johnson was a native of Henderson but had
lived in Texas several years immediately preceding the war.

When they had recruited twenty-seven men they went
about boldly, and were chased by Federal cavalry from one
county to another, but always managed to escape. Being
hotly pressed, Johnson and Martin managed to slip across
Green River above Spottsville, in Henderson County. They
learned that there was a force of infantry at Newburg, Indiana, just above the mouth of Green River, and with their
force of twenty-seven men were piloted through the wooded
bottom-lands of the Ohio River on the Kentucky side to a
point opposite Newburg. They mounted a piece of stove
pipe two joints long on the hind part of a wagon and put it
in position to fire on Newburg. The twenty-seven men
were openly displayed around the artillery, moving back and
forth from the open space into the woods to make the impression that a strong force was at hand. Johnson and

Martin, and Amphleus Owen took a skiff with an oarsman and crossed over to Newburg with a flag of truce. The Federal garrison gathered at the wharf, when the party landed, to see what on earth could be the matter. Johnson asked for the commander, who presented himself. They then notified him that Col. Adam R. Johnson was across the river with artillery and a large force and demanded the surrender of the garrison, otherwise he would shell and destroy the town of Newburg. A great many citizens had gathered in the crowd and were panic-stricken over the prospect. After parleying for some time the terms of surrender were agreed to, being largely influenced by prominent citizens to save the town, and the ferry-boat was carried over to bring the men across to take charge of the arms.

Meanwhile, Johnson, Martin, and Owen guarded the stack of arms and equipments of every description. The ferry soon returned with the men, and the boat being loaded with everything Johnson and Martin wanted, the remainder of the spoils were destroyed. The captain and his men were paroled, when Johnson, Martin, and Owen, taking friendly leave, entered their skiff and were rowed to the Kentucky shore. They got a light wagon and before the next day had dawned were far up Green River in its wildest woods, where the surplus was secreted, and the little band was soon on the other side of the river, loaded with all they could carry.

The fame of this exploit spread rapidly, and the restless Southern spirits were hunting everywhere for Johnson and Martin to join their command. Within a short time their force had grown to several hundred, and companies were being secretly organized in several counties to enlist with the proposed regiment. In a brief period a regiment was actually organized, with Adam R. Johnson as colonel and Robert M. Martin, lieutenant-colonel, and practically occupied the counties of Hopkins, Muhlenburg, McLean, Daviess, Henderson, Union, Webster, and Christian, at will, outside the county-seats, where Federal garrisons were in force too strong to capture.

During the summer Johnson and Martin attacked and captured many garrisons and scouting commands. It was their tactics to surprise the enemy and never be surprised. Colonel Johnson was awakened one night by a messenger with the news that Col. James M. Shackelford, commanding a force of Federal cavalry, had left Madisonville to attack the camp. Johnson at once mounted his command and departed.

Colonel Shackelford reached the point early in the forenoon and found a deserted camp. He rested here to feed his horses, and in a little while the Rebel citizens began to slip across the waters of Wiers Creek flats, to Johnson's camp on Walnut Hill, loaded with breakfast for Johnson's men. One by one they were unloaded and pointed to a spot selected for prisoners. Up to the time Shackelford was ready to move he had caught about twenty of these patriotic Southerners in his net.

The next day Colonel Johnson's regiment was thirty-five miles away, beyond Morganfield, and at daybreak the following morning surrounded and captured the garrison at Uniontown, on the Ohio River.

Colonel Shackelford heard of this event and went in pursuit. When he reached the locality Colonel Johnson had retired to a secluded dense woods around Geiger's Lake in Union County. Shackelford moved with his command upon the Confederate rendezvous and an engagement ensued in which Colonel Shackelford was shot in the heel. Johnson escaped with his command in good order and without loss, eluding immediate pursuit. Colonel Johnson attacked the garrison at Clarksville, Tennessee, capturing Colonel Mason and his regiment, with an immense quantity of army supplies stored there for shipment by railroad to General Grant at Oxford, Mississippi.

With reference to this affair General Grant says:

On the 22d, Col. Rodney Mason surrendered Clarksville with six companies of his regiment.

* * * * * * *

When he was summoned to surrender by a band of guerrillas, his constitutional weakness came over him. He inquired the number of men the enemy had, and receiving a response indicating a force greater than his own he said if he could be satisfied of that fact he would surrender. Arrangements were made for him to count the guerrillas, and having satisfied himself that the enemy had the greater force he surrendered and informed his subordinate at Donelson of the fact, advising him to do the same. The guerrillas paroled their prisoners and moved upon Donelson, but the officer in command at that point marched out to meet them and drove them away.

The daring and successful operation of this force, for six months, 250 miles in the rear of Grant's army in north Mississippi, and of Buell's at and east of Huntsville, Alabama, kept alive the spirits of the friends of the South and terrorized the Union element all over this section of Kentucky between the Cumberland and Green rivers and west of the Louisville and Nashville Railroad to the Ohio River. It was the first anyhow, and perhaps the only regiment that ever boldly occupied territory far in the rear of the Federal armies.

After the battle of Perryville Col. John H. Morgan swept down toward western Kentucky as far as Hopkinsville. Colonel Johnson now followed on out to Middle Tennessee after the retreat of Bragg's army from Kentucky, and attached his regiment to Morgan's forces and commanded one of the brigades on the Ohio raid in 1863.

The Federals were now in undisputed possession and visited retribution upon the "Secesh" citizens. Colonel John W. Foster* of Evansville, Indiana, with an Indiana regiment occupied Madisonville and notified all Southern sympathizers in the county of any standing to report at his headquarters. These were required to pay an assessment of $100 to $500 on the spot or go to prison. My father and next younger brother, only sixteen years old, were required to go. My father was assessed $200 for himself and $100 for my

---

*Resided at Washington, D. C., 1905. He was Secretary of State in President Harrison's Cabinet, having been Minister to Mexico and Russia.

brother and both required to take a non-combatant's oath. The receipt for the money recited that it was collected to reimburse Union men who had lost horses or provisions by the depredations of guerrillas. The Union men were boldly riding around with the squads of cavalry to summon citizens to Foster's headquarters at Madisonville.

This was the condition of affairs I found to exist, and I could not remain. I sent a message to Bowers. After being equipped with clothing, etc., I rode my father's best horse away to the South again. I started at sunset through the woods, reaching the house of Wm. Mills, an enthusiastic friend, and spent the night. The next day I crossed Tradewater at White's Mill and reached Allen Baker's, where I found Bowers. We started after supper and traveled all night by our now familiar route to a point near Palmyra. We learned, however, that a garrison of Federals was now stationed at Palmyra. We were directed to the right and arrived at the house of Squire Fletcher a while before sundown. Fletcher went with us by a blind path around Mrs. Outlaw's place to the river bank, and shouted across to a man named Murray who lived in a cabin surrounded by timber on the opposite bank. Murray came over with his skiff. We stripped our horses and put our luggage in the skiff. Then getting in we led our horses into the water by halters and pushed out, swimming our horses on the upper side.

At the house of Mr. Dickson, in Charlotte, we met our old friend John B. Walker of Madisonville, Kentucky, who was a refugee. His wife and two daughters, Mary and Blanche, were with him for a brief visit.

We left Charlotte the next day and stopped a while in the afternoon at Franklin. Forrest's command still occupied the same position, but he was commanding a brigade of four regiments now, and one or two smaller commands, besides a battery. And this fine brigade had been recruited since Forrest returned from Kentucky, two months before, one each by Col. James W. Starnes, Col. George G. Dibrell, and

Col. J. B. Biffle of Tennessee, and one from Alabama, by Col. A. A. Russell, which included four companies of Forrest's original regiment, that had been with him at Sacramento, Donelson, and Shiloh.

We were greatly tempted to enlist here with Forrest, but concluded to go and enter the Kentucky command of Morgan, which we learned was now on the other side of Murfreesboro, to which point we then proceeded.

CHAPTER VII

Bragg's army at Murfreesboro—Secret service for General
  Bragg—Purchases at Lafayette, Kentucky—Surprise, flight,
  and narrow escape—Battle at Murfreesboro—Discontent in
  the army and feeling against General Bragg—Col. R. C.
  Tyler wounded—Death of Tyler—Bragg and his generals.

At Murfreesboro we found all the commotion incident to
a great army. The army of General Bragg had been concentrated here. Among our old acquaintances Bowers met
Maj. James M. Hawkins, commissary on the staff of Maj.-
Gen. Frank Cheatham. In the afternoon, when we were
about ready to start in the direction of Morgan, Major
Hawkins met us and I was introduced. He told Bowers
he had just come from Col. Robert C. Tyler of Nashville,
who was provost-general of the army, and wanted to know
how it would suit us to enter the secret service for General
Bragg and scout in the direction of Clarksville. After discussing the question for a while we went with Hawkins to
see Colonel Tyler. It was finally agreed that we would
undertake the service, it being understood that we should
continue to represent ourselves as discharged soldiers from
Kentucky, as a matter of protection in case of capture. And
to further conceal our character we should endeavor to bring
out contraband goods of any kind that would be useful, and
Hawkins would help us sell them at headquarters and
otherwise so as to pay expenses.

At this period it was almost impossible to purchase a
pocket-knife, tooth-brush, comb, suspenders, handkerchief,
or any of the real necessary articles used by the soldiers or
people. There was no such thing as tea or coffee. Sub-
stitutes for coffee were made of sweet potatoes, rye, and
wheat. Colonel Tyler issued each of us a pass "By order

of General Bragg," attested by himself as provost-general. We were thus authorized to pass through the lines of Bragg's army at will. It was agreed that Hawkins should receive one-third of the net profits of the articles we might bring out.

Our general instructions from Colonel Tyler were that we should go as near Nashville as possible, on both sides of the Cumberland River, below the city, and all important news should be reported to Forrest or the commander of the post at Franklin, who would forward our report promptly to Bragg or Tyler, except when we should have supplies to bring through. Tyler proposed to notify Forrest of our mission and gave us a note to him, that was to be then destroyed, so that no writings would exist on the subject that might implicate us in the event of falling into the enemy's hands.

We hurried on to Franklin and had the good luck to find General Forrest in town. He was now a brigadier-general. He read the note from Tyler and tore it up. We briefly told him our business and promised to keep him posted as we passed back and forth, then hastened on through Charlotte to Mrs. Batson's. Here we learned from reliable citizens that the Federal company which had been stationed at Palmyra had gone to Clarksville, which left the river without a garrison between Clarksville and Dover. Scouting bodies of cavalry had made several trips to this locality from Clarksville within a week, arresting a number of refugees and soldiers. And another from Dover had been along Yellow Creek some eight miles away.

Bowers and I went through the "coalings" to Palmyra, and finding the situation clear we concluded to go across and on to Lafayette, Kentucky, where we could perhaps find a supply of such articles as we wished to buy. We made the trip, reaching the town just after dark. It had been learned that Horace Kelly carried a large stock of goods and was a strong Union man. So we introduced ourselves as Union men, from Stewart County, Tennessee, and ten miles from Dover. He cheerfully sold us anything we wanted. We invested $175 in silk handkerchiefs, suspenders, gents' hose, pocket-knives, pins, needles, combs, buttons, etc., each filling a two and a half bushel cotton sack. These we put across our saddles like a turn of corn was carried to mill in old times. We crossed over at Palmyra, and hurrying through the "coalings" arrived safely at Mrs. Batson's. Somewhat weary from the journey we concluded to rest a day. Misses Rebecca Abernathy and Dora Watkins were here when we arrived but soon departed. However, Mrs. Batson invited them to meet one or two others and spend the following day at her house, we agreeing and proposing to remain to meet the company.

The next forenoon we were in the parlor awaiting the expected company, when Mrs. Batson appeared at the door, saying, "Yonder comes the Yankees." Bowers and I ran out into the hall and saw a company coming in a gallop up the lane in front about one hundred yards from the house. We went bareheaded out the back door and into the orchard and a little up hill across it to the woods. The distance from the back gate of the yard was near two hundred yards. When we were half way Bowers was perhaps ten steps ahead of me, as he could run the fastest. I was nearly out of breath. I heard the enemy behind, and looking back saw they were on each side of the house, throwing down the fence to get inside the orchard. When I got on the fence to go over, Bowers was out in the woods going like a deer, and the enemy shouting "Halt!" was coming at full speed not more than one hundred yards behind me now and gaining fast. The woods appeared naked and I felt that there was no escape. Just outside the fence wild weeds had grown up between it and the woods, and going through this strip six or eight steps I ducked and ran to the right about thirty feet and then crawled back to the fence, where I lay as close as possible alongside the bottom rail. The pursuers made a gap in the fence where we got over and rushed forward into the woods. They were gone a long time, and when I heard them returning it appeared they were coming direct to my location. But they struck the fence I judged about seventy-five feet on the other side of me from the gap. There they made another gap into the orchard and went on back to the house. One or two rode along on the opposite side of the fence from me. They could hardly have seen me if they had looked down, as the rails from their view-point obstructed the cracks, while I peeped up into their faces not more than ten feet away.

I could not determine whether they had Bowers or not, as part of their force went back on the outside around beyond the negro cabins. I saw several of them go out into the stable lot, and presently they came out with our horses, saddled. After searching the house and getting our saddlebags, but not our sacks of goods, they fell into ranks and rode off to the left toward the Clarksville road. Just as they passed the orchard they shouted, "Good-by, boys!" This indicated that Bowers also was safe. There were about forty in the company. I got up and looked all around but saw nothing of Bowers. Presently I heard his signal, a peculiar whistle, and went to him. He was in the top of a large fallen tree, where he had concealed himself under the piles of dead leaves on the ground, though several of the cavalrymen had ridden within a few feet of him.

We secured horses and saddles in the neighborhood at reasonable prices and hurried through to Murfreesboro, and quickly disposing of our merchandise we returned to Mrs. Batson's without incident. A man named Dickerson had a somewhat run-down country store on Barton's Creek two miles distant. It was found that he had a stock of canned pine-apples, cove oysters, sardines, pepper, spice and ginger not ground; a lot of hammers, hinges and other hardware; a few hats and other useful articles, in the army. We bought a two-horse wagon load, with Confederate money, and hired a man to haul the load to Murfreesboro for $50 in Confederate money. Bowers went to Charlotte to hear from Nashville, only thirty miles away, and learned that a battle was being fought at Murfreesboro. Some one had brought the news from

Franklin to Charlotte. He went on far enough to learn that the battle lasted two days and that Bragg was falling back. We then turned our team and went to Columbia, from where we sent our teamster home.

At Columbia we found that Forrest's brigade was encamped near by and just returned from his famous raid into West Tennessee. The Federals now occupied Franklin, Triune and Murfreesboro, while Bragg's army was located at Tullahoma, with his advance posted north of Shelbyville. We hired a team from Mr. Miles Mays and hurried forward through Farmington to Shelbyville. We secured board for a few days at the residence of Dr. Blakemore, until we could dispose of our load, which, with the aid of Major Hawkins, was readily done at a large profit.

We learned that the battle of Murfreesboro was the same old story, of winning the victory and then a retreat. It was Shiloh and Perryville over again. The spirit of the army was unbroken, but there was a universal clamor for the removal of Bragg.

Major Hawkins advised us that the army would hold the line of Shelbyville and it was agreed that we should return to the "neutral zone" and endeavor to get in communication with Nashville, on the other side, through citizens who might go inside the lines.

We were sorry to learn from Major Hawkins that our friend Col. Robert C. Tyler, commanding his Tennessee regiment, in the battle, was seriously wounded and a leg had been amputated. It was never our pleasure to meet him again, though he recovered and was made a brigadier-general. He was killed in one of the last fights of the war at West Point, Georgia.*

*"About one hundred and forty-five old war-worn soldiers were at the hospital at West Point, Ga., on the 16th of April, 1865, totally unconscious of General Lee's surrender on the 9th inst. General Tyler, of Tennessee, who had lost a leg at Murfreesboro, was also there sick. About a dozen of Waller's Charleston, South Carolina, battery, and fourteen of the Coupee, Louisiana, battery were also there. When the report came that Colonel Griffin, with two regiments of Wilson's Federal cavalry, a battery, and two thousand men, was marching on them, Gen-

The following authentic correspondence is given as showing that the discontent in the Army of Tennessee and of the citizens was recognized and definitely stated to General Bragg by the brigade and division commanders of his army.

HEADQUARTERS ARMY OF TENNESSEE.
TULLAHOMA, TENN., January 11, 1863.

GENERAL: Finding myself assailed in private and public, by the press, in private circles by officers and citizens, for the movement from Murfreesboro, which was resisted by me for some time after advised by my corps and division commanders, and only adopted after hearing of the enemy's reinforcements by large numbers from Kentucky, it becomes necessary for me to save my fair name, if I cannot stop the deluge of abuse which will destroy my usefulness and demoralize this army. It has come to my knowledge that many of these accusations and insinuations are from staff-officers of my generals, who persistently assert that the movement was made against the opinion and advice of their chiefs, and while the enemy was in full retreat. False or true, the soldiers have no means of judging me rightly or getting the facts, and the effect on them will be the same—a loss of confidence and a consequent demoralization of the whole army. It is only through my generals that I can establish the facts as they exist. Unanimous as you were in council in verbally advising a retrograde movement, I can not doubt but that you will cheerfully attest the same in writing. I desire that you will consult your subordinate commanders and be candid with me, as I have always endeavored to prove myself with you. If I have misunderstood your advice and acted against your opinions, let me know it in justice to yourselves. If, on the contrary, I am the victim of unjust accusations, say so, and unite with me in staying the malignant slanders being propagated by men who have felt the sting of discipline.

General Smith has been called to Richmond, it is supposed, with a view to supersede me. I shall retire without a regret

---

eral Tyler got out on his crutches and commanded all the old soldiers present, who could stand up, to fall in line of battle. He threw up some hasty breastworks, and divided the ammunition among the men, which amounted to forty-three rounds apiece. The enemy charged and were repulsed. General Tyler hobbled on his crutches along his lines, encouraging his men to stand their ground and never surrender. He took no thought of himself. Seven of his men were killed. The enemy repeated their charge and were driven back again, and commenced firing from a if I find I have lost the good opinion of my generals, upon whom I have ever relied as upon a foundation of rock.

Your early attention is most desirable, and urgently solicited. Most respectfully,

Your obedient servant,
BRAXTON BRAGG,
General C. S. A.

I enclose copies of a joint note, received about 2 o'clock a. m., from Major-Generals Cheatham and Withers, on the night before we retired from Murfreesboro, with Lieutenant-General Polk's indorsement and my own verbal reply to Lieutenant Richmond, General Polk's aide-de-camp.

B. B.

Lieut.-General HARDEE,
    Commanding Hardee's Corps.

TULLAHOMA, TENN., 12th January, 1863.

GENERAL: I have the honor to acknowledge the receipt of your note of yesterday, in which, after informing me of the assaults to which you are subjected, you invoke a response in regard to the propriety of the recent retreat from Murfreesboro, and request me to consult my subordinate commanders in reference to the topics to which you refer.

*   *   *   *   *   *   *

You also request me to consult my subordinate commanders, stating that General Smith has been called to Richmond with the view, it was supposed, to supersede you—and that you will retire without regret if you have lost the good opinion of your generals, upon whom you have ever relied as upon a foundation of rock. I have conferred with Major-General Breckinridge and Major-General Cleburne in regard to this matter, and I feel that frankness compels me to say that the general officers whose judgment you have invoked are unanimous in the opinion that a change in the command of this army is necessary. In this opinion I concur. I feel assured that this opinion is considerately formed, and with the highest respect for the purity of

---

distance. First Sergeant Hearn, the only man there of the First Louisiana Infantry Regulars, C. S. A., who was then sick and wounded in the leg, had his arm shot off. A Minie ball struck the noble old General Tyler, who was standing a few paces in the rear of the Sergeant, and passed through the center of the forehead, killing him instantly. Then Captain Gonzales, of Pensacola, fell. Colonel Gillespie then took command and fought with this little remnant of the Confederacy till their ammunition gave out, and the Federals, finding there was no return to their fire, charged over the works and their brave defenders. They

your motives, your energy and your personal character; but they are convinced, as you must feel, that the peril of the country is superior to all considerations. You state that the staff officers of your generals, joining in the public and private clamor, have within your knowledge persistently asserted that the retreat was made against the opinion and advice of their chiefs. I have made inquiries of the gentlemen associated with me, and they informed me that such statements have not been made or circulated by them. I have the honor, General, to assure you of my continued respect and consideration, and to remain,   Your obedient servant,

W. J. HARDEE,
Lieutenant-General.

Official.
T. B. ROY, Chief of Staff.
Indorsed: Letter to General Bragg.

then heard for the first time, from their captors, that they were fighting after the war was over. Their loss was about twenty killed and wounded; the enemy's about forty-five.

"The Federals, on finding who they were fighting, took good care of the wounded and returned the sick to the hospital. There was not a man among them who had not borne the hardships of four years of war, and had faced death in many shapes. This was only a little skirmish; nobody has ever thought it worth while to mention it till now, some twenty years after. This tale is told by one of the old boys." (F. L. Richardson, in *Southern Bivouac,* 1885.)

CHAPTER VIII

Situation changed in "neutral zone"—Secret negotiations with
the Federal commander at Clarksville—Surprised at Mrs.
Batson's—Capture and escape—Another narrow escape—
Escape of Bowers from prison at Clarksville.

On the way to Columbia we overtook Captain Bill Forrest,
at Farmington, near Duck River, who had been north of it
with his scouts, as far as Triune. He said the Federals were
encamped at Nolensville on the pike to Nashville. At Co
lumbia we found that the entire command of General Forrest
was encamped, with the Federal advance posted at Franklin.

We found the situation somewhat changed when we
arrived in the neighborhood of Charlotte. Several scouting
commands from Clarksville had been scouring the country,
one of them coming to Charlotte. A number of Confederates, at home on furlough, were hiding in the secluded places
of every neighborhood. And there were a few parties of
"Partisan Rangers" organized, that had been annoying the
garrison at Dover. One of them was under command of a
Captain Ray, of McLean County, Kentucky, and made its
rendezvous on Yellow Creek, some fifteen miles from Charlotte. And the Confederate conscript officers had been at work
in the "neutral zone." These different attractions had been
receiving attention from the Federal commanders at Dover
and Clarksville.

In our absence Mr. Walker had been down to Mr. Russell's, near Palmyra. Russell as a Union man had been twice
to Clarksville and had managed to get into the confidence of
the commander of the garrison and post. He thought he
could arrange with him to bring a supply of articles down the
river or by wagon to Palmyra, that were even contraband
of war. We went to Russell's and he heartily entered into

an arrangement to bring out a lot of articles from Clarksville, but he wanted a partnership. We agreed to his proposition. We arranged with Russell to secure information for us at Clarksville. We had paid $3,000 in Confederate money for $1,000 in Tennessee good money, at Columbia, then went back to Mrs. Batson's to wait until Russell returned from Clarksville.

Misses Abernathy and Watkins happened here again. I was playing chess with Miss Abernathy in the parlor, the rest engaged otherwise. "Yonder's the Yankees!" some one said, looking out toward the front. There they were sure enough, dismounting at the front gate about sixty feet distant. Bowers stepped out in the hall, and all the others except Miss Abernathy. She was greatly distressed on my account. I quietly admonished her to keep quiet a moment. I surveyed the room. There was a large old-fashioned mahogany press, a fine piece of furniture, against the wall behind the door leading out into the hall. The piano, a couple of divans, and parlor chairs completed the articles of furniture in the room. I motioned Miss Abernathy to say nothing, then got down and crawled under the press, pushing back against the wall. I then told her to leave the door open and go in the hall. The soldiers were talking at the hall door to Mr. Walker and the others by this time, and asked for Bowers and Headley. I slipped my pass from Bragg under the edge of the carpet. Mrs. Batson told the captain that we were there but that we had gone out from the parlor. They came in and searched the house from top to bottom. Some of them aggravated the ladies, who quarreled with them all the time.

Several soldiers walked to the parlor door, looked in, and seeing it was practically vacant, passed on. I heard them up-stairs going from room to room, and finally they cheered. They had found Bowers in a dark garret over the diningroom, where Mrs. Batson had put him through a small door, that connected with it, from the hall up-stairs. They had fun over Bowers when he came down. He was jolly, and put the ladies in good humor while the soldiers were still looking for me. They got candles and went into the cellar under me and prowled around among barrels and boxes, for some time, until they were satisfied I was not in the house. Some of them went out to the negro cabins and searched there. They filled the house and hall and seemed to be a good-natured lot. They finally gave me up and the captain ordered them to mount, our horses having been brought out also. One of the soldiers straggled into the parlor, and after looking at the chess-men a moment walked to the very large mirror on the mantel and looked at himself. The mirror leaned forward at the top and I could see his face as plainly as he could see it. And in a moment he saw mine. He turned around quick and shouted, "Here he is!" The other soldiers had all started out and some were on their horses. I felt pretty cheap, but I got out before the others came in. I at once made it a good joke and got on good terms with the crowd. The ladies tried to enjoy the performance after we appeared so comfortable in our trouble.

There were about sixty men in the command. It went from Mrs. Batson's to the Barton's Creek neighborhood, and chased and captured several others they had orders to capture. It rained during the afternoon and we all got quite cold and wet, though the soldiers wore gum coats.

I was riding in the ranks with Monroe Adams, who, as I remember, was from Casey County, Kentucky. They were all Kentuckians, the garrison at Clarksville being a Kentucky regiment.

I saw we were now headed for Clarksville after leaving Mrs. Batson's, and night soon came on. The rain continued and most of the men began to wish they were in Clarksville. We had twelve miles to ride and all settled down to a dreary trip. I kept my guard, Adams, cheered up for an hour or so, when he too got stupid. It was very dark and very muddy. We passed through a long lane and then entered a woods. I could not see anything but the road dimly. After going perhaps a hundred yards the idea occurred to me, and

I turned my horse into the woods and urged him forward with both feet jogging his sides. There was confusion in the ranks instantly and a gun fired. I did not hear any bullet, but the noise frightened my horse. I suppose he thought it was in front, for he stopped suddenly and I went on over the horn of the saddle to his neck, but I got back quick and crowded him into the woods. I pushed through the bushes for fifty yards perhaps and stopped. The column of soldiers had been halted and every one was trying to find out what was the matter. I sat on my horse and listened. The commander was some time discovering that a man had escaped, and then the trouble was to locate or identify the other prisoners. He lectured Adams severely and then referring to me, said, "Let him go." He ordered all the soldiers who were guards to lead the horses of the prisoners. I calculated that they could accomplish nothing by coming into the woods.

The command resumed the journey, and as the sound of their marching began to die away I came into the road and started my horse on the back track. I did not know the road, but the horse went right back to Mrs. Batson's by two o'clock that night. She and Mr. Walker insisted that I would be safe till morning, when she would give me breakfast at sunrise and I could then go to Sim Talley's, her son-in-law, and sleep all day. I had already fed my horse before I waked any one in the house. I had a change here and with dry clothes on I slept well till waked at dawn. I had my breakfast before all the family got up. As I came out of the dining-room and into the front hall to get my hat I saw about twenty-five Federal cavalry coming up the front lane at full speed not over one hundred yards from the house. I crouched close to the wall and went out the back door without saying a word to any one. It was but about twenty steps to the back yard gate into the orchard and then only a few steps farther on the right was a log hen-house. I noticed the door stood open and that there were no boards on the cracks. I knew I could not cross the orchard, and going into the hen-house climbed up and stood on the top log over the door, my head reaching to the comb of the roof at the gable end.

The soldiers were all round the yard on horseback within two or three minutes. One of them halted between the hen-house and the yard fence and sat there on his horse. I could see from his knee downward by stooping with a hand-hold above. Most of the men were searching the house. They were mad this trip and abused the family to some extent for harboring rebels. But Mrs. Batson argued with the captain that we did not belong to the army. He said we must come to Clarksville and take the oath or leave this country. They searched the negro cabins and made some trouble down there trying to make the negroes tell where I was hid. They did not know. I heard one soldier say that one of the negro men coming from the house had met them in the lane and told them I was up-stairs asleep then and I must be hid on the premises somewhere. But finally the whole command mounted and rode away toward the Clarksville road.

I held my position for at least three hours until a hen came off her nest and cackled, when Mrs. Batson came out there to look for eggs. I told her to put my hat and overcoat in the back yard at a certain spot. Walker had taken care of these things for me. I got down and went through the yard, taking my hat and coat quickly and ran off to the right across the front woodland.

Mr. Walker arranged to board at the house of Mr. Watkins, which was an elegant home. And a few days afterwards I went there. He went through to Russell's and found that he had been successful in a measure. We arranged with Mr. Watkins for his wagon and a negro man to drive, whom we could trust. We intended to get the load from Russell's as soon afterwards as the roads would freeze, it being too muddy then. I did not stay about the house of Mr. Watkins all the time, but found a place on the hillside where I had a view of all the roads that approached the dwelling through the coalings, and kept up a good camp-fire. One forenoon I observed a lone horseman coming, a quarter of a mile away. I soon recognized the familiar form of Ike Bowers. I went near the road and called him. He sat down and told me his experience. I will give it substantially, as I remember, he told the story:

"After you ran into the woods on the road," he said, "I felt that I must escape too. I thought of a good many plans and finally decided, as the guard was carrying my bridle reins, that I would slip back over my saddle behind it, and holding to the saddle skirt let myself off easy behind my horse and run into the woods. In a bunch of woods I got behind the saddle all right and was ready to go in a second, when my guard said, 'Whoa, there, get back.' And then he jerked the long skirt of my overcoat. He said he had been holding it all the time as he had an idea I would try some trick of that kind. I gave it up then and bided my time. All the prisoners in the crowd were registered at headquarters in Clarksville and then sent to prison. This was in a lawyer's office up-stairs. We entered an open stairway from the pavement and at the top on the right were two large rooms with a connecting door.

"I learned that David Scott, our old friend from Madisonville, kept the leading hotel in town. I wrote him a note to come and see me. He came promptly and I arranged for three meals a day for myself and the other eight prisoners. A servant came with the loaded waiter at the regular time and I fared well. The guard stood down-stairs at the entrance and one in the back of the hall up-stairs. These I observed were changed at six o'clock every evening. I decided on a plan to escape. The servant brought the supper at five o'clock every day. I had him to leave it yesterday evening because I was not then hungry, telling him he could take the dishes in the morning. At the same time I gave him a quarter. As soon as the sentinels were relieved at six o'clock and new men on watch I blackened my face and hands with charcoal from the fireplace and arranged my

clothes so as to look like a darky. We had already eaten
the supper. I picked up the waiter and went down and out.
The guard asked me where I was from. I told him I came
from the hotel with supper for the prisoners up-stairs."
(Bowers could imitate a darky's talk perfectly.) "I then
went to the vacant market-house, where I put the waiter
down and walked off. I came out of town between the
roads all right, but got lost outside and wandered around
in the country nearly all night, finally getting to the river
only four miles from Clarksville. But I found a friend,
Samuel Stewart, who put me across in a canoe fifteen miles
from here. I walked to the first house, a cabin, and found
the man had this white horse, which had fallen overboard
and come ashore from a passing transport. I bought him
for $50 in Tennessee money, with the saddle and bridle in-
cluded in the bargain, but it was the enemy's property and
if I had been armed I would not have paid anything for
the horse."

The sudden reappearance of Bowers enabled us to proceed with our affairs. We lost no time in going to Russell's
with a wagon and were ready for what appeared to be our
last trip to Shelbyville, as we doubted if General Bragg's
army would be enabled to hold its position in Middle
Tennessee.

We found Mr. Russell had just been to Clarksville again,
not to obtain further supplies, immediately, but with reference to other matters. However, it happened that his previous close relations with the commander brought the opportunity for a confidential conference, which resulted in an
arrangement for unexpected facilities to handle contraband
articles to the South. It was agreed that a friend of Russell
in Clarksville might order from Cincinnati a shipment of
merchandise by steamer to Clarksville, with a permit to
deliver the consignment to Russell at Palmyra, before reaching Clarksville. The shipment was to be marked to Clarksville but consigned to Palmyra in the bill of lading. We at

once departed with the wagon-load already at Palmyra, in a vacant store-room, but agreeing to secure current money and make the order without delay.

At Charlotte it was determined that Mr. Walker should remain there with most of our Confederate money and endeavor to make exchange for greenbacks or Tennessee bills. He arranged to board with a citizen named Trotter, near town, while we went on to Shelbyville as before.

Forrest was still near Columbia and there seemed to be no particular change at Shelbyville when we arrived. Major Hawkins was delighted with the Clarksville arrangement, and hastily placing our load at a fair profit we left for Charlotte. It was deemed best for Bowers to push on and help Walker and Russell, while I moved leisurely with the team. We stopped the first night with Mr. Hill, at the crossing of a creek, seven miles from Columbia. We went on to Columbia, and as our wagon was delayed Bowers left me there. I called on General Forrest and told him of our arrangement through Russell and the colonel in Clarksville and the chance of capturing the place and then making a demonstration on the north side of the river against Nashville and the communications of Rosecrans. He highly appreciated the information. I told him we had reported the situation to General Bragg at Shelbyville, through Major Hawkins.

CHAPTER IX

Captured at Louisa Furnace—Capture of officers of Lee's army—Escape from prison and captivity in Nashville—Notes on Rosecrans's army—Departure from Nashville on a pass—Escape of other prisoners.

I was two days in reaching Charlotte, and sending the team on home I went out to Mr. Trotter's. He had exchanged $1,000 in Tennessee bills, with Mr. Walker, for $3,000 in Confederate money. Walker and Bowers had gone to Mr. Watkins's. I went on there, arriving about dark. I found that Walker and Bowers had gone to Mr. Russell's. Here I met Will Baxter, a brother of Mrs. Watkins, Robert Mockbee, her nephew, and Captain Hick Johnson, on furlough from Lee's army in Virginia. Johnson was the son of Hon. Cave Johnson, who was Postmaster-General in the Cabinet of President James K. Polk, and was a cousin of Baxter and Mrs. Watkins. The home of these young men was in Clarksville, but they had not considered it safe to venture beyond this point. Two sisters, Misses Bettie and Nannie Garland, had come out from Clarksville to meet their friends.

We did not retire till after ten o'clock and it was only twelve o'clock when Mockbee shook me and said the yard was full of Yankees. I asked the others what they intended to do. Captain Johnson said there was nothing to do but surrender. I then arranged with them to say they never saw me before and knew nothing about me, and that I came there after supper. They lighted a candle and began to dress. I cut a small slit in the under side of the bed-tick and pushed my pass from Bragg inside without attracting the attention of the others. They were about dressed when the Federals came up. I stayed in bed perfectly unconcerned. The officers in charge questioned the others and got a straight story of their character and the reason of their presence. They were soon ready to go. The officer then asked Johnson, "Who is that other man?" Johnson answered as I had suggested. I then raised a little and said, "Good-evening." He spoke, asked my name, where I lived, and what I was doing there. I told him my name was Williams, that I was from near the cotton mills on Duck River below Waverly; that the conscript officers were scouring the country to take every one to the Southern army; that I hid out for two weeks until it looked as if I could not stay there any longer and I was now on my way to Shawneetown, Illinois, where I expected to do something until the trouble was over in my section. He looked at my clothing and was satisfied, but several others came up and joined the captain's party and one of them recognized me as the prisoner who ran out of ranks on the way to Clarksville, two weeks before. He called Monroe Adams, who was below, and who identified me without hesitation. It was another joke on me, but the captain told me if I tried to escape this time I would be killed, and he gave orders accordingly.

The command had several other prisoners, and rode around the neighborhood toward Palmyra for others. We stopped at an iron furnace about three o'clock and were kept sitting there in a room until morning.

At Clarksville we were registered at headquarters and sent to the same prison rooms where Bowers had been confined. A great number of friends came promptly to see Johnson, Baxter and Mockbee, and they were furnished every luxury in abundance. As I was taken into their mess I had no occasion to notify my friends, of whom I had several in Clarksville.

The next day we were taken down to the river and on board a steamer for Nashville. A crowd of citizens gathered on the wharf as we went down, and Lafayette Wilson, a friend from Madisonville, Kentucky, recognized me, and coming to greet me walked down to the boat. He touched me on the hand as we walked along, my guard being on the other side. I looked and he was trying to put a ten-dollar bill, of greenback money, in my hand. I thanked him in a whisper, telling him I did not need it.

It was late in the afternoon when we started from Clarksville and it was sixty miles up the river to Nashville. I had a great many plans to escape from the boat in the night, but none seemed feasible. The best one, I thought, was to take a plank and jump overboard, but I was afraid I would freeze before I could paddle the plank ashore with my hands. When we reached Nashville the next morning we were marched to the State Capitol, where we were registered at headquarters after ten o'clock, and then marched down to the market square and sent up into the third story of the market-house building, which was used as a temporary prison. This was a three-story brick building. There were two rooms and a wide hall between on each floor. A winding stair ran up in the hall with iron railing and banisters. The two rooms on the third floor were used for the prisoners and about twenty guards were stationed in the hall. Prisoners were brought in every hour, in squads, and both rooms were crowded. Rosecrans's army was here and at Murfreesboro, and of course a few prisoners on both sides were taken every day. I learned from a guard that the prisoners were sent North every morning at eight o'clock. I noticed a rather rude restaurant on the first floor as we were brought up. I asked the guard about it and he told me any of us could go down there under guard and buy a meal. This was good news, as the sleeping and cooking were going to be horrible in our prison rooms. I suggested to Baxter that we go down and get a hot dinner. We selected the youngest guard in the bunch, a boy about nineteen years old, to go with us. We made the guard eat with us, which he appreciated, and when we spoke of coming down for supper, he asked us to let him come with us and that arrangement was made.

We could see from our windows that citizens and soldiers crowded the pavements and army wagons crowded the streets. And it seemed a poor prospect for making our escape even from the prison, and still worse for getting out of Nashville. I told Baxter in the afternoon we would go late to supper on the idea that we were not hungry yet, and after dark would try to bribe our guard to let us go in the crowd, while he could slip back, and this was agreed to. We put every small article of our baggage in our overcoat pockets and inside of our other clothing.

At dark we went down and at the bottom of the stairs I turned to Baxter, as if it made no difference to the guard, and told him that the restaurant in the building was a sloppy place to eat and that we would go across the street to a nice restaurant. I had seen the sign from a window. Baxter agreed, but the guard said he was not allowed to take us over there. He stood by it for a long time through fear, only on his own account, for disobeying orders. I pleaded with him that in such a crowd we would not be noticed and they would never know up-stairs, but he had taken us to the river bank where he had a right to go with us. He finally consented. We went to a restaurant about the middle of the block between the market square and the Commercial Hotel. While there was a crowd along the pavement there were very few in the restaurant. We sat at a table which stood against the wall, making room for three. The guard sat next to the door, Baxter next to his right, and I on the back side facing the guard and the front door. The cashier's desk was across by the opposite wall and ten feet nearer the front door than our table. I took the lead and ordered a nice supper. While we waited for it Baxter drew a half pint bottle of whiskey a friend had given him at Clarksville, and we all made a toddy. We had a good time eating our supper and talking about the war.

An idea of escape occurred to me, and I finished my meal first and carelessly got up, saying I would settle with the cashier and we would be ready to go when they were through eating. I walked on without any more ceremony, getting out my money as I went. I stood for my change with my face turned to the back of the restaurant so the guard would not be uneasy. Taking my change I fumbled with it, turning toward our table. The guard was looking at me, so I took a step slowly while putting my money away. At this moment the guard put his fork to his mouth, bowing his head slightly, which took his eyes from me. I turned and walked to the front door so as not to attract the attention of passers-by. I looked back and the guard had grabbed his gun, which stood against the wall, and was rising hurriedly, but I was out and in the crowd the same as any other person. I knew the guard could not leave Baxter to follow me, and felt safe after going a few steps as no one noticed me. Several details of soldiers were passing in both directions, but I passed on in the crowd as though I lived in Nashville. I went several squares toward Broad street and observed that I was getting into the residence part of town. I believed any old citizen would be a friend and I wanted to find one without delay. I went into the first substantial home where there was a light. When the servant answered the door-bell I got a glimpse inside and observed a number of Federal officers in the parlor. I asked the servant if Mr. Wilson lived there. She said, "No, sir," and told me who did; but I begged pardon, saying I was mistaken in the house, and excused myself.

A little farther on I came to a small family grocery on the corner. I walked in, and buying a cigar sat down with the proprietor to smoke, which he said was agreeable. I soon learned that he was an old resident and a strong Southern sympathizer. He did not care who knew it. I assured myself fully and then told him the story of my escape. He told me of the large encampments all around the city on both sides of the river. I felt that it was much better for me to go out between picket posts and risk their shots in the dark if I could find any woods. He directed me how to go, to the left of the Charlotte pike, where I would probably have the best chance to evade the pickets. I followed his directions for fully a mile and the woodland he had described was in my front. As I approached a fence, at the edge of it I discovered tents on the other side among the trees. I stopped, but had been heard by a sentinel not more than forty feet on the inside of the fence. He shouted "Halt!" It was pretty dark, but I could see my way a few yards. I stooped and ran on tip-toe, swerving to the right, so that I would not be in the range if he shot where he heard me. It was my calculation that he would do that if he shot at all. However, I presume he concluded he was mistaken as I heard nothing more.

My new friend in the grocery had told me every one caught on the streets after ten o'clock was arrested. I judged it to be half past eight now, and concluded it would be better to abandon the idea of going out that night. The houses were very scattering in the neighborhood and mostly cottages, where I thought best not to apply for accommodations. When I got on Broad street I found it was after nine o'clock. I met an old darky, from whom I learned the location of the cemetery on the Nolensville pike inside the city. He said houses extended to the grounds. I went out that way briskly without seeing a light in any dwelling on the street, and began to regret that I had not tried to arrange with my grocery friend for lodging. I looked for his place again in my wanderings but failed to find it.

At the entrance to the cemetery I stopped to look in all directions for a light. I was going into the cemetery and sit up all night among the cedars, because I did not believe I would be disturbed in there. But I saw a light and went to it. I entered the yard gate and saw a two-story dwelling with a hall and room in front. The light was in the front room. When I looked in at the window I saw a lady sitting at the hearth knitting and a man in bed reading by a lamp on a table near by. I sounded the door-bell and the lady came to the door with the lamp in her hand. I bowed, and apologized for being late, but just wanted to speak to her husband a minute. She appeared a little frightened and said he had retired. In a sort of pleading manner I suggested that I would not think of having him get up and would just go in only for a minute. She balked along and showed plainly that she did not want me to come in. I asked her what time it was and tried to relieve her of any apprehension.

We were at the entrance to the door of their bed-room by this time, when her husband spoke up to inquire who was coming in. His wife quickly said she did not know. I laughingly said, "It's a friend; you'll be surprised to see me." His wife stopped in the middle of the room so the light would shine on my face to let her husband see if he could recognize me. I then candidly explained that I had come in for some information only because they had a light burning and I did not think it would be considered an intrusion. I felt that I did not want a gentleman to get up and dress to talk with me a few minutes. I then said frankly that I was a Confederate and told him how I had escaped and the predicament in which I was placed. His wife instantly declared that her husband had taken the oath and could not afford to violate it. I finally got a hearing and told so fair a story that the husband, Mr. Metcalf, said he didn't care if I was a Rebel or a Yankee or neither, if I simply wanted lodging and breakfast and proposed to pay for the accommodation he had a right to entertain me and would do it. After his wife became satisfied she got interested in my story, and when we retired it was midnight. I was put in their best room up-stairs. Mr. Thomas Metcalf was the name of my host. He became thoroughly satisfied that night, and when he left me it was agreed that I should be known to the cook, a negro woman, as the cousin of Mrs. Metcalf. The next morning everything was easy. It was agreed that I should stay there until I got tired unless I had a chance to leave the city. As there were no children in the family I felt perfectly safe.

Mr. Metcalf came home in the afternoon from his business, and had told a friend, who was a grocer, of my case, and after supper we went down town and spent an hour or so in the counting-room of the establishment. I arranged to go the next night to the store of a clothing merchant, who was a friend, where I could fit myself out as a citizen, in the style of a young man. I had been wearing my hair rather long and cropped around the edge. This I had shingled to change my appearance in every respect as much as possible. I then went about the city freely, having no fears except from Kentucky soldiers from my own locality, who might recognize me on sight. But I carried my discharge from the army for such an emergency.

I soon realized that there was no possible way of escape from Nashville except to get a pass northward. There were over 50,000 soldiers in the army of General Rosecrans, from Nashville to Murfreesboro. The Confederate cavalry under Forrest, Morgan and Wheeler had threatened the east and west picket posts of the city so continually that three different posts were stationed on every road leading to the country, with camp sentinels between the roads. During the next three weeks I visited in the neighborhood, with Mr. and Mrs. Metcalf, attending several social parties, and made very pleasant acquaintances. However, during the first week, I got an introduction to a Captain Rhodes, of Michigan, who understood from me that I was from Bourbon County, Kentucky, and was visiting relatives in the city and some in the Seventeenth Kentucky Cavalry. We did not talk politics, but he was led to infer that I was a Union man. I managed to impress the fact that I would need a pass when I got ready to go home and he very promptly volunteered to say that he would arrange that for me. I now cultivated this gentleman, who was a good man. I was introduced by him to other officers and in a general way, without exciting suspicion, I learned the names of all the brigadiers and major-generals in Rosecrans's army, not only those at Nashville, but at Murfreesboro, Triune,

Lavergne, Brentwood, and Franklin. I managed to meet men from nearly all the commands by "raking up" acquaintances in a casual way and by a little liberality at times with cigars and refreshments. I knew the number of brigades with this information, and while I did not make any notes there was little else on my mind and I remembered all.

There were funerals every day in the cemetery opposite Metcalf's (my home), and I attended several of these to form casual acquaintances among the soldiers and learn their commands. I frequented all the hotels, where I had generals pointed out to me by soldiers. Here I first saw Governor Andrew Johnson. I was now possessed of information on which a safe estimate could be made, within a few thousand, of the strength and location of the army, and I was ready to go out, but I could not afford to show any special anxiety, though I felt confident now I would have no trouble to use Captain Rhodes.

I was afraid to apply too soon after his offer for fear he might possibly become suspicious. About the third time I met him, after I was ready, the matter came up and I told him when I wanted to start. He cheerfully went with me and introduced me to his personal friend, the provost-marshal, who issued the pass without hesitation. My name was William C. Sims during this sojourn in Nashville.

Before going I bought a gross of good pocket-knives, of small size, that were put up one dozen in a package. These I distributed in my pockets and boot-legs. I managed also to conceal two dozen silk handkerchiefs in my clothes. I passed through two sets of pickets beyond the bridge on my way out on the Louisville pike. Just beyond Edgefield I turned off to the left on the White's Creek pike. After going about one mile from the pike I met an old gentleman on horseback. His name was Squire White. He lived on White's Creek near by, five miles from Nashville. He eyed me pretty closely and said I looked like a Rebel. I could tell by his look that he hoped I was one. When I concluded it was safe to tell him so it made me a friend. I went to his home to dinner. He directed me to a man two miles ahead whom I could get to take me to Cumberland River without traveling any public road. I found the place and before sundown I was on the bank of Cumberland River, fifteen miles below Nashville. I was soon rowed across in a skiff and spent the night at the home of Mr. Robertson. The next morning he sent me to Charlotte, his son-in-law going with me to bring back the horse I rode. At Charlotte I found a company of about one hundred Confederate cavalry, from Forrest's command at Columbia, on a scout.

I learned afterwards from Mrs. Watkins, at Louisa Furnace, that Baxter went with the guard back to the prison room after failing in an effort to bribe him for liberty. But the next night Johnson, Baxter, and Mockbee succeeded in making their escape, and Mrs. Watkins gave me the particulars. I have them now from an authentic source after a lapse of thirty-eight years. I submit a correspondence that gives the story just as I heard it at the time:

MEMPHIS, TENN., July 2d, 1901.
MR. JOHN W. HEADLEY,
          Louisville, Ky.
    DEAR SIR: I inquired at Kentucky Headquarters during the late reunion of Confederate Veterans here for one Mr. Headley, who was captured with Major J. Hick. Johnson, Lieutenant William Baxter and myself, in March, 1863, at the home of Mr. S. D. Watkins, on the south side of Cumberland River, twelve miles from Clarksville, Tennessee, in Montgomery County, and your address was given me as the only person of the name known to those with whom I talked. If you are the same person as the one I speak of, please write me here for the next ten days and after that at Cornwells, S. C. Or if you know of the party of whom I speak, please write me as to his whereabouts, if still living. The Headley I knew was at that time quite a young man but exceedingly bright and attractive in his manners, and, I think, engaged in a blockade secret service for the Confederates, going in and out through the lines frequently. Although it is only a matter of good feeling I cherish for one whom I

shared a short term of prison life with, I would be greatly pleased to hear from him, and especially to know that he is alive and prospering.

By answering this at your convenience you will oblige,

Yours very truly,

R. T. MOCKBEE.

MEMPHIS, TENN., July 29th, 1901.

MR. JOHN W. HEADLEY,

Lyndon, Jefferson County, Ky.

DEAR FRIEND: I was more than delighted to receive your letter of 22d inst., directed to me at Cornwells, S. C., where I expected to be some time ago when I wrote you, but have been detained here on account of Mr. Baxter, my son-in-law, and family making a visit to Middle Tennessee, and he wished me to stay and overlook his business during their absence.

And now, my dear friend, let me express to you my sincere pleasure and gratification at knowing that you are one and the same person as my comrade and fellow-prisoner, and especially that the world has used you well, and that you have been blessed with good health during all the years since those eventful days when we were together as prisoners at Clarksville and Nashville. I suppose in the lapse of years your memory has failed to keep what really occurred as to William Baxter, Major Johnson and myself after your escape. About the third night after you got away we all three went down to the "restaurant," accompanied by a poor "green" Yankee boy as our guard, and, after having our supper, in which our guard shared, we went out as if we were going back up-stairs into the prison. When we reached the entrance at the foot of the stairway we halted (as had been prearranged) and Major Johnson said, "Boys, we ought to have a bottle of brandy for to-night," and, turning to the guard, said, "Here, you take this money and go over to the saloon across the square and get us a bottle of brandy and bring it up. We will go on up-stairs. Just put your gun behind the door there until you come back." And the poor simpleton did just as he was told, in the mean time Johnson having given him a five-dollar bill. He walked out into the dark and Baxter a.. I followed him just as soon as we thought it safe. Major Johnson stopped to pull off his Confederate overcoat, which he threw behind the door, and took the Yank's gun to guard Baxter and me, after we got outside. In the mean time, Baxter and I had gotten out in the dark and went around the market-house on the side next to the river, and when Johnson came out with his gun he went the other way and so missed us entirely, and putting the gun down he hurriedly made his way to his sister's, Mrs. Hickman, the mother of John P. Hickman, the present secretary of our Tennessee Confederate Association. And she secured a pass from the provost-marshal, took him over the river in a buggy, dressed as a lady, to a sister's, Mrs. Dortch, where he had such a good time he stayed too long, and an old negro servant went in and reported him and the Yankees sent a squad of cavalry out and took him in, putting him in a cell in the penitentiary, until he was sent North.

Baxter and I, after getting safely away, secured us a complete outfit of the latest style citizen's clothes from a friendly Jew and each of us carried a well-stuffed valise. After going to a barber shop and getting clean shaved and trimmed up we sallied forth and joined a procession of people who had just come on the train from Louisville, and went with the largest crowd to the Sewanee House, then one of the leading hotels of the city. There we registered, Baxter as Charles H. Haynes, and I as John C. Smith, of Louisville, Ky., secured a room and a bottle of brandy, to help keep our nerves quiet, and spent the night. We went down to breakfast the next morning and the room was filled with Yankee officers, at least a hundred at breakfast. Afterwards we went out in the city to try to find some avenue of escape into the country, but failed completely and had to remain two days and until the third night. We succeeded in getting a skiff and went down the river to Hagwood's Landing, where we stopped within ten miles of Mr. Watkins's, where we had been captured. I remained in that section for several weeks getting information, and also some recruits for my regiment in Virginia. I, like you, had orders from the War Department at Richmond, countersigned by General Lee, and slipped them between the feather bed and mattress, and quietly told Mrs. Watkins where to find them. I got back to Richmond just as the battle of Chancellorsville was being fought, and was with my command until Appomattox, with the exception of about two months' sickness, in 1864.

* * * * * * *

I am,

Very truly, your friend,

ROBERT T. MOCKBEE.

CHAPTER X

Situation after return from captivity—Forrest at Palmyra—
    Wheeler at Fort Donelson—Plain talk of Forrest to
    Wheeler—Report to Forrest and Bragg of Rosecrans's
    army—Van Dorn over Forrest and others, on the left, and
    Wheeler over Morgan and others, on the right, of Bragg's
    army—Morgan's raid to Kentucky in December, 1862—
    Infantry armies being exhausted in drawn battles and in
    camp—Spirit of vengeance—Colonel Streight marches out
    from Palmyra and encamps on Yellow Creek.

At Charlotte I found Ike Bowers on the day of my arrival
from the Nashville captivity. He and Walker had duly
received the shipment from Cincinnati to Russell at Palmyra.
Teams had been furnished by Mr. Watkins, of Louisa Furnace, and the trip was made to Shelbyville. Major Hawkins
and Bowers had promptly disposed of the stock. I received
$3,318 in Confederate money as my share of the profits
from the beginning.

I learned now that Forrest had acted on my information in February, and moving along our route had passed
through the coalings to Palmyra with his command. Bowers
had fallen in with him and acted as guide through to Russell's. There, Forrest, being fully advised of the situation
at Clarksville, was waiting to capture a passing transport
and cross over the river, then to reach Clarksville within a
few hours and capture the garrison. He would then pass
between Ashland and Springfield, and striking the railroad
and burning all the bridges he could destroy, and the "Morgan" tunnel, near Gallatin, north of Nashville, and then make
his way to a crossing of the river above Hartsville or Burkesville, if necessary. But General Wheeler overtook Forrest
at Palmyra, and, assuming command, went down to cap-

ture Dover. Bowers told me it looked to Forrest and all his men that Wheeler had followed to assume command and get the credit of a victory or a raid somewhere. Forrest and Morgan had made such brilliant successes of their December raids that Wheeler seemed anxious to "catch up." This expedition now turned down the river and went twenty miles to the attack of Fort Donelson. It will be interesting to quote extracts from a graphic and authentic account of the engagement and the result from "Wyeth's Life of Forrest," as follows:

Near Palmyra, Forrest, who had masked his guns and ambushed his men, and was all ready for a bout with any passing craft, was overtaken by the chief of cavalry, who brought with him a portion of Wharton's brigade. General Wheeler having concluded that the Federals had become apprised of the Confederate position along the river, and would not, for the present, send any more boats on that stream, and having nothing else in hand, determined upon an expedition for the capture of the Federal garrison at Dover. In his official report he says: "After maturely considering the matter, we concluded that nothing could be lost by an attack upon the garrison at Dover, and from the information that we had there was good reason to believe that this post could easily be captured."

In the "Campaigns of General Forrest," which was edited under his personal supervision, it is stated that some difference of opinion existed as to the propriety of this attack upon the fort at Dover, and that General Forrest submitted to his chief that he was not only poorly supplied with ammunition, but that the effort did not promise results commensurate with the losses that an assault upon such a formidable position would entail, and earnestly advised that the effort be abandoned. The premonition of disaster weighed upon Forrest so heavily that on the morning of the engagement he spoke of the matter in strict confidence to his chief-of-staff, Major Charles W. Anderson, and to Dr. Ben Wood of Hopkinsville, Kentucky, then a surgeon connected with his command. He said: "I have a special request to make of you in regard to the proposed attack on Fort Donelson. I have protested against this move, but my protest has been disregarded, and I intend to do my whole duty, and I want my men to do the same. I have spoken to none but you on this subject, and I do not wish that any one should know of the objections I have made. I have this request to make: If I am killed in this fight, you will see that justice is done me by officially stating that I protested against the attack, and that I am not willing to be held responsible for any disaster that may result." (From a personal communication from Major Charles W. Anderson, living at Florence, Tennessee, in 1898.) General Wheeler believed, however, that by a simultaneous and quick rush from two sides the garrison could be overcome with trifling loss, and immediately ordered the advance.

* * * * * * *

General Wheeler says: "Just as I left General Forrest, he, thinking the enemy were leaving the place, and being anxious to run in quickly, remounted his men and charged on horseback. The fire from the enemy was so strong that he was repulsed and obliged to retire."

The discomfited troopers were again formed for assault, this time on foot, and, simultaneously with the advance by Wharton's column, they rushed forward, Forrest again on horseback at the head of his dismounted detachment. * * * They pressed forward with courage to the breastworks, but were unable to gain a footing within the fort. Forrest's horse was shot down, being the second animal killed under him that day, and the General was badly shaken up in falling. A number of men were killed within a few feet of the breastworks.

* * * * * * *

On the left, Wharton's command easily drove the Federals into their works, capturing a few prisoners and one fine twelve-pounder brass rifled cannon, which was brought from the field. The stubborn resistance made by the garrison had, however, succeeded in holding off their assailants until near nightfall, when, as General Wheeler states, his troops had a secure position not more than ninety yards from the main rifle-pits of the garrison. Before making a third assault a conference was held, and it was decided that there was not enough ammunition left in the entire command to justify a further attack. It was also learned at this crisis that reinforcements for the garrison were arriving, and had already fired upon the Confederate outposts. Before retreating a detachment was sent to the river landing near the fort, and there set fire to a boat loaded with supplies, which was soon destroyed. As they retired, other details were made to gather up all the wounded who could be carried away on horseback or in wagons, and to bring off the captured gun and other property, among which was a generous supply of blankets found in the Federal quarters, which were greatly needed, as the weather was intensely cold.

* * * * * * *

Major Charles W. Anderson says: "It was late when I reached headquarters at Yellow Creek Furnace. Arriving there, I asked for General Forrest. The General, recognizing my voice, came to the door, and as I was too near frozen to dismount, he came out and helped me down and into the house. Without any ceremony he went to the only bed in the room, jerked the covering from two officers who were occupying it, and brusquely ordered them to get out. My boots were pulled off, I was rolled up in blankets and put in the vacated bed. General Wharton was sitting on the side of the fireplace opposite General Wheeler, who was dictating his report to one of his staff. Forrest had resumed his place, lying down on his water-proof coat in front of the fire, his head on a turned-down chair and his feet well on the hearth. General Wharton said: 'When the signal was given, my men moved forward, but were met with such a severe fire that, with the Fourth Georgia and Malone's battalion, they gave way. As we fell back I noticed the garrison from our side of the fort rush across to the other side to take part against General Forrest's attack, and, as his command caught the fire of the entire garrison, he must have suffered severely.' Forrest interrupted him, saying in an excited and angry tone, 'I have no fault to find with my men. In both charges they did their duty as they have always done.' At this moment General Wheeler remarked, 'General Forrest, my report does ample justice to yourself and to your men.' Forrest replied, 'General Wheeler, I advised against this attack, and said all a subordinate officer should have said against it, and nothing you can say now or do will bring back my brave men,lying dead or wounded and freezing around that fort to-night. I mean no disrespect to you; you can have my sword if you demand it; but there is one thing I do want you to put in that report to General Bragg—tell him that I will be in my coffin before I will fight again under your command.' Neither the soldier nor the man in 'Fighting Joe Wheeler' was ever more in evidence than on this occasion. He both knew and appreciated Forrest, admired his wonderful genius, and loved him devotedly. He proved this in many ways in after years. Moreover, he knew that when the tempest was raging in this wild and rugged nature he could appeal to it more by gentle word and manner than by the strict rules of military discipline. 'Forrest,' he said quietly and with great feeling, 'I cannot take your saber, and I regret exceedingly your determination. As the commanding officer I take all the blame and responsibility for this failure.' "

*   *   *   *   *   *   *

The losses at Dover on the part of the Confederates were very heavy for the number of the troops engaged. In Wharton's command 17 were killed, 60 wounded, and 8 missing.* Forrest, who had not quite 1,000 men in the engagement, lost in killed, wounded, and captured 200; and among these Col. Frank Mc-Nairy, of his staff, was killed; Col. D. W. Holman, of Napier's battalion, wounded, and three captains of this command wounded and captured. The Federal commander, Colonel Lowe, on February 4th reported that 135 Confederate dead had been found, and that they then held 50 prisoners. Major C. W. Anderson says the lost officers in Starnes's Fourth Tennessee was so great that he was ordered to command a detachment of this regiment, and led it in the last charge. Colonel Harding, in his official report, gives his loss as 13 killed, 51 wounded, and 46 prisoners. On the morning of February 4th the Confederates resumed their march in the direction of Columbia. Being informed of the approach of a column of infantry and cavalry under General Jefferson C. Davis, they were compelled to make a wide detour in the direction of Centerville toward Duck River, and there succeeded in crossing this stream. On the 17th they were once more in camp at Columbia.

I left Bowers at Mr. Trotter's, riding Bowers's horse, agreeing to remain until my return from Shelbyville, where I proceeded with haste to send a full report of the situation, in and around Nashville, to General Bragg. In passing through to Shelbyville I forwarded a copy to General Forrest, who was then encamped above Columbia. I learned here that General Van Dorn was now commanding the cavalry forces on the left wing of Bragg's army. It was encamped from Columbia toward Spring Hill and consisted of five brigades with a strength of some 6,000 men. Forrest was commanding a division of two brigades.

---

*Official Records, Vol. xxiii, part i, p. 41.

General Wheeler was now commanding the cavalry forces on the center and right flank of the army, including a division commanded by General Morgan.

There had been sanguinary battles here about Spring Hill and the Confederates had gained decisive victories over all the forces sent against them.

At Shelbyville I stopped at Dr. Blakemore's for three days. I arranged with Major Hawkins to take my report and send it forward to General Bragg at Tullahoma. Here I met a number of General Morgan's command and learned the particulars of his December raid into Kentucky.

General Duke says:

The results of this expedition were the destruction of the railroads, which has been described, the capture of eighteen hundred and seventy-seven prisoners, of a large number of stores, arms, and government property of every description. Our loss was only twenty-six in killed and wounded (only two killed) and sixty-four missing.

* * * * * * *

It seemed to me that Morgan and Forrest had inaugurated the only effective warfare that had been of material advantage to the Confederacy, between the Mississippi River and the mountains. It seemed strange that Bragg and the government would not back them in every way possible and encourage all other similar commands of cavalry to actually live in the rear of the Federal armies and even cross the Ohio River into every State from Iowa to Pennsylvania. I had heard Capt. William Forrest say at Columbia that his brother, General Forrest, had often remarked that it could be done successfully.

I felt sure of the fact that the infantry armies would give out if we must rely on them to take and hold the country from the Mississippi River to the mountains. It was only necessary to instance our experience at Fort Donelson, Shiloh, Perryville, Corinth, and Murfreesboro in order to understand that our volunteer armies were already practically exhausted for any aggressive warfare. Our losses in killed, wounded, and prisoners in these battles had been about equal to those of the enemy, and now the Federals would not exchange prisoners. They wanted to keep ours and did not need their own. The enemy had over two men to our one in the field in this department. But half of them at least were required to guard the railroad bridges, trestles, and posts in Kentucky and Tennessee against the raids of Morgan, Forrest, and other smaller cavalry commands. We knew that Colonels Johnson and Martin had operated, with never over six hundred men, between Clarksville and Henderson, Kentucky, for six months, when the nearest Confederate lines were at Corinth and Chattanooga, and had defied thousands of the enemy, who were still stationed all over that section of Kentucky to intimidate the citizens and prevent Confederate organizations by a reign of terror. These ideas were not original with me. They could be heard in every camp and were freely spoken out by soldiers and by citizens. No man was ever heard to condemn the December raids of Forrest into West Tennessee or of Morgan into Kentucky. And notably no man was ever heard to applaud the march of Bragg to Kentucky and back again. He and Kirby Smith had demonstrated that 50,000 Confederates, all volunteers, and the flower of Southern manhood, could not stay in Kentucky over one month. It was believed they were not doing any good now in Middle Tennessee. The Federals could stand equal losses of infantry and were glad to fight our armies on those terms. But Bragg somehow had learned no lesson from the experience of six months before when Forrest with 1,500 men and Morgan with 900 men had, by one month's work, reduced Buell's army of over 50,000 men to ten days' rations with starvation staring them in the face. They were doing this while Bragg with about 30,000 men rested in safety at Chattanooga.

Nearly every soldier thought Bragg ought now to go to Chattanooga at once and let Forrest and Morgan with divisions, while Duke, Wharton, Armstrong, and Johnson, each with a brigade, roam all over Kentucky and Tennessee with the 15,000 cavalry now doing nothing around the army except to watch the front and flanks of Bragg. They were willing for him to keep General Wheeler. It was believed by the soldiers that these veteran raiders with their veteran and daring troops would not only terrorize everything they did not capture in the rear of Rosecrans, but would recruit ten thousand men in the two States before the summer was over. Some suggested that the infantry and artillery could fortify and hold the mountain gaps, from Huntsville to West Virginia, while the cavalry harassed every army that might attempt to break over. And many thought horses ought to be brought out to mount Bragg's infantry and let it have a chance to win. But from my observation and the opinion of all the other soldiers I ever talked to on the subject, Bragg was the pet of the President, and would be kept in control until our backbone was broken. The time had already arrived when no man would volunteer to enlist in the infantry to serve under Bragg or any one else and no recruits could be had except by conscription. Morgan had enlisted or secured as many recruits on the Kentucky campaign as Bragg and Kirby Smith combined. Every man who wanted to devote his services and his life if necessary to the Southern cause was ready for active, determined warfare. It made no difference about the weather or hardships so there was a chance to get the best of the enemy. But the slavish monotony of life in a big army, that could not now expect to gain victories in the West, was already abhorred and believed to be a fatal mistake. And then there was a spirit of vengeance being bred in the Southern breast by the atrocities of the invaders in the Southern States and by commanders of posts in Kentucky.

In hearty sympathy with this universal feeling, I was without a settled plan. Bowers entertained the same views when

I rejoined him near Charlotte. We concluded to leave the vicinity of Charlotte and watch developments for a short time. I bought a splendid bay mare from Mr. Nix, a blacksmith, three miles from Charlotte, for three hundred and twenty-five dollars in Confederate money, and we went west about fifteen miles to a good neighborhood on Yellow Creek.

We started back to Charlotte, where we thought more could be observed with less risk. We had not gone far until we learned that a large force of Federal cavalry was crossing the Cumberland River at Palmyra that morning, only twelve miles distant. We halted at a safe place until we could learn the direction the column would take. We did not have to wait long.

The enemy, marching from Palmyra, suddenly appeared on Yellow Creek in the afternoon. We were in the highway when refugees reported the advance within a mile. The little wooded hills that bordered the creek bottoms furnished a secluded rendezvous and we stationed ourselves with several citizens about half a mile from the highway along the creek, on a projecting hill, where we could have an extended view. The column soon approached with detachments on each flank that galloped about from house to house and gathered up stock, especially mules and horses; but the news went ahead of the column and the people stampeded with their animals. They did not come nearer than a few hundred yards of our hiding-place, where we sat mounted with vi-dettes on our flanks and a good line of retreat. But the Federals made a sweep of everything they could use. We estimated the force at about 2,500, though the command was too much scattered to be counted. After it had passed we ventured out at sundown and learned that the force was under command of Colonel Streight and had encamped three miles up the creek.

We camped in the neighborhood with others, getting supper at the house of a brother-in-law of Colonel Lockhart of Dover, who was commanding a Tennessee regiment in the South, and met his wife here. After a casual glimpse of the enemy's camp we departed for Charlotte at midnight and reached Columbia the next evening, where we reported to General Forrest. He ordered a company of scouts on the march at once toward Centerville. But we inferred that he expected to follow with a stronger force. He said it would not be necessary for us to report to General Bragg, as he would send a courier post-haste.

CHAPTER XI

Famous raid of Col. Abel D. Streight through Alabama to Georgia—Famous pursuit and capture by Gen. N. B. Forrest—Ovation to Forrest at Rome, Georgia—Federal prisoners attest the kindness of Forrest.

We went out to the house of Mr. Miles H. Mays, our friend, and remained a week or more, hoping General Forrest would be sent after Streight and we would go along. But it finally appeared that Forrest's scouts had lost Streight's track where he embarked on transports at Fort Henry and went up the Tennessee River. But, besides, Forrest had no orders to do anything else. We now returned to Charlotte to await events. After we had been at Mr. Talley's about a week we heard from Columbia, that the Federals were marching up the Tennessee River Valley, from Tuscumbia toward Decatur, opposed by General Roddey's brigade of cavalry, and that Forrest had gone to his aid.

The pursuit of Streight by Forrest and the capture of his entire command was the most marvelous performance of the war. Forrest at no time had as many troops as Streight and less than one-third as many when Streight surrendered. The particulars are of special interest and I quote extracts from a graphic account from "Wyeth's Life of N. B. Forrest":

At Spring Hill, on April 23d, a message arrived from General Braxton Bragg, directing Forrest to make a forced march with his old brigade to Decatur, Alabama, and uniting there with the brigade of General Roddey, to take charge of all the Confederate troops and check the Federal advance. On receipt of this order, Colonel Edmondson's Eleventh Tennessee was hurried off with directions to reach Bainbridge on the Tennessee River as soon as possible, cross there, and effect a junction with Roddey. Following with the Fourth, Ninth, and Tenth Tennessee regiments, and Morton's battery, Forrest crossed the Tennessee River at Brown's Ferry, near Courtland, Alabama, on the 26th, and was soon in position to dispute the farther advance of General Dodge. * * * General Dodge had pushed out with his legions, and on Monday, April 27th, had driven the Confederates across Town Creek, when he ascertained that the enemy were in force under Forrest on the opposite bank.

On the 28th, although "the resistance of the enemy was very strong, and their sharpshooters very annoying," the Union commander succeeded in crossing the creek, the Confederates retiring toward Courtland. Notwithstanding his advantage, Dodge again withdrew to Town Creek that night and there encamped.

It was here, about dark on the evening of the 28th of April, when the fighting had ceased and the Union forces were going into camp on Town Creek, that a well-known citizen of Tuscumbia, Mr. James Moon, after a hurried ride around and through various Federal detachments, reached General Forrest with the startling intelligence that a very considerable body of mounted Union troops, estimated at about two thousand, had passed through Mount Hope in the direction of Moulton, and were probably now at the latter place. In his original plan, General Rosecrans had intended that Dodge should advance no farther than Tuscumbia in aid of Streight, but when at this point he informed the leader of the raiders that Forrest was at Town Creek, Streight insisted that Dodge should attack the latter and drive him at least as far as Courtland, or even to Decatur, and thus hold Forrest off. Streight says, moreover: "It was understood that in the event Forrest took after me in the direction of Moulton, Dodge and his cavalry were to follow Forrest." Swinging loose from all support, and taking advantage of the darkness of night to conceal his departure, Streight's "lightning brigade" marched out of Tuscumbia in the direction of Mount Hope on the 26th of April.

*　*　*　*　*　*　*

Sergeant H. Briedenthal, of Co. A, Third Ohio Inf., says: "On the night of the 27th, at Mount Hope, Colonel Streight received the cheering news from Dodge that he had Forrest on the run, that he had crossed east of Town Creek, had driven the Confederates away, and that he must now push on. Colonel Streight did push on through mud and slush and rain, and late on the afternoon of the 28th of April woke up the sleepy village of Moulton with the largest procession of Union troopers that secluded spot had yet entertained. Here he fed and rested his weary cavalcade until 1 a. m. (29th), when, saddling up, he moved eastward, with Blountsville as his next objective."

*   *   *   *   *   *   *

When Forrest, at dark on the 28th of April, received the information as to the presence of so large a body of mounted troops so far detached from their main column, his quick perception took in the situation at a glance.

*   *   *   *   *   *   *

Three days' rations were cooked, and shelled corn issued for two days' forage.

*   *   *   *   *   *   *

By one o'clock on the morning of the 29th of April all was ready, and as the cavalcade rode out of the town of Courtland, in the cold, drizzling rain which was falling and making the muddy roads still more difficult, there began a race and running fight between two bodies of cavalry which, in the brilliant tactics of the retreat and stubbornness in defense on one side, and the desperate bravery of the attack and relentlessness in pursuit upon the other, has no analogue in military history.

*   *   *   *   *   *   *

Steadily throughout that night, and well into the daylight of the 29th, the Confederate leader rode without a halt.

*   *   *   *   *   *   *

On the morning of the 30th, Forrest, with about 1,000 of his command in advance, overtook Streight and his 2,000 at the top of Day's Gap on Sand Mountain. Forrest's men rushed to the attack with Capt. Bill Forrest and his company of scouts in the lead. They went yelling right up against Streight's force, which had formed to receive the onset. Forrest's orders were, "Shoot at everything blue and keep up the scare!"

But Forrest was repulsed, and Streight, making a gallant charge with his whole line, drove the Confederates back. Among Forrest's losses was Capt. Bill Forrest, seriously wounded, and two pieces of artillery.

However, Colonel Streight immediately got his command off and pursued his journey in the direction of Blountsville. In this fight fifty to seventy-five were killed and wounded on each side. Lieutenant-Colonel Sheets, of the Fifty-first Indiana, mortally wounded, was among Colonel Streight's losses.

But Forrest pressed forward as before, and nine miles from Day's Gap came in sight of the blue-coats. A running fight ensued for several miles, until finally Streight was compelled to give battle at Hog's Mountain, which was desperate and lasted into the night and until Colonel Biffle, with a strong detachment, in the darkness flanked Streight and got in his rear. Colonel Streight now managed to escape with his command, leaving the two pieces of artillery behind that he had captured from Forrest. Forrest had one horse killed and two wounded under him in this desperate engagement.

The pursuit and skirmishing was hot and continuous from Day's Gap to Blountsville for twenty-eight hours without sleep—a distance of forty-three miles. And still Forrest kept at the heels of the raiders. Colonel Streight says:

After resting about two hours we resumed our march in the direction of Gadsden. The column had not got fairly under way before our pickets were driven in and a short skirmish ensued between Forrest's advance and our rear-guard under Captain Smith in the town of Blountsville.

Forrest still crowded Streight for ten miles to the Black Warrior River, where Streight was obliged to fight in order that his men could pass the ford. Forrest got a little behind here but soon caught up.

Streight reports that it was about five p. m. on the 1st day of May when he crossed the Black Warrior. He says:

With the exception of small parties who were continually harassing the rear of the column, we proceeded without further interruption until nine o'clock next morning, May 2d, when the rear-guard was fiercely attacked at the crossing of Black Creek near Gadsden.

But Colonel Streight got across the wooden bridge over Black Creek and had it in flames before Forrest could get to it.

Wyeth says:

> There was no other means of crossing the stream (deemed impassable except by bridge or boat) nearer than two miles.

It now appeared that Streight would leave Forrest behind, but it turned out otherwise. Wyeth says further:

> Close by the roadside was a plain farm-house in which lived a widow and two daughters. Here a brave girl only sixteen years old, Emma Sanson, rode behind General Forrest, under fire, and showed him at a secluded place an old ford where he could cross his command.

The "lost" ford was soon cleared and made passable. Forrest's advance-guard caught up with Streight at Gadsden, only four miles from Black Creek, and started him on another all-night march, although Colonel Streight says:

> The command was in no condition to do so. Many of our animals and men were entirely worn out and unable to keep up, and were captured. It now became evident to me that our only hope was in crossing the river at Rome and destroying the bridge, which would delay Forrest a day or two and allow the command a little time to sleep, without which it would be impossible to proceed.

Colonel Streight being sorely pressed, set an ambuscade about fifteen miles from Gadsden, but Forrest was not caught in it in making his attack. Here Colonel Gilbert Hathaway was killed. He was Colonel Streight's chief support in the command. Colonel Streight says:

> His loss to me was irreparable. We remained in ambush but a short time, when the enemy, who by some means had learned of our whereabouts, commenced a flank movement. I then decided to withdraw as silently as possible.

Wyeth says:

> From Gadsden, by a parallel route, he (Forrest) had dispatched on horseback, to go right through to Rome, a courier who would arrive there in time to warn the citizens to guard or burn the bridge and thus stop the raiders.

Colonel Streight was overtaken beyond Gaylesville, where he had halted, as his command could go no farther. Here he dismounted his men and let them sleep in line of battle.

But Forrest came up by nine a. m., and his men yelled incessantly to create the impression of a large force. Forrest now had less than six hundred men left to follow him. He did not attack but made a bluff.

Colonel Streight, in his official report, says:

Nature was exhausted. A large portion of my best troops actually went to sleep while lying in line of battle under a severe skirmish fire.

Wyeth says:

It was at this propitious moment that General Forrest sent Captain Henry Pointer, of his staff, with a flag of truce to the Union commander, demanding the surrender of himself and command. * * * Colonel Streight replied that he would meet General Forrest to discuss the question, and in the conference asked what his proposition was. Forrest replied: "Immediate surrender—your men to be treated as prisoners of war; the officers to retain their side-arms and personal property." Colonel Streight requested a few minutes in which to consult his officers. Forrest said: "All right, but you will not require much time. I have a column of fresh troops at hand, now nearer Rome than you are. You cannot cross the river in your front. I have men enough right here to run over you." In all of this there was not one word of truth; but this is war, and in war everything is fair.

Just then one piece of a section of Ferrell's battery, under Lieut. R. G. Jones, came in sight.

    *   *   *   *   *   *   *

Soon Sergeant Jackson came up with the other piece and took position in the other half of the roadway.

Streight returned to his command, called his officers together, and talked over the situation. They voted unanimously to surrender, and their commander, though personally opposed to it, and still ready to fight to the death, yielded to the decision of his subordinates. The men stacked their guns, and were marched away to an open field or clearing, but it was not until the Confederate general got his small command between the Federal troopers and their arms that he felt himself secure.

    *   *   *   *   *   *   *

Moving in front, the Federal commander had cleared up the country of all horses and mules, and in this way kept his men supplied with fresh mounts. He says: "I do not think that at the time of the surrender we had a score of the mules drawn at Nashville left." On the other hand, Forrest had no opportunity of supplying his men with animals. When, from casting a shoe or other injury, or from exhaustion, one of his horses gave out, that was the end of both man and horse as far as this expedition was concerned.

*   *   *   *   *   *   *

Major-General Richard J. Oglesby, in his official report, says: "One of Dodge's men who was with Streight and escaped, says that when taken they were worn out, and Forrest captured them with five hundred men. Streight thought a large force was after him."

*   *   *   *   *   *   *

General Braxton Bragg reported to the War Department, at Richmond: "May 3d, between Gadsden and Rome, after five days and nights of fighting and marching, General Forrest captured Colonel Streight and his whole command, about sixteen hundred, with rifles, horses, etc."

The Congress of the Confederate States of America resolved that: "The thanks of Congress are again due to General N. B. Forrest and the officers and men of his command for meritorious service on the field, and especially for the daring skill and perseverance exhibited in the pursuit and capture of the *largely superior forces* of the enemy near Rome, Georgia, etc."

*   *   *   *   *   *   *

It is safe to say that there entered into Rome, Georgia, on the 3d of May, 1863, the hungriest triumphal procession in the history of this borough. The victorious troops were royally entertained by the citizens, and the men and horses soon forgot the severe ordeal to which they had been subjected. Even the unfortunate prisoners were not neglected. Sergeant Briedenthal, in his diary, from which I have already quoted, says on May 5th: "We have been treated well since our surrender, by Forrest's men, who have used us as a true soldier should treat a prisoner."

This testimony of a Federal soldier as to the treatment of prisoners is noteworthy.

Colonel Streight and General Dodge had just desolated the Alabama Valley between Eastport and Town Creek, as will appear from the next chapter.

CHAPTER XII

Conduct of the invaders—Devastation of the country in Tennessee, Alabama, and Mississippi—Cruelty to non-combatant sympathizers with the South.

The army of General Bragg had now been resting over four months on the line of Shelbyville. General Van Dorn had been killed by a citizen of Spring Hill. The operations of Forrest between Columbia and Brentwood and of Morgan from McMinnville toward Lebanon had been the only activity in Middle Tennessee.

But during this period the citizens of Kentucky, Missouri, Tennessee, Louisiana, Maryland, Mississippi, Alabama, and Virginia had suffered from all the horrors of war.

It would be fair to leave the story of these features of the conduct of the invaders to be told by some of the Federal officers and commanders who issued, or executed, the orders to imprison and execute citizens, pillage and burn the barns, mills, and homes of the people, use or destroy all provisions, hogs, cattle, and horses, and terrorize non-combatants, and in fact devastate the country. I submit the testimony (taken from official reports) of a few of the Federal commanders as follows:

HEADQUARTERS, THIRD DIVISION, FOURTEENTH ARMY CORPS.
TRIUNE, TENN., April 15, 1863.

COLONEL: The enemy have been remarkably reserved for the past four days.

* * * * * * *

Van Dorn is quiet at Spring Hill with his force.

In the destruction of property, under the order of Major-General Stanley to his command to burn the houses of all citizens who have sons or near relatives in the Confederate service, a large amount of forage was burned.

* * * * * * *

Respectfully, your obedient servant,
JAMES B. STEEDMAN,
Brigadier-General Commanding, Third Division.

Lieut.-Col. GEORGE E. FLYNT,
Chief of Staff, Fourteenth Army Corps.

CAMP NEAR MURFREESBORO, TENN.
April 16, 1863.

SIR: I have the honor to submit the following report of the late scout to Franklin, Tenn.:

Left camp with my command, consisting of the Second East Tennessee Cavalry and a detachment of the Fourth Indiana Cavalry, on the morning of Thursday, April 9, 1863; halted at night about four miles south of Triune.

* * * * * * *

On the 11th instant, advanced as far as where the Fourth U. S. Cavalry were engaged on the 10th. Returned from that place to where we halted on the morning of the 10th instant. Resumed march on the 13th for Murfreesboro at twelve a. m.; arrived at camp at nine p. m., burning on our way ten dwellings and outhouses belonging to persons who had sons in the Confederate army, as per order of Major-General Stanley.

I am, very respectfully,
Your obedient servant,
D. M. RAY,
Colonel Commanding, Third Cavalry Brigade.

Capt. W. H. SINCLAIR,
Assistant Adjutant-General.

HEADQUARTERS, DISTRICT OF CORINTH.
May 2, 1863.

GENERAL: My command is coming in. I send brief report. We had four fights, viz., at Bear Creek, Little Bear, Leighton, and Town Creek. Captured about forty prisoners, 900 head of mules and horses, 60 bales of cotton, and a large amount of provisions, and destroyed at least 1,500,000 bushels of corn and a large quantity of bacon, three tan-yards, and five mills; took the towns of Tuscumbia and Florence, and destroyed about 60 flat-boats on Tennessee River, breaking up every ferry from

Eastport to Courtland. A large number of refugees and negroes joined us, and we have rendered useless for this year the garden spot of Alabama.

*   *   *   *   *   *   *

I turned over 500 animals to Colonel Streight, and broke down at least 400 more. Cattle, sheep, cows and hogs we captured and used by the thousands, and I did not leave a thing in the valley that I considered would in the least aid the enemy.

*   *   *   *   *   *   *

G. M. Dodge,
Brigadier-General.

Maj.-Gen. R. J. Oglesby, Jackson, Tenn.

Corinth, Miss., May 5, 1863.

Sir: I have the honor to submit the following report of the expedition up the Tuscumbia Valley to Courtland, Ala.

*   *   *   *   *   *   *

On my return, I burned all provisions, produce and forage, all mills and tan-yards, and destroyed everything that would in any way aid the enemy. I took stock of all kinds that I could find, and rendered the valley so destitute that it cannot be occupied by the Confederates, except provisions and forage be transported to them.

*   *   *   *   *   *   *

G. M. Dodge,
Brigadier-General.

Capt. S. Wait,
Assistant Adjutant-General, Left Wing, Sixteenth Corps.

General Grant says:

Up to the battle of Shiloh I, as well as thousands of other citizens, believed that the rebellion against the Government would collapse suddenly and soon, if a decisive victory could be gained over any of its armies.

*   *   *   *   *   *   *

But when Confederate armies were collected which not only attempted to hold a line farther south, from Memphis to Chattanooga, Knoxville, and on to the Atlantic, but assumed the offensive and made such a gallant effort to regain what had been lost, then, indeed, I gave up all idea of saving the Union except by complete conquest. Up to that time it had been the policy of our army, certainly that portion commanded by me, to protect the property of the citizens whose territory was invaded, without regard to their sentiments, whether Union or Secession. After this, however, I regarded it as humane to both sides to protect the persons of those found at their homes, but to consume everything that could be used to support or supply armies. Protection was still continued over such supplies as were within lines held by us and which we expected to continue to hold; but such supplies within the reach of Confederate armies I regarded as much contraband as arms or ordnance stores. Their destruction was accomplished without bloodshed and tended to the same result as the destruction of armies. I continued this policy to the close of the war.

* * * * * * *

On the 20th, General Van Dorn appeared at Holly Springs, my secondary base of supplies, captured the garrison of 1,500 men commanded by Colonel Murphy, of the 8th Wisconsin Regiment, and destroyed all our munitions of war, food and forage. The capture was a disgraceful one to the officer commanding, but not to the troops under him. At the same time Forrest got on our line of railroad between Jackson, Tennessee, and Columbus, Kentucky, doing much damage to it.

* * * * * * *

After sending cavalry to drive Van Dorn away, my next order was to despatch all wagons we had, under proper escort, to collect and bring in all supplies of forage and food from a region of fifteen miles east and west of the road from our front back to Grand Junction, leaving two months' supplies for the families of those whose stores were taken. I was amazed at the quantity of supplies the country afforded.

* * * * * * *

On the 2d of August I was ordered from Washington to live upon the country, on the resources of citizens hostile to the Government, so far as practicable. I was also directed to handle rebels within our lines without gloves; to imprison them, or to expel them from their homes and from our lines.

* * * * * * *

A similar and worse condition of affairs had been suffered by the people of Virginia during the past year, as may be seen from the following orders of Gen. John Pope, commanding the Federal army:

HEADQUARTERS OF THE ARMY OF VIRGINIA.

July 18, 1862.

General Orders No. 5.

Hereafter, as far as practicable, the troops of this command will subsist upon the country in which their operations are carried on. * * *

By command of Major-General Pope.

GEORGE D. RUGGLES,
Colonel, A. A.-General, and Chief of Staff.

*   *   *   *   *   *   *

HEADQUARTERS ARMY OF VIRGINIA.

July 18, 1862.

General Orders No. 7.

The people of the Valley of the Shenandoah and throughout the region of the operations of this army, living along the lines of railroad and telegraph, and along routes of travel in the rear of United States forces, are notified that they will be held responsible for any injury done the track, line, or road, or for any attacks upon the trains or straggling soldiers, by bands of guerrillas in their neighborhood. * * * Evil-disposed persons in the rear of our armies, who do not themselves engage directly in these lawless acts, encourage by refusing to interfere or give any information by which such acts can be prevented or the perpetrators punished. Safety of the life and property of all persons living in the rear of our advancing army depends upon the maintenance of peace and quiet among themselves, and upon the unmolested movements through their midst of all pertaining to the military service. They are to understand distinctly that the security of travel is their only warrant of personal safety. * * * If a soldier or legitimate follower of the army be fired upon from any house, the house shall be razed to the ground and the inhabitants sent prisoners to the headquarters of this army. If such an outrage occur at any place distant from settlements, the people within five miles around shall be held accountable, and made to pay an indemnity sufficient for the case; and any person detected in such outrages, either during the act or at any time afterward, shall be shot, without waiting civil process. * * *

By command of Major-General Pope.

GEORGE D. RUGGLES, Colonel.

HEADQUARTERS ARMY OF VIRGINIA.

Washington, July 23, 1862.

General Orders No. 11.

Commanders of army corps, divisions, brigades, and detached commands will proceed immediately to arrest all disloyal male citizens within their lines, or within their reach in the rear of their respective stations.

Such as are willing to take the oath of allegiance to the United States, and will furnish sufficient security for its observance, shall be permitted to remain at their homes, and pursue in good faith their accustomed avocations. Those who refuse shall be conducted south beyond the extreme pickets of the army, and be notified that, if found anywhere within our lines or at any point in the rear, they will be considered spies, and subjected to the extreme rigor of the military law.

*   *   *   *   *   *   *

GEORGE D. RUGGLES,
Colonel, A. A.-General, and Chief of Staff.

The operations of Gen. Benjamin F. Butler at New Orleans were of a different character. Much might be given in detail from many sources to portray the sufferings of the Southern people in that locality, but an extract, which is taken from the account of Jefferson Davis, will state the case sufficiently.

Of New Orleans, May 1, 1862, and afterwards, he says:

*   *   *   *   *   *   *

The United States forces were under the command of Maj.-Gen. Benjamin F. Butler. Martial law was declared, and Brig.-Gen. George F. Shepley was appointed military governor of the State.

*   *   *   *   *   *   *

Peaceful and aged citizens, unresisting captives, and non-combatants were confined at hard labor with chains attached to their limbs, and held in dungeons and fortresses; others were subjected to a like degrading punishment for selling medicine to the sick soldiers of the Confederacy. The soldiers of the invading force were incited and encouraged by general orders to insult and outrage the wives and mothers and sisters of the citizens; and helpless women were torn from their homes and subjected to solitary confinement, some in fortresses and prisons—and one, especially, on an island of barren sand, under a tropical sun—and were fed with loathsome rations and exposed to vile insults.

*   *   *   *   *   *   *

Egress from the city was refused to those whose fortitude stood the test, and even to lone and aged women and to helpless children; and, after being ejected from their houses and robbed of their property, they were left to starve in the streets or subsist on charity.

* * * * * * *

By an order (No. 91), the entire property in that part of Louisiana west of the Mississippi River was sequestrated for confiscation, and officers were assigned to the duty, with orders to gather up and collect the personal property, and turn over to the proper officers, upon their receipts, such of it as might be required for the use of the United States Army; and to bring the remainder to New Orleans, and cause it to be sold at public auction to the highest bidders. This was an order which, if it had been executed, would have condemned to punishment, by starvation, at least a quarter of a million of persons, of all ages, sexes, and conditions. The African slaves, also, were not only incited to insurrection by every license and encouragement, but numbers of them were armed for a servile war, which in its nature, as exemplified in other lands, far exceeds the horrors and merciless atrocities of savages. In many instances the officers were active and zealous agents in the commission of these crimes, and no instance was known of the refusal of any one of them to participate in the outrages.

The order of Major-General Butler, to which reference is made above, was as follows:

HEADQUARTERS DEPARTMENT OF THE GULF.
New Orleans.

As officers and soldiers of the United States have been subjected to repeated insults from women, calling themselves ladies, of New Orleans, in return for the most scrupulous non-interference and courtesy on our part, it is ordered hereafter, when any female shall, by mere gesture or movement, insult, or show contempt for any officers or soldiers of the United States, she shall be regarded and held liable to be treated as a woman about town plying her vocation.

By command of Major-General Butler.

This order was issued on May 15, 1862, and known as General Order No. 28.

As a rule no report was made of the outrages committed by the detachments sent out to pillage and burn by Stanley, Payne, Turchin, Grierson, Milroy, Hunter, Merritt, etc.

But, No. 42, Rebellion Records, published at New York during the war, contains among a large number a report of an expedition by Colonel Montgomery, commander of a negro regiment on the coast of Georgia. Montgomery detailed his expedition on June 11, 1863, on an improvised gunboat with a force of negro soldiers, up the Altamaha River to Darien, to pay his "compliments to the rebels of Georgia." As he approached the town he says he threw shells into it which drove the inhabitants "frightened and terror-stricken in every direction." Then here is what he says his negro soldiers did:

Pickets were sent out to the limits of the town. Orders were then given to search the town, take what could be found of value to the vessels, and then fire it. Officers then started off in every direction, with squads of men, to assist. In a very short time every house was broken into, and the work of pillage and selection was begun. * * * Soon the men began to come in in twos, threes, and dozens, loaded with every species and all sorts and quantities of furniture, stores, trinkets, etc., etc., till one would be tired enumerating. We had sofas, tables, pianos, chairs, mirrors, carpets, beds, bedsteads, carpenters' tools, coopers' tools, law books, account books in unlimited supply, china sets, tinware, earthenware, Confederate shin plasters, old letters, papers, etc., etc., etc. A private would come along with a slate, yard stick, and a brace of chickens in one hand, a table on his head, and in the other hand a rope with a cow attached. * * * Droves of sheep and cows were driven in and put aboard. * * * Darien contained from seventy-five to one hundred houses—not counting slave cabins, of which there were several to every house, the number varying evidently according to the wealth of the proprietor. One fine broad street ran along the river, the rest starting from it. All of them were shaded on both sides, not with young saplings, but good sturdy oaks and mulberries, that told of a town of both age and respectability. It was a beautiful town; and never did it look so grand and beautiful as in its destruction. As soon as a house was ransacked, the match was applied, and by six o'clock the whole town was in one sheet of flame.

*   *   *   The South must be conquered inch by inch; and what we can't put a force in to hold, ought to be destroyed. If we must burn the South, so be it.   *   *   *   We reached camp next day, Friday, about three o'clock p. m. The next morning the plunder was divided, and now it is scattered all over the camp, but put to good use the whole of it. Some of the quarters really look princely, with their sofas, divans, pianos, etc.

CHAPTER XIII

Organization to raid western Kentucky and recruit a regiment—
Fight and defeat at Dixon—Return to Tennessee.

At this period the operations of troops in Tennessee had
been confined to the commands of Forrest and Morgan on
the left and right wings of Bragg's army and Wheeler in
the center.

Our location at Charlotte was within 27 miles of Nashville.
Nothing of interest occurred until June, when John W.
Head of Providence, and Rev. William Dimmitt of Madisonville, came through from their homes and reported the situation in Kentucky. Dimmitt had been chaplain of Colonel
Johnson's regiment. Head was a lieutenant in the regiment, but had been one of those who had been cut off and
had been hiding about in the woods with others, expecting
Johnson to return. Dimmitt was the foremost minister in
his church—the Christian denomination. They reported
great persecution of the citizens by the Federals. Mr. Dimmitt's home was four miles from Madisonville and he reported the garrison to be sixty-five cavalry at that place.

About this time Colonel Ross of West Tennessee, who had
been wounded some months before, stopped in the neighborhood. And next came my uncle, Capt. F. M. Headley,
from the army in Mississippi, on leave to go into Kentucky
and endeavor to secure recruits for his company. He had
carried out the first and only infantry company from Hopkins County in 1861.

It was suggested by Parson Dimmitt that a company of
thirty men could make its way through the lines and capture
the garrison at Madisonville by attacking at daylight. He
proposed to go if the men could be gathered together. This

expedition was at once approved. The prospects of the exploit filled us all with the idea that its success would enable us to recruit a regiment before we could be expelled from the territory.

It was soon agreed that Dimmitt should be colonel, Ross, lieutenant-colonel. Head was to recruit a company, and Captain Headley likewise to serve temporarily. Bowers and I agreed to accompany the expedition and help. We soon secured the pledges of twelve in all, and within a week or ten days about twenty were ready, and most of them had arms. But no one had ammunition. Head knew where Col. Adam Johnson had buried two kegs of powder and several sacks of buckshot in a cavern not far from Cerulean Springs, in Trigg County, Kentucky, and he and I were selected to go on the trip for the supply of ammunition, while the others would endeavor to fill out as large a command as possible.

Head and I reached the cabin of our friend Murray on the bank of the Cumberland River on the first day, where we spent the night. We made a night ride of it by Brewer's Mill and on to Baker's near White's Bridge, where Bowers and I had stopped. We told Baker our plans and arranged with him to go to Madisonville, or go over to Thompson Hamby's in Hopkins County and send him to get the exact location of the camp of the garrison in town by the time our command came in. The friend who assisted in the burial of the ammunition promptly aided us, and we soon got as much as we could carry in saddle-bags duly wrapped up for safe carriage. We traveled through by the same route and reached Talley's, near Charlotte, in safety.

Arrangements were now about complete to take our departure for Kentucky. But, unfortunately, the next day about ten o'clock three of our men were run out of Charlotte by a cavalry company of Federals. One of them, our friend Walker, came to Talley's, where sixteen of our company had met, at full speed, to give the alarm. We all mounted our horses and went around the farm into a dense woods, where we felt safe, and dismounted to await events, leaving a picket on our track to watch the house and road toward town. We had been here but a little while when we heard a noise back in the woods that sounded like horses coming. It was the Federal cavalry within seventy-five yards of us. By the time we got mounted we were running, and we made as much noise among the bushes as would be made by a hurricane. The woods were too thick for the enemy to shoot, even if ready, and no doubt they thought they were getting into an ambuscade. Our party stampeded about three hundred yards and halted on a hill in the woods, as some of the men had pistols and the guns were loaded. We wanted to give the enemy a few shots. I now discovered that in the race the weight of my powder and shot, being jolted, tore my saddle-bags apart in the middle and away went half of our supply of ammunition. We saw the Federals stop just in sight and turn back. No doubt they had expected to surprise us at the house and capture the crowd, which might have been an easy job, but since we were mounted and wide awake on a hill in thick woods, the matter was different. The Federals retraced their steps to Charlotte and returned to Clarksville without going to Talley's house.

We were in trouble when we found they had picked up the ammunition I had lost. However, it was decided to try and make our way into Kentucky by traveling at night to the place where we left the greater part of the ammunition.

Starting after supper, we rode through Charlotte and on to Barton's Creek and encamped in a secluded wood. We remained here a couple of days and in the interim got a supply of ammunition from parties on Yellow Creek. We then moved down near the road that leads from Clarksville to Dover on the south side of the river. Here we camped in a safe retreat. Colonel Brewer, a daring Confederate, whose command had been scattered north of Clarksville, joined us here, but for the trip to Christian County only. We now had twenty-eight in our force, exclusive of Brewer, and all pretty well armed with pistols and double-barreled shotguns. When we were ready for our march, Colonel Dimmitt formed the party in line and delivered a patriotic and inspiring address, in which he demonstrated the absolute necessity for strict obedience of orders and attention to duty even more important on this perilous raid than in an encampment of the Regular Army. He then proposed that an oath be administered by which every person connected with the command should bind himself not to leave the ranks on the journey, either to visit or stop at his home, or for any other purpose. He invited those who were unwilling to enter into this obligation to ride to the front out of ranks. Not a man went. The oath was then administered by Colonel Dimmitt to all the command and then by Colonel Ross to Dimmitt.

We crossed the Cumberland River at Murray's by swimming the horses after dark, and camped near Squire Fletcher's. We made an early start next morning and were across the Dover and Clarksville road by sunrise. We followed the private route to the Hurricane timber and rested until night, arranging for supper and forage in the neighborhood. We made it convenient, of course, to conceal our presence from all save friends on this trip, as we were now in the enemy's country. After night we pushed forward to the neighborhood of the ammunition and supplied all with powder and buckshot.

At Cerulean Springs we met a party of Confederates, and recognized an officer as they approached. This was Lieut.-Col. Robert M. Martin, commander of the Tenth Kentucky Cavalry in Morgan's command. He told us he was wounded at McMinnville, Tennessee, just before Morgan started on the Ohio raid, and was left behind. He was shot in the right lung with a Minie ball, which lodged in his lung and was still there. He said he had been on a "fly" to the old stamping-ground. We offered him the command of our crowd if he would go back, but he declined.

It was arranged that Colonel Dimmitt and I go off the road to Allen Baker's and get his report of the situation at

Madisonville. After sunset we came to the fork of the road and left the command, which was to travel along slowly across White's Bridge over Tradewater River, then to Charleston, four miles, and take the Madisonville road, which place was twelve miles farther on.

When Dimmitt and I reached Baker's we got a good supper and our horses were well fed. The situation was unchanged at Madisonville and the camp was in an old livery stable. Baker belonged to Bro. Dimmitt's church in that locality, so I rested while they talked. We left there at 8 o'clock at night and jogged along four miles to White's Bridge, when I suggested that we should hurry on; but Dimmitt said he could not stand the jolting of a fast gait and we had plenty of time. He was elated over the idea of surprising the enemy at daybreak. We now knew the exact location of the camp, and both being familiar with the approach we planned every detail of the arrangement for the attack.

At daylight we overtook our column six miles from Madisonville, where it had halted on the roadside in an open woodland. I had been feeling discouraged and Dimmitt had declared that, if we were too late, we could conceal our men during the day and take Madisonville the next morning. The men were all furious when we arrived. Dimmitt made his explanation in a very sorrowful manner and expressed his painful regrets at the delay. Dimmitt proposed that we go through a by-road to Mrs. Kirkwood's, four miles distant, where we could arrange for breakfast in the woods and camp in a secluded place. This was decided on, and, to my astonishment, Dimmitt said he would go through the woods two miles to his home, spend a few hours with his family, and join us in camp during the afternoon. The command then devolved upon Colonel Ross and we moved away on the road to Mrs. Kirkwood's.

I soon saw that the men did not intend to allow Dimmitt to have any further connection with our expedition. Several other men were as near their homes as Dimmitt, and yet he was the first and only one to forget his oath, taken in Tennessee. I felt sorry for him when I came to reflect that this was his first experience, but we were not in condition to allow him to learn the business at our expense. We arranged without trouble with Mrs. Kirkwood and a neighbor for breakfast, and spent the day in a secluded woods, resting ourselves and the horses. Dimmitt did not make his appearance by sunset, so we recognized Colonel Ross as our commander, who decided to move six miles farther west and encamp above Stoney Point on Clear Creek, just below Burnett's Bridge. We moved that night across toward Providence to wild woods in Wiers Creek flats and encamped. The next morning we arranged with Kerney G. Rice for breakfast, and he entertained us all at his hospitable home two and a half miles from Providence. We passed through Providence, exciting a good deal of curiosity, as several of us were at home; but we only tarried a few moments, none dismounting. We took the road to Caseyville, on the Ohio River, but bore to the right and went to Clayville, nine miles, where we halted for half an hour and bought a lunch of cheese, crackers, and cove oysters at a family grocery. I bought a pocket-knife from Joel Blackwell, a Union man. We then turned toward Dixon, the county-seat of Webster County, after learning it was not occupied by a garrison. We traveled the ten miles to Dixon by twelve o'clock, including a stoppage to feed our horses. At Dixon we rested an hour, perhaps, and mingled with our friends among the citizens, giving it out that we were going to Providence.

We had calculated that forty or fifty of the garrison at Madisonville would be on our trail about half a day behind. And except for an accident our idea would have been correct. Kerney Rice, where we got breakfast, was one of my mess-mates at Hopkinsville and at Fort Donelson, where he surrendered with those who remained behind when Forrest took the rest of us out. When the year expired for which we enlisted, he was still in prison, and taking the oath of allegiance was released and came home. He told me we were

welcome to anything on his place but he was obliged, under
his oath, to send a man to Madisonville and report us. It
was sixteen miles, however, to Madisonville, and the Federals could not come to the locality before night.

It was our plan on leaving Dixon after our circuit to go
four miles on the road toward Providence, then turn square
to the left on the Madisonville road and follow this to the
Shake-Rag hills, very near Madisonville, and we would go in
next morning at daybreak and capture all that were left in
camp, while at least half of the garrison was out on our trail.

It happened that the man Rice sent to Madisonville met
the pursuing force on the Rose Creek road, only six miles
from Rice's house, near Wm. Peyton's. They questioned
him, of course. He had been sent to report. Peyton, the
leading Union man of that section, lived two miles from
Nebo and knew several of us intimately. He joined in the
chase as the guide. At most, they were only eight miles
behind us, and followed at full speed. We rode leisurely out
of Dixon, all the men closing up but two, who came rushing
after us just as we reached a thick woods in the edge of the
town on a ridge. We looked back at the first sound of running horses and saw the two men were closely pursued by a
company of blue-coats. Colonel Ross ordered us into the
edge of the woods and tried to form us into line quickly.
Our two men rushed by us and entered the woods beyond.
The enemy came in column of fours and I heard the commander order a charge. We opened fire with our shot-guns
when they were within fifty yards, but they did not pause.
Colonel Ross ordered us to dismount and get behind trees.
About half of us dismounted and balked the rush of the
enemy. Nearly half our men had given way and Colonel
Ross ordered us to mount. I was up in a second and off at
full speed. Colonel Ross, I noticed, was wounded, and Captain Headley's horse being shot, he was captured; but Ross
mounted and escaped. There were over fifty in the attacking
party and not over half our men fired a gun; but they were
not to blame as we were taken by surprise and had no time
to take position for a fight.

Most of the Federals, without stopping, dashed after the rest of us through the thick woods. I had gone about a hundred yards and was getting away on my fast-running mare, when I felt my saddle come loose. I found the girth had broken and I must go off with the saddle or get rid of it. I turned off to the right to get out of the track of the pursuers, and grasping my mare's mane I managed to let the saddle off behind. I had slacked up a little, but the blue-coats followed the crowd, and now I pushed forward without a saddle or baggage. I soon came to a field and turned to the right still farther, but presently came upon another fence running squarely to my right as far as I could see. The cheering Federals were a hundred yards to my left going on the other side of the little field after the main body of our men and firing all the time. I could not see far behind me and decided that I was hemmed in if any of the enemy were after me. I rode to the right some thirty yards, dismounted, and hitched my mare to the fence, under a tree, and ran under that much cover to the right until I reached the woods in a thick place, when I got over and climbed a sugar-tree with low spreading branches, that a man could not see into unless he got under it. From this tree I had a glimpse of my mare. I thought I might meet the enemy if I went in any direction. The cheering and shooting went on away from me until they appeared to be half a mile distant. I now felt safe unless they should look for me as they returned. But they did not come near me, though I could hear them going back.

After sunset I slipped along through the woods and found my saddle and baggage undisturbed. Presently I heard a man calling cows about two hundred yards distant across the field, and saw that his house was not far off. I ventured out a short distance and called to him. He came to me and I recognized him as Joseph Jenkins, who had been one of my father's customers for merchandise in my boyhood. He brought me feed for my mare and a good supper, mended my saddle girth, and gave me a hat—I having lost mine in the chase. It was eight miles to my father's house. Jenkins directed me through the woods to the highway, and I reached home about nine o'clock. My parents were glad to see me alive after the events of the day. My father had learned from Providence that the Federals, after our fight, had gone back by way of Clayville and then to Providence, where they had halted a few minutes. My uncle, Captain Headley, was their only prisoner. His feet were tied together under the horse he rode, to prevent his escape. When my uncle surrendered, Wm. Peyton, the guide and acquaintance, became ferocious, and rushed forward to shoot him, but the captain of the company interfered and saved Captain Headley's life. After leaving Providence the Federal command came along the big road by my father's farm, en route to Madisonville.

We learned the next day that a young man named Pate, from Tennessee, had been wounded severely during the retreat and was hid in a cabin on the farm of Andrew Bruce, one mile from my father's house on the road to Madisonville. He finally recovered and went to the South.

I managed to have inquiries made in all directions for my comrades, but it appeared that none had stopped in Hopkins County. After spending a few days at home, I started south again and traveled by the familiar route to Squire Fletcher's, and crossing by canoe at Murray's, arrived safely at the home of Mr. Watkins. Thus ended in disaster the expedition of Colonel Dimmitt into Kentucky. I learned that a number of friends were boarding on Barton's Creek at a farmhouse near Dickerson's store. I went there and arranged to stay with the crowd a few days before proceeding toward Bragg's army at Chattanooga. I found Capt. John H. Christy, of the Tenth Kentucky Cavalry, and we traveled together, reaching the army a few days after the battle of Chickamauga.

CHAPTER XIV

Bragg's retreat from Shelbyville to Chattanooga—Wheeler's fight and escape at Shelbyville—Morgan starts on Ohio raid—Federal commanders lose Morgan in Kentucky, except those on his trail—Morgan crosses into Indiana, passes near Cincinnati—Morgan surrenders, and with his officers is confined in Ohio Penitentiary.

The monotony in General Bragg's army had been broken by the retreat to Chattanooga, where it was now safely located. In the retreat from Shelbyville, General Forrest's command was unable to reach the bridge over Duck River in time to cross there, and General Wheeler, seeing that Forrest was cut off, led 500 cavalry across the bridge and soon encountered the enemy, whom he fought back until he and his command were cut off from the bridge and it looked like he would be captured; but Wheeler, calling upon his men to follow him, rode to the steep river bank and plunged his horse over into the deep water fifteen feet below. His men followed. Horses and riders went under and some were drowned. The enemy swarmed upon the bank and poured volley after volley upon the struggling masses, but Wheeler and most of the men reached the other bank and escaped. Forrest, finding the enemy in his front, made a circuit and crossed his command over the river in safety. Now all were at Chattanooga with Bragg's army. Rosecrans's army had followed to the mountains.

I now learned some of the particulars of the raid of General John H. Morgan and his capture in Ohio with about 1,800 of his command. I had heard of it in Kentucky, and it was said at Madisonville, his home, that Gen. James M. Shackelford claimed the honor of making the capture.

Although the expedition had resulted in disaster to General Morgan and his command it had been of great advantage in many ways. It had surprised and mystified the Federal commanders in Kentucky and terrorized Indiana and Ohio, besides creating widespread consternation all over the North. It had prevented reinforcements to Rosecrans and prevented the advance of Burnside through Cumberland Gap to East Tennessee. The result did not alter the romance and grandeur of the expedition. It had attracted the attention of the South as well as the North above all other events, especially in the closing scenes, when it was known that he had eluded and escaped from all pursuers, and had reached the Ohio River at Buffington Island, where it was expected he could ford the river. It was estimated that over 30,000 regular troops, besides over 50,000 militia, were in front and rear of Morgan during the twenty-five days from the time he crossed the Cumberland River, at Burkesville, until he surrendered. It will be remembered that Colonel Streight with 2,000 men left Tuscumbia, and with a start of twenty-four hours was pursued by Forrest with only one small brigade, and surrendered 1,600 of his men at the end of five days, when Forrest had but 500 men.

General Morgan's raid was perhaps unparalleled in the annals of warfare. It was intended at the outset, by General Bragg, that Morgan would cross the Cumberland, threaten or capture Louisville, and make such a diversion as would hamper and check General Rosecrans, or in the event that Rosecrans advanced Morgan would turn upon his rear. But when Morgan had crossed the Cumberland River, half a dozen brigades of infantry and cavalry began to close on him from all directions. He ran the gauntlet, captured garrisons, burned bridges, tapped and cut telegraph wires, and managed to elude and mystify the enemy as to his movements and the number of his troops until they had lost him entirely, except those on his trail. When he captured two steamboats at Brandenberg, forty miles below Louisville, and crossed his command over to Indiana, it stampeded the enemy on the river. It was believed at first, by the Federal commanders, that Morgan had gone down the Ohio River on the steamboats. Even the commander at Cairo, Illinois, called on the commander at Columbus, Kentucky, for 800 infantry reinforcements.

Gen. Basil W. Duke, who commanded one of the two brigades of General Morgan's division on the Ohio raid, says:

He (Morgan) had ordered me three weeks previously to send intelligent men to examine the fords of the upper Ohio—that at Buffington among them; and it is a fact, of which others, as well as myself, are cognizant, that he intended—long before he crossed the Ohio—to make no effort to recross it, except at some of these fords, unless he found it more expedient, when he reached that region, to join General Lee, if the latter should still be in Pennsylvania.

* * * * * *

As it turned out only the unprecedented rise in the Ohio caused his capture—he had avoided or had cut his way through all other dangers.

On the 2d of July, 1863, the crossing of the Cumberland began, the first brigade crossing at Burkesville and Scott's Ferry, two miles above, and the second crossing at Turkey-neck Bend. The river was out of its banks, and running like a mill-race. The first brigade had, with which to cross the men and their accoutrements, and artillery, only two crazy little flats, that seemed ready to sink under the weight of a single man, and two or three canoes. Col. Adam R. Johnson, commanding the Second Brigade, was not even so well provided. The horses were made to swim.

Just twelve miles distant upon the other side, at Marrowbone, lay Judah's cavalry, which had moved to that point from Glasgow, in anticipation of some such movement upon Morgan's part as he was now making. OUR ENTIRE STRENGTH WAS TWENTY-FOUR HUNDRED AND SIXTY EFFECTIVE MEN—THE FIRST BRIGADE NUMBER- ING FOURTEEN HUNDRED AND SIXTY, THE SEC- OND ONE THOUSAND.

It should be observed that General Morgan and his command appear to have been lost to the Federal commanders after crossing the Cumberland River. A number of official despatches of the Federal officers, covering this period, are given below:

LEXINGTON, KY., July 4, 1863—8 a. m.

Received 8.45 a. m.

General BURNSIDE:

Following just received:

"MARROWBONE, July 3—8 p. m.

"The developments of the past two hours verifies my conjecture, and justifies the movements I ordered toward Columbia and Greensburg. The Eighth Kentucky Cavalry has been in Burkesville. No enemy in my front. I have arranged to have Mason's brigade in Glasgow by a forced march some time to-morrow night. Cavalry entire to precede infantry and artillery, and go on to Greensburg. Hobson's brigade I have ordered to follow up Shackelford. You will perceive the necessity for the different movements of the two brigades. Morgan's whole force, from 4,000 to 5,000, has advanced toward Columbia. If Carter can check them until my force can come, all will be well. I think it will, anyhow. Bacon Creek Bridge will be the point struck, I believe, just above Munfordville. I think Morgan may now be permanently disposed of, by checking him beyond Columbia until I can get at him and partly behind him. I will be in Glasgow to-morrow, and, unless I receive contrary orders, continue to direct Shackelford's movements, as well as those of my division. Forces at Russellville and Bowling Green should be returned, and surplus concentrated at Munfordville.   M. H. JUDAH."

     A. E. BURNSIDE,

       Major-General.

LOUISVILLE, July 4, 1863—10.20.   (Rec. 10.45.)

General BOYLE:

If there are any troops at Indianapolis or in Ohio, had they not better be sent here? Morgan has got on around our forces, and threatens the railroads. Morgan has 4,500 men. I have no force under my command to protect the road. I regret the troops have moved from Columbia, and believe part of Carter's division will have to be moved to Lebanon or other point. Morgan's men are mounted, and it will be difficult to engage them except at his option.

     J. T. BOYLE,

       Brigadier-General.

CINCINNATI, July 4, 1863.

General HARTSUFF, Lexington, Ky.:

I do not think any improvement can be made upon the dispositions made by yourself and Judah. I am satisfied there can be no force to come through Cumberland Gap. If we can succeed in whipping Morgan, it is my intention to make a quick and rapid movement into East Tennessee. Use all your available force to operate against him.

A. E. BURNSIDE,
Major-General.

LOUISVILLE, July 10, 1863.

General HARTSUFF (Lexington, Ky.):

Wires all cut in Indiana. Morgan's force reached the railroad. I cannot communicate with General Burnside.

*   *   *   *   *   *   *

J. T. BOYLE,
Brigadier-General.

Col. B. W. Duke, having surrendered with part of his brigade, says:

On the next day, the 20th, we were marched down the river bank some ten miles to the transport which was to take us to Cincinnati, and she steamed off as soon as we were aboard of her. A portion of the Ninth Tennessee had been put across the river in a small flat before the fight fairly commenced and these men, under command of Captain Kirkpatrick, pressed horses and made their escape. Colonel Grigsby and Captain Byrnes also crossed the river here and succeeded in escaping. Between eleven and twelve hundred men retreated with General Morgan, closely pursued by Hobson's cavalry, the indefatigable Woolford, as usual, in the lead. Some three hundred of the command crossed the river at a point about twenty miles above Buffington. Colonel Johnson and his staff swam the river here and got safely ashore, with the exception of two or three of the latter, who were drowned in the attempt.

The arrival of the gunboats prevented the entire force from crossing. General Morgan had gained the middle of the river, and, having a strong horse, could have gained the other shore without difficulty, but seeing that the bulk of his command would be forced to remain on the Ohio side, he returned to it.

*   *   *   *   *   *   *

General Morgan surrendered in a very peculiar manner.

In the extreme eastern part of Ohio (where he now was), he came into the "district" of a Captain Burbeck, who had his militia under arms. General Morgan sent a message to Captain Burbeck, under flag of truce, requesting an interview with him. Burbeck consented to meet him, and, after a short conference, General Morgan concluded a treaty with him, by which he (Morgan) engaged to take and disturb nothing, and do no sort of damage in Burbeck's district, and Burbeck, on his part, covenanted to guide and escort Morgan to the Pennsylvania line. After riding a few miles, side by side, with his host, General Morgan, espying a long cloud of dust rolling rapidly upon a course parallel with his own (about a mile distant), and gaining his front, thought it was time to act. So he interrupted a pleasant conversation by suddenly asking Burbeck how he would like to receive his (Morgan's) surrender. Burbeck answered that it would afford him inexpressible satisfaction to do so. "But," said Morgan, "perhaps you would not give me such terms as I wish." "General Morgan," replied Burbeck, "you might write your own terms, and I would grant them." "Very well, then," said Morgan, "it is a bargain. I will surrender to you." He accordingly surrendered to Captain Burbeck, of the Ohio militia, upon condition that officers and men were to be paroled, the latter retaining their horses, and the former horses and side-arms. When General Shackelford (Hobson's second in command, and the officer who was conducting the pursuit in that immediate region) arrived, he at once disapproved the arrangement and took measures to prevent its being carried into effect. Some officers, who had once been Morgan's prisoners, were anxious that it should be observed, and Woolford generously interested himself to have it done. The terms of this surrender were not carried out. The cartel (as Morgan had anticipated) had been repudiated, and the terms for which he had stipulated, under that apprehension, were repudiated also.

Although this expedition resulted disastrously, it was, even as a failure, incomparably the most brilliant raid of the entire war.

General James M. Shackelford, in his official report, says:

Learning that Morgan, with about four hundred men, had crossed the railroad and was going in the direction of Smith's Ford, I ordered Major Rue to return, with the advance, to the head of the column, then on the New Lisbon road. We had gone about seven miles when a courier from Major Rue announced that Morgan had run into the New Lisbon road ahead of him. Within a few minutes a second courier came from Major Rue, stating that he had come up with the enemy and wished me to send forward reinforcements immediately. The whole column was thrown forward at the utmost speed of the horses. We came to where the roads forked. The enemy had gone to the left, and was between the two roads. My advance had taken the right-hand road. I moved the column on the road the enemy had gone. On our approach, several of the enemy started to run. Just at this moment a flag came from the enemy, the bearer stating that General Morgan wanted a personal interview with me. I caused the firing to cease, and moved around to where Morgan and his staff were standing in the road. Morgan claimed that he had surrendered to a militia captain. Major Rue had very properly refused to take any action in the premises until I came up. I ordered Morgan and his staff to ride forward with Colonel Woolford and myself, and ordered Major Rue to take charge of the balance of the prisoners.

Morgan stated to me, in the presence of Colonel Woolford and other officers, that he had become thoroughly satisfied that escape from me was impossible; that he himself might have escaped by deserting his men, but that he would not do so. He also stated in the same conversation that he did not care for the militia; that he could, with the command he had, whip all the militia in Ohio; yet he said that since crossing the Ohio he had found every man, woman, and child his enemy; that every hill top was a telegraph and every bush an ambush. After traveling back two miles we halted, to have the prisoners dismounted and disarmed. General Morgan then desired a private interview. He called three or four of his staff and Colonel Cluke. I asked Colonel Woolford to attend the interview. He claimed that he had surrendered to a militia captain, and the captain had agreed to parole him, his officers and men. I stated that we had followed him thirty days and nights; THAT WE HAD MET AND DEFEATED HIM A NUMBER OF TIMES; we had captured nearly all of his command; that he had acknowledged, in the presence of Colonel Woolford, that he knew I WOULD CAPTURE HIM; that he himself might have escaped by deserting his men, but that he would not do so; that we were on the field; that Major Rue had gone to his right and Captain Ward to his left, and the main column was moving rapidly upon his rear; that he had acknowledged the militia captain was no impediment in his way, showing by his own statement that he could, with the force of men he then had, whip all the militia in Ohio; that I regarded his surrender to the militia captain, under such circumstances, as not only absurd and ridiculous, but unfair and illegal, and that I would not recognize it at all. He then demanded to be placed back on the field as I had found him. I stated to him that his demand would not be considered for a moment; that he, together with his officers and men, would be delivered to Major-General Burnside, at Cincinnati, Ohio, and that he would take such action in the premises as he might think proper. The number of prisoners captured with Morgan was about 350.

*   *   *   *   *   *   *

General B. W. Duke says:

While we were waiting in the hall, to which we were assigned, before being placed in our cells, a convict, as I supposed, spoke to me in a low voice from the grated door of one of the cells already occupied. I made some remark about the familiarity of our new friends on short acquaintance, when by the speaker's peculiar laugh I recognized General Morgan. He was so shaven and shorn that his voice alone was recognizable, for I could not readily distinguish his figure. We were soon placed in our respective cells and the iron-barred doors locked.

*   *   *   *   *   *   *

When we returned to the hall, we met General Morgan, Colonel Cluke, Calvin Morgan, Captain Gibson, and some twenty-six others—our party numbered sixty-eight in all. General Morgan and most of the officers who surrendered with him, had been taken to Cincinnati and lodged in the city prison (as we had been), with the difference, that we had been placed in the upper apartments (which were clean), and he and his party were confined in the lower rooms, in comparison with which the stalls of the Augean stables were boudoirs. After great efforts, General Morgan obtained an interview with Burnside, and urged that the terms upon which he had surrendered should be observed, but with no avail. He and the officers with him were taken directly from Cincinnati to the Ohio Penitentiary, and had been there several days when we (who came from Johnson's Island) arrived.

CHAPTER XV

Col. Robert M. Martin—Record in Morgan's cavalry—
Morgan's men under Martin open and close battle of
Chickamauga—Forrest loses his division.

Among the daring spirits of the Southern cavalry it is
due that more than ordinary mention be made of the
personal record of Col. Robert M. Martin. And it may be
pardonable for the reason that we were companions from
this period to the close of the war and ever afterward.

Robert Maxwell Martin was born January 10, 1840, near
Greenville, Muhlenburg County, Kentucky, and was some
months over 23 years of age at this time.

Martin was six feet in height and straight as an Indian
until wounded in the right lung at McMinnville. He was
now a little bent, but his form was shapely, his weight being
about 160 pounds. His eyes were bluish gray with very
light or blonde hair, mustache and goatee. In camp he was
playful and mischievous. In battle or in time of peril he was
at his best and had no superior. He belonged to the only
class of the Southern people to whom General Sherman paid
a compliment in a letter to General Halleck when asked for
his opinion of the disposition that should be made of the
population after the war.

General Sherman says:

The young bloods of the South, sons of planters, lawyers
about towns, good billiard-players and sportsmen, men who
never did work and never will. War suits them, and the rascals
are brave, fine riders, bold to rashness, and dangerous subjects
in every sense. They care not a sou for niggers, land, or anything. They hate Yankees per se, and don't bother their brains
about the past, present or future. As long as they have good

horses, plenty of forage, and an open country, they are happy. This is a larger class than most men suppose, and they are the most dangerous set of men that this war has turned loose upon the world. They are splendid riders, first-rate shots, and utterly reckless. Stuart, John Morgan, Forrest, and Jackson are the types and leaders of this class. These men must all be killed or employed by us before we can hope for peace. They have no property or future, and therefore cannot be influenced by anything, except personal considerations. I have two brigades of these fellows in my front, commanded by Cosby, of the old army, and Whitfield, of Texas. Stephen D. Lee is in command of the whole.

They are the best cavalry in the world, *but it will tax Mr. Chase's genius for finance to supply them with horses.*

Colonel Martin had rendered service in General Morgan's cavalry since December, 1862, of which General Duke says:

Shortly after the Hartsville fight, Col. Adam R. Johnson reached Murfreesboro with his regiment. It had been raised in western Kentucky, and was very strong upon the rolls, but from losses by capture, and other causes, had been reduced to less than four hundred effective men. It was a fine body of men, and splendidly officered. Martin, the lieutenant-colonel, was a man of extraordinary dash and resolution, and very shrewd in partisan warfare. Owens, the major, was a very gallant man, and the disciplinarian of the regiment.

*   *   *   *   *   *   *

Lieutenant-Colonels Huffman and Martin were especially enterprising during the early part of February, in the favorite feat of wagon catching, and each attacked with success and profit large foraging parties of the enemy. * * * I have heard an incident of one of the dashes of Martin, related and vouched for by reliable men who witnessed it, which ought to be preserved. Martin had penetrated with a small force into the neighborhood of Murfreesboro, and upon his return was forced to cut his way through a body of the enemy's cavalry. He charged vigorously, and a mêlée ensued, in which the combatants were mixed all together. In this confused hand-to-hand fight, Captain Bennett (a dashing young officer, whose coolness, great strength and quickness had made him very successful and celebrated in such encounters), was confronted by an opponent who leveled a pistol at his head, and at the same time Bennett saw one of the men of his company just about to be shot or sabered by another one of the enemy. Bending low in his saddle to avoid the shot aimed at himself, Captain Bennett first shot the assailant of his follower and then killed his own foe.

* * * * * * *

General Morgan, in his official report of the fight which ensued on the next day at Milton, says:

"On the evening of the 19th inst. I reached Liberty, Tennessee, and learned that the Federals were moving upon that place from Murfreesboro, their numbers being variously estimated at from two thousand to four thousand infantry, and two hundred cavalry, with one section of artillery. At the time I reached my videttes on the Milton road, the enemy was within five miles of Liberty. It being near night, they fell back to Auburn, and encamped. Determining to attack them next morning, I ordered Colonels Breckinridge and Gano, who were in command of brigades, to move within four miles of the enemy, and hold themselves in readiness to move at any moment. * * * In a short time I arrived upon the ground. * * * I therefore ordered Lieutenant-Colonel Martin to move to the left with his regiment, and Colonel Breckinridge to send one to the right—to go forward rapidly and when within striking distance, to move in and cut off the pieces. Having two pieces of artillery, I ordered them to go forward on the road, supported by Colonel Ward's regiment, dismounted, and the remainder of the command to move in column in supporting distance."

* * * * * * *

"They went forward gallantly, supported by a part of Ward's regiment. Lieutenant-Colonel Martin, who still occupied his position on the left, was ordered to threaten the right of the enemy. At the same time, I ordered the command under Colonel Gano to move up, dismount and attack the enemy, vigorously, immediately in front. Colonel Breckinridge was ordered to move to the right with his command and attack their extreme left. Captain Quirk, in the mean time, had been ordered to get upon the pike, immediately in the rear of the enemy, which he did in a most satisfactory manner, capturing fifteen or twenty men.

"He remained in the rear of the enemy until reinforcements came to them from Murfreesboro (being only thirteen miles distant), when he was driven back. When our artillery opened, the whole command moved forward. Colonel Martin charged up in most gallant style, and had a number of his horses killed with canister, as the guns of the enemy were turned upon him. The remainder of the command was moved up to within one hundred yards of the main column of the Federals and dismounted. Moving rapidly to the front, they drove in the enemy's skirmishers, and pushed forward in the most gallant manner upon the hill occupied by the enemy."

* * * * * * *

The scanty supply of ammunition, however, and its failure at the critical moment, was the principal cause of the repulse, or rather withdrawal of our troops. All who have given any account of this battle concur in praising the conduct of the combatants. It was fought with the utmost determination, and with no flinching on either side.

One incident is thus described by an eye-witness: "Just here Martin performed one of those acts of heroic, but useless courage, too common among our officers. When his regiment wavered and commenced to fall back, he halted until he was left alone; then at a slow walk, rode to the pike, and with his hat off rode slowly out of fire. He was splendidly mounted, wore in his hat a long black plume, was himself a large and striking figure, and I have often thought that it was the handsomest picture of cool and desperate courage I saw in the war."

It has been related that Col. Adam R. Johnson, commander of the Second Brigade in General Morgan's division, made his escape across the Ohio River in West Virginia at the close of Morgan's Ohio raid.

Colonel Martin having arrived at Chickamauga from his recent trip to Kentucky found Colonel Johnson absent on leave. While yet unable to report for regular duty he volunteered to serve through the battle, and commanded the little remnant of Morgan's division which had been collected by Johnson.

General Duke says:

An officer who was a valuable assistant to Colonel Johnson in collecting Morgan's men previous to the battle of Chickamauga, says: "From Calhoun we were ordered to Lafayette, from Lafayette to Dalton, thence to Tunnel Hill. On the morning of the 18th of September, the whole army marched

out for the battle. Our small force was ordered to report to
General Forrest, and did so about ten a. m. on the field. We
were immediately deployed as skirmishers, mounted, in front of
Hood's division, of Longstreet's corps, just come from Virginia. As the men galloped by Forrest, he called to them in
language which inspired them with still higher enthusiasm. He
urged them to do their whole duty in the battle. He spoke of
their chief, who had been insulted with a felon's treatment, and
was then lying in the cell of a penitentiary. He gave them
'Morgan' for a battle-cry, and bade them maintain their old
reputation.

"The enemy first engaged fell back upon a supporting regiment. We soon drove them back upon a third. By this time
our small 'layout' found the fighting rather interesting.
Engaging three times our number, and attacking every position
the enemy chose, was very glorious excitement, but rather more
of it than our mouths watered for. Yet no man faltered—all
rushed on as reckless of the opposing array of danger as of
their own alignment. * * *

"The enemy had formed in the edge of a woods, in front of
which was an open field. This field was fought over again
and again, each side charging alternately, and forced back. At
last a charge upon our part, led by Lieutenant-Colonel Martin,
was successful. The enemy fell back still farther. We now
saw clearly from many indications, and were told by prisoners,
that the Federal line of battle, the main force, was not far off.
We, therefore, moved more cautiously. Just about sundown,
we found the enemy's cavalry drawn up directly in front of
the infantry, but they made little resistance. After one or two
volleys, they fell back behind the protecting 'web-feet.' Night
falling stopped all further operations for that day. We camped
in line of battle, and picketed in front.

                    *   *   *   *   *   *   *

"The fighting of the next day was very similar to that of the
previous ones—the enemy falling back slowly with his face
toward us. But late in the evening the retreat became a rout.
The army made no attack on the 21st. In the afternoon
Colonel Scott was sent with his brigade over Missionary Ridge
into the valley, and engaged a few scattered cavalry and an
Illinois regiment of infantry—capturing nearly all of the latter
before they could reach the works around Chattanooga. Forming his brigade, Colonel Scott sent a portion of our command,
on foot, to reconnoiter the enemy's position. The reconnoiter-
ing party drove in the pickets, took the outside rifle pits, and
forced the enemy to their breastworks and forts.

"This closed the battle of Chickamauga—Morgan's men firing the first and last shot in that terrible struggle."

Colonel Martin related to me the trouble that was caused by the attempt of General Bragg to appropriate the horses of the orphan soldiers of the Confederacy, from far-away Kentucky, and how General Forrest stood by Captains Dortch and Kirkpatrick, and their men. When the order came for the surrender of their horses, Forrest swore he would surround Morgan's men with his division and protect them. The horses were not taken, but in consequence Forrest lost his own command.

Wyeth's "Life of Forrest" says:

It was while in pursuit of the retreating enemy, on September 30th, that Forrest received from General Bragg the following order:

"MISSIONARY RIDGE, September 28, 1863.

"Brigadier-General FORREST, near Athens.

"GENERAL: The general commanding desires that you will without delay turn over the troops of your command, previously ordered, to Major-General Wheeler."

Upon the receipt of this message he flew into a violent rage, at the height of which he dictated a letter to Major Anderson, who says: "The general dictated a letter which I wrote to Bragg, resenting the manner in which he had been treated, and charging the commander of the army in plain, straight language with duplicity and lying, and informing him *that he would call at his headquarters* in a few days to say to him in person just what he had written. He concluded by saying he desired to shirk no responsibility incurred by the contents of his letter. When Forrest read the letter over and signed it, it was sealed and handed to the courier, and, as he rode away, the general remarked to me, 'Bragg never got such a letter as that before from a brigadier.'"

Before President Davis assigned Forrest to another field of duty General Bragg had been succeeded by Johnston.

Wyeth says:

Gen. Joseph E. Johnston wrote: "He will, on arriving there, proceed to raise and organize as many troops for the Confederate service as he finds practicable."

*   *   *   *   *   *   *

From Rome, and thence westward, along the route over which, a few months before, he had pursued and captured Streight's raiders, Forrest marched with his handful of men—a brigadier-general with an army of two hundred and seventy-one men, as follows:

Field and staff.................................. 8
Escort company 65
McDonald's battalion..................... 139
Capt. J. W. Morton's battery...... 67
                                                        ———
Total effectives 271

CHAPTER XVI

Martin's expedition to Kentucky—Exciting adventures—
Skirmish with an old friend—Surprised and routed near
Greenville—Loss of horses and equipments—Rendezvous in
Henry County, Tennessee—Expedition on foot to Golden
Pond—Recapture of horses, and home-guards paroled.

Upon my arrival with Captain Christy, in Bragg's army,
we were installed by Colonel Martin as members of his mess,
the others being Cyrus W. Crabtree, Lieut. Arthur Andrews,
Lieut. Oscar L. Barbour, Lieut. Meade Woodson of Independence, Missouri, and a young man named Bryson from
Macon, Mississippi. Captain Helm of Texas, with sixteen
men, composed a company of scouts for Col. Adam R. Johnson, brigade commander. Andrews, Barbour, and Woodson
belonged to Johnson's staff.

This remnant was all that now remained here of Morgan's
men. The battalions of Captains Kirkpatrick and Dortch
had been sent away, one with Wheeler and the other with
Forrest. Wheeler had gone on a raid into Middle Tennessee, where he terrorized the garrisons that he did not
defeat and capture. Forrest was operating in the direction
of Kingston, on the way to Knoxville.

Colonel Martin discussed the situation with us all and
said he was perhaps as well now as he would ever be, the
Minie ball having lodged in his lung. It could not be ex-
tracted. But Martin did not know what to do. His regiment was in prison with the most of Morgan's division and
no prospect of their exchange, as the Federal Government
did not want to give up the Southern prisoners in return
for their own. They preferred to keep our ranks depleted

in that way and fill their own by draft and bounties, leaving their men in our prisons to suffer like our soldiers for the necessaries of life.

Martin determined that he had better try to recruit a command in the mean time, as he and Johnson had done the year before. He now proposed to take us and Captain Helm's men and go to western Kentucky.

There was no baggage or other luggage to pack, and with the men I have named, twenty-five in all, Colonel Martin rode away about daylight, passing over Lookout Mountain and then down the valley toward Gadsden, Alabama.

We crossed Tennessee safely, and arriving within five miles of Lafayette, Kentucky, learned there was a garrison of about thirty encamped in a stockade. Colonel Martin at once decided to attack and endeavor to capture this garrison if we could get to them before they could reach the stockade. The hour fixed was eight o'clock next morning, when it was calculated the men would be more or less scattered about the village, as was their custom, and that very few could beat us to the stockade, where their arms were always kept.

We started at 6.30 and were guided by pathways through timber between farms, and reached the designated point within one hundred yards of the stockade undiscovered. We were formed in column of fours. Martin selected Crabtree, Christy, Barbour, and myself to form the first set and go in front, with Martin commanding on our left. The stockade was on the right and about forty feet from the fence along the pike. We quickly observed that the garrison was nearly all outside, but there were several squads around fires not more than ten steps from the stockade. Martin did not hesitate a moment, and ordered us to go at full speed and commence firing and yelling. It was a dash. The Federals looked at us a moment as if astonished, and then darted toward the stockade. We got nearly even with it before they got in and began to fire from the port-holes.

Martin had directed that if we reached the position opposite the stockade before many got into it we were to dismount and run in around it so as to cut the others off who would be unarmed. The first shot struck Crabtree's horse, which groaned considerably. Martin ordered us to go on, and the whole command dashed by under fire. We escaped without a man being hurt, and stopped a hundred yards distant, in the business portion of the town, among the population, which had congregated there en masse. Horace W. Kelley, the leading merchant, was reported to Colonel Martin as the chief informer and persecutor of the Southern sympathizers in that vicinity. Martin directed Captain Helm to take a detail and go to Kelley's store and get some boots for his men, who were nearly barefooted, also socks, underwear, and hats. Mr. Kelley had locked up his store, but opened it and waited on his enemies just as cheerfully as if they had been cash customers. He seemed pleased to get off so easy.

We passed through Roaring Springs and reached the neighborhood of Canton, on Cumberland River, before night, and stopped to feed our horses and rest. We heard a steamboat whistling below and were enabled to determine that it was coming up stream.

Colonel Martin decided to go into Canton, where there was no garrison, and fire into it from the nearest safe place when it landed, provided it was loaded with troops, otherwise we would go aboard and perhaps capture some officers and burn the boat.

We were four miles from town and it was just night when the steamer came in sight. Meanwhile, we had halted within half a mile of the landing. We moved around to the river bank just above. The lights on the boat and on shore gave us a good view of the cabin deck, and no soldiers appeared and but few persons of any class. We dismounted, and with twenty men Colonel Martin went down the bank in the darkness. When the boat was securely tied up two men were sent to guard the deck-hand at the stab

and see that the boat was not cut loose. Colonel Martin
led the way and followed the boat's agent and others on the
gang-plank. One man went to the capstan to guard the
rope and see that it should not be cut. We followed Martin
up the stairway to the cabin and took possession. Several
soldiers were taken and paroled. A few government stores
were destroyed and thrown overboard. Colonel Martin told
me the captain pleaded for his boat not to be burned. But
as a matter of fact the captain was not a Union man. We
knew the government was pressing boats into the service no
matter who might be the owners. The barkeeper treated
the crowd to toddies and cigars and the steward brought
out some lunch.

It was reported to Colonel Martin that a Union man,
named Ford, who was a regular informer on Southern men,
had a very fine chestnut-sorrel mare. Captain Helm went
with a squad and got her, leaving Martin's animal instead.

We rode quietly into Cadiz, after a ride of nine miles,
at ten o'clock. There was a stampede of the prominent
Union men and several soldiers who were at home on furlough when they heard that "Bob Martin" was in town.
Colonel Martin sent a detail to get the postage stamps and
stamped envelopes at the post-office.

The weather had grown extremely cold, but we pushed
on to the house of my friend Allen Baker, in Caldwell
County. Colonel Martin intended now to capture the garrison at Madisonville and hold Hopkins County long enough
to get some recruits. After going a few miles the Colonel
decided to go off the road half a mile to some hollow in the
woods and build fires. We soon had regular log-heaps
blazing. The ears of one or two of our party were frost-
bitten.

"Cy" Crabtree had a brother-in-law, William B. Parker,
who lived three miles from the road on our way, and six
miles from Madisonville. Colonel Martin sent Crabtree
ahead to arrange for breakfast there and get a friend to go
early to town and find out all about the garrison.

We went through the country to Parker's by sunrise and were entertained handsomely by Mrs. Parker, the sister of Crabtree. It was then deemed best to camp in a secluded part of adjacent hilly, timbered country and await the return of the messenger Crabtree had sent to Madisonville. He did not return until night, as per instructions, in the event the garrison was kept in camp. He learned that Martin's capture of the steamboat at Canton was known and that the men were on the lookout for a surprise at any time. The garrison numbered about eighty cavalrymen and kept their horses in an old livery stable, one square from the courthouse.

It was now deemed best to draw the enemy out in pursuit, and for that purpose we left our camp before night, and went to the highway six miles from Madisonville, and eight miles from Vanderburg on the Henderson road. We turned off beyond the Shake-rag Hills before reaching Vanderburg and camped in an impregnable position on a bluff not far from the farm of a friend, Robert Washington. We remained there all the next day, hoping the company from Madisonville would follow our trail. We had arranged to have our presence at Parker's reported.

In this camp we were joined by two recruits, one of them a young man named Ashley, who had neither horse nor gun. He rode behind the other recruit, as he had a plan for a mount and arms. He guided Martin a few miles through the hills to the house of his cousin, who had turned to be a strong Union man and guide for the Federals. I knew nothing about the arrangement until we left his cousin's house. When we reached it, his cousin, Andrew Ashley, came out in the dark. Colonel Martin, as I was told, represented himself as a captain from Greenville, in pursuit of Bob Martin; that he had heard in Madisonville that Martin was camped at Vanderburg and the purpose in coming here was to get him (Ashley) to go along as a guide. Ashley promptly volunteered and said he would take his double-barreled shotgun. He caught his horse and was ready in a few minutes. Meanwhile, Martin had sent Captain Helm and two men with young Ashley, who took them to another place, Jack Burton's, near by, to get his fine animal, and they succeeded.

We started off without delay, Andrew Ashley riding with Colonel Martin. After going a short distance Martin undeceived Ashley and put him in ranks as a prisoner, turning over his gun and ammunition to young Ashley. We then headed for Madisonville to make a midnight attack and create a sensational fright. Several offensive Union men were arrested on the way, the purpose of Colonel Martin being to demoralize some of them. They were treated with perfect kindness, but they were in mental agony as to their fate, as Colonel Sam Johnson had shot several Confederate prisoners at Hopkinsville, in retaliation for the killing of his own men. Before we had gone very far, Andrew Ashley learned that I was in the command and urged Martin to let him meet me. He was brought back and I was surprised. I knew him well, and he was a Southern sympathizer when I left home. He asked me to have him released. When I learned the circumstances I told him Martin wanted to take him farther on, but I assured him he should not be hurt. He had been one of my customers in the store at Nebo and was a good citizen.

We arrived in the suburbs of Madisonville about midnight, near the dwelling-house of Nathan Hibbs, between the Ashbyburg and Henderson roads. We had learned that two pickets were out on all the roads. Those on the Henderson road stood at an elbow of the lane opposite the residence of Mrs. Bishop. Christy and Crabtree were sent to charge them as soon as Martin's command opened fire on the camp in town. We moved from the Hibbs place down across the common which extended nearly to the public square. Just as we had reached a point nearly opposite the old Eagle Hotel, on a corner of the public square, and were ready to dismount and creep around the camp to open fire, we heard two shots on the Henderson road. This was unexpected. In a moment we heard horses running and suddenly a great commotion in the camp, one square away. The pickets came at full speed and ran to the camp. We listened to the uproar for a few minutes, when Martin concluded it would be better not to attack now. We retraced our tracks to the Hibbs house, where we had left our prisoners under guard. Christy and Crabtree were there. It was understood that if their plans or ours miscarried, all should rally there. The pickets had heard the horses of Christy and Crabtree, a hundred yards away, and fired and then ran, because they were expecting Martin. We traveled a circuitous route with Captain Christy and Crabtree as guides and reached the house of Hugh McNary by sunrise, on the other side of Pond River, at the point where the Madisonville and Greenville road crosses the ford. We were in position to guard the ford against pursuit and were royally entertained here by the truest of friends. The young ladies, the Misses McNary, treated us to the first piano music we had heard in many a day.

It was a comfort to look back, as we rode away toward Greenville, and cheer the waving white handkerchiefs of this enthusiastic household. Our prisoners were released here and started home, feeling safer but mad. Greenville is the county-seat of Muhlenburg County and Colonel Martin's father lived three miles from the town. His father was a strong Union man and two brothers were captains in the Federal army.

The weather was unusually cold for the time of the year, December, which retarded our speed and subjected us to unusual hardships in our night rides and in our efforts to rest and sleep in the open air.

We stopped six miles from Greenville, off the road, where Colonel Martin knew a friend, and slept until night, two citizens volunteering to stand on guard where they had a long view of our track and could give us warning of a pursuing enemy without taking any risk. At sunset we started for Greenville, where there was no garrison, and charged into the town, about eight o'clock, yelling like Indians. There was a general stampede and great excitement among the population. This was a hotbed of Unionism and the offensive Union men dreaded Martin. Others greeted us cordially. A detail went to the post-office and got the postage stamps and envelopes. We now had over $20 worth of U. S. spoils. After Colonel Martin had spent an hour with his friends we rode out toward Hartford, soon turned, made a circuit around Greenville toward Hopkinsville, and camped with good fires until sunrise the next morning. After breakfast we went toward the Greenville and Madisonville road to learn if we had been pursued. It was the purpose now to go back to Madisonville if any of its garrison had followed us to Greenville. We entered a long lane through a farm and Colonel Martin inquired at the house, about midway. He heard of three different companies that were in pursuit, but got no information as to where they belonged. Just before we reached the end of the lane it was observed that dense woods were in front and extended around to the right over a hilly region. It was determined to pass on out of sight of the farm-house, scatter on the left of the road for a hundred yards in the woods and get across to the other side of the road, making a dim impression on the frozen ground and to some extent obscure our trail.

The fence on the left extended about fifty yards farther than on the right side of the lane we were in. Crabtree, wearing a Federal overcoat, was the advance guard, and at the end of the lane he observed a company of Federals about 200 yards to the left, across a little old unfenced field. There was a small ravine that ran through it about midway between our ridge and the one where the Federals had halted. Crabtree stopped and motioned back to us. Martin halted the column and galloped up to Crabtree, then called out to the Federals and asked who was in command. "Capt. Jeff Rouark," was the response. "Where from?" inquired Martin. "Hopkinsville," was the answer, and followed with the inquiry, "Who are you?" "Captain Wilkes from Henderson," answered Martin. "Send a man down half way," said Martin. "All right," said Rouark. Martin directed Crabtree to go and get all that Rouark knew about us. Crabtree and Rouark met down in the little ravine, while both sides sat quietly and looked on. Colonel Martin called out to "Cy" and asked, "Is it all right?" "Yes," responded Crabtree; "he wants to see you, Captain." Martin trotted his horse down to meet his old friend. They had been boys together in the same neighborhood. Captain Rouark was astonished when he recognized Col. Bob Martin. I heard Martin laughing as he said, "Well, Jeff, we ought to shake hands over a joke like this." "I think so too, Bob," said Rouark, and they greeted each other cordially. They then talked for a few minutes, and separated, each galloping back to his command. I had counted the enemy and made the number forty-two besides the captain.

Martin announced that he was going to fight. He ordered us to dismount in the woods on the right and hitch our horses quick. The ground sloped downward on that side. We then ran back to the fence on the enemy's side of the road and opened fire while Rouark was forming on horseback. Some of our men were behind trees farther to our right than the fence extended. Our long-range guns only were fired, it being deemed advisable to reserve our double-barreled shotguns for closer quarters if Rouark should charge on horseback. Most of Captain Helm's men were Texans and fine shots. I noticed some commotion in the enemy's ranks and was satisfied that men or horses were being struck. We were so well concealed, lying down behind fence corners and trees, that none of our men were touched and the bullets passed over our horses. Presently Rouark dismounted his men, and coming closer they got behind trees. Colonel Martin concluded we were wasting ammunition. He told us to be ready when he gave the word and that he wanted us to get up and run to our horses, mount quick and follow him; that he intended to form in ambush. He told me to mount and remain, to see if they pursued, and then fall back, keeping in sight of them. At the command all arose and ran as if stampeded, mounted and galloped away in good order and out of sight. I sat on my horse and watched. Rouark's men ceased firing and mounted their horses. There was a parley of several minutes and then they marched away in the opposite direction. I reported to Colonel Martin at once and it was now thought best to travel till our trail would be lost for a night. Martin knew the country and made a circuit around Greenville, keeping five miles from it, to the side toward Russellville, and stopped seven miles from town about ten o'clock in the night. We entered a thick woods, and going perhaps 400 yards made a gap in a rail fence around a cornfield. The gap was fixed up behind us. We then went along the fence inside for two hundred yards and then out through a gap into the woods again, camping about a hundred yards from the field. The movement inside the field was made to protect us from surprise, as our guard was placed at the last gap and could see the enemy come through the first gap. It was our purpose to go toward Russellville the next morning, making a circuit toward Madisonville.

I was the first man to awake the next morning. Our lonely picket down at the fence had his horse hitched and was stamping about to warm his feet. I was eating some lunch when I saw the picket mount his horse hurriedly and start to camp. Martin did not need to order the horses saddled. The picket rushed up and reported the enemy coming through at the place where we had entered the field. Colonel Martin directed me, as I was ready, to ride down within fifty yards of the gap, where we came out, and as the enemy came up to fire and fall back. I had hardly reached the spot when I got a glimpse through the brush of the approaching column, quietly riding along on our trail. I was sitting on my horse fairly well covered by a large white-oak tree. When the column arrived at the place where we had come out it halted and I fired, or thought I was firing, with deliberate aim, but the cap failed to go off. I then galloped back to camp. My animal was a handsome chest-nut-sorrel pony, but I knew nothing yet of his speed. I judged the enemy to number about fifty men.

Martin had the men nearly ready and was forming a line to fight, but on my report he decided to charge before the enemy could get through the fence, which they had begun to throw down, and then withdraw. We went with a yell, but they received us with a volley. Martin then ordered us to fall back and keep together. As we passed over the ridge beyond our camp the enemy was peppering away at those in the rear. Martin on his fine mare could have run away in the lead, but hung back and encouraged the boys to keep cool and close up. I observed a branch in a small ravine ahead of us and that the bank on the opposite side was steep and the men in front were making their horses climb to get up. I also observed that men from the rear were passing me and the shooting was coming nearer every step. It was only a question of a few jumps until I would be the hindmost man. My horse was too weak. I looked back and the Federals were only about seventy-five yards behind and not many of our men were now behind me. The ridge on which we had camped wound around on my left and broke down not far from the branch that crossed our path in front. I turned my horse around this little hill to the left, lying down on my horse's neck to hide if possible from the view of our pur-suers. I ran upon a small field. The branch our men were crossing ran out of it and where it passed under the fence a considerable drift had accumulated inside. I jumped down, and turning my horse's head toward our crowd, got over the fence quick and hid in the drift pile. Not more than half a minute had passed since I left the path. I peeped out and saw our men scrambling up the bank of the branch, about fifty yards away, and observed Colonel Martin was off his mare as she clambered up the hill, but he had her by the tail and was holding fast with both hands. Somebody grabbed her by the bridle-bit. At this moment the shout-ing pursuers were up even with me, and their firing and up-

roar frightened my loose horse back my way and he went
trotting around the hill along the fence. They got a glimpse
of him, and two men came rushing around after him and
passed within ten feet of me. This frightened him and he
stampeded into the woods with the two men in pursuit.

Everybody was now out of sight, but I could hear the
yelling and shouting the same as before. I moved my position a little, as I was on the ice, and crept as far under as
possible without leaving any fresh signs behind. I remained
in this position until I began to freeze. I could still hear
the firing and yelling a mile or two away, which had never
ceased at any point since the retreat commenced.

I got out and crossed another field to the woods and went
some distance until I came in sight of a log cabin. This was
out of view from the battle-ground. I went to the house and
warmed. I told the housewife I had been fox hunting and
came for a chunk of fire as my companion, who was at the
fox hole, thought we ought to have a fire. She asked me
what all that shooting meant. I was of course in another
direction and had not heard it. I got the fire and found a
secluded hiding-place, where I kept comfortable till night.

I wandered around after sunset, and coming near a farm
I waited until after dark and went to the house. I had lost
everything except my gun and pistol. I found the farmer
to be a friend of the Confederates and regret that I have forgotten his name. When he heard my story he said he had
one poor horse that he did not need and I was welcome to
him. I was supplied with an old saddle and bridle and given
directions around Greenville to the Madisonville road. I
reached the point before morning, got breakfast, and traveled
neighborhood roads to the house of a friend, five miles from
McNary's ford on Pond River. That night I called at
McNary's and learned that Lieutenant Andrews had been
there two hours before, having escaped in the chase. They
had directed him to James L. Brown's, who was a wealthy
farmer living seven miles to the right of Madisonville. I
went there and found Andrews. We safely passed Madi-

sonville and through Nebo to my father's house. We were obliged to go on, as it was agreed that all would rendezvous in Jordan Stokes's hollow, in Caldwell County, one mile from White's bridge on Tradewater. We reached there before morning, traveling my private route by Fisher's Spring, Rush's and Fox's. After waiting a week we scouted to Grubb's cross-roads and to Wolf's store, where we learned that Martin's party had gone through a week before. We now pushed through, traveling at night, crossing the Cumberland River at Murray's, and then up Yellow Creek and over to Piney Creek. We saw friends who had been in all directions, but none had heard of Martin's party. We concluded he must have fallen back across the rivers into the Kentucky Purchase or into West Tennessee, which were not occupied by garrisons now, and we headed in that direction.

Lieutenant Andrews remembered that he had a friend in Paris, Mr. Caldwell, formerly of Bowling Green, Kentucky, who had married a lady of Paris and had settled there in business. He entertained us at his elegant home on Christmas day. In the afternoon we heard that we might find our party in the neighborhood of Mr. Edwards's, five miles from Paris, on the road to "Mouth of Sandy." To our delight we learned upon reaching the home of Mr. Edwards that Colonel Martin, Christy, Barbour, and others had been there. The others had stopped with a Mr. Kendall and his neighbors farther on. We soon learned that the command had arrived in the neighborhood after losing their horses and baggage. They were now gone on foot into the enemy's country to mount and equip themselves.

Andrews and I found a home with a Mr. Kendall, who was a good farmer and a gentleman.

A few days afterwards Colonel Martin and his men returned from the expedition and were quartered in the neighborhood for two weeks. The events which had occurred in the command since the attack on our camp near Greenville, Kentucky, were narrated to me by Martin, Christy, Barbour and others.

"After you turned off the track," they said, "our worst trouble was at the embankment of the branch where you saw Colonel Martin on the ground. His mare shied under the limbs of a tree that swept him off behind, when he grabbed her tail and clung to it till we caught her, and he remounted under fire. But the pursuers could take no aim running at full speed through bushy woods and their shots did not hit anybody. We gained distance on them while they were having our experience at the embankment, and we would have been out of their reach very soon but for the presence of another company of Federals in front that was trying to find our camp. We got within fifty yards of them before they were discovered. When we turned at right angles they took the lead in the pursuit. They were in firing distance for a mile perhaps, and in this chase Andrews left us.

"We made our way to the mouth of Little River, on the Cumberland, between Canton and Eddyville, and the command crossed over to the narrow section between the Cumberland and Tennessee rivers. We reached the neighborhood of Golden Pond, where we concluded to rest, as there was no garrison of Federals nearer than Paducah, Hopkinsville, and Princeton. It was an out of the way locality where scouting parties seldom had any occasion to go.

"We went into camp in the afternoon," they said, "and made our beds as comfortable as possible, retiring early to get a much needed rest for one entire night.

"The moon was shining every night, going down about midnight. About that time our camp was fired into by a force of home-guards. We all made a dash away from the firelights and kept together in the woods. We opened fire on the enemy and scattered them on the side where we escaped. "Cy" Crabtree was shot in the hip and captured. The rest of us made our way through the country to the Tennessee River and crossed over. After resting here a week or more Colonel Martin decided to march back and surprise that same neighborhood. We crossed the river about sundown and arrived near Fungo or Golden Pond after a couple of hours. It was easy to capture one man at a time and recover our horses or get better ones. We captured Captain Bogard, who commanded the attack on our camp. He had returned Martin's fine animal to its owner, Mr. Ford, at Canton, only five miles distant, but Martin managed to find a good one. Martin had paroled that entire company of home-guards."

The news of the escape of Gen. John H. Morgan, from the Columbus, Ohio, Penitentiary, and his safe arrival in the Confederacy, had reached us. He had established an encampment at Decatur, Georgia, where it was proposed that the scattered remnants of his old division should rendezvous for organization and service in a new command to be made up for General Morgan while most of his own was still in Northern prisons.

It was decided that Andrews, Barbour, and Captain Helm, with his men, should proceed up the Tennessee River on the west side, pass between Shiloh battlefield and Corinth, and then across Alabama to Decatur, while Martin, Christy, and I would go around Nashville and then south with the view of giving General Morgan the situation in Middle Tennessee, which might induce him to make a raid with his force and attack the communications of Sherman.

CHAPTER XVII

Journey to Kentucky, then around Nashville and into Alabama —Narrow escapes—Luxurious homes of an Alabama valley— Johnston succeeds Bragg.

In leaving Henry County, Tennessee, on the journey to Georgia, Colonel Martin, Captain Christy, and I crossed the Tennessee River at Paris Landing. We then traveled to Murray's on the Cumberland River. The horse and outfit my friend had furnished me near Greenville was about as shabby as any I ever saw in the army. The animal was small, slow and in poor order. My companions proposed that our first adventure should be to improve my mount.

That night we stopped with my friend Squire Fletcher, one mile from the river, and left his house with directions to the home of his nephew, Jasper Fletcher, in Christian County, Kentucky, between Hopkinsville and Clarksville. We learned that a company of negro soldiers were encamped at the State line of Kentucky on the pike we must travel, on the direct route, and were directed to the house of Dr. Thomas, which we would reach within half a mile of the camp, and he could direct us through his farm to "Jap" Fletcher's. We went on four miles and entered the front gate of the yard of Dr. Thomas. The house stood back about fifty yards, and we were to go on through his farm. The Doctor was delighted to meet us. We sat on our horses in front of the portico and he sat on the steps. His wife and two other ladies came out to greet us and were enthusiastic over our presence. The Doctor gave us particular directions of our route, the way being often through gates into and out of wooded pastures and along neighborhood roads. He said we could not afford to tarry there, as the negro soldiers frequently came over to his negro cabins at night. About this moment we heard a treading sound toward the front gate, and looking that way saw a dark mass moving toward us. It was a body of the negro soldiers.

When we discovered the soldiers so close upon us, Martin and Christy darted off to the left. My weak animal was so slow to move that it looked to me as though the soldiers would get there before I could pass around and follow without being shot. It was a cloudy night and quite dark. I concluded instantly to go to the right and try to reach the gate by going around the rear of the house.

The cry of halt and shooting commenced as soon as Martin and Christy started. I rushed my horse off to the rear of the house, but a light in the kitchen blinded me to objects when looking in the dark, and I presume it had the same effect on the horse, for, to my surprise, he ran with all his force against the back yard fence, and I thought he would fall down. I heard them crying halt behind me. I jumped off and left the horse, but took my saddle-bags along. I got over the fence quickly, but at this moment I heard the darkies in the negro cabins at their doors and knew the instant they were opened the light would shine on me and expose me to a volley. I put my saddle-bags by the fence and then on all fours I crept along the fence. I did not hear any of the enemy getting over the fence but could hear them out about the stable and at the front of the dwelling. Within an hour everything was perfectly quiet. I got out and ventured to the door on the side of the house next to the stable lot. A servant opened it, when I asked for Dr. Thomas. He came in very bad humor. I asked him if I could employ any one there or near by to take me to Fletcher's. He said he could not assist me in the matter and I ought to get away. He told me that he had been arrested, taken over to the negro camp and put under bond to appear at headquarters in Clarksville the next day. He began to close the door and I had to leave without telling him good-by.

I walked to Jasper Fletcher's with my baggage over my shoulder, a distance of ten miles, by a little after midnight. He told me that Martin and Christy were encamped at the back of the farm, refusing to stay at his house, on account of the darkies. I thought I would be safer elsewhere and walked a mile to Mrs. Clardy's, who entertained me cheerfully. She was delighted when she found I was the friend of her two sons, Mont and Henry Clardy, in the First Kentucky Cavalry. I joined Martin and Christy early next morning and we decided to spend the day in their hiding-place.

Fletcher told us of a prominent Union man who was an informer and had guided the Federal cavalry around to places where they took horses, corn, and other supplies from Southern sympathizers, and pressed wagons to haul away all they wanted. He said if we wanted horses that man had two fine ones. We did not want a better arrangement, and just after dark we started after them. Fletcher and I walked in front and he went a near route between farms through the open woods. The stars afforded very good light. Christy rode up and sat on his horse at the front gate. Martin and I went into the stable lot and found the horses running loose. They were hard to catch and of course made considerable noise. The barking dogs brought the old gentleman to the door, but Christy told him to go back, the rebels were getting his horses and might take him.

Fletcher had described two large chestnut-sorrels. Martin having lost his fine mare at Golden Pond didn't like the one he had gotten from Captain Bogard, and so we took both. We found the place where the saddles were kept and I was now well mounted.

We then traveled without incident a little north of the Tennessee line, and stopped at a farm-house three miles from Mitchellsville, on the Louisville and Nashville Railroad. We learned that a garrison of one company of infantry occupied a stockade at this place, with picket posts half a mile from their camp on all the public roads. Having received minute directions that would enable us to make a circuit of the town and come into our road on the other side, we started on after supper. We were often guided in our course by the stars. It must have been near midnight when we reached the Mitchellsville and Gallatin road. We discovered the fire of the picket post and went into the road some two hundred yards farther out. The road ran through unfenced woods here. After we had gone about fifty yards along the road we noticed a horse standing on the right by a small tree, and as we rode up also observed a soldier sitting against a large tree with his gun standing beside him. He was fast asleep. Martin halted and handed me his bridle-rein. He went quietly to the horse, and getting the halter came and re-mounted. The horse did not appear to realize that he was loose and the soldier did not awake. We rode on without any disposition to hurt the poor fellow. A few miles from here we changed our course so as to leave Gallatin seven or eight miles to our right in turning to the south. We camped soon afterward, but were up at sunrise next morning to seek a secluded place, as we found we were now within twelve miles of Gallatin, where Gen. E. A. Paine commanded, and was having prisoners and citizens shot at his pleasure.

Mr. Lyon lived on the south side of Cumberland River, where we were entertained. He got us to order everything, as though we were pressing our way, in the presence of a negro man, and then sent him to Nashville to report us. After resting a while we traveled the public road to Lebanon, where there was no garrison. We passed through the town after midnight and undertook to make our way through the country, when we got lost in the cedars five miles out.

We traveled through the country toward McMinnville, passing localities where Colonel Martin had fought with Morgan the summer before. Martin met some old acquaint-ances among the citizens, and several straggling Confed-erates, from whom we learned a good deal about the garri-son and general situation at Nashville, without hinting the idea of a raid by General Morgan. We now felt that Morgan with 1,500 men and two pieces of artillery could surprise Nashville, sweep into western Kentucky, where he could stay two weeks anyhow to recruit, and escape across the Cumberland and Tennessee rivers to a place of safety in West Tennessee.   There would not be a telegraph line on his route and he could only be pursued by his trail.   We could guide him on the entire trip.

The next night we stopped within five miles of Manchester, where there was no garrison and none nearer than Tullahoma.   The next morning we rode into town, and to our surprise came upon a company of Federal cavalry, formed in line, on one side of the public square.   Although they saw us wheel and run we were at least 200 yards ahead when they came in sight.   We aimed to circle around the right side of the town through a common, but we discovered a small river and followed the big road out parallel with it for a quarter of a mile.   Then we came to the woods and left the road on the left side, but the river wound back toward the road.   Here there was a large frame dwelling on the road and a farm lying in the rear.   We saw a bridge, just beyond the house, which the road crossed.   To reach it we must pass near the house, and when within seventy-five yards of it we observed several of the cavalry, mounted, in the yard and others, on foot, in the stable lot.   There was nothing for us to do but charge and pass or surrender, and without delay we rushed up at full speed as though they were not there.   They looked at us a moment in surprise and ran back toward the stable lot.   We were across the bridge before they were ready to shoot or could decide what to do.   The crowd behind us in pursuit was coming at full speed, but we had gained on them since we left the edge of the town.   A short distance beyond the river we turned into the woods on the left, where there was no road, and passing around a little field reached the summit of a considerable hill that was thickly timbered, and then waited a while to see if we would be followed.   We crossed the Nashville and Chattanooga Railroad at a point between Wartrace and Tullahoma, then crossed Elk River below Fayetteville, and passed across the Tennessee Valley to the same crossing on the river where we were ferried over in going to Kentucky.

We now set out over the mountains and in a few days reached Asheville, a small county-seat among the fragmentary mountains. The next day we were at Blue Mountain, a station at the terminus of the railroad from Selma. We went on fifteen miles to Talladega, which was a substantial town in a locality of great wealth among the planters in the surrounding valley of the Coosa River.

It was now our purpose to travel toward Decatur, Georgia, but if a convenient arrangement could be made it was deemed better to leave our horses and go by rail, as we believed General Morgan would act on our information and come by this route on a raid into Middle Tennessee and Kentucky. Meanwhile, our horses would rest.

There were no marks of war in this section, and everything indicated a prosperous population of planters. We were passing elegant homes all along the road from Talladega. Near sunset we came upon a broad plantation that stretched far on either side of the road. The planter's home was on the right. This was the home of Walker Reynolds. We enjoyed every attention and comfort here and the family seemed to appreciate the acquaintance of volunteers from Kentucky. We made known to Mrs. Reynolds our plans, and on account of the absence of her husband at Selma she referred us to her brother, Dr. William Welch, near Alpine, the station on the railroad for this neighborhood, who she was sure would take an interest in us. Mrs. Reynolds invited us to remain until after dinner and we accepted. During the forenoon we were delightfully entertained by her daughters, Misses Eppie, Pink, and Bessie, who were about twenty, sixteen, and fourteen years of age; and also by Miss Kathleen McConnell. It was the first day of real pleasure that came to us after our troublous wanderings of many weeks. We had the good fortune to meet Dr. Welch at the station and also Mr. Thomas Reynolds, a married son of

Walker Reynolds. Both gave us cordial invitations to their homes. After a brief conference we concluded that Martin and Christy would go with Dr. Welch and leave their horses there, while they were gone to Decatur, Georgia, and I would go with Mr. Reynolds to remain until their return. I found a most enjoyable home with Mr. Reynolds, and also with Mr. William Mallory.

CHAPTER XVIII

Mission for General Morgan to vicinity of Nashville—Miss
Mary Overall secures information in Nashville—Death of
Dee Jobe—Wounded Union soldier dies and is buried, by
enemies, in family graveyard—Safe arrival at Rome, Georgia.

When Martin and Christy returned to Alpine an order
was brought from General Morgan directing me to proceed
to Guntersville, Alabama, where a detail of four picked men
would be furnished me by the commander of the post.   I
was to cross the Tennessee River near Guntersville, and go
to a safe point near Nashville, leaving my men stationed as
couriers, about one day's ride apart, between me and Guntersville.   It was his desire that I secure through friends,
who could go into Nashville, the location of each encampment and of the government stores, with the number of
troops as nearly as possible; also full information of the
garrisons as reported at all points near the route I traveled.
At Guntersville four young men volunteered when they
learned my mission. The Federals occupied the valley across
Tennessee River opposite Guntersville, with about a regiment of infantry, artillery and two companies of cavalry.   I
was directed to a friend near the mouth of a creek, five miles
above Guntersville. He had a small ferry-boat hid in the
creek and put us over after midnight and directed me to the
cabin home of a noted guerrilla, who lived just across the
valley—five miles, on the side of the mountain, nearly in the
rear of the camp of the enemy and not far from the road
that leads from Scottsboro to Guntersville ferry. I was told
that he was a typical mountaineer and could guide me across
the mountains, through the woods, never being in sight of
a road. I have forgotten his name.

I found his place, and, just after daylight, left my men in the woods, and went across his field to the rear of the house, whistling. His wife was in the back yard when I came up. She too was a shrewd mountaineer. It required considerable explanation before she would agree to find her husband for me. She told me to go back and stay near a tree that she pointed out, farther up the mountain, and he would come there from another direction. She cautioned me that I, only, should go to him when he appeared in sight and called, otherwise the shooting would commence. I waited fully an hour, when we heard a voice on the mountain side above us. I looked and saw a man, about one hundred yards distant, on a large rock in plain view. I started toward him, when he sat down and waited for me. I had a note to him from the captain at Guntersville which, with my explanations, satisfied him that there was no deception. He came down and remained with us until his wife could cook our rations and feed our horses, as we would pass no houses during the day.

We were within two miles of the northwest side of the mountain, where we were to descend, when a storm, which had been threatening, now burst over us. My guide told me he would have to turn back at the point of descent in order to make his way to a road he intended to travel all night and reach his den before morning. He put us into the big road at the parting place and in the darkness we started down the mountain. The way became so slippery that our horses had trouble to keep on their feet and several went down, one man being quite badly bruised. I finally halted and we hitched the horses and stood under big trees until the rain ceased, about midnight, and the stars came out. We found a dry place under a large projecting rock, on the mountain side. It was comfortable here and we remained until daylight.

We struck the valley seven miles above Huntsville. At the base of the mountain I found a good friend with whom one of the couriers was left to be kept secluded on the mountain side. I instructed him to make a circuit around Huntsville in going out with my report and cross Tennessee River in a safer locality. I then traveled to the right of Fayetteville, crossing Elk River five miles above the town and just below a mill-dam. Some twelve miles beyond, on White's, or Lynn's Creek, as I remember the name, I located another man, and, five miles east of Lewisburg, another. With the remaining man I went through Farmington, expecting to travel the Nashville pike, crossing Duck River at the bridge. I learned it had been destroyed. I went a few miles below and forded the river. Near by was the plantation of Lieutenant-Colonel Haynes, of a Tennessee regiment in Johnston's army. His wife entertained us and agreed to keep my man supplied if he would conceal himself in the woods. She directed me to Squire Boyd, on the pike five miles north. He had not retired when I arrived and directed me beyond Triune, within twenty miles of Nashville.

I was directed to Dr. Clem Jordan, to call for his son Ned, one mile north of Triune. I traveled the pike, as the nearest garrisons were at Franklin and Murfreesboro, reaching Dr. Jordan's place at one o'clock that night. In talking with Ned, at an upper window, I heard some ladies talking in an upper room at the other end of the house and caught the remark, "That is Headley's voice." Mrs. John A. Jordan and her daughters, Sophia and Mary Overall, were the ladies I met at my friend Ellis Suttle's, near Murfreesboro, just after my escape from Fort Donelson. Mr. John A. Jordan was the son of Dr. Clem Jordan, who lived here, and Ned was his brother.

After calculating the chances of getting in and out of Nashville with Ned Jordan it seemed that my best arrangement would be to send the ladies to the city, as they frequently went now without difficulty.

Miss Mary Overall was an enthusiastic Southern girl, about nineteen years of age, and when I confided my mission to her and her mother they said she could go and get their friend, Dr. Hunter, in a drug store, to secure all the information. She arranged with Miss Lucy King to accompany her to Nashville.

I moved a mile from the pike into a brier thicket on a ridge in a large field. Ned Jordan came to my camp nearly every day. He went with me across the field to the nearest house, farther back, in which a widow, Mrs. Warren, lived with a family of children. Mrs. Warren had a neighbor over the hill, a Mrs. Cherry. Mrs. Cherry's oldest son was a sort of roving soldier, a daring fellow, who was said to have killed a number of the enemy from ambush. And "Buck" Cherry, as he was called, was being hunted by every party of scouting cavalry that raided in the neighborhood. Between the two places I got my meals.

The right wing of General Rosecrans's army, under General Gordon Granger, occupied Triune after the battle of Stone River and many of the homes of the citizens had been destroyed in this locality. In my watches on the pike I occupied a wooded hill in the rear of Mr. Moss's place on the west side opposite the Page place on the hill across the pike. Dee Jobe, a noted scout of Johnston's army, was with me the last day I spent on this hill. He had achieved local fame by a number of daring exploits with a few men during the Murfreesboro campaign. I should record here that he was surprised by Federal cavalry scouts on the same hill, shortly after I was gone, while asleep, and riddled with bullets. He was left for dead, but revived after the enemy was gone, and the citizens learned from him that he was asleep and did not know who shot him.

Mrs. Jordan and her daughters, the Misses Overall, related to me their experience in the battle of Murfreesboro. They were at the home of Mr. Ellis Suttle near Asbury church on Overall's Creek where I first met them. When the Federal right wing was engaged in this immediate locality and toward the Wilkerson pike half a mile distant, these ladies with Mr. and Mrs. Suttle sought safety down in the baling box of the cotton-press below the surface of the ground. They heard the battle raging all day long. After the firing had ceased around the premises they came out and found the yard, dwelling, and negro cabins filled with Federals.

It was a command which claimed to have been raised in
Philadelphia, of select, first-class young men, to serve as the
body-guard of General Buell.   One of their number was
found in the house on a bed, mortally wounded.   His name
was Walter Oak Edye, from Hamburg, Germany.   His father
was an English merchant and ship owner who had removed
to Hamburg.   A brother, Henry Oak Edye, was located in
New York as the agent of the ship line to Hamburg.   This
younger brother was highly educated, speaking fluently
several languages, and coming over to this country enlisted
in the crack command in Philadelphia.   His right arm was
crushed above the elbow.   The wound was received in the
morning but did not have attention from a surgeon until
after night.   The troop to which he belonged was captured
about sunset, in the yard, being surprised by a force of Confederate cavalry.   He lingered for two weeks and died, having been nursed by this family the same as if he had been a
friend.   He was buried and still sleeps in the family burial-
ground of the old Overall homestead.   The Misses Overall
wrote his parents in Hamburg of his fate, with assurances
that his grave was duly marked and would be kept green
under the bluegrass of Tennessee.   The brother in New
York sent a man to recover the body and remove it to that
city, but when he learned it had received decent burial in a
family graveyard he was proud to let it continue there forever, though the National cemetery of Stone River is but a
mile and a half distant.   The parents in Hamburg wrote the
Misses Overall a grateful letter and sent a present for both.
To one a gold locket set with diamonds and pearls containing a picture of the father and of his boy.   To the other a
gold locket set with a spray of pearls containing the picture
of the mother and of her boy.

I had been in the neighborhood of Triune about a week
when Miss Overall informed me she was ready to go into
Nashville.   She drove from Dr. Jordan's down to Flat Rock
within three miles of the city, where she and Miss King
were guests of Mrs. Angie Claude.   The son-in-law of this

lady, Mr. Henry Tanksley, was taken into Miss Overall's confidence. He cheerfully agreed to serve her in the matter.

The next morning he drove the conveyance of the young ladies into the city and left them at the residence of his relatives. It happened that his two nieces, by engagement, were about ready to accompany some Federal officers up to Fort Negley, and Misses Overall and King were invited to join the party. The officers took pains to display everything about the fort to the ladies. Not even Miss King had a hint of the mission of Miss Overall.

Mr. Tanksley, however, being familiar with the city, had, himself and through his friends, obtained full information on every point, so that I could guide General Morgan into the city on one side and out on another side in the event he should fail to compel a surrender, and Miss Overall returned with the information in detail. I promptly sent a complete report to General Morgan without signing my name, as Colonel Martin and Captain Christy would know my handwriting. I continued to secure additional information, all of which corresponded with that furnished Miss Overall by Mr. Tanksley.

I had suggested a route by which General Morgan could reach and surprise Nashville with an even chance to enter the city without being discovered. It was about as follows: March through Alabama, cross the Tennessee River between Florence and Waterloo, then go north to Lawrenceburg, Newburg and Centerville, on Duck River. This route was thirty to forty miles west of the Nashville and Decatur Railroad. Then from Centerville the way was clear of the enemy for a straight ride across the country to the neighborhood of Mr. Robinson's, on Cumberland River, fifteen miles below Nashville, which point he would reach ready to go right on to Nashville at night, entering the city at a vacant place on the west side. He could send a few picked men, when he crossed the Tennessee River, through to cut the telegraph wires, between Decatur and Nashville every day, and come on to the place I had named six miles from Triune in the cedar hills. Then send a man from Lawrenceburg naming the night Morgan would reach Nashville. He could safely calculate the time by the distance, Duck River, at Centerville, being the only stream to cross, and might be forded, as the Harpeth River was bridged on the Charlotte and Nashville pike.

Dee Jobe, who was with me, knew every private road through all the hills between the pikes from Triune and Murfreesboro to Nashville and could gather about fifteen good men, who were hiding in that section, to pilot an attacking party on our side and cut the wires between Murfrees boro and Nashville. With Dee Jobe as a guide we would go at night and rendezvous, five miles from Nashville, in the hills and spend a day secreted and then be near enough to hear a fight in town, when we would drive in or capture the pickets on the Triune and Murfreesboro pikes, and cause an alarm that would help mystify the enemy.

I went back and forth along my line of couriers after waiting seventeen days, but they did not report . I finally learned that Morgan had gone to western Virginia.

The next day I crossed the mountains, arriving at Mr. Henry's, two miles from Guntersville, where I spent one night. I found the Confederate garrison gone. I traveled all day across Sand Mountain. There were only three houses on the road in a day's ride. I stopped ten miles from Gadsden and the next day reached Rome, Georgia. I learned here that General Morgan had been ordered to western Virginia. The command had marched from Decatur, Georgia, through western North Carolina to Abingdon, Virginia. I could hear of no orders for me, and proceeded to sell my horse and follow by railroad to Abingdon.

CHAPTER XIX

Raid of Kilpatrick and Dahlgren to capture Richmond, release
  Federal prisoners, pillage and burn the city, and kill President
  Davis and his Cabinet—Vengeful views of the Confederate
  soldiers at this period over the devastation of their country.

One of the notable events that had attracted universal
attention among citizens and soldiers was the raid of General Kilpatrick and Colonel Dahlgren upon Richmond with
the purpose of releasing the Federal prisoners and turning
them loose upon the city to pillage and sack it and then burn
it. Meanwhile, they were to kill President Davis and his
Cabinet. The attempt had been made in March, 1864.

Colonel Dahlgren had been detached with 500 picked men
to execute the plan, while Kilpatrick would threaten and
endeavor to enter the city with his large force of cavalry on
another side from Dahlgren. It appeared that Dahlgren's
men were provided with Greek fire and other combustible
material with which they might readily destroy the city.

The soldiers I met in Virginia were growing desperate.
Many of them knew their homes were being pillaged or destroyed by the invaders, that their families were being persecuted and subjected to cruel and inhuman treatment, that
their mothers, wives, and sisters were being driven from the
burning homes and set adrift in a barren waste to seek food
and shelter. The spirit of vengeance was more pronounced
in the infantry, where the men led an idle life and brooded
over the woes they could not avert. Many a man would
express his hope that the day would come when there would
be a chance to retaliate. It seemed to aggravate every one
that the public sentiment of the North gloried in the persecution of non-combatants, the total devastation of homes and

all personal property; and especially the subjugation and degradation of the Southern people. This Northern spirit seemed to be intensified by the conviction that the South could only be conquered by ruin and starvation.

It happened that Colonel Dahlgren was killed after the failure at Richmond and that upon his body the papers were found that disclosed his plans and purposes. These papers were delivered by Lieutenant Pollard to the authorities at Richmond and were published all over the South and in many Northern papers.

It appears that General Kilpatrick and Colonel Dahlgren came directly from a conference in Washington with President Lincoln and acted by his authority and approval, just as the army commanders were doing who were burning the homes and property of the citizens of the South.

It also appears that the secret of the expedition was not entrusted to General Meade, who was commanding the Army of the Potomac; and that when he ordered General Sedgwick with a corps of infantry and General Custer with 2,000 cavalry to make demonstrations on the left of Lee's army, he was simply obeying orders from Washington and was ignorant of the mission of Kilpatrick and Dahlgren.

The papers found on the body of Colonel Dahlgren were as follows:

(From "Life of Gen. R. E. Lee," by James D. McCabe, Jr.)

HEADQUARTERS THIRD DIVISION CAVALRY CORPS.
OFFICERS AND MEN:

You have been selected from brigades and regiments as a picked command to attempt a desperate undertaking—an undertaking which, if successful, will write your names on the hearts of your countrymen in letters that can never be erased, and which will cause the prayers of our fellow-soldiers now confined in loathsome prisons to follow you and yours wherever you may go.

We hope to release the prisoners from Belle Isle first, and having seen them fairly started we will cross the James River into Richmond, destroying the bridges after us, and exhorting the released prisoners to destroy and burn the hateful city, and do not allow the rebel leader Davis and his traitorous crew to escape. The prisoners must render great assistance as you cannot leave your ranks too far or become too much scattered, or you will be lost.

Do not allow any personal gain to lead you off, which would only bring you to an ignominious death at the hands of the citizens. Keep well together, and obey orders strictly, and all will be well, but on no account scatter too far; for in union there is strength.

With strict obedience to orders, and fearlessness in the execution, you will be sure to succeed.

We will join the main force on the other side of the city, or perhaps meet them inside.

Many of you may fall; but if there is any man here not willing to sacrifice his life in such a great and glorious undertaking, or who does not feel capable of meeting the enemy in such a desperate fight as will follow, let him step out, and he may go hence to the arms of his sweetheart, and read of the braves who swept through the city of Richmond.

We want no man who cannot feel sure of success in such a holy cause.

We will have a desperate fight; but stand up to it when it does come, and all will be well.

Ask the blessing of the Almighty, and do not fear the enemy.

U. Dahlgren,
Colonel Commanding.

Besides this address were the following "special orders and instructions," which were written upon a similar sheet of paper, giving an outline of the whole plan of Kilpatrick and Dahlgren:

Guides—Pioneers (with oakum, turpentine, and torpedoes)—Signal-Officer—Quartermaster—Commissary:

Scouts and pickets—Men in rebel uniform:

These will remain on the north bank and move down with the force on the south bank, not getting ahead of them; and if the communication can be kept up without giving alarm, it must be done; but everything depends upon a surprise, and NO ONE must be allowed to pass ahead of the column. Information must be gathered in regard to the crossings of the river, so that should we be repulsed on the south side we will know where to recross at the nearest point.   All mills must be burned, and the canal destroyed; and also everything which can be used by the rebels must be destroyed, including the boats on the river. Should a ferry-boat be seized and can be worked, have it moved down.   Keep the force on the south side posted of any important move of the enemy, and in case of danger some of the scouts must swim the river and bring us information.   As we approach the city, the party must take great care that they do not get ahead of the other party on the south side, and must conceal themselves and watch our movements.   We will try and secure the bridge to the city (one mile below Belle Isle), and release the prisoners at the same time.   If we do not succeed, they must then dash down, and we will try and carry the bridge from each side.

When necessary, the men must be filed through the woods and along the river bank.   The bridges once secured, and the prisoners loose and over the river, the bridges will be secured and the city destroyed.   The men must keep together and well in hand, and once in the city it must be destroyed, and JEFF. DAVIS AND CABINET KILLED.

Pioneers will go along with combustible material.   The officer must use his discretion about the time of assisting us.   Horses and cattle, which we do not need immediately, must be shot rather than left.   Everything on the canal, and elsewhere, of service to the rebels, must be destroyed.   As General Custer may follow me, be careful not to give a false alarm.

The signal-officer must be prepared to communicate at night by rockets, and in other things pertaining to his department.

The quartermasters and commissaries must be on the lookout for their departments, and see that there are no delays on their account.

The engineer-officer will follow to survey the road as we pass over it, etc.

The pioneers must be prepared to construct a bridge or destroy one.   They must have plenty of oakum and turpentine for burning, which will be rolled in soaked balls and given to the men to burn when we get in the city.   Torpedoes will only be used by the pioneers for destroying the main bridges, etc.   They must be prepared to destroy railroads.   Men will branch off to the right, with a few pioneers, and destroy the bridges and rail-roads south of Richmond, and then join us at the city.   They must be well prepared with torpedoes, etc.   The line of Falling Creek is probably the best to work along, or, as they approach the city, Goode's Creek; so that no reinforcements can come up

on any cars.   No one must be allowed to pass ahead for fear of
communicating news.   Rejoin the command with all haste, and,
if cut off, cross the river above Richmond, and rejoin us.   Men
will stop at Bellona Arsenal and totally destroy it, and anything
else but hospitals; then follow on and rejoin the command at
Richmond with all haste, and, if cut off, cross the river and
rejoin us.   As General Custer may follow me, be careful and
not give a false alarm.

In addition to the above, the private note book of Colonel
Dahlgren contained the following memoranda, some of
which seemed to have been written with great haste:

Pleasanton will govern details.
Will have details from other commands (four thousand).
Michigan men have started.
Col. J. H. Devereaux has torpedoes.
Hanover Junction (B. T. Johnston).
Maryland Line.
[Here follows a statement of the composition and numbers
of Johnston's command.]
Chapin's farm—seven miles below Richmond.
One brigade (Hunton's relieved Wise, sent to Charlestown).
River can be forded half a mile above the city.   No works on
south side.   Hospitals near them.   River fordable.   Canal can
be crossed.
Fifty men to remain on north bank, and keep in communication, if possible. To destroy mills, canal, and burn everything of
value to the rebels.   Seize any large ferry-boats, and note all
crossings, in case we have to return that way.   Keep us posted
of any important movement of the rebels, and, as we approach
the city, communicate with us, and do not give the alarm before
they see us in possession of Belle Isle and the bridge.   If engaged there, or unsuccessful, they must assist in securing the
bridges until we cross.   If the ferry-boat can be taken and
worked, bring it down.   Everything that cannot be secured or
made use of must be destroyed.   Great care must be taken not
to be seen or any alarm given.   The men must be filed along off
the road or along the main bank.   When we enter the city the
officer must use his discretion as to when to assist in crossing
the bridges.
The prisoners once loosed and the bridges crossed, the city
must be destroyed, burning the public buildings, etc.

Prisoners to go with party.

Spike the heavy guns outside.

Pioneers must be ready to repair, destroy, etc. Turpentine will be provided. The pioneers must be ready to destroy the Richmond bridges, after we have all crossed, and to destroy the railroad near Frederick's Hall (station, artillery, etc.)

*   *   *   *   *   *   *

Fifteen men to halt at Bellona Arsenal, while the column goes on, and destroy it. Have some prisoners. Then rejoin us at R.; leaving a portion to watch if anything follows, under a good officer.

Will be notified that Custer may come.

Main column, four hundred.

One hundred men will take the bridge after the scouts, and dash through the streets and open the way to the front, or, if it is open, destroy everything in the way.

While they are on the big bridges, one hundred men will take Belle Isle, after the scouts instructing the prisoners to gut the city. The reserve (two hundred) will see this fairly done and everything over, and then follow, destroying the bridges after them, and then destroy the city; going up the principal streets and destroying everything before them, but not scattering too much, and always having a part well in hand.

Jeff Davis and Cabinet must be killed on the spot.

The proof afforded by these papers will not admit of a doubt of the murderous intention of the Federal commander. The authenticity of the papers has been denied by the father of Colonel Dahlgren, but the denial was accompanied by no proof. The genuineness of the papers is well shown by the following letter from General Fitz Lee, in transmitting them to the War Department:

HEADQUARTERS LEE'S DIVISION,
Cavalry Corps, Army Northern Va.,
March 31, 1864.

General S. COOPER, Adjutant and Inspector-General.

GENERAL: I have the honor to enclose to you Colonel Dahlgren's note book, just sent to me by Colonel Beall, commanding Ninth Virginia Cavalry. Had I known of its existence it would have been forwarded with the "papers."

His name and rank is written on the first page, with the date (probably) of his purchasing it. The book, amongst other memoranda, contains a rough pencil sketch of his address to his troops, differing somewhat from his pen and ink copy. I embrace this occasion to add, the original papers bore no marks of alteration, nor could they possibly have been changed except by the courier who brought them to me, which is in the highest degree improbable; and the publications of them in the daily Richmond papers were exact copies, in every respect, of the original.   Very respectfully,

Your obedient servant,

(Signed)   Fitz Lee,

Major-General Commanding.

This raid of Kilpatrick and Dahlgren attracted universal attention all over the North as well as the South.

Besides the death of Dahlgren, his command was scattered and many of them fell into the hands of the Confederates. With reference to these Mr. Davis says:

The prisoners, having been captured in disguise, were, under the usages of war, liable to be hanged as spies, but their protestations that their service was not voluntary, and the fact that as enlisted men they were subject to orders, and could not be held responsible for the infamous instructions under which they were acting, saved them from the death-penalty they had fully incurred.   PHOTOGRAPHIC COPIES OF THE PAPERS FOUND ON DAHLGREN'S BODY WERE TAKEN AND SENT TO GENERAL LEE, with instructions to communicate them to General Meade, commanding the enemy's forces in his front, with an inquiry as to whether such practices were authorized by his Government, and also to say that, IF ANY QUESTION WAS RAISED AS TO THE COPIES, THE ORIGINAL PAPER WOULD BE SUBMITTED.   NO SUCH QUESTION WAS THEN MADE, and THE DENIAL THAT DAHLGREN'S CONDUCT HAD BEEN AUTHORIZED WAS ACCEPTED.

Many sensational stories, having not even a basis of truth, were put in circulation to exhibit the Confederate authorities as having acted with unwarrantable malignity toward the deceased Colonel Dahlgren.   The fact was, that his body was sent to Richmond and decently interred in the Oakwood Cemetery,

where other Federal soldiers were buried. The enormity of
HIS OFFENSES WAS NOT FORGOTTEN, but resentment
against him ended with his life. It was also admitted that,
however bad his preceding conduct had been, he met his fate
gallantly, charging at the head of his men when he found himself inextricably encompassed by his foe.

It would be fair to give the explanations made by the
friends of Colonel Dahlgren, who, however, do not appear to
have ever published any explanation from any officer or
soldier of Colonel Dahlgren's force of 500 picked men. The
defense seems to have been made by persons who felt called
upon to exonerate General Meade.

A major-general of the Federal army* writes as follows:

The only other event of note, before the arrival of General
Grant, was the Kilpatrick-Dahlgren raid upon Richmond. *It
was authorized directly from Washington,* and was not the
suggestion of General Meade, nor did it have his approval;
however, he set about carrying it into effect with all proper
spirit and energy. The movement depended largely for its
success upon its secrecy, and, therefore, *when Colonel Dahlgren
arrived from Washington before the preparations were completed,* and asked to be permitted to accompany Kilpatrick,
Meade was annoyed to learn that the expedition was currently
discussed in the Capital. *The plan was* for Kilpatrick to move
generally from our left, passing the right flank of Lee's army,
and to proceed to Richmond by as direct routes as possible,
while, as diversions, and to cover his movement, Custer, with
2,000 cavalry, was to make a raid beyond Gordonsville, and the
Sixth Corps and Birney's division of the Third were to move in
support of Custer to Madison Court House on Robertson's
River. No effort was made to conceal this movement, as it was
intended to convey the impression to the enemy that a formidable
attempt was to be made upon his left flank. Upon the arrival
of Sedgwick and Birney at Robertson's River at nightfall of the
27th of February, Custer went by with his command, with
instructions to proceed toward Charlottesville, and, if possible,
to destroy the railway bridge near that place.

*   *   *   *   *   *   *

*General Martin T. McMahon in Century War Series, No. 26.

His movement had certainly had the desired effect as a diversion. While these operations were taking place Kilpatrick had advanced in the direction of Richmond and had divided his forces, sending a portion under Dahlgren to strike the James River above Richmond, retaining the main body under his own command until he was satisfied that the experiment was not feasible. He made his way down the Peninsula in the direction of Butler's command, and was subsequently transferred by boat to rejoin the Army of the Potomac, or more properly the horse-hospital camp, near Washington. Aside from our losses in men, and among them the gallant and heroic Dahlgren, the result of this movement was to disable for the time being 3,000 or 4,000 of the very flower of our cavalry.

A gentleman* who appears to have investigated the particulars of the expedition of Kilpatrick and Dahlgren writes as follows:

On the night of Sunday, the 28th of February, 1864, Gen. Judson Kilpatrick, leaving Stevensburg with 4,000 cavalry and a battery of horse artillery, crossed the Rapidan at Ely's Ford, surprised and captured the enemy's picket there, and marched rapidly by Spottsylvania Court House toward Richmond.
"His object was to move past the enemy's right flank, enter the Confederate Capital, and release the Union captives in its military prisons. This bold project had grown out of PRESIDENT LINCOLN'S DESIRE TO HAVE HIS AMNESTY PROCLAMATION CIRCULATED WITHIN THE CONFEDERATE LINES; AND GENERAL KILPATRICK, WITH WHOM MR. LINCOLN DIRECTLY CONFERRED, HAD REPORTED TO GENERAL MEADE, ON THIS OFFICER'S APPLICATION, A PLAN WHICH INCLUDED THE RELEASE OF THE RICHMOND PRISONERS AND A RAID UPON THE ENEMY'S COMMUNICATIONS AND SUPPLIES. His force was to be chosen from the cavalry corps, mostly from his own—the Third—division; and Col. Ulric Dahlgren, separating from him near Spottsylvania, with five hundred picked men, was to cross the James, enter Richmond on the south side, after liberating the Belle Isle prisoners, and unite with Kilpatrick's main force entering the city from the north at 10 a. m. of Tuesday, March

---

*George E. Pond in Century War Series, No. 26.

1st. General Meade aided the enterprise with simultaneous demonstrations of the Sixth Corps and of Birney's division of the Third against Lee's left, and of Custer's cavalry division toward Charlottesville."

The publication of the Dahlgren papers did not materially add to the now revengeful feelings of the Confederate soldiers. They did not think that Dahlgren had attempted to do anything worse than many Federal officers and soldiers were doing every day in many parts of the South. They thought the homes in Richmond no more sacred than those of the Shenandoah Valley that were in ashes; and while President Davis and his Cabinet were of greater value to the Confederacy it would be no worse to kill them than for Gen. Stephen G. Burbridge to shoot innocent prisoners, at Lexington, Kentucky, because his raiding parties were fired on from ambush and men killed or wounded. The same policy was being pursued by Col. Sam Johnson at Hopkinsville, Kentucky, and by Gen. E. A. Paine at Gallatin, Tennessee. This was Gen. John C. Fremont's policy in Missouri, even in 1861, toward men who might be caught with arms in their hands, though they might wear a so-called Confederate uniform.

It appeared that the war party in the North claimed a monopoly of this mode of warfare. The slightest innovation by Confederates was regarded as infamous and "unparalleled in the annals of war." General Morgan and sixty-eight of his officers were subjected to penitentiary treatment and discipline on the charge of being "horse thieves." Their heads were shaved or cropped close to the skin and likewise mustaches or beards. They occupied convicts' cells and received the dungeon treatment of convicts at the option of guards or wardens upon any infraction, real or supposed, of the penitentiary rules. They were not recognized as prisoners of war. They were not in a military prison even suffering the privations there under military discipline. But they had been delivered by Major-General Burnside, after their capture in battle or on the march, to Governor Tod of Ohio to be confined in the penitentiary as felons.

These and many other like views were common subjects now among the best men in the Confederate Army. It seemed a bitter fate to the Southern people according to the opinions of the Confederate soldiers.

It was some consolation to them, however, that about half the Northern people were opposed to the cruel war upon the Southern people and seemed ready to fight against being drafted into the Union Army.

The riot in New York City against the enforcement of the draft was a notable instance. On this occasion the mob had held sway in the city for several days. Governor Horatio Seymour, of New York, appeared upon the scene and appealed to the rioters for peace and good order, promising to have the "order for the draft suspended," but by way of warning to the authorities at Washington or rather to President Lincoln, he exclaimed, in a public address in New York City:

Remember this, that the bloody, and treasonable, and revolutionary doctrine of public necessity can be proclaimed by a mob as well as by a government. * * * When men accept despotism, they may have a choice as to who the despot shall be!

It was this condition of affairs that animated the Southern citizens and soldiers in extending so warm a welcome to General Morgan upon his escape from captivity. Indeed, the presence of Morgan in the Confederacy was an inspiration to the soldiers.

CHAPTER XX

Morgan at Abingdon—General Jenkins wounded and his command routed—Martin leads a charge—Morgan defeats enemy near Wytheville—His last raid to Kentucky—Captures garrison at Mt. Sterling—Martin's command surprised by Burbridge—Defense and escape with severe loss—Fight and capture of garrison at Cynthiana—Capture of Gen. E. H. Hobson and his command at Cynthiana—Morgan defeated by Burbridge—Escape to Virginia.

The universal manifestation of confidence by the people and soldiers in General Morgan seemed to inspire him with fresh enthusiasm, and he at once proceeded to organize a division out of the fragments of his old division that had not been captured and other detachments and commands of Kentucky cavalry that were available in western Virginia.

Since the arrival of General Morgan at Abingdon some exciting events had occurred. I learned from my comrades at the hotel in Abingdon that two expeditions of the Federals had attacked the line of railroad, from Abingdon to Richmond, at Dublin near New River bridge. General Jenkins commanded the Confederate garrison stationed at this place. Upon the approach of the Federals under command of General Crook, General Morgan sent the dismounted fragments of his old division, about four hundred men, under Col. D. Howard Smith and Lieut.-Col. Martin to the assistance of Jenkins. When they arrived at Dublin Depot General Jenkins had been attacked by a superior force and his troops were in retreat toward the depot from their line of battle. In a vain endeavor to rally his men, General Jenkins was seriously wounded. Colonel McCausland, who succeeded to the command, was making the same attempt, when Morgan's men rushed from the cars, and forming quickly Colonel Martin led them in a charge upon the enemy, who were rushing forward wildly upon the idea that the garrison was at their mercy. They were driven back in confusion, though the retreating troops of General Jenkins did not halt to help their rescuers. Finally the enemy after reforming advanced with a large force, when Smith and Martin withdrew their men and safely crossed New River, where they remained until the next morning and then returned to Abingdon. Captain Cleburne, a young brother of Maj.-Gen. Pat Cleburne of Bragg's army, was killed in the charge of Morgan's men at Dublin Depot.

The enemy under General Averill at the same time had advanced against Wytheville, where a Confederate force was posted.

General Morgan had hurried from Abingdon, with his mounted force, to Wytheville and arrived in advance of the enemy. A sharp engagement ensued as the enemy approached, which resulted in a victory for the troops under General Morgan's command, including a brigade of cavalry commanded by General Jones that was stationed at Wytheville. The Confederates lost between fifty and sixty killed and wounded. But they had inflicted a heavier loss upon Averill's force, besides taking over one hundred prisoners and nearly two hundred horses. Generals Crook and Averill retreated northward after these engagements and General Morgan returned to Abingdon.

I had arrived at Abingdon a few days after these occurrences, and while the enemy had fallen back from our territory they still occupied advanced positions in West Virginia and threatened Saltville, which had been guarded by General Morgan, and he was still expected to protect the salt works located there.

There was now an active effort to equip General Morgan's troops. But for the first time in its history the Government at Richmond was furnishing supplies to General Morgan's command, though in scant measure.

Martin got permission from General Morgan to go to the country and recruit the horses of his staff. We went some fifteen miles distant in the mountains, where we located on a fertile plateau. In leaving Abingdon I with a number of others traveled in a two-horse wagon.

Colonel Martin went by General Morgan's headquarters and when he overtook us on the road he handed me an envelope. It contained my commission from General Morgan as 1st lieutenant in the Tenth Kentucky Cavalry. Martin told me afterwards that General Morgan appreciated my trip to Nashville. He also told me that he was to command the dismounted men organized into a brigade on the raid to Kentucky which would be made within a few days. He said he wanted me to serve on his staff.

The command started about the first of June. There were two mounted brigades, one commanded by Colonel Giltner and the other by Col. D. Howard Smith. These of course went ahead of our dismounted men and cleared the route.

Colonel Martin's staff was made up as follows: Lieut. Arthur Andrews, assistant adjutant-general; Capt. Bob Berry, commissary; Capt. Orville West, quartermaster; Lieut. John W. Headley, inspector-general; Lieuts. Oscar L. Barbour and Meade Woodson, aides-de-camp. There was nothing for this staff to do on the march to Kentucky. I simply fell into ranks and marched in the column for four days, when I began to fag, and took my place among the stragglers, who were loaded down with swollen feet and legs. When I reached Hazel Green I learned I was half a day behind the head of our column. But I pushed on, stopping to wade in cool streams occasionally, hoping that might take out some of the swelling. At Ticktown I was informed that our brigade would camp in Mt. Sterling that night and wait for the column to close up. Also that General Morgan had captured the garrison the night before and several hundred horses for our men. This news stimulated me to try and reach camp before the horses were distributed. I arrived at about eleven o'clock at night.

The command was camped in a woodland on a ridge that crossed the pike about half a mile before reaching Mt. Sterling. Nearly every man in camp was fast asleep. I did not go ten feet from the pike, but spread my pallet and tried to sleep or rest, but could do neither. Many others were in equally bad condition. I learned that Colonel Martin's headquarters were across the pike.

At daylight I got up and lighted my pipe, concluding I would smoke for consolation. Just then two or three shots were fired about half a mile down the pike on which we had come into camp. I heard several horses coming at full speed and then a storm began to roar in the same direction. It was a column of horses on the pike after the pickets. Only a few men in the whole command seemed to be awake or to have heard the shots. I began to shout aloud, forgetting my heavy legs, and wabbled around in the camp to rouse the soldiers. Others spread the alarm, but objects could hardly be seen very far as daylight was barely breaking. On came the uproar up the pike. The pickets ran by, yelling the alarm, and there was confusion all over the camp. I hardly had an idea of our location, but discovered a plank fence back from the pike about seventy-five yards. There was none along the pike on our side. I and other officers called to the men to get over the fence and lie down. Those who got up went in a run for the fence. The enemy was coming into the camp now, shooting men as they got up or as they lay asleep. It looked like a slaughter. But from the fence the fire opened and we began to pour buckshot into the crowded enemy and they were falling fast. They spread all over the camp in a few minutes, and kept shooting our men who were trying to escape. Our fire from over four hundred guns was telling on their ranks all the time. They were not over a hundred feet from us. Suddenly a horseman from their crowd galloped toward us bareheaded, shouting, "Come over the fence, boys, and charge quick!" Every one recognized the form and voice of Col. Bob Martin. There was no hesitation. The line went over the fence in an instant and went right up to them with shotguns and pistols.

The enemy got so blocked they ran over each other as well as the dead and wounded. We yelled and fought still, crowding them so closely that they were in such confusion they could not shoot, and there was no room for them to spread and get out of each other's way. Martin was yelling, and fighting with his pistol along with the rest. It was light enough to see some distance now, and the enemy's column seemed to have clogged in the lane, which was hedged by a strong plank fence on both sides, and they could not get off their horses nor out of the lane, so Martin led the charge on the crowded head of their column so furiously that it stampeded for a hundred yards at least. They got a piece of artillery through the fence about two hundred yards distant and began to throw canister into the camp. But we were fifty yards down the lane now and pushing ahead. I saw Colonel Martin and his horse go down some ten steps from me, but he arose quickly and within a few minutes was on another horse. Rushing toward me on the right he told me to take some men and get that cannon while he rushed the column back on the pike. I called on the men around me to follow, and they sprang forward in a run, loading their guns and firing as they went. I had no gun and held my pistol fire for closer quarters.

Martin was going with the main force right on the enemy in the pike and had them nearly back to the cannon. Their whole column along the lane was jammed. My party was inside the field and we went along as fast as we could load and shoot. My men fired in the rear of the head of the column, as I thought that would increase the confusion. We were already beyond the head of the column, but it had no time to give my crowd any attention, while our column on foot was all around the stampeding front. We then made a rush for the cannon and stopped firing. Three of my men reached the cannon ahead of me.

A number of shots were falling around us from the rear, some distance back, where I noticed several men were over in the field on foot, having turned their horses loose in the crushing crowd along the lane. The horses were gone from the cannon and one of those hitched to the caisson was dead in the harness, while the other one seemed frightened nearly to death but could not go anywhere with his load. Unfortunately, none of my party knew how to load and shoot the cannon or we would have turned it on their struggling masses in the lane as far as we could see. The men were cutting the harness off the dead horse, as our fighting column had now passed us; but I observed, not over a hundred yards from us, the enemy was putting men into the field, dismounted, and knew they would· not be long in coming. We thereupon hitched ourselves to the cannon and went up the slope as fast as we could, some of the men bringing what they could carry from the caisson.

The firing had lulled somewhat by the time we got into our camp, where we hoped a squad might be ready to load and open on the masses in the lane. I then saw that the enemy had dismounted about a hundred yards from us and formed on both sides of the lane and were about ready to move forward. More were still going over the fences on each side farther in the rear. Martin was now falling back slowly, still firing. We took the cannon and pushed on, my aim being now to get away with it. I supposed the other two brigades were near by and was expecting every minute they would come to our rescue.

We hurried forward with the cannon and were out of danger, when we stopped to see if we had better go to help the men with Martin and try to find some one who could shoot the cannon.

Bullets began to pepper the ground around us and to pass higher from the dismounted enemy in the field. One struck me on the shin of the left leg. It must have struck a rail or something else, however, as it only half buried itself in the flesh and dropped in my boot leg. It hurt about like the lick of a stone thrown hard at a short distance.

Martin was now bringing the men back rapidly, and galloping to me said we would have to leave the cannon. He told me he was shot in the foot and hurried away. I did not know the other six men who went with me to capture the cannon, but I have since learned they were from Carroll County, Kentucky.

With my swollen limbs, I soon dropped to the rear, but the enemy was not pressing us. Their mounted column that was jammed in the lane could not pursue without trampling their own dead and wounded.

There was a common between our camp and Mt. Sterling and I now had several hundred yards to go before reaching the suburbs. Just as I reached the foot of the ridge and the edge of the common, several loose horses, with their halters dangling, came running around from the right, and I spread myself to coax one to stop. I finally secured one, and mounting him bareback guided him by the halter rein. I galloped through town and soon reached Martin, who was trying to get all the men closed up. We went out the Winchester pike and half a mile from town passed through a cut in a ridge that crossed the pike. It seemed to be the same ridge that wound round toward our camp. Just behind this ridge we came upon the mounted brigade of Colonel Giltner standing in line. The Colonel rode to us, and he and Colonel Martin agreed to make a stand here. Martin turned his column and formed a line on the right of the pike facing Mt. Sterling. We could see the enemy in town and presently a dismounted line moved forward with skirmishers in advance. The pike curved somewhat in Giltner's front, or rather it circled so that Giltner was first to be engaged.

As the enemy pressed forward, Colonel Martin endeavored to move forward and to turn the enemy's left flank, but was met with a volley from a line of skirmishers that covered our front. Driving these back we came in sight of a dismounted line of battle some two hundred yards from the ridge. The line officers in Martin's remnant reported the ammunition exhausted. This was no surprise after the engagement of the early morning. Giltner's brigade repulsed the advance against his position while we were simply holding ours. But soon the enemy advanced upon us slowly and our remaining shots were fired, after which Colonel Martin withdrew his line and part of Giltner's brigade occupied our position. We did not know whether or not Giltner could resist the advance, so Colonel Martin ordered his men to hasten to reach the woods half a mile farther back. Meanwhile, Captain West, the quartermaster, was endeavoring to get a supply of ammunition from Giltner's stock. The enemy, from an elevation to our right, sent a volley at our mounted party as we were leaving the ridge and Martin and I had to go under fire for about fifty yards. The weary officers and men were getting away in droves; perhaps half of the command was bareheaded. I asked Martin why Giltner had not come to our assistance in the morning when he had only a mile to go and we were fighting from daybreak until after sunrise. "I do not know," he said, laughing; "I did not ask him why he didn't."

I asked Martin how we happened to be surprised. He said General Morgan had captured Mt. Sterling the night before we arrived, taking 400 prisoners, a lot of horses, teams and supplies; and had gone to Winchester to take that place and try to mount our men without delay, leaving Colonel Brent with 50 men for guard posts. He said he directed Brent to post the picket at least a mile from camp. I then told him that I reached the camp at eleven o'clock and the pickets told me the camp was not over two hundred yards ahead, which I found to be true. He said he didn't know anything about Brent, except that he ought to be court-martialed, etc.

Colonel Martin now complained of his foot giving him pain. A bullet had furrowed across on top at the base of the instep and it was bloody. We thought best for him to get a surgeon. He went off after one and to have it examined.

Our little command had reached the pike and halted near the woods while Giltner's brigade still held the ridge, but the firing had about ceased.

We discovered a command of cavalry on the pike toward Winchester coming at full speed, and in a few minutes the men shouted, "Morgan, Morgan, that's Morgan!" The boys yelled for joy, and Morgan's men came yelling. Their princely commander was recognized in the lead, bareheaded, but waving his hat and cheering as he pushed forward. He was the first to reach us. Halting his column, he rode around among our 450 men until they quieted. I sat by the side of the pike on my naked horse and watched him. I had never seen General Morgan before. Everything in his appearance denoted elegance and gallantry. He had the exquisite form of perfect manhood, with the fair complexion, the mellow blue eyes, and the charming features of a handsome woman. He listened to the stories of our disaster for a few minutes. Then with words of sympathy for the men he exclaimed, "I'll get them yet," and told them they should not walk any farther. He called to Colonel Smith and said a few words. I overheard the remark that these men must have something to eat at once and drinking water. He ordered Smith's brigade forward to support Giltner. It had been standing in a column of fours for ten minutes, while one of Morgan's staff officers had been to confer with Giltner, whose brigade had ceased firing. Morgan then asked for Colonel Martin. Some one said, "Yonder is Lieutenant Headley, he can tell," at the same time calling me. I went forward and Morgan said he was glad to know me. I told him I had just learned Martin was at the house not far away, to which I pointed in Giltner's direction. He galloped away. It was soon rumored that Morgan was going to attack the town.

A supply of rations arrived, fires were started in the woodland, and we were soon eating a meal. I had not eaten a mouthful since noon of the day before. In a little while a man brought me a saddle and bridle which Colonel Martin had sent, and a message for me to join him. His foot had been dressed but was swollen and, some of the bones being broken, he was suffering.

MAJOR-GENERAL JOHN H. MORGAN
1864

After an hour or so Martin received a message from Morgan, by a staff officer, that it was deemed inexpedient to attack the enemy in town, having ascertained that they had occupied and barricaded the court-house and principal brick buildings. It would be necessary to burn the town, which Morgan was unwilling to do.

The entire command was now formed on the pike and moved toward Winchester. Most of our little brigade had been furnished horses and the rest rode in wagons.

Before we had gone far Colonel Martin sent for me. He wanted me to go and ask General Morgan to assign our remnant to one of the other brigades. Morgan studied a moment and said all right, he would put the men with Colonel Smith's brigade. He sent me to tell Smith, but said he would see him also. I caught up with Smith and reported the arrangement. He invited me to serve with him and said the others on Martin's staff could do likewise. His inquiries as to myself brought out the fact that he had served in the State Senate of Kentucky with my father, so we became good friends.

Colonel Smith told me of the fight at Mt. Sterling the morning before our arrival, when they captured 400 prisoners, supplies, etc. He explained that his brigade went with General Morgan to Winchester, twelve miles, leaving Giltner's brigade with horses and supplies for Martin's dismounted brigade.

These events occurred on the 9th day of June, 1864.

Marching from Mt. Sterling we passed through Winchester and entered Lexington after midnight. The garrison of the enemy there was driven into a fortification on one side of the city. We only remained here a short time.

Early next morning we marched into Georgetown and halted for several hours. Meanwhile, several details had been sent toward Frankfort and in other directions to make feints and deceive the enemy. We left Georgetown on the pike toward Cynthiana.

At sunrise the next morning, the 11th, we approached Cynthiana on the Leesburg pike, with Giltner's brigade in front. The pickets were driven in, the command going forward at a gallop. There was some firing at the fleeing pickets. A brisk fight was raging when the head of our brigade came to the suburbs, at a point where the pike descended from a ridge and entered the town. Just beyond a brick residence on the right, inside a blue-grass meadow, General Morgan sat on his horse with members of his staff around him. The meadow sloped down to the railroad depot, a distance perhaps of two hundred yards on the right. The depot was in the edge of the town and occupied by the enemy. Giltner had reached the town and his men were now fighting on the other side of the depot from us. Smith's brigade was dismounted and entered the meadow, charging toward the depot. Lieutenants Andrews, Barbour, and I went along on horseback. We were received with a storm of bullets from the depot and were obliged to halt about fifty yards from it; some lying down, others finding shelter along a fence to the left were thus enabled to creep closer. Here a courier from General Morgan brought a message for me and others on horseback to come back. He said we were exposing ourselves and doing no good.

This position was held for perhaps half an hour, when Giltner's men, having set fire to the houses near the depot, were now in the act of setting it on fire when the white flag was hoisted by the enemy. The doors were opened and our men entered the building from all sides.

The enemy had suffered severely inside the depot. Their commander, Colonel Berry, was among the killed. He was a wealthy farmer of the county near Berry Station, which had been named for him by the railroad company some years before. He had been straightened on his back by some of his men, with a piece of plank under his head, when I went to see him as he lay on the floor. He was a large, tall, fine-looking man, apparently about forty-eight years of age. Some one remarked that he had a son in Morgan's command.

I immediately thought of Capt. Robert Berry, who was commissary on the staff of Colonel Martin and now with Colonel Smith. I went at once to find him and he proved to be the son. It was sad to see him look upon his father's face in death for a moment and then come away. He did not know until then that his father had entered the service on the other side, though a Union man from the beginning of the war.

Not long afterward it was reported that a force of the enemy had arrived on the other side of the town by railroad from Cincinnati. Giltner's brigade formed and engaged them for a while, then General Morgan with Smith's brigade followed. We found the forces nearly a mile from town. The enemy's force consisted of infantry. After they disembarked their train had gone back. When our brigade moved up in full view, the Federal commander formed his force in a hollow square about the middle of a large blue-grass pasture. Their flag was planted on each side. The commander and his staff sat mounted in the center. The enemy, as nearly as I could estimate, numbered about 1,500 men. General Morgan's force here present numbered about 1,800 men, and he at once formed a hollow square, mounted, facing to the inside all around the enemy and about two hundred yards away. This consumed some time, but the display was an attractive dress-parade. General Morgan now sent a flag of truce and, without firing a gun, the enemy surrendered. The commander who surrendered this force was Gen. E. A. Hobson, whose command had captured General Morgan's command in Ohio. But General Morgan did not retaliate upon Hobson for his own treatment as a felon in the Ohio Penitentiary, as he was satisfied General Hobson had not inspired it and should not be held responsible.

General Duke says:

General Hobson was paroled and sent, under escort of Capt. C. C. Morgan and two other officers, to Cincinnati, to effect, if possible, the exchange of himself and officers for certain of

General Morgan's officers then in prison, and, failing in that, to report as a prisoner within the Confederate lines. He was not permitted to negotiate the exchange and his escort were detained for some weeks.

It was now nearly night, and General Morgan proceeded to commit the first mistake in his hitherto brilliant career, which had never been equaled except by the indomitable Forrest. After detailing, including the detachments which had been sent in different directions, guards for the prisoners and wagon-train, perhaps 600 men altogether, the remainder of about 1,500 were moved out on the Paris pike less than a mile from town, where they were encamped in a woods pasture. We were only thirty miles from Mt. Sterling, where Burbridge with 4,000 cavalry had surprised Colonel Martin's camp two days before. Giltner's brigade was near the pike on the right and Smith's brigade still farther to the right—all on a ridge that crossed the Paris pike.

At daylight next morning I was awake and heard several rifle shots two or three hundred yards up the pike in front of Giltner's camp. Andrews, Barbour, and I were ready, as we had not taken off any clothing when we retired and our horses were saddled and ready. I awakened Colonel Smith nearby—we were all sleeping under the same tree—who directed us to wake up the camp and have the command formed. We found Colonel Bowles, Captains Kirkpatrick and Cantrill already up and their commands falling into line as fast as the men could get ready and mount.

The enemy had reached Giltner's command, which had formed hastily, and an engagement was in progress. The enemy began to appear about four hundred to five hundred yards distant, moving from the pike in our direction, and presently their mounted line swung around in our front. Lieutenant Andrews, who had gone for Colonel Smith, came with orders for our line to move forward. We did not go far when the command was dismounted and sent forward on foot. Barbour and I went with Colonel Bowles's command, which was on the extreme right. The Federal line was stretched from our front all the way to the pike. The conflict with Giltner was in plain view but the line in our front was standing still. Our line went forward yelling, the right going over a rock fence into a small woods pasture. Just to the left of this was a rail fence and a big gate in line with the rock fence. Soon after we passed this line of fencing, to my surprise Colonel Martin passed us shouting, "Charge!" I had not seen him for two days. He was riding with one foot in the stirrup and the other on a pillow and hooked around the horn of his saddle. Barbour and I went with him, but the enemy soon halted us all. They opened fire and stood firm.

When we were within one hundred yards of their line, they started a charge upon the front of Bowles, to our right, and their whole line moved forward. Colonel Martin ordered our line to fall back. Bowles's men formed behind the rock fence. Cantrill and Kirkpatrick were not so well protected, but the first charge was directed at Bowles. Before we could get through the gate my hat was knocked off in the rush and the gateway was choked for a minute. Colonel Martin held my horse while I got my hat, as I was just as safe on the ground while waiting to get through the gate. The Federals rushed into the little woods pasture and came within fifty feet of the rock fence under fire as if they were going to ride over it, but Bowles's men did not waver or slacken a continuous fire. He sat his horse and rode along his line, while Colonel Martin and others aided in encouraging the line to hold that fence. It was too hot for the enemy. They recoiled, but, after halting about one hundred yards distant and reforming under fire, they came rushing forward again—with the same result. On our left, Colonel Alston, Captains Cantrill and Kirkpatrick were holding their ground against the superior force in their front which had apparently hesitated to await the attempt to turn our flank.

Presently a force of several hundred fresh men galloped up behind the enemy's line which was in front of the rock fence, and swung around to our right. We had no force to oppose this flanking charge. At the same time the enemy, with an overwhelming force, moved forward all along the line. I observed that Giltner's line was broken away to the left, and the enemy was charging with yells. It was now a race for our men to reach their horses ahead of the enemy. Many of the horses were turned loose by the horse-holders, who were determined to escape. From this moment there was a stampede of the entire command. Lieutenant Barbour, Major Gassett, of General Morgan's staff, and I were the last to cross the bridge over the Licking River on the Leesburg pike. The Federals then took possession of it and stopped to take prisoners as our men came up.

We went about two hundred yards up the pike and then halted to see if we were pursued. We saw half a dozen of our men plunge into the stream one hundred yards from the bridge, when the Federals opened fire on them as they swam across. We recognized Colonel Martin and Captain Christy in the squad. Several Federals galloped from the bridge to capture them as they came out. Martin was off his horse as it came up the bank, but was trying to mount and succeeded. He then led the squad, and opening fire on the enemy, who seemed to be waiting for a surrender, charged through, scattering them; but a reinforcement from the bridge turned Martin's party up the river. We saw they could not get with us, so we galloped away to get a good start. We only went along the pike to the first woods on the left and turned off, making our way some fifteen miles through the country before we camped.

We made the journey safely through the mountains to Abingdon, Virginia. Within a day or two Colonel Martin and Lieutenant Andrews arrived. Many others arrived singly or in crowds under some officer, and finally General Morgan with a large number of the command reached Abingdon.

CHAPTER XXI

Morgan reestablishes headquarters at Abingdon—Reorganizing his command—Officers recuperate—Richmond authorities aroused against Morgan—Skirmish of Major Cantrill with scouts—Detached by Secretary of War.

The result of the expedition of General Morgan into Kentucky was unfortunate in its effect at Richmond, more than in the losses the command had suffered. Although the troops came in fragments, except the considerable force with General Morgan, it seemed that nearly all the command, except the killed and wounded, finally reached Abingdon and really better equipped than when they started on the raid. All were well mounted and armed.

Colonel Martin's wounded foot had not fully healed and he was practically off duty. A number of us who belonged to his staff while he commanded a brigade were now out of a job. Martin proposed that we go down toward Bristol and recuperate our horses. Lieutenant Barbour and I joined him and we arranged for board with Mr. Thomas near Bristol, who was a prosperous farmer. Within a few days we were joined by Lieut.-Col. Robert A. Alston, of South Carolina, and Adjutant Andrews. Alston had been adjutant-general on the staff of General Morgan and had commanded a battalion on the Kentucky raid.

At this time most of the command had reached Virginia and General Morgan immediately began its reorganization. A battalion was put in camp near our location under command of Maj. James E. Cantrill.

General Morgan had reestablished his headquarters, however, at Abingdon and that was the chief rendezvous of the command.

It was now common talk that the authorities at Richmond had broken out afresh against General Morgan, it being claimed that he had not asked or received permission to make the raid into Kentucky. We had been expecting this turn of affairs, although none could understand why the Government should ever be in readiness to handicap General Morgan as had been done with Forrest. They had both recruited more soldiers, had killed, wounded, and captured more of the forces, and captured and destroyed more of the stores, arms, equipments, and railroad bridges of the enemy since the war began than any other brigadier or major-general in the Southern army. They had displayed as much practical military capacity and rendered more effective service. And yet there seemed to be an insatiable determination to subordinate and restrain their untiring endeavors to aid the Southern cause. The unwillingness to trust them apparently appeared to be caused by the fact that neither was a graduate of West Point. The same spirit no doubt had promoted and upheld General Wheeler, who had never recruited a regiment or won a battle, but on the contrary had made a worse blunder, in attacking Fort Donelson, in January, 1863, where he was defeated, than could be charged against Forrest or Morgan. There was no record that General Wheeler had ever won a battle. All the soldiers, however, believed General Wheeler to be a true soldier and a good fighter, but could find no reason for giving him the forces of other commanders. He was but little over twenty-five years of age and the soldiers thought he ought first to recruit a regiment and learn something of practical warfare before becoming a lieutenant-general. Still, there was no disposition to reflect upon him for accepting all the distinction in the Confederacy for that matter, but the strange partiality was spoken of as the "lone love" of General Bragg.

It was well known that General Bragg, after the Missionary Ridge disaster, had been taken to Richmond and made chief military adviser to President Davis. It was also remembered that Bragg and Wheeler had reflected on General Morgan for going into Indiana and Ohio. It was pretty generally understood among the soldiers that Morgan did use his own discretion after he got to Kentucky and learned that Bragg had begun his retreat to Chattanooga on the 30th of June. While the soldiers were ignorant at the time of the position that would be taken by Bragg and Wheeler with reference to General Morgan's failure to return and help Bragg on his retreat, it was believed that the opportunity to strike him a lick would not be lost. For it had been seen that Bragg would hold on over his own army, at Tullahoma, when even his generals of the highest rank and character had told him in writing that he ought to give up the command. It was equally clear that Bragg and Wheeler were determined to dominate Morgan and Forrest when it was notorious that neither was satisfied to serve under Wheeler. And equally notorious that the troops of both had volunteered to fight under Forrest and Morgan and did not want to follow Wheeler.

Over four months after Morgan started on the Ohio raid, and while he was confined as a felon in the Ohio Penitentiary, General Wheeler made an official report to Bragg's adjutant-general on the subject of General Morgan's orders given him at the time the raid into Kentucky was authorized. The report is as follows:

HEADQUARTERS CAVALRY CORPS,
Cleveland, Tenn., November 7, 1863.
COLONEL: I have the honor, in obedience to your instructions, to state that, about June 13 last, I received a despatch from Brigadier-General Morgan, stating that the enemy at Louisville, Ky., were but 300 strong, and asking permission to march upon said place, and take and destroy the public works, etc. I immediately presented the matter to the general commanding this army, who had also learned from other sources of the small garrison at Louisville, and he directed me to send the following order to General Morgan, viz:

"HEADQUARTERS CAVALRY CORPS,
"Shelbyville, Tenn., June 14, 1863.
"GENERAL: Your despatch was received last night, and the facts communicated to General Bragg, and I visited him to-day

on the subject. He directs that you proceed to Kentucky with a sufficient number of regiments to make up 1,500 men, and that you use your own discretion regarding the amount of artillery you take. He directs that you take Kentucky troops and those which will be most likely to get recruits. The remainder of your command will be left under the command of the senior officer. Should you hear that the enemy is advancing for a general engagement, General Bragg wishes you to turn rapidly and fall upon his rear.

"I regret exceedingly the circumstances which render it impossible for General Bragg to detach your entire division, but the probability of an advance upon the part of the enemy makes it necessary for him to retain enough force to enable him to hold his position should a general engagement take place, and he hopes, since the enemy's forces in Kentucky are so reduced, you may be able to accomplish much good with the proposed detachment. General Bragg wishes the movement to take place as soon as possible.

"With great respect,
"Your obedient servant,
"JOSEPH WHEELER,
"Major-General.
"Gen. JOHN H. MORGAN,
"Commanding Cavalry Division."

This was sent, and its receipt acknowledged by General Morgan, with the request that he might take 2,000 men, stating that with these he could accomplish everything which he had proposed, viz., the capture of Louisville, Ky. General Bragg acceded to this request, and I sent the following order to General Morgan:

"Special Orders, }
    No. 44. }
"HEADQUARTERS CAVALRY CORPS,
"Near Shelbyville, June 18, 1863.

"1. General Morgan will proceed to Kentucky with a force of 2,000 officers and men, including such artillery as he may deem most expedient. In addition to accomplishing the work which he has proposed, he will, as far as possible, break up and destroy the Louisville and Nashville Railroad. He will, if practicable, destroy depots of supplies in the State of Kentucky, after which he will return to his present position.

*   *   *   *   *   *   *

"By order of Major-General Wheeler.
"E. S. BURFORD,
"Assistant Adjutant-General."

Prior to General Morgan's departure, I wrote him one or two letters, in which I urged his rapid movements, stating that I hoped his movements would be so rapid that he would be on his return to our army before General Rosecrans could be certain he had left Kentucky. The retained copies of these letters were unfortunately mislaid. In these letters to General Morgan and General Morgan's letters to me, not one word was said about his crossing the Ohio River; but, on the contrary, he was urged by me to observe the importance of his returning to our army as rapidly as possible. I make *this point apparent,* as it is *one to which my attention* was particularly called.

I am, Colonel, very respectfully,
Your obedient servant,
JOSEPH WHEELER,
Major-General.

Col. GEORGE WILLIAM BRENT,
Assistant Adjutant-General, Army of Tennessee.

It might be fair to observe that a great deal of stress is laid upon the point that General Morgan was charged to go to Kentucky and return, with instructions in advance to fall upon the rear of Rosecrans if that general should advance, which he was expected to do, and thereby assist General Bragg in retiring his army to Chattanooga, which he expected to do.

Unfortunately for this plea of General Wheeler, Bragg began his retreat on June 30th and Morgan did not get his command across the Cumberland River until the 2d of July. Besides this, it does not appear that Bragg needed Morgan. He had over 10,000 cavalry after the departure of Morgan's force and there seems to be no record that any of it fell on the rear of Rosecrans. General Forrest was ordered to reconnoiter in force at Triune from Duck River. He went there and skirmished in the village with the enemy until confronted by an infantry force, when he retired and, being cut off from the bridge at Shelbyville, made a circuit and reached Bragg at Tullahoma. There seemed to be a sufficient force of cavalry under General Wheeler and it was not apparent that General Bragg's army could have retired across the mountains in better order if Morgan had been in the column. If Morgan had immediately turned back from Columbia or Lebanon he could have done nothing but find his way across the mountains into East Tennessee in search of Bragg and Wheeler. It therefore appeared to most persons that Morgan had missed nothing by his Ohio raid except his own calculation that there would not be a big rise in the Ohio River the last week in July, when he expected to reach Buffington Island.

The presence now of General Bragg at Richmond as chief military adviser of the authorities accounted for the sudden condemnation of General Morgan and the indignation of the Secretary of War over this last raid to Kentucky, which was soon manifested with spirit, and with the unceremonious ill treatment of General Morgan.

The arduous labors of reorganizing his troops, which were continually arriving in squads from Kentucky, so engrossed the time and attention of General Morgan that his friends contended that he should give little heed to the clamor of this unfriendly manifestation at Richmond.

Capt. John L. Sanford, who was adjutant-general on the staff of General Morgan, in a letter to Gen. Basil W. Duke says:

I remember, too, my visit to Richmond during the month of August, 1864, on which occasion, at the General's request, I called upon the Secretary of War to lay before him some papers entrusted to my care, and also to make some verbal explanations regarding them. The excited, I may say the exasperated, manner in which the Honorable Secretary commented upon the documents, left but one impression upon my mind, and that was, that the War Department had made up its mind that the party was guilty and that its conviction should not be offended by any evidence to the contrary. The determination to pursue and break the General down was apparent to every one, and the Kentucky expedition was to be the means to accomplish this end (the reasons for a great deal of this enmity are, of course, familiar to you). I endeavored to explain to Mr. Seddon the injustice of the charge that General Morgan had made his expedition without proper authority (I felt this particularly to be my duty, as I was the only person then living who could bear witness upon this point), but being unable to obtain a quiet hearing, I left his office disappointed and disgusted.

Senator Benjamin H. Hill of Georgia, in 1878, writing of the campaign of Gen. Joseph E. Johnston in front of Atlanta, shows that President Davis authorized General Morgan's expedition to Kentucky. He says:

On Wednesday or Thursday, I think the 28th or 29th of June, 1864, a messenger came to my house, sent, as he said, by General Johnston, Senator Wigfall of Texas, and Governor Brown of Georgia.

The purpose of his mission, as he explained, was to persuade me to write a letter to President Davis urging him to order either Morgan or Forrest with five thousand men into Sherman's rear, etc.   *   *   *

The result of this interview was a determination on my part to go at once to see General Johnston, and place myself at his service. I reached his headquarters near Marietta, on the line of the Kenesaw, on Friday morning, which was the last day of June or the first day of July. We had a full and free interview, and I placed myself unreservedly at his disposal.

He explained at length that he could not attack General Sherman's army in their entrenchments, nor could he prevent Sherman from ditching round his (Johnston's) flank and compelling his retreat.

The only method of arresting Sherman's advance was to send a force into his rear, cut off his supplies, and thus compel Sherman either to give battle on his (Johnston's) terms or retreat. In either case he thought he could defeat Sherman, and probably destroy his army.

I said to him, "As you do not propose to attack General Sherman in his entrenchments, could you not spare a sufficient number of your present army, under Wheeler or some other, to accomplish this work?"

He said he could not—that he needed all the force he had in front. He then said that General Morgan was at Abingdon, Virginia, with five thousand cavalry, and, if the President would so order, this force could be sent into Sherman's rear at once.

He also said that Stephen D. Lee had sixteen thousand men under him in Mississippi, including the troops under Forrest and Roddey, and that, if Morgan could not be sent, five thousand of those under Forrest could do the work. Either Morgan or Forrest, with five thousand men, could compel Sherman to fight at a disadvantage or retreat, and there was no reason why either should not be sent if the President should give the order.

* * * * * * *

I was delayed en route somewhat, and reached Richmond on Sunday morning week, which I think was the 9th day of July. I went to the hotel, and in a few moments was at the Executive Mansion.

This interview with Mr. Davis I can never forget.

I laid before him carefully, and in detail, all the facts elicited in the conversation with General Johnston, and explained fully the purpose of my mission. When I had gone through, the President took up the facts, one by one, and fully explained the situation. I remember very distinctly many of the facts, for the manner as well as matter stated by Mr. Davis was impressive. *"Long ago,"* said the President, "I ordered Morgan to make this movement upon Sherman's rear, and suggested that his best plan was to go directly from Abingdon through East Tennessee. *But Morgan insisted that, if he were permitted to go through Kentucky* and around Nashville, he could greatly recruit his horses and his men by volunteers. *I yielded, and allowed him to have his own way.* He undertook it, but was defeated, and has returned back, and is now at Abingdon with only eighteen hundred men, very much demoralized, and badly provided with horses."

There was a surplus of officers and several of the best in Morgan's division were without a command. We learned that Gen. Adam R. Johnson, who had been detached by the Secretary of War to operate in western Kentucky, would not again return to the division until he could recruit another command, or his old brigade should be exchanged.

Colonel Martin met a Mr. Frank Phipps, who lived down in the bend of the Holston River on a splendid farm, and who invited him to bring us and make a visit where we could fatten our horses. All went except Colonel Alston. Mr. Phipps was at home alone, his family being away at some mineral springs in the mountains. We found a luxurious home with Mr. Phipps, and remained until his family returned and then moved to the house of an uncle of his, nearer Rogersville, Tennessee. Meanwhile, we had gone with Frank Phipps by invitation to dine with his sister, Mrs. Bynam, who was a widow, in the suburbs of Rogersville. She was one of the handsomest ladies, and hers one of the most elegant homes, in Tennessee. She had furnished her house with splendor—all that wealth could supply. She afterwards married Capt. Harry Clay, of Morgan's command.

A short while after we located with the elder Phipps, the battalion from Bristol with Major Cantrill in command arrived and camped about two or three miles from Rogersville. Colonel Martin and Lieutenant Andrews received orders to report to General Morgan at Bristol. Lieutenant Barbour and I were ordered by Major Cantrill to report to him. He assigned me to the command of a company of 28 men. Lieutenant Barbour was assigned to another company with more men but under a captain.

It appeared that General Morgan was moving all his troops in this direction on account of an advance of the Federals from Knoxville. Within a week after I went into camp here a Federal command of cavalry appeared in Rogersville early one morning and created a sensation, several of our men making narrow escapes from the town.

Major Cantrill promptly moved with his battalion to meet the enemy. We came upon them in the suburbs of the town. Our column was then in a long lane. It was formed across the lane through gaps in the fence on either side. I was in the field with my company on the right-hand side. As soon as Major Cantrill started his skirmishers forward, the enemy, about one hundred and fifty yards distant lying behind a fence, fired once or twice along their line without doing us any damage. Cantrill then moved his line forward, when we discovered the enemy had fled. We occupied the town for a while, learning that the enemy's force consisted of about one hundred cavalry on a scout. Major Cantrill then returned to camp.

The next day Major Cantrill sent for me to come to his headquarters, and showed me an order from General Morgan directing me to report to Colonel Martin at Bristol. I started without delay and reached there the next day in the forenoon. Bristol had one very wide main street running east and west. The line of Virginia and Tennessee was in the center of this street. I entered at the west end and found a great many soldiers mounted and forming in this street. In the center of the town I came upon General Morgan, mounted. After a greeting he told me Colonel Martin was at the hotel, to which he pointed. He then bade me good-by, saying he was just leaving for Tennessee and that I was going to leave his command, but I was yet ignorant of the fact and wondered what had happened.

Colonel Martin informed me he had been to Richmond, having gone from Abingdon, with Hon. Henry C. Burnett, our old Congressman when the war commenced and now one of the Confederate States Senators from Kentucky.

After a conference with Secretary of War James A. Seddon, and then with President Davis, Colonel Martin was detailed, and at his request I was also detailed, to report to Colonel Jacob Thompson in Toronto, Canada, for service under his orders along the northern borders of the United States.

He brought a letter, written by the Secretary of State, Judah P. Benjamin, to Colonel Thompson, introducing us and cautiously stating our mission.

CHAPTER XXII

Departure for Canada—Death of General Morgan—Forrest in Mississippi—Journey from Corinth to Toronto.

This appointment for special duty in Canada, as we understood the mission, would end our service in the South. Still, we only knew that we would be expected to engage, with other young officers, in expeditions and in heading forces in the event of a prospective uprising of our friends in the Northern States. It was of course a perilous journey to Canada, as we must travel in citizen's clothes to go through the United States and our letter from Mr. Benjamin to Colonel Thompson must be concealed. Our capture meant death. It was therefore decided that we would go as far west as convenient, in the Confederacy, and turn north beyond the range of our acquaintances in the Federal army. Colonel Martin had about seventy and I about one hundred and twenty dollars in greenbacks, which we agreed to advance for expenses, the amount to be repaid by Colonel Thompson.

We rode to Abingdon to sell our horses but could only get Confederate money. We sold the two horses for seventeen hundred dollars. This was the first of September.

The Secretary of War had issued to each of us a pass through our lines and to go anywhere in the Confederacy. We stopped over one night in Lynchburg and then went by rail without delay to Augusta, Georgia, where we were obliged to wait over an afternoon and night. Here at the hotel we met our friend Senator Burnett, from Kentucky, who had been away from Richmond several days. While we sat out in front of the hotel talking about the prospects for the Confederacy he received a telegram from the Secretary of War announcing the death of Gen. John H. Morgan, at Greeneville, Tennessee.

At Meridian, Mississippi, we found General Forrest starting up the railroad. He had about completed the organization of his command, which he told us was moving or stationed all along the Mobile and Ohio Railroad up to Corinth.

Forrest, in recalling to Martin the order of Bragg taking the horses of Morgan's 200 men that Martin commanded at Chickamauga, said, "I lost my division by taking the part of your men, but when Bragg doubled the dose on me I went to his headquarters and gave him h—l and told him he could go there."

When we told him our mission and showed him our papers he said, "Now look here, Colonel, you can't go ahead of my men. I'm going to do something up yonder but I've got to break the ice myself. I can't risk any mortal man to go up there from here. You have got to stay along here till we get to Corinth."

We went up to Columbus and stopped until most of Forrest's command had gone forward to Corinth. We went along on the train as he did and stopped at Corinth one night. When we left Forrest at Corinth, he told us that he was going to Middle Tennessee to attack Sherman's communications.

We walked five miles to the house of a good farmer, where we bought an ordinary horse and mule. Here I bought an old-fashioned black coat, with long waist, short skirt and broad collar. Martin got a pair of trousers that were a little too short, and a linen duster.

There were at this time no Federal garrisons in West Tennessee, and we passed through Jackson and Trenton, stopping at a farm-house three miles before reaching Troy, where the road turns squarely to the right toward Troy. Here we left with the family a lot of trinkets, our passes, and such things as might identify us as Confederates.

There were Federal garrisons at Hickman, Columbus, and Paducah. We wanted to reach St. Louis. Traveling toward Hickman we stopped at ten o'clock in the night within four miles of the town. Our friend waked us an hour before day and at sunrise we were on the bank of the Mississippi, two miles below Hickman. The distance was two miles to the point where we landed on the Missouri side. The horse and mule panted like lizards when they came out of the water. We were directed to the house of an old bachelor, named Miller, on the road to Charleston. This was the Sabbath day and when we reached Miller's place he had gone up the road to church. The congregation was dispersing as we came up and we rode along with the crowd toward Charleston. We met Mr. Frank Miller and stopped at his home for dinner. We stayed here until night. Mr. Miller did not need our animals but gave us a hundred and twenty dollars for the outfit.

There was a garrison of the enemy in Charleston eight miles distant. We walked eighteen miles that night to Price's woodyard on the Mississippi River above Cairo, Illinois. It was kept by Captain Price, a large land owner, who had been discharged from the Confederate Army on account of wounds. We were fagged out when we arrived at his place on the bank of the river. He let us sleep until ten o'clock in the forenoon, when a steamer, coming up, whistled for his landing. It stopped for two hours to wood. We observed that it was loaded with infantry, even all over the roof. We went aboard with our bundles and one common carpetbag or satchel. The cabin was full of soldiers. We arranged with the clerk for a stateroom to St. Louis and paid our passage. We strolled around looking at the boat. I bought a cigar at the bar and smoked. Several soldiers were drinking at the time and I engaged one in conversation, a gentlemanly sergeant. I learned that Gen. Sterling Price was marching on St. Louis with a large army and the city was in danger of capture. These troops were being forwarded to reinforce the army at St. Louis. I winked at Martin and presently he straggled around and said to me that he was a little "dry." He took in the party, three soldiers, and we all had toddies. We did not notice any of the officers. We concluded it was best to not patronize the barber shop though we needed a hair-cut and shave. It was not long before I got into a game of euchre with the sergeant and two others. After dinner Martin and another soldier proposed to play against us for five cents a corner. We carried on this game until the next afternoon, when we reached St. Louis. Martin and I purposely managed to pay the expenses.

Soon after we reached a hotel in St. Louis we happened to discover a friend. Martial law had been declared, business houses all closed, and details were pressing every able-bodied citizen, without regard to politics, into the ranks to defend the city. Our friend found a retail merchant who kept clothing and furnishing goods. He slipped us in at his back door. We had treated ourselves to bath, hair-cut and shave at the hotel. Now we got a complete wardrobe, that is, all we could wear; and carried no baggage. A hack was secured and we drove from this store in time to reach the transfer steamer for Alton, Illinois, ten miles up the river, where we caught the train for Chicago. We arrived the next morning and spent the day looking at the city. At night we took a train on the Michigan Central Railroad and reached Detroit, Michigan, next morning, and crossed over safely to Windsor, Canada. After breakfast we boarded the train for Toronto.

The Queen's Hotel where we stopped fronted on Toronto Bay. It may be said that we found Confederate headquarters here at this hotel. Colonel Jacob Thompson, and secretary, Walter W. Cleary, occupied a suite of rooms.

Among the first Kentuckians we met were Dr. Stuart Robinson, the famous Presbyterian minister from Louisville; Dr. Luke P. Blackburn, Mrs. W. C. P. Breckinridge, with her children, her sister Miss Mollie Desha, and Miss Maria Hunt of Lexington.

Within a few days we had met, perhaps, a hundred Confederates and prominent citizens of Kentucky, Missouri, West Virginia, and Maryland, who were refugees.

Colonel Thompson cautioned us on our arrival against any stranger who might claim an acquaintance, etc., as a swarm of detectives from the United States, male and female, were quartered in Toronto. An intelligent gentleman, Larry McDonald, from New York, was one of Colonel Thompson's closest friends, and also a gentleman from Little Rock, Arkansas, Mr. G. J. Hyams, who had escaped from prison and was reputed to be wealthy. These were especially commended by Colonel Thompson.

It was deemed a wise precaution that Martin and I should separate and secure boarding-houses, where we would only be known as escaped prisoners, and not frequent the Queen's Hotel, in order that our connection with Colonel Thompson would not be especially noted by the detectives in the employ of the Washington authorities. And that our association with other prominent Confederate officers should only be casual in public. We cultivated the acquaintance of refugee citizens and the Canadians.

Colonel Martin secured a room at the boarding-house of Mr. Withers, from Covington, Kentucky, a brother of Maj. Al Withers of General Morgan's staff. Dr. Stuart Robinson and Dr. Luke P. Blackburn boarded here. I boarded with Mr. Inglis, a Canadian. In a few days Capt. Thomas H. Hines took the room adjoining mine. And about the same time Mrs. J. Russ Butler and her children arrived. Her husband, Col. J. Russ Butler, was then the commander of the First Kentucky Cavalry. He had escaped from prison and his family joined him here. I spent the time in reading, and playing chess with Mrs. Butler.

After Captain Hines had been here a few days he left, and, being absent about two days, returned with his bride. He had been to Cincinnati, where his sweetheart, Miss Sprowle, from Woodbury, on Green River, Kentucky, had met him by agreement and they were married.

I met a young Confederate soldier, Charles C. Hemming, from Jacksonville, Florida, who was an expert oarsman. He

had escaped from prison and had managed to reach Toronto.
He had enlisted in the select forces of Colonel Thompson.
I enjoyed a skiff ride with him as he did all the pulling. The
city presented a grand front when viewed from a distance
out in the bay.

There was everything in the prospect at Toronto to make
a sojourn enjoyable. The leading newspapers of Canada
were published here and the South got a friendly comment
on the course of events. All the news of the war and from
the front of the armies was published daily. We also received the New York, Chicago, Buffalo and Detroit papers.

CHAPTER XXIII

Capt. Thomas H. Hines—Purposes of mission to Canada—Col. Jacob Thompson's mission—Coalition with leaders of Sons of Liberty—Concentration at Democratic National Convention in Chicago—Fruitless endeavor to release Confederate prisoners at Camp Douglas and Springfield.

Capt. Thomas H. Hines related to me much of the experience of himself, Capt. John B. Castleman, Lieut. George B. Eastin, Lieut. Bennett H. Young and others, and Col. Vincent Marmaduke of Missouri, on an expedition to Chicago in August. He also described the organization, character and purposes of the order known as Sons of Liberty who had cooperated with the Confederates in the plans to liberate the Confederate prisoners confined at Camp Douglas and Springfield, Illinois.

Thomas Henry Hines was a native of Woodbury, a village on Green River, in Warren County, Kentucky, some twenty miles below Bowling Green. He enlisted in Capt. John H. Morgan's squadron of cavalry at the time when Gen. Albert Sidney Johnston commanded at Bowling Green. In personal appearance Hines was effeminate, though above the medium height, with blue eyes and black hair. Though not formed for strength, he was athletic and capable of endurance. In manners he was captivating, though modest and unassuming. He was endowed with varied talents and unflinching courage. I judged him to be about twenty-four years old. Before his escape with General Morgan from the Ohio penitentiary, which gave him wide fame, he was noted in Morgan's cavalry as one of the many daring young officers of that romantic command. His exploits recorded in Duke's History of Morgan's Cavalry are too numerous to be recorded here.

Captain Hines was the first Confederate officer to be selected by President Davis for the service along the northern borders of the United States for the release of prisoners, and started from Richmond soon after the death of Colonel Dahlgren, whose daring attempt against that city had ended in disaster in the first days of March, 1864.

It is deemed more appropriate that the purposes of his mission and his efforts should be given as related by himself in the *Southern Bivouac,* as follows:

In March, 1864, Mr. Davis determined to send into Northern territory some Confederate officers who should especially undertake to effect the release of Confederate prisoners. He selected for that purpose Capt. T. H. Hines, of the Ninth Kentucky Cavalry, C. S. A. (Morgan's division). Other Confederates, both of the army and navy, were afterwards detailed for similar service. Hines was given authority to collect and organize, for the accomplishment of his mission, all of the Confederate soldiers then in Canada, most of whom were themselves escaped prisoners. He was to be in active command of any force so created, but was subsequently ordered to report to and receive general instructions from the commissioners, whose appointment has already been mentioned, and who reached Canada in May.

Captain Hines had escaped with General Morgan from the Ohio penitentiary. Mr. Davis's attention was attracted to him by this circumstance, which perhaps contributed to suggest the idea of a general release of prisoners. After a conference, in which the situation was fully discussed, and the character of the attempt desired thoroughly explained, the following order was given Hines, in accordance with Mr. Davis's directions, by the Secretary of War:

"CONFEDERATE STATES OF AMERICA,
"WAR DEPARTMENT,
"RICHMOND, VA., March 16, 1864.

"Capt. T. H. HINES.

"SIR: You are detailed for special service to proceed to Canada, passing through the United States under such character and in such mode as you may deem most safe, for the purpose of collecting there the men of General Morgan's command who may have escaped, and others of the citizens of the Confederate

Thomas H. Hines
1864

States willing to return and enter the military service of the Confederacy, and arranging for their return either through the United States or by sea.

"You will place yourself, on arrival, in communication with Hon. J. P. Holcomb, who has been sent as special commissioner to the British Provinces, and in his instructions directed to facilitate the passage of such men to the Confederacy. In passing through the United States you will confer with the leading persons friendly or attached to the cause of the Confederacy, or who may be advocates of peace, and do all in your power to induce our friends to organize and prepare themselves to render such aid as circumstances may allow ; and to encourage and animate those favorable to a peaceful adjustment to the employment of all agencies calculated to effect such consummation on terms consistent always with the independence of the Confederate States. You will likewise have in view the possibility, by such means as you can command, *of effecting any fair and appropriate enterprises of war against our enemies,* and will be at liberty to employ such of our soldiers as you may collect, in any *hostile operation offering,* that may be consistent with the strict observance of neutral obligations incumbent in the British Provinces.

"Reliance is felt in your discretion and sagacity to understand and carry out, as contingencies may dictate, the details of the *general design* thus communicated. More specific instructions in anticipation of events that may occur under your observation cannot well be given. You will receive a letter to General Polk in which I request his aid in the transmission of cotton, so as to provide funds for the enterprise, and an order has been given to Colonel Bayne, with whom you will confer, to have two hundred bales of cotton purchased in North Mississippi and placed under your direction for this purpose.

"Should the agencies you may employ for transmitting that be unsuccessful, the same means will be adopted of giving you larger credit and you are advised to report to Colonel Bayne, before leaving the lines of the Confederacy, what success has attended your efforts for such transmission.

"Respectfully,

"(Signed.) 'JAMES A. SEDDON,

"Secretary of War."

Instructions were also forwarded to Lieut.-Gen. Leonidas Polk, as follows :

"CONFEDERATE STATES OF AMERICA,
"WAR DEPARTMENT,
"RICHMOND, VA., March 16, 1864.

"Lieut.-Gen. L. POLK, Commander, etc.

"GENERAL: I shall have occasion to send Capt. T. Henry Hines, an enterprising officer, late of General Morgan's command, who was so efficient in aiding in the escape of that general and others from the Ohio penitentiary, on special service through the lines of the enemy. To provide him with funds for the accomplishment of the purpose designed, it will be necessary that I shall have transferred to Memphis some two hundred (200) bales of cotton, which I have ordered an officer of the bureau to have purchased at some convenient point in North Mississippi.

"Captain Hines will himself arrange the agencies by which the cotton can be transferred and disposed of, so as to place funds at command in Memphis, and I have to request that facilities, in the way of transportation and permission to pass the lines, may, as far as needful, be granted him and the agent he may select. You will please give appropriate instructions to effect these ends to the officers in command on the border.

"Very respectfully,
"(Signed.) JAMES A. SEDDON,
"Secretary of War."

* * * * * * *

In pursuance of these instructions Captain Hines immediately proceeded to Canada, making his way through the United States.

* * * * * * *

The Commissioners appointed by Mr. Davis were Messrs. Clay of Alabama, Holcomb of Virginia, and Thompson of Mississippi.

The following letter was sent Mr. Thompson, requesting his immediate departure upon the mission for which he was selected:

"RICHMOND, VA., April 27, 1864.

"Hon. JACOB THOMPSON.

"SIR: Confiding special trust in your zeal, discretion and patriotism, I hereby direct you to proceed at once to Canada; there to carry out the instructions you have received from me verbally, in such manner as shall seem most likely to conduce

JOHN B. CASTLEMAN
1864

to the furtherance of the interests of the Confederate States of America which have been intrusted to you.

"Very respectfully and truly yours,

"(Signed.) JEFFERSON DAVIS."

Messrs. Thompson and Clay, with Mr. W. W. Cleary, of Kentucky, who was appointed secretary of the Commission, left Richmond on the 3d of May for Wilmington, and sailed from Wilmington on the 6th, running the gauntlet of armed United States cruisers stationed at and near the mouth of the harbor.

In pursuance of this necessity of making the authority of the commission absolute in all matters pertaining to Confederate interests in Canada, or operations to be directed thence, a necessity foreseen even before Mr. Thompson sailed from Wilmington, the following order, directed to Captain Hines, who had then taken his departure, was issued. It will be seen to what extent it modified the one previously given him of March 16th.

"CONFEDERATE STATES OF AMERICA,

"WAR DEPARTMENT,

"RICHMOND, VA., May 27, 1864.

"Capt. T. Henry Hines, of the Army of the Confederate States, will report to and confer with Hon. Jacob Thompson, Special Commissioner of the Confederate States Government in Canada, and be guided by his counsel in his proceedings and action on his present service. He may consider his instructions from this department subject to modification, change, or revocation by the said Commissioner, and will take further direction from him.

"JAMES A. SEDDON,

"Secretary of War."

Mr. Thompson established his headquarters at Montreal on the 30th of May, 1864, and opened an account with the Bank of Ontario in that city. Before *resorting to other and more extreme measures,* he endeavored to carry out Mr. Davis's primary idea of negotiating "with such persons in the North as might be relied on to aid the attainment of peace." He sought, therefore, to secure conferences, not only with influential men representing the peace party in the Northern and Eastern States, but also with leading public men who were identified with the political party in power, and might be supposed to reflect the views of Mr. Lincoln and his Cabinet.

* * * * * * *

Soon as it was definitely ascertained that it was impracticable to open negotiations looking to the cessation of hostilities and truce in any form between the contending sections, the Commissioners prepared to utilize the feeling existing in the Western and border States, inimical to the Administration, and to organize it for active and practical opposition to the further prosecution of the war. On the 9th of June Captain Hines had been sent to confer with Mr. Clement L. Vallandigham, then at Windsor, Canada, in order to obtain such information on that subject as that gentleman could furnish.

On the 11th of June Mr. Thompson himself met Mr. Vallandigham, and the two thoroughly discussed the existing disaffection, which had already crystallized into the semi-military organization popularly known as the "Sons of Liberty." Mr. Vallandigham was the Grand Commander of this order, and he represented that it was in all three hundred thousand strong. There were eighty-five thousand members, he said, in Illinois, fifty thousand in Indiana, and forty thousand in Ohio.

* * * * * * *

As early as January, 1861, Hon. Fernando Wood, then mayor of New York City, addressed a message to the Common Council, in which he recommended that New York should secede and constitute herself a free city, and formulated the idea, then so prevalent, in very striking terms: *"It may be said that secession or revolution in any of the United States would be subversive of all Federal authority, and, so far as the central government is concerned, the resolving of the community into its original elements*—that, if part of the States form new combinations and governments, *other States may do the same. California and her sisters of the Pacific* will no doubt set up an independent republic, and husband their own rich mineral resources. *The Western States,* equally rich in cereals and other agricultural products, will probably do the same. Amid the gloom which the present and prospective condition of things must cast over the country, *New York, as a Free City, may shed the only light and hope of a future reconstruction of our blessed Confederacy."*

* * * * * * *

Mr. Thompson, of course, and the Confederates acting under his directions, would have preferred to see the whole tendency of the movement directed toward the establishment of a separate confederacy of Northwestern States.

* * * * * * *

JACOB THOMPSON
1864

So far as possible, they encouraged this idea among the parties who seemed most sensible of the stimulus of personal ambition.

* * * * * * *

At this time Mr. Vallandigham introduced to Mr. Thompson a prominent official of the order who occupied somewhat the position of its adjutant-general, thoroughly indorsing his reliability and energy. Through this gentleman Mr. Thompson subsequently arranged for the distribution of funds to be used in arming and mobilizing the county organizations.

* * * * * * . *

Conferences with very many Northern men who at that period visited Canada, who were not connected with the order of the "Sons of Liberty," nor informed in any wise of the purposes of the Commissioners, further developed the fact that there was a widely spread feeling of fatigue, to use the mildest term, with the war and those who were profiting by it. A subsequent investigation of the character and sentiment of the "Sons of Liberty" confirmed perfectly all that Mr. Vallandigham had said, and revealed a feverish desire of the general membership to assert and maintain their rights.

Mr. Lincoln's call, about this time, for five hundred thousand more men for the army, and the proposed draft to provide them, intensified the wish to resist a further prosecution of the war, and seemed to have ripened it into resolve.

Mr. Thompson became thoroughly convinced that the movement could be induced, and that it would be successful. But there was always the doubt whether men bound together merely by political affiliations and oaths, behind which there was no real legal authority, could be handled like an army.

* * * * * * *

Mr. Vallandigham returned to Ohio about the middle of June. He made speeches immediately, which seemed intended to invite his rearrest and the action he had predicted.

In his first speech, after his return, at Hamilton, he almost declared the existence and purposes of the order. He said:

"But I warn also the men in power that there is a vast multitude, a host whom they cannot number, bound together by the strongest and holiest ties, to defend, by whatever means the exigencies of the times shall demand, their natural and constitutional rights as freemen, at all hazards and to the last extremity."

The 20th of July seemed to have been determined upon as the date of outspoken declaration of resistance. The inclination to prevent the enforcement of the draft pervaded all classes who would probably be subjected to it, and might unite all such men in an effort to prevent it.

It was understood that a simultaneous movement would be concerted in Illinois and Indiana, and that in each of those States the State officers would be practically deposed and provisional governments organized.

In his first report to Richmond, made in July, Mr. Thompson said: *"Though intending this a Western confederacy and demanding peace, if peace be not granted, then it shall be war.* There are some choice spirits enlisted in this enterprise, and all that is needed for success is unflinching nerve. For our part, it is agreed that Capt. T. Henry Hines shall command at Chicago, and Capt. John B. Castleman at Rock Island. *If a movement could be made by our troops into Kentucky and Missouri,* it would greatly facilitate matters in the West. The organized forces of the Federal Government would thus be employed, and this would give courage and hope to the Northwestern people. The rank and file are weary of the war, but the violent abolitionists, preachers, contractors, and political press are clamorous for its continuance. If Lee can hold his own in front of Richmond, and Johnston defeat Sherman in Georgia prior to the election, it seems probable that Lincoln will be defeated. Nothing less, however, can accomplish this end. It is not improbable that McClellan will be nominated by the war Democrats. His recent war speeches have broken him down with the peace party, but in my opinion no peace candidate can be elected unless disaster attend the Federal armies in Virginia and Georgia. In short, *nothing but violence can terminate the war."*

*   *   *   *   *   *   *

On the 22d of July the Commissioners, with Captains Castleman and Hines, met, at St. Catharines, certain delegates from this Chicago conference, who reported that it was proposed to take decided action on the 16th of August, but expressed a fear that unless there was such movement of the Confederate forces into Kentucky and Missouri as would occupy the attention of the Federal military authorities, troops would be immediately employed and on hand to suppress any action attempted.

*   *   *   *   *   *   *

So it was agreed that another council should be held at London, Canada, on the 7th of August. When that conference was held, the representatives of the State and county organizations present insisted that there should be a further postponement until the 29th of August, the date of the assembling of the National Democratic Convention at Chicago. At Chicago they urged, and on that date, the vast concourse of people drawn together would be the best cover for their action, and it would be easy to concentrate a large body of reliable and determined men in aid of their design, without attracting attention or suspicion.

* * * * * * *

An earlier date than the 29th had been suggested by Hines and Castleman, but the point was yielded in deference to a communication received from the representatives of the "Sons of Liberty," which clearly indicated that they were beginning to regard the situation as a very grave one, and to feel profoundly the responsibility they had incurred. It was as follows:

"LONDON, C. W., August 8, 1864.

"HON. JACOB THOMPSON, HON. C. C. CLAY, T. H. HINES, JOHN B. CASTLEMAN.

"GENTLEMEN: We have thought on the conclusion of this morning, and feel constrained to say a few words more. We told you that we could not approve the plan, and the more we think of it the more thoroughly are we convinced that it will be unsuccessful. The time is too short to expect assistance, however willing we may be to assist. It will require some two days to travel back to places of residence and make arrangements about cashing drafts and procure messengers of the right sort to go into different counties and give notice. This will require until Thursday to get the ear of our chiefs, which will give only one day to select and notify men that they are in for a perilous and uncertain campaign under men who they know but little about. Of course few will respond to the call made so suddenly and unexpectedly, and we shall have to depend almost entirely upon what cooperation we can get from the organization in Chicago. Under these circumstances we are powerless to render the needed aid. A movement unsupported by vigorous cooperation at Indianapolis and Springfield had better not be undertaken. We are willing to do anything which bids fair to result in good, but shrink from the responsibility of a movement made in the way now proposed, and have concluded to frankly communicate this to you. You underrate the condition of things in the Northwest. By patience and perseverance in the work of agitation we are sure of a general uprising which will result in a glorious success. We must look to bigger results than the mere liberation of prisoners. We should look to the grand end of adding an empire of Northwestern States. We leave for Chicago to-night to do our best, but with heavy hearts and drooping hope for the cause in which we have thrown our very souls and existence."

In the mean time, enough had been learned to warrant the belief that, in the event of an organized and resolute *Northwestern revolt,* there *was a sentiment in New York and the neighboring States* which would induce a formidable opposition to the transportation of troops over their territory for the purpose of coercing their Western sisters. *Influential men were ready to formulate measures to meet such a necessity,* and *those who could be trusted were informed by the Commissioners that they would be willing to render substantial assistance.*

The means to purchase arms for those who were committed to such opposition to coercion were solicited and provided. *A prominent citizen of New York undertook to purchase and distribute the arms which would be required there.* On this subject the Hon. James P. Holcomb wrote from Montreal as follows, to Mr. Thompson at Toronto, July 27th:

"DEAR SIR: Our friends are here and urge the promptest measures, as the time is very brief. They have contracted for five thousand; these will cost thirty thousand in gold. No payment until they are received. Bills Canada bank on England, payable to their order, can be cashed, and should be sent in small denominations *at once to New York.* The other party for whom we were anxious has gone home to see others among the initiated. It is immaterial *which of the two* has the fund about which you consulted me. All now depends upon prompt action."

* * * * * * *

In August the garrison was largely increased at Chicago, and three thousand troops were placed on duty. This led to an apprehension that the Administration intended to interfere with the meeting of the Democratic Convention on the 29th of August, and this fact was used to stimulate the prejudice throughout the West and justify the assembling of a large body of men, outspoken in their determination to resist the possible outrage. There was thus furnished sufficient excuse for the county commanders of the Order of the Sons of Liberty to mobilize the members of their organization on the plea that they should attend the convention, and ought to resist any attempt to interrupt its deliberations. Mr. Vallandigham's representatives were furnished means for transportation, and had ample time to make proper distribution and explain to the more faithful and courageous county commanders why the rank and file should come to Chicago and resist any further attempt on the liberties of the citizens. These representatives were further urged to make provision for keeping reasonably in hand the delegations from the various counties; but it must be confessed that events fully justified the belief that some of the principal agents employed were lacking either in fidelity or courage, or in both.

In Canada there were less than one hundred Confederate soldiers, and to the discretion of some of these it was not altogether safe to trust the success of the enterprise. Sixty men were chosen for service at Chicago. Many of these men had escaped from prison under circumstances which illustrated their daring and fertility of resource. One of them, Lieut. George B. Eastin, was well known in Morgan's command as the hero of a desperate hand-to-hand combat with the Federal Colonel Hallisey, in which the latter was killed.

Lieut. Bennett H. Young had been sent by President Davis to report to the Commissioners for service on the Lakes.

* * * * * * *

"TORONTO, C. W., August 24, 1864.

"JOHN B. CASTLEMAN, Captain C. S. A.:

"By virtue of the authority vested in me, and having confidence in your courage and fidelity, you are hereby appointed to special service and made responsible with Capt. Thomas H. Hines for an expedition against the United States prisons in the Northwestern States, and *such other service as you and he have been verbally instructed about.* To you and Capt. T. H. Hines is left the selection of such Confederate soldiers in Canada as are probably suited for use in so perilous an undertaking. You are expected to take with you all those on whose courage and discretion you are willing to rely.

"Your obedient servant,

JACOB THOMPSON."

* * * * * * *

On the 27th and 28th of August the Confederates detailed for this important service proceeded to Chicago, traveling in small parties and assuming the appearance and conduct of men attracted there by the political interest of the occasion. They stopped at places designated in advance, the greater part of them having been instructed to go to the Richmond House.

*   *   *   *   *   *   *

Men commended to us by Mr. Vallandigham had been entrusted with the necessary funds for perfecting the county organizations; arms had been purchased in the North by the aid of our professed friends in New York; alliances offensive and defensive had been made with peace organizations, and though we were not misled by the sanguine promises of our friends, we were confident that with any sort of cooperation on their part success was reasonably possible. During the excitement that always attends a great political convention, increased as we supposed it would be by the spirit of opposition to the Administration, we felt that we would be freer to act unobserved, and that we could move with promptness and effect upon Camp Douglas. With nearly five thousand prisoners there, and over seven thousand at Springfield, joined by the dissatisfied elements in Chicago and through Illinois, we believed that at once we would have a formidable force, which might be the nucleus for much more important movements. Everything was arranged for prompt action, and for the concentration and organization of all these bodies. It was, as we felt, the first step that was the most difficult and the most serious. Success was only possible by prompt and concerted action during the convention. The Confederates were ready. The men chosen for this work were no mere adventurers; they had enlisted in an enterprise where they knew success was doubtful, and that failure meant probable death; and these men have since shown by their success in civil life that they were men of no ordinary capacity. The roster of this little band was made up on the occasion of the distribution of arms, which had been obtained by Judge Cleary, and it does not contain the full names of all. That roster is as follows:

Bennett H. Young, Wood, Price, Doty, Stone, George Young, B. Steele, G. A. Elsworth, C. M. Swager, George E. Cantrill, R. F. Smith, J. M. Trigg, H. B. Hibble, W. M. Wordward, Keller Thomas, Allen M. Kiser, C. E. Wasson, Crumbaugh, William Cooper, Henry Sampson, M. Huntley, S. Gregg, M. Major, Denny, Hays, Mock, Squire Tevis, William T. Tevis, Lackey, Marcus A. Spur, Bruce, B. Magoffin, Jr., Kiester, Wallace, Daniel, P. M. Hansbrough, Ben M. Anderson, Webster, Denny, T. H. Hines, McGuire, Theodore Schultz, Ignatio, Higbee, Hillborn, J. C. Hill, Joseph Elbert, Hunt, Bell,

John Maughir, Frank O. Anderson, George B. Eastin, John T. Ashbrook, R. B. Drake, John B. Castleman, Leavel, H. Seabring, J. T. Harrington, Joseph Harrington, John H. Thomas, W. E. Mumford, J. T. Buttersworth, V. Marmaduke.

The National Democratic Convention met at Chicago, August 29th.

* * * * * * *

Arms were ready, and information had been conveyed to the prisoners of war of our intention. Chicago was thronged with people from all sections of the country, and among this vast crowd were many of the county officers of the secret organization, on whom we relied for assistance. Most of these present at our Chicago conference were from Illinois; men well known in their own localities, whose influence, once they were committed to our plans by some overt act, would be of vast service.

It was essential to the success of any undertaking for us to know definitely what armed forces the representatives of Mr. Vallandigham could provide. For this a meeting of the officers of the organization was held at the rooms of Hines and Castleman at the Richmond House the night before the convention, August 28, 1864.

* * * * * * *

The evening of the 29th of August came, but on the part of the timid timidity became more apparent, and those who were resolute could not show the strength needed to give confident hope of success. The reinforcement sent by the Administration to strengthen the Chicago garrison had been vastly exaggerated, and seven thousand men was the number rumor brought to the ear of the Sons of Liberty. Care had been taken to keep informed as to what troops came to Camp Douglas, but the statement made by Hines and Castleman, to the effect that only three thousand were present, did not counteract the effect produced by the rumor that the Federal forces there numbered more than double that number. When, therefore, a count was taken of the number of the Sons of Liberty on whom we could rely, it seemed worse than folly to attempt to use them. There were not enough to justify any movement which would commit the Northwestern people to open resistance, and not even enough to secure the release and control the organization of the prisoners at Camp Douglas as the nucleus of an army which would give possible relief to the Confederacy.

* * * * * * *

The immediate influence of the vast convention assembled was **exactly** contrary to what had been expected.

With this state of things existing, it could not be safe or wise for the Confederates to linger in Chicago after the disappearance of the great throng which had assembled; it was necessary, therefore, to look beyond Chicago for a field of action. Captains Hines and Castleman accordingly proposed to the officers of the Sons of Liberty to furnish a detail of five hundred Northwestern men, to be accompanied and controlled by their own officers, and it was proposed with this aid to liberate the prisoners confined at Rock Island, and take possession both of that town and of Springfield. The two Confederate officers named had agreed that Castleman should take charge of these forces, and on the following evening assume quiet possession of the passenger train which left Chicago at nine o'clock for Rock Island, running through on schedule time, and cutting the wires with the hope of surprising and capturing that town. The garrison there had been weakened to protect Chicago, and Rock Island seemed an easy conquest.

*   *   *   *   *   *   *

Hines and Castleman had agreed that if the detail was furnished, some ten chosen Confederates should accompany the latter to Rock Island, where, if the prisoners were released, regiments should be hastily organized and equipped and thrown across to Springfield. Hines, with the remaining Confederates, about fifty, was to organize them into ten squads, mount them, cut the wires, destroy the bridges out of Chicago, on every road, and send to the outer world such telegrams of his own choosing as would account for the condition of things in Chicago. For the purpose of effect on the public mind, it was determined to inform the people outside of the responsibility of the Administration for the interference with the political convention in its deliberations, trusting that communication might not be reopened under a fortnight. But no one experienced in army life will be surprised to observe the difference between the soldier and citizen, even though the citizen may formerly have been a soldier. The contingent which we asked could not be promised us with any certainty, and all hope of success in this direction had to be abandoned, at least for the time. The Confederate officers accordingly deemed it wise to leave Chicago, as the safety secured by the presence of the convention was removed, and the agents of the Government had been aroused to greater vigilance and activity.

CHAPTER XXIV

Plan for capture of gunboat *Michigan* on Lake Erie and release of prisoners on Johnson's Island—Captain Cole and Acting Master Beall undertake the adventure—Lieutenant Young sent with funds to Buffalo—Cole, at the moment of success, is betrayed and arrested and imprisoned at Sandusky City—Thompson and Clay to the rescue—Cole finally recognized as prisoner of war.

Colonel Thompson explained to Martin and me the character of expeditions in which the Confederates with his approval and support had been engaged. The story of the attempt of Hines and Castleman to release the prisoners at Chicago on the 29th of August was gone over in substantially the same form as told by Hines.

Colonel Thompson had indulged the hope that the gunboat *Michigan,* which was anchored near Johnson's Island, might be captured and thus give the Confederates the mastery on the Lakes. It would put the cities and towns of New York, Ohio, Illinois, Michigan, and Wisconsin, that were upon the shores of the Lakes, at the mercy of this warship under Confederate command.

The capture of this gunboat had been undertaken by Capt. Charles H. Cole, of Forrest's command, and Capt. John Yates Beall, an officer of the Confederate Navy. The attempt was made just before our arrival in Toronto.

Captain Cole had first investigated the situation as follows*:

Soon after, Captain Cole made a special report showing the prospect of an early capture of the steamer *Michigan,* and Lieut. Bennett H. Young was sent to Sandusky, Ohio, to report

---

*T. Henry Hines in *Southern Bivouac.*

to Captain Cole for duty, and to provide him with the necessary funds. After investigating the matter with which he was charged, Captain Cole made a report, from which the following are extracts:

"Buffalo is poorly protected; one regiment and a battalion of invalids. The regiment is at Camp Morgan, opposite Port Huron, and between North and South Buffalo, and the battalion doing hospital duty and guarding the stores. There is a very large amount of government stores there, a large quantity of ammunition in United States arsenal, and also some cannon, mortars, and small arms. The arsenal is situated on Oak street. I left for Cleveland, and on the passage met a gentleman who will be of benefit to our cause at Chicago. He assisted me materially in Cleveland, and took me around the government works, and introduced me to the foreman of the cannon shops, who told me there were about two hundred and fifty men employed there, and that they were shipping large cannon to Sandusky, Milwaukee, and Chicago, with one hundred rounds of ammunition to each gun. I learned the bearings of the lake around Cleveland. I met the engineer of the *Pacific*, who, I think, money can influence. I concluded my information from him and left for Detroit with him. From Detroit I went to Chicago, meeting with Mr. Charles Walsh.

"I ascertained there the water needed for crossing the bars, and the amount of tonnage of the tugs, which would be most serviceable in time of need. The new steam tugs are of, say one hundred and seventy-five tons, one screw engine, and are capable of carrying coal for thirty-six hours' run; will mount two guns, one large gun at the stern and a small field-piece at the bow; are easily managed, and will make ten knots an hour even in the severest weather. There is little difficulty in bringing vessels to bear against Camp Douglas. We can run the tugs up the river, and an armed vessel on the lake, bringing guns to bear on the camp. There is an immense amount of shipping, and among the first things would be to destroy the different draw-bridges, and then the whole city is accessible by water.

"Milwaukee is an easy place to take possession of. They have no fort, and twelve feet of water up to the first draw-bridge. The Milwaukee and Detroit steamers are below the first draw-bridge; there is a large amount of grain shipment and quantities of coal. Sheboygan supplies all the country from

Fond du Lac; sends grain and produce there for shipment. Port Washington is a small settlement with little of advantage, but its people are strong friends, and determined in their resistance to the draft. Mackinaw has a natural fortification, and mounted at the observatory are three guns bearing on the straits. * * * Lake Erie furnishes a splendid field for operations. * * * Erie is a difficult place to get at, more so than any city on the Lakes. * * * I made the acquaintance of Captain Carter, commanding United States steamer *Michigan.*

"He is an unpolished man, whose pride seems to be touched for the reason that, having been an old United States naval officer, he is not allowed now a more extensive field of operation. I do not think that he can be bought."

Captain Cole, desiring formal authority before undertaking the capture of the *Michigan,* addressed Mr. Thompson from Sandusky, Ohio, as follows:

"Hon. JACOB THOMPSON.

"SIR: I have the honor to ask to be placed in secret detached service, in undertaking the capture of the gunboat *Michigan* at Johnson's Island. Combination can be made without infringing the neutrality laws of Canada. I send this by special messenger. An immediate answer requested.

"CHARLES H. COLE,

"Captain, C. S. A."

To this Colonel Thompson replied:

"Captain CHARLES H. COLE, Captain C. S. A., and Lieutenant C. S. Navy.

"SIR: By the authority in me vested, specially trusting in your knowledge and skill, you are assigned to the secret detached service for the purpose mentioned in your letter. To aid you in this undertaking, John Y. Beall, master in the Confederate States Navy, has been directed to report to you for duty. In all you may do in the premises, you will carefully abstain from violating any laws or regulations of Canada or British authorities in relation to neutrality. The combinations necessary to effect your purposes must be made by Confederate soldiers, with such assistance as you may draw from the enemy's country. Your obedient servant,

"JACOB THOMPSON."

It should be said, with reference to the statement that Lieutenant Bennett H. Young was sent to Sandusky with funds, that Thompson and Clay had sent Young with twenty-five thousand dollars in greenbacks, which he delivered to Captain Beall at the Genesee House in Buffalo. Young then returned to Toronto and Beall to Sandusky.

Captain Cole had located at the West House, in Sandusky, and hailed from Philadelphia. After Cole and Beall had agreed upon the plan to capture the *Michigan,* Beall departed to carry out his part of the undertaking.

The plan provided that Beall with a force of twenty Confederates should take passage on the steamer *Philo Parsons,* at or below Detroit, put the passengers and crew ashore, and then steam ahead in the usual way as if going to Sandusky until near the *Michigan,* when they would turn and run alongside, board and capture the gunboat. The prisoners on Johnson's Island would then be released. Captain Cole meanwhile would perform his part and have a messenger at Bass Island for Beall and Burley upon their arrival.

The acquaintance formed with Captain Carter of the *Michigan,* when Captain Cole made his initial tour around the Lakes, had been cultivated until a congenial association had made them the best of friends. Cole had also ingratiated himself in the esteem and confidence of the other officers of the gunboat. He often entertained them at sumptuous dinners at his hotel and dispensed the choicest wines with lavish but discreet hospitality. Cole was often an invited guest on the *Michigan,* and added the engineer to his list of friends, with whom he finally made safe and satisfactory terms. It might be said with truth that Cole was now a privileged character on the gunboat and was freely allowed to visit the prison on Johnson's Island and converse with the officers, among whom were Maj.-Gens. Edward Johnson and J. R. Trimble, Brig.-Gens. Jeff. Thompson, Archer, Jones, Beall and Frazer, Colonel Scales of the Thirtieth Mississippi, Major Thompson of Morgan's command, Captain Breckinridge, son of John C. Breckinridge of

Kentucky, Col. Lucius Davis, who officiated in the John Brown war, and Capt. Robert Cobb Kennedy of the First Louisiana Infantry. These gentlemen were let into the secret of the proposed capture of the *Michigan* and had all the arrangements perfected for a revolt in the prison at the critical moment, in aid of their rescuers, if the gunboat should be secured. A signal was to be fired from the gunboat by Cole and Beall which the prisoners would understand to mean that the vessel was in their possession.

Cole had established relations with the citizens of Sandusky who were members of the "Order of the Star." These were at his service in a social way. They frequently joined him in extending hospitality, and he never missed an opportunity to fete any of the officers of the gunboat when they appeared in Sandusky.

The time had now arrived for action and Cole arranged with the officers of the *Michigan* to be his guests, on their own gunboat, at a special champagne dinner he was to give on the evening of the 19th of September. Meanwhile, he had arranged with the engineer to derange the machinery of the gunboat. Cole's plan at his dinner was to drug the wine of the officers and put them to sleep. He, with a Confederate companion, would then be on board to await the arrival of Beall. A signal was to be sent up from the gunboat when Beall approached, besides the messenger to Middle Bass Island.

There was a small arsenal on the gunboat where the arms, etc., of the men were kept. Cole and one friend proposed with two pistols each to take position at the door of the little armory and hold the unarmed men at bay when Beall arrived on the *Philo Parsons* and boarded the gunboat. In this way it was expected to obtain possession without a conflict or any loss of life.

It happened that some one in the confidence of Colonel Thompson had betrayed Cole. The officers were advised in time to arrest him promptly and put him in irons. The *Michigan* was put in order for battle with steam up for the pursuit of the *Philo Parsons* if she approached. It developed, however, that the engine did not work at this critical juncture, but Captain Carter never knew the cause. The engineer had been true to his bargain with Captain Cole.

The imprisonment of Captain Cole and the other important fact that he had been betrayed was at once communicated by a messenger to Colonel Thompson and Mr. Clay at Toronto. They promptly addressed the United States commander as follows:

TORONTO, September 22, 1864.
To Colonel HILL, Commandant of Post, Johnson's Island.

SIR: We have just learned that Captain Cole, an escaped prisoner, has been arrested by the military authorities at your post, and is to be tried on the charge of being a public spy. As the agents and commissioners of the Confederate States, we protest against his being tried on this charge. As a prisoner he was brought into your lines against his will, and since his escape he has not been able to return to his own country, and therefore he was legitimately where he was found and taken into your lines. Whatever business he might have conceived, he has done nothing whatever violative of the laws of nations, the laws of the United States, or any regulation of the army, and it will be contrary to every principle, either of public, common, civil, or statutory law, to punish him for his designs or purposes, provided he had carried none of them into execution. On the hypothesis, then, that you have reason to believe that he contemplated any act of violence, if he failed to carry it out or make any attempt looking to that end, he cannot surely be judged guilty of any offense. If you proceed to extremities with Captain Cole we shall find it our duty to call on the authorities of the Confederate States to adopt proper measures of retaliation. If you can justly condemn Captain Cole as a spy, every soldier and officer of the army of the United States coming within the lines of the armies or limits of the Confederate States could be tried and condemned as such. We admit your right to return him to prison as a recaptured prisoner, but any other punishment, in our judgment, would be against justice and the law.

If any importance is attached to his being within your lines without wearing his uniform, the circumstances which surround him as an escaped prisoner will very well explain the reason of its absence. He had no uniform to wear. He did not even change his name, which is usual in such cases. He had conducted himself with the boldness, courage, and frankness of the true soldier in all his associations. He deserves this fate and none other.

Very respectfully,

(Signed.)   JACOB THOMPSON,
                                                      C. C. CLAY,
                                                           Commissioners.

The contention made in this communication was eventually effective and Captain Cole suffered no worse fate than that of a prisoner of war. He had frankly acknowledged his true character and purposes to release the prisoners on Johnson's Island.

The plans and purposes of Captain Cole were related to me by Colonel Thompson and afterwards by Captain Beall.

The Federal official proceedings were as follows:

WAR DEPARTMENT, BUREAU OF MILITARY JUSTICE.
                                                    July 18, 1865.

Bvt. Brig.-Gen. W. HOFFMAN, U. S. Army,
     Commissary-General of Prisoners, Washington, D. C.

GENERAL: I have the honor to acknowledge the receipt of your communication of the 15th instant, with which, pursuant to the direction of the lieutenant-general of the Army, you inclose the papers in the cases of Charles H. Cole and John E. Robinson (held as prisoners of war) for the opinion thereon of the Judge-Advocate-General as to their proper disposition, and in reply thereto would respectfully submit as follows:

It is clearly disclosed by the report of Col. Charles W. Hill, U. S. Army, and the testimony accompanying the same, that Cole was an active co-conspirator with Jacob Thompson, C. C. Clay, Jr., W. Norris, and others in Canada and the neighboring States of the Union, in a scheme to release in September last the rebel prisoners confined on Johnson's Island, and to seize the United States steamer *Michigan*, then stationed at Sandusky, Ohio; that Cole had, for a considerable period before his arrest (on 19th of September), been engaged in the preparatory details of the expedition, and that while so engaged he was directly in the pay of the rebel Government, receiving from Thompson, its "agent and commissioner," sundry sums of money in gold and U. S. Treasury notes, amounting in all to about $4,000; further, that Robinson was a subordinate of Cole in the general plan, and, though possessed of less intelligence, was actively employed in the plot.

What the details alluded to precisely were, beyond passing to and fro between the representatives of the rebellion in Canada and the United States, and acting principally at Sandusky as a principal and director of the parties on the United States side of the lake who were to co-operate in carrying out the scheme, does not clearly appear. The seizure, however, of the steamers *Island Queen* and *Philo Parsons* by Canadian rebels on the same day as that on which Cole was arrested was a signal overt act of the conspiracy, for which he is no doubt to be held responsible equally with those immediately concerned therein.

The only direct testimony connecting Cole actively with the plot is, indeed, his own confession. This confession was oral, and does not appear in written form, but having been made, and, as it is understood, voluntarily, in the presence of Colonel Hill and Captain Carter, of the *Michigan,* and carefully noted, in substance, by the former, it may readily be introduced in evidence.

No confession or statement by Robinson appears to have been presented, and the only proof against him is found in the declarations of Cole.

Upon the arrest of the latter a communication was addressed by Thompson and Clay, from Toronto, Canada West, to Colonel Hill, protesting against Cole's being treated as a spy, and claiming that he was an escaped rebel prisoner who could merely be returned to captivity by the U. S. authorities, but could not be proceeded against for any crime.

But there is no evidence that Cole was technically a spy, yet that he is to be treated as a criminal, and not as a prisoner of war, is abundantly shown by the papers found in his possession upon his apprehension. From these it appears that when a prisoner of war at Memphis in April, 1864, he subscribed both to a formal parole not to take arms against the United States or give any aid or comfort to the enemy, and to an oath of allegiance to the Government, and that thereupon he was granted, under the designation of "Charles Cole, late a captain in the rebel army," a permission to proceed to Harrisburg, Pa., with the condition only that he should report to the provost-marshal there. He was, therefore, to be deemed, from and after that time, as a citizen, under military surveillance, perhaps, but no less a citizen and owing allegiance as such to the United States.

It follows, therefore, that this party is triable, as follows:

For a treasonable conspiracy with Robinson, Thompson, Clay, Norris, and others.

For a violation of the laws of war in engaging in an attempt to seize Government property and release prisoners of war.

For a violation of his oath of allegiance.

For a violation of his parole.

Upon any and all of these charges he is believed to be triable by a military commission.

* * * * * * *

It would appear, however, that the criminality of Robinson is of a character much less grave than that of Cole, and also that he is not a person of influence or much intelligence. It is suggested, therefore, that the privilege be offered him of appearing as a witness against Cole, upon the usual terms of pardon, provided he fully and frankly discloses all the facts within his knowledge; and that should he so appear and disclose, the trial of Cole upon all the charges indicated be proceeded with.

That this man—at once a secret agent and hireling of the rebellion and a false and perjured traitor—should escape punishment would appear to involve a deplorable failure of justice.

In absence of the Judge-Advocate-General:

A. A. Hosmer,
Major and Judge-Advocate.

Captain Cole was afterwards removed to Fort Lafayette, New York, and his case was disposed of as follows:

Headquarters Fort Lafayette,
New York Harbor, February 5, 1866.

Bvt. Brig.-Gen. E. D. Townsend,
Assistant Adjutant-General, U. S. Army, Washington, D. C.

Sir: I have to state that I allowed the writ of habeas corpus in the case of Charles H. Cole to be served on me this day, and that I have to present him in the City Hall at the court-house in Brooklyn on the 10th instant at 9 a. m.

Very respectfully, your obedient servant,

Martin Burke,
Brevet Brigadier-General, U. S. Army, Commanding Post.

HEADQUARTERS FORT LAFAYETTE,
New York Harbor, February 10, 1866.

Bvt. Brig.-Gen. D. T. VAN BUREN,
Assistant Adjutant-General, Headquarters Department of the East.

SIR: I have to state that Charles H. Cole, late prisoner at this post, has been discharged by Judge Gilbert at the Brooklyn court-house this day.

Very respectfully, your obedient servant,
MARTIN BURKE,
Brevet Brigadier-General, U. S. Army, Commanding Post.

(Indorsement.)

HEADQUARTERS DEPARTMENT OF THE EAST,
New York City, February 12, 1866.

Respectfully forwarded to Adjutant-General's Office. Cole was confined as one of the party who attempted to seize the U. S. steamer *Michigan* on Lake Erie in 1864, etc.

JOSEPH HOOKER,
Major-General Commanding.

By D. T. VAN BUREN,
Assistant Adjutant-General.

CHAPTER XXV

Capt. John Yates Beall—His home in Virginia—Early career in the Confederacy with Bennett G. Burley—Capture of steamer *Philo Parsons* on Lake Erie—Capture of *Island Queen*—Attempt to release prisoners on Johnson's Island—Mutiny of men when signals failed to appear—Compelled to return and destroy vessels—Men disperse in Canada—Arrest of Burley—Confederate steamer *Georgiana* on Lake Erie.

The betrayal and arrest of Captain Cole necessarily doomed the expedition of Captain Beall, and yet he proceeded in ignorance of the fact. As an officer of the Confederate Navy Beall was adapted to the particular part of the adventure to which he had been assigned.

John Yates Beall was born January 1st, 1835, at Walnut Grove, the farm of his father, in Jefferson County, Virginia. It is said of this home that it took the first premium at a State Fair as the "model farm" within the limits of the Old Dominion. Beall graduated at the University of Virginia about 1856. He espoused the cause of the South and was ready for service when hostilities began in Virginia. His first experience was with Stonewall Jackson in a skirmish at Falling Waters. He was attached as a private to the Second Virginia Infantry, but was at home on leave when his regiment went from the Shenandoah Valley to the battle of Bull Run, July 21, 1861. A Federal force having occupied Harper's Ferry and the county of Jefferson, Col. Turner Ashby with a command of cavalry was contesting their advance and a number of engagements were fought. In one of these near Beall's home he was a volunteer and commanded an improvised company of militia in the engagement. The Confederates were successful. As the Federals fell back, a party of them halted, and turning fired upon their pursuers. Beall was among the foremost and received a shot in the right breast which broke three ribs and went around his body.

During the long period he was an invalid he went to Richmond, thence to Tallahassee, Florida. "Here he met Gen. R. W. Williams and his wife. Upon their urgent invitation he accompanied them to their plantation on Pascagoula Island, in Louisiana, where he remained for several months a welcome recipient of their hospitality."

Beall finally passed through the United States and located at Riley's Hotel, Dundas, C. W., in November, 1862. Early in January, 1863, his preparations were made to return to the South. He says in his diary:

John Morgan had played such havoc in Kentucky with the railroads and communications, that it was deemed impossible for me to go South by that route. I then thought of West Virginia, but the steamboats were seized to carry subsistence to Rosecrans's army, and I took the cars to Baltimore. After a false start I got on a pungy owned and run by blockaders, and about the last of February landed in Virginia. My comrade, Mr. Schluder, of St. Louis, Missouri, had escaped from the Yankees—was from Price's army. We got to Richmond, and found Dan Lucas and all the boys at Fredericksburg.

*   *   *   *   *   *   *

From a "Memoir of J. Y. Beall" (author unknown) I quote the following:

Upon Beall's arrival in Richmond he set about to make a digest of his views. 1st. In regard to privateering on the Northern lakes, and levying contributions on the adjacent cities; and 2d, by privateering on the Potomac and Chesapeake. It is the belief of the author, that Beall was the first to suggest to the authorities in Richmond the feasibility of successful attack on Johnson's Island, and the rescue of the prisoners there held in confinement. In conjunction with a gallant young officer of the Confederate Army, then on the retired list owing to ill-health, Beall submitted his project to the President, embracing both of the above-named objects. His ideas were bold, but not visionary. A privateer, secretly armed and manned, once set afloat on the Lakes could, he maintained, sweep their waters, and

JOHN YATES BEALL
1864

lay their cities from Chicago to Detroit in ashes, unless redeemed by heavy contributions; or could surprise the steamer off Johnson's Island, release the prisoners, and with this steamer sweep Erie from Toledo to Buffalo, and burn these cities, or lay them under contributions. Beall, and the young officer above alluded to, laid this project before the President, and it was by him referred to Hon. S. R. Mallory, Secretary of the Navy. Mr. Mallory, after due consideration, informed Beall that his scheme upon the Lakes was regarded as feasible, but did not think it could be accomplished without endangering our neutral relations with England. The project upon the Potomac was approved, and Beall was handed a commission as acting master in the Confederate States Navy. He was assured that if at any time in the future the Secretary should conclude to execute the Lake scheme, he (Beall) and the young officer who was acting in conjunction with him were to be assigned positions in the enterprise. Whether the honorable Secretary kept his promise or not, may interest the future historian to inquire.

Thus held in abeyance as to his favorite enterprise on the Lakes, Beall and his colleague, with their naval commissions in their hands, set about organizing an expedition for privateering on the waters of the lower Potomac and York rivers, and on Chesapeake Bay. Meantime, it should have been mentioned that Beall had gone before a medical examining board, and received a final discharge from the military service on the ground of disability arising from a wound received on the 16th day of October, 1861, which penetrated the right lung, and increased a hereditary tendency to consumption.

* * * * * * *

The conscription was now being rigorously enforced in the Confederacy, and Beall was restricted in recruiting to those not liable to military duty under existing law. Among his earliest recruits were two young Scotchmen; one was a stout, round-shouldered, deep full-chested man of two and twenty, with brown hair, blue eyes quick with intelligence, and a fair beardless face—this was Bennett G. Burley, afterwards Beall's lieutenant in the famous Lake Erie expedition, and subsequently delivered up on the requisition of the United States authorities, by Chief Justice Draper of Canada West; delivered up on a charge of robbery to be tried for piracy; a rendition illustrative of what Junius so much admired as represented in Lord Mansfield—*the independence of the English judiciary in political*

trials. Burley, even at this early day, had not been without his
experience in prison life. The son of a master mechanic of
Glasgow, he had left the land of the pibroch and thistle, landed
in New York, and finally strayed into the Confederacy with a
sub-marine battery in his pocket. It was on paper—the inven-
tion of his father.

*   *   *   *   *   *   *

He had also a torpedo which required to be attached to the
side of the vessel attacked, by screws, and then ignited by a
fuse; such attachment could only be effected by approaching
the vessel by night in a small boat with muffled oars, and swimming the remainder of the way, and screwing the torpedo to
the vessel—returning to the skiff or small boat, and thence
igniting the fuse. Brooke thought that Diogenes with his lamp
might as soon find the object of his search, as he a man willing
to swim to an enemy's vessel, screw on a torpedo, and light
the fuse. One such man, however, was found, who afterwards
swam to a war vessel in the ——————, screwed on the
torpedo, retired, and sprung the lanyard, but the fuse would
not ignite; in this way the torpedo found its way again to New
York; from Burley's pocket in Castle Thunder, corner of 21st
and Casey, Richmond, to the northwest corner of Fulton and
Nassau streets, New York, whence in the columns of the *Herald*
it duly issued in large capitals: "CURIOUS INFERNAL
MACHINE, FOUND ATTACHED TO THE BOTTOM OF
THE WAR STEAMER ———— on ———— RIVER!"
The look-out declared he had heard oars as of a bateau dipping
near the ship that night, and next morning the officer found
the infernal machine fastened to her prow.

The Scotchman who fastened this torpedo on the vessel of
war was John Maxwell, accompanied by Burley, whose companion he was when he enlisted with Beall. Maxwell was the
larger of the two—he was full six feet, with broad square
shoulders, black hair, moustache, and whiskers. If Burley
would have done to set for Lydon the supple Pompeian
gladiator, Maxwell on the other hand would have represented
the almost Herculean Niger. Burley was the Lowlander from
Glasgow and the banks of the Clyde, but Maxwell looked for
all the world as though he might have just stepped from the
side of Ben Lothian with bare legs, the plaid upon his shoulder,
and the purse about his waist.

Such were specimens of the non-conscripts who composed the
first privateering expedition on the waters of the York,

Potomac, and Chesapeake, which Beall originated, but, in command of which, at his own request, he was ranked by the gallant young soldier before alluded to. This expedition met with but partial success. Their numbers only reached nine or ten, and they were not armed or equipped in a style which would justify extensive operations. They started from Richmond about the 1st of April, 1863, and proceeded to Mathews Court House. Beall returned to Richmond about the 15th of June, to procure cutlasses, and other necessary equipments. The company was of a partisan character, the Government furnishing nothing but arms, uniforms, and equipments, while the party furnished their own boat, received no pay, but were entitled to all they could capture. In the first month nothing more was done than to surprise a camp of armed "Contrabands," killing one, capturing one, and putting to flight the remainder. This exploit occurred on Black River, in Elizabeth City County, Virginia, and within ten miles of Fortress Monroe.

Upon his return to Richmond Beall's superior in command received an appointment with the rank of colonel of cavalry, and, accepting it, Beall was left thenceforth in command of the adventurous squad upon the Potomac. His aim was to render his command upon the waters of the Peninsula, in the bays, and inlets of the eastern shore of Virginia, what Mosby's was on land, in the fastnesses of the Blue Ridge, and in the forests of Piedmont, and the Northern Neck.

*   *   *   *   *   *   *

On the 18th of September Beall set out from Mathews. His party now numbered eighteen. Roy McDonald had been promoted to the rank of acting master. Beall himself was generally known as "Captain Beall," from the time he assumed entire command of the party; though he never at any time during the war held any other commission than that of acting master, dating from the 5th of March, 1863. His two gallant little boats, one black, the other white, were christened respectively the *Raven* and the *Swan*. Dividing his party, taking half in the *Swan* with himself, and assigning McDonald to command the *Raven* with the remainder, he left Horn Harbor, Mathews County, and proceeded first to Raccoon Island near Cape Charles; lying off here he found a Yankee sloop, the *Mary Anne*, and two fishing scows, all of which he captured. Thence with his prizes, he proceeded to Watch Spring Inlet on the coast of Accomac. On the night of the 21st of September, notwithstanding the equinoctial storm had set in, and a heavy northwester was blowing, he boarded and captured the *Alliance,* a large sloop, Capt. David Ireland, Staten Island, New York, bound from Philadelphia to Port Royal, South Carolina, laden with sutler's stores. McDonald with the *Raven* was to tackle the sloop on the starboard, and Beall on the port. The night was fearfully dark and stormy; the hour selected was eleven; the crew had turned in; the captain and mate were playing dominoes in the cabin. The *Raven* was dashed against the side of the schooner, her tiller broken, and McDonald thrown headlong into the water. He regained the boat, which was washed back by the heavy sea, and came up with the *Swan* on the port; Beall and McDonald therefore boarded on the same side; the former conducted his crew to the forecastle to capture the schooner's crew, while the latter struck for the cabin, where he found the captain and mate, unsuspicious of danger, quietly enjoying their game. Captain Ireland was a bold, brave man, and, watching his opportunity, started for his own stateroom to get his arms; in doing so, however, he had to pass McDonald, who, observing the movement, called him to halt, with a cocked pistol, and told him to go back to the cabin; the Captain promptly obeyed.

The next day, September 22d, the equinox continued, and, all hands being brought on board the *Alliance,* both anchors were cast away to keep her steady. That night, however, they again took boat, and just out the inlet captured three Yankee sloops, the *Houseman, Samuel Pearsall,* and a third, name not remembered, commanded by Capt. Rushman Craft. On the night of the 23d they ran these three vessels, last named, out of the inlet, stripped them of all valuables, scuttled them, and sent them to sea. On the 24th all hands took to the larger schooner *Alliance,* and sailed westward to Cobb's Island. Here Beall obtained a reliable pilot, and announced his intention, hazardous as might seem the undertaking, to run his prize through the blockade, and up the Pianketank River to North End or about that point, where he would be enabled to land his whole cargo, and transport the same to Richmond. Accordingly he paroled the crews of the *Mary Anne* and fishing smacks, sent McDonald with the other prisoners to Mathews, and set out for the mouth of the Pianketank with the *Alliance.* His pilot was a Canadian, experienced and true; but whether owing to the presence of a Federal gunboat within a mile of the mouth of the Pianketank, or some other cause, on this occasion he missed the channel by twelve feet, and grounded the vessel.

Beall promptly landed what goods he could run ashore in boats, and burnt the schooner to the water's edge. He reached Richmond with what remained of his cargo, about the same time that McDonald arrived there with seventeen prisoners. From the sale of the cargo the party realized a handsome dividend, as the goods captured were at this time very valuable in the Confederacy.

Captain Beall's operations now began to attract attention, and to call down heavy denunciations upon him in the North. Brigadier-General Wistar was sent down to Mathews and the neighboring counties for the special purpose of capturing Beall and his marines. Wistar's force for this purpose consisted of one regiment of negro infantry, two of white cavalry, and a battalion of artillery; also three gunboats in North River, three in East River, two in the Pianketank, and one or two off New Point Comfort. * * * He (Beall) found the Peninsula, for the present, too hot for him, and, dispersing his party through the country, he returned to Richmond. * * *

Beall collected his small band of marines, and, leaving Richmond about the 10th of November, proceeded cautiously, almost stealthily, to the coast, and again took boat. He crossed the bay again with his two gallant little birds, the *Raven* and the *Swan;* he struck Tangier Inlet, on the coast of Accomac, and captured there a schooner. Daylight coming on, Beall sent a squad of his men with one boat to conceal themselves, while he remained with the captured schooner and only a sufficient number of men not to attract attention. The result was, the party sent out were by carelessness captured, and one of them in terror disclosed who they were. Forthwith the enemy armed all the small boats and pungies in the neighborhood, and with four or five hundred men went in pursuit of Beall. The latter could have escaped, but waited so long to see what was the fate of his detachment, that escape became impossible, and he found himself surrounded. Recognizing the fact that he was no longer master of the situation, Beall threw overboard everything of value, and surrendered. His capture was heralded throughout the North as an achievement of no small moment, and was the subject of a special despatch from General Wistar. The "notorious Captain Beall" was at last caught, and the enemy proposed to deal out summary, or as the Neapolitans call it, "economical," justice to him and his band of "pirates." * * * He and his party remained in irons for forty-two days. At the end of this time they were released, and placed upon the footing

of other prisoners of war.   Beall was allowed to write a communication to Richmond, which being laid before Mr. Mallory
and Commissioner Robert Ould, was speedily followed by a
reprisal by placing in irons seventeen captive Federal marines,
and two commissioned officers as hostages.   This "taste of
retaliation" soon had the desired effect.   Gen. Benjamin F.
Butler himself gave the subject his attention, and ordered these
so-called "pirates" to be released from their irons, and placed
on the footing of other prisoners of war.   This being done,
Beall was forwarded along with other officers from Fort
McHenry to City Point on the 20th of March, where he
remained until the 5th of May ensuing, when he was duly
exchanged, and returned to Richmond.   McDonald, however,
and the balance of the party, among whom was Beall's brother
William, were not exchanged until the following October, when
a general exchange of naval prisoners took place between the
respective governments.   *   *   *   On the very day on which
Beall was exchanged commenced the battle of the Wilderness.
        *   *   *   *   *   *

On the succeeding day he temporarily attached himself to
the Engineer Corps under charge of Lieutenant Henderson, a
friend; and being thus enabled to draw rations, etc., he remained
near the defenses around Mechanicsville for some days.   When,
however, both armies were sufficiently exhausted to require rest,
Beall, his patience exhausted by the neglect of the department,
and his spirit chafing for that action which his health denied
him on the field, suddenly left the camp on the Chickahominy,
reappeared on the coast in Mathews County, crossed over to
the Eastern Shore, and came leisurely on through Baltimore to
New York, and thence to Canada West.

There was everything in the military experience of
Beall to fit him for the expedition to release the prisoners
at Johnson's Island.   In company with Bennett G. Burley, the
Scotchman who had been his comrade on the shore of Virginia, and eighteen other Confederate soldiers, Captain Beall
made every preparation and took position to embark upon
the expedition to capture the gunboat *Michigan* at Johnson's
Island.

On Sunday evening, the 18th of September, 1864, Bennett G.
Burley took passage on board the *Philo Parsons* at the wharf of
Detroit.   This steamer plied regularly between Detroit and

Sandusky City. Burley inquired whether the boat stopped regularly at Sandwich, a small town on the Canadian side of Lake Erie; upon being informed that it did not he requested the clerk and part owner of the boat, W. O. Ashley, to stop there the next morning and take on three friends of his, who, with himself, were bound for Sandusky. (Memoir of Beall.)

This arrangement was made and at 8 o'clock the next morning Captain Beall with two men jumped on the boat as she came near enough without a *regular stop*.

At Amherstburg 16 men came on board without baggage except an old trunk tied with ropes. This was 9.30 o'clock. About 4 p. m. the steamer touched at Kelley's Island. Immediately after leaving Kelley's Island Captain Beall was talking with the mate, who was at the helm. Glancing around to see that his men were ready, Beall exclaimed that he took possession of the boat in the name of the Confederate States and that any man who resisted would do so at his peril.

In a moment Beall and Burley with their eighteen men flashed out their navy sixes and commanded the situation. There was a prompt surrender on the part of all the passengers, who were corralled in the cabin under guard. Ashley, the clerk, obeyed the command to surrender. Beall then took possession of the papers, books, and money of the boat. There was over one hundred dollars in money belonging to the boat. Burley with sixteen men cleared the deck for service at Johnson's Island by throwing overboard all the heavy freight.

Beall now had the steamer headed for Middle Bass Island, which is ten miles from the Ohio shore and the same distance from Johnson's Island. Soon after the *Philo Parsons* reached the island and the prisoners were put ashore, the *Island Queen* from Sandusky landed alongside the *Philo Parsons*. Beall with fourteen men boarded her immediately and took possession in the name of the Confederate States, proclaiming the fact in a loud voice. It looked for a few minutes as if there would be a fight, as there was some resistance and several shots were fired before the crew and passengers surrendered. Mr. Haynes, the engineer, was wounded in the neck. The passengers and crew were sent on board the *Philo Parsons* and held for an hour, when they were landed with their baggage. Among them were several Federal soldiers unarmed belonging to the One Hundred and Thirtieth Ohio Regiment of "hundred day" men who were on their way to Toledo to be mustered out of service. These were paroled. One of the passengers had eighty thousand dollars on his person. He asked Beall to let him keep a part of it. Beall told him to keep it all and told all that they wanted nothing from any of them. But that the boats and their money were a prize of war on the lake and would be appropriated accordingly. The two vessels were lashed together, but after running some five miles Beall scuttled the *Island Queen* and sent her adrift. She sunk just above Chichanolee Reef.

Beall was disappointed in not finding a messenger at Middle Bass Island from Captain Cole and was now proceeding without any advices whatever. As he reached the mouth of Sandusky Bay he was looking for the agreed signal lights or rockets, either from Johnson's Island, on the *Michigan,* or on the Ohio shore. But he looked in vain and his men looked in vain. The moon was shining brightly and the length of the *Michigan* could be discerned. The lights were burning on the gunboat and Beall proceeded slowly and cautiously. Suddenly seventeen of Beall's men mutinied. They declared that they were going into the battle blindly with a gunboat and that none of the promises of Captain Cole had been fulfilled. There had been no messenger and there were no signals. The steamer was halted for a parley. Beall expostulated and threatened but without avail. The men then drew up an instrument of writing and all signed it as follows:

ON BOARD THE PHILO PARSONS,
September 20, 1864.

We, the undersigned, crew of the boat aforesaid, take pleasure in expressing our admiration of gentlemanly bearing, skill, and courage of Capt. John Y. Beall as a commanding officer and a gentleman, but believing and being well convinced that the enemy is already apprised of our approach, and is so well prepared that we cannot by possibility make it a success, and having already captured two boats, we respectfully decline to prosecute it any further.

J. S. Riley, M. D.	William Byland,
H. B. Barkley,	Robert G. Harris,
R. F. Smith,	W. C. Holt,
David H. Ross,	Tom S. Major,
R. B. Drake,	N. S. Johnston,
James Brotherton,	John Bristol,
M. H. Duncan,	F. H. Thomas,
W. B. King,	J. G. Odoer.
Joseph Y. Clark,	

Burley and one other stood by Beall. There was no alternative now but for Captain Beall to return up Lake Erie. He was compelled to abandon the attack though he did not believe Captain Cole had failed. Beall contended that he would surprise the gunboat in any event and if he failed to board her he could escape. He now proceeded to Fighting Island in Detroit River, where he landed several prisoners, among whom was Captain Orr of the *Island Queen*. These had been confined in the hold of the *Philo Parsons*. He then proceeded to Sandwich, Canada.

Having removed everything of value from the steamer, Beall scuttled the *Philo Parsons* and left her to her fate. The men dispersed and all escaped arrest except Bennett G. Burley. His extradition was demanded by the United States authorities and his arrest followed. He was confined at Toronto.

Captain Beall managed to confer with Colonel Thompson and give a full account of the failure of his expedition.

The attempt of Captains Cole and Beall had caused great excitement in the United States, especially along the northern borders. There were now many detectives in Toronto and other places from the United States endeavoring to locate and identify the parties who composed the force of

Captain Beall on the *Philo Parsons*. Beall went northward in Canada on a hunting and fishing journey, spending a couple of weeks in camp.

Martin and I had crossed the ferry at Detroit, on our way to Toronto, only three days after Beall scuttled the *Philo Parsons* at Sandwich.

A brief account of this expedition under Captain Beall and a letter he wrote to a Canadian editor, who had severely criticised the conduct of Beall, are recorded in his diary, and are striking illustrations of his character and sentiments:

RAID ON LAKE ERIE.

Immediately on my arrival in Canada I went to Colonel Thompson at Toronto, and made application to start a privateer on Lake Huron. He informed me of a plan to take the *Michigan* (14 guns), and release the Confederate officers confined at Johnson's Island. I immediately volunteered, and went to Sandusky, Ohio, to meet Captain Cole, the leader. We arranged our plans, and separated. Cole stayed at Sandusky. I came to Windsor to collect men, and carry them to the given point. On Monday morning we started, some from Detroit, some from Sandwich, some from Amherstburg. When off Kelley's Island, I seized the *Philo Parsons,* and mustering my men, found only some twenty there.

We went back to Middle Bass Island to procure wood and wait for the time when the steamer *Island Queen* came up, and we took her. I then started back to attack the *Michigan,* when seventeen of my twenty men mutinied, and refused to go forward, and this necessitated my turning back, thus abandoning Cole to be hung, a most cowardly and dishonorable affair.

Communication to a Canadian Journal.

"Mr. Editor: You condemn the conduct of those who captured the two steamers on Lake Erie as infringing the laws of Canada. Cognizant of the facts, I wish to present them to you, hoping to win you to reserve your decision.

"The United States is carrying on war on Lake Erie against the Confederate States (either by virtue of right or sufferance from you), by transportation of men and supplies on its waters; by confining Confederate prisoners on its islands, and lastly, by the presence of a 14-gun steamer patrolling its waters. The

Confederates clearly have the right to retaliate, provided they can do so without infringing your laws. They did not infringe those laws; for, first, the plan for this attack was matured, and sought to be carried out in the United States, and not in Canada; there was not a Canadian, or any man enlisted in Canada.

"Secondly. No act of hostility was committed on Canadian waters or soil. Any man may lawfully come into, or leave Canada as he may please, and no foreign government can complain of the exercise of this right here. These men embarked on an American vessel from Detroit, or sprang on to it while in motion, from Canadian wharves. The boat did not properly stop at Sandwich, or Amherstburg at all, as the Customs will show. It touched at two American ports, and was not captured until within range of the 30-pounder Parrott guns of the 14-gun steamer. What act of hostility had been committed up to this time? Another boat containing thirty or forty United States soldiers was captured in an American port. After wooding up, the *Philo Parsons* proceeded to the mouth of Sandusky Bay for the purpose of attacking the *Michigan,* when six-sevenths of the crew refused to do duty, and thus necessitated the abandonment of the enterprise.

"Thirdly. What is this *Michigan* that she cannot be attacked? Is the fact that she carries thirteen more guns than the treaty stipulation between the United States and England allows, a sufficient reason why she is not to be subject to attack? England allows this boat to remain guarding Confederate prisoners, though she carries an armament in violation of the treaty.

"Before these men are condemned, judge if they have broken your laws. No 'murder' was committed, indeed not a life lost. There was no searching of prisoners, no 'robbing.' It is true the boats were abused; but, sir, they were captured by Confederates, enemies of the United States, and however questionable the taste, the right is clear. These men were not 'burglars,' or 'pirates,' enemies of mankind, unless hatred and hostility to the Yankees be taken as a sin against humanity, or a crime against civilization."

Immediately after the expedition of Beall and Burley had failed, Colonel Thompson decided to secure a vessel on the Lakes and equip her secretly, to be manned by a crew under command of Captain Beall.

The steamer *Georgiana* was purchased by Dr. J. P. Bate, of Kentucky, who had been a steamboat captain. Beall was organizing his crew and force. He was now about ready. The *Georgiana* was anchored off the Canadian shore and equipments ready to be taken on board.

Colonel Thompson now told us that Beall would pick up his crew and men at different points and begin operations at the east end of Lake Erie. Martin and I agreed to go on the expedition under Beall. It was intended that Beall should shell and capture Buffalo, if possible, or make the authorities ransom the city. He would at all events capture several other good steamers at Buffalo and destroy all the others at the wharf. Then our navy would take the towns along the shore to Cleveland, where a few additional Confederates would come aboard at each place to help man the vessels. At the earliest moment, after two or more vessels could be equipped, the fleet would be divided and the one under Beall would make straight along the Canadian shore for the west, destroying every vessel he met. He would reach Toledo as soon as possible unless, by a scouting vessel, which he would send to Sandusky, he found the gunboat *Michigan* had gone east to capture us about Buffalo. In such event he could go direct to Johnson's Island before the garrison could be reinforced and release the Confederate prisoners by attacking with the guns of two vessels. It was understood that every available Confederate soldier in Canada or Kentucky would come to join the crews. The chief reliance upon which the enterprise was expected to succeed was that four armed vessels would be ready in advance of the enemy when an effort would be made to surround the *Michigan,* and then in a battle at least one of our vessels would reach and board the gunboat, and capture her. It was not believed the gunboat could overtake our vessels by a chase and sink them in detail. According to the calculations it was believed that our forces would number 300 to 400 men on the boats, within one week after we struck Buffalo.

Martin and I were ready to go and the only man we selected was George S. Anderson from Pittsylvania County,

Virginia. He had been a courier for Colonel Martin on Morgan's last raid to Kentucky and was afterward in the company that I commanded in Cantrill's battalion near Rogersville, Tennessee, at the time I was detailed for service in Canada. He had heard of our coming to Canada, and being captured near Greeneville, East Tennessee, about the time General Morgan was killed, he escaped from a train in Ohio en route to Camp Chase, and made his way to Canada and found us at Toronto.

Martin and I, with Anderson, proceeded to Port Colburn, on the north shore of Lake Erie, to get on the *Georgiana*. That place was fifteen miles from Buffalo and was the last Canadian port at which Beall would touch before making the attack. We waited for him two days and nights. His failure to come (he being twenty-four hours overdue) became a mystery and we returned to Toronto. We now learned from Colonel Thompson that the Canadian authorities had instituted such surveillance of the vessel that it had been impossible to get arms or other supplies on board the *Georgiana*. And besides the United States authorities, after the purchase, had alarmed all points on the lake and tugs were being fitted up at Buffalo and other cities, with artillery for her destruction. The panic could not have been greater if we had captured a city. In this dilemma this last enterprise was abandoned and disposition was made of the *Georgiana* without delay.

CHAPTER XXVI

Lieutenant Young's raid upon St. Albans, Vermont—Retreat and pursuit—Capture by Americans in Canada—Rescued by a British officer—Sympathy for prisoners in Canada—Extradition demanded—Preparations for defense.

A profound sensation was created all over the United States and Canada on the morning of October 20, 1864. The papers published the particulars of a raid upon St. Albans, Vermont, by a band of Confederate soldiers. It appeared that the attack was made by a party under command of Lieut. Bennett H. Young of Kentucky. The town had been fired, several citizens had been shot in the mêlée, and a large sum of money taken from three of the banks. The guerrillas had been chased by the citizens into Canada, according to reports in the newspapers.

I soon learned that Colonel Thompson knew nothing of the expedition, but knew Lieutenant Young. A few days afterwards Mr. Clay came up from Montreal to Toronto and gave us all of the particulars, as reported to him by Lieutenant Young and his men. I met him in Colonel Thompson's rooms at the Queen's Hotel. He said he had authorized the expedition, which had been a success except that a large part of the money had been taken from the men who were arrested. Lieutenant Young had surrendered to a party of pursuers who came near taking his life. The expedition which had brought Lieutenant Young into great notoriety, in the United States and Canada, had produced alarm in all the towns in the United States, from Maine to Minnesota. This was the condition which was desired by the Confederates.

BENNETT H. YOUNG
1864

Lieutenant Young, who conducted this enterprise, was 21 years of age at the time. He was a native of Jessamine County, Kentucky, and had enlisted in Gen. John H. Morgan's command. On General Morgan's raid into Ohio, Young was captured and imprisoned, first at Camp Chase, and later at Camp Douglas, from which place he escaped and made his way to Canada in the early spring of 1864. After considering all the routes and risks of returning to the Confederacy, he concluded to go by sea from Nova Scotia. It was late in the spring before the ice broke up and navigation was resumed on the St. Lawrence River. Lieutenant Young went by the earliest vessel and landed at Halifax. Here he met Mr. Clay en route to Canada on his mission as Confederate Commissioner. It was soon agreed that Young should proceed on his journey to Richmond and arrange to return for service in Canada.

Lieutenant Young sailed from Halifax early in June, and arrived safely at the Bermuda Islands. He then secured passage on a blockade runner, and passed safely into Wilmington, North Carolina, though under a brisk fire from the blockading ships of the enemy.

At Richmond the' authorities cheerfully agreed to the recommendation of Mr. Clay. Young was commissioned a first lieutenant in the Confederate Army, with an assignment to service in Canada. He immediately departed with a sealed communication from the Secretary of War, James A. Seddon, to Mr. Clay. At Wilmington he found the same vessel, and having been furnished transportation by the Government, he proceeded without incident to the Bermuda Islands, and thence to Canada.

Lieutenant Young went on to Upper Canada and stopped a few days at Toronto, but in due time reported for duty at St. Catharines, where Mr. Clay and Mr. James P. Holcombe were residing and had been engaged in peace negotiations with Horace Greeley and Judge Black of Pennsylvania. Several conferences were also held here between the Confederates and the leaders of the "Sons of Liberty."

Lieutenant Young organized quite a number of escaped prisoners and went to Chicago on the expedition of Capt. Thomas H. Hines, for the release of prisoners at Camp Douglas, when the revolution of the "Sons of Liberty" was also to occur during the Democratic National Convention, of which an account is given in a preceding chapter.

Soon after this Lieutenant Young was sent by Mr. Clay to Columbus, Ohio, to arrange for an uprising of the prisoners at Camp Chase, when the signal should be given that the arsenal outside and four miles distant, had been captured. Young made the journey alone and found but a small garrison at the arsenal, which he felt could be overcome readily by thirty Confederates. It was thought that the prisoners after breaking out could reach the arsenal before any Federal troops could arrive from any other point. Young proposed after capturing the garrison at the arsenal, to go with over half of his men to the prison and make the attack suddenly upon the guard on the prison walls, thus opening a way out for the prisoners. The attack was to be made at midnight, telegraph lines were to be cut, and the bridges over the river were to be blown up. The 6,000 prisoners, as soon as armed at the arsenal, would then mount themselves in the city and country around, when they could march to the Confederacy.

Lieutenant Young finally enlisted thirty men, the number needed, but a third of them were raw or elderly, and at the appointed time for action these weakened and caused the abandonment of the enterprise.

Lieutenant Young, after a conference with Mr. Clay, went into Vermont alone and selected St. Albans for an attack which could be made with the twenty reliable men who were now under his command. By arrangement, his men, two and three in a party, went by different routes and trains so as to arrive all together on the night of the 18th of October, 1864. There was no disappointment this time. Every man arrived, and each party found rooms at the several hotels, where they remained most of the time. Lieutenant Young and one or two others went out the next forenoon and located the banks and livery stables.

CLEMENT CLAIBORNE CLAY
1867

Promptly at 3 o'clock in the afternoon the little command suddenly rallied and formed in the street, with overcoats off and Confederate uniforms on. Each man wore a pair of navy sixes belted on outside. They proclaimed that they took possession of St. Albans in the name of the Confederate States. The public square in the center of the city contained several acres, and all the citizens on the street were ordered to go into the square and remain. This was ridiculed by a number of citizens, when the Confederates began to shoot at men who hesitated to go, and one was wounded. The citizens now realized that the exhibition was not a joke.

The Confederates were prepared with fifty four-ounce bottles of Greek fire each, and while three men went to each bank and secured their money, the others were firing the hotels and other buildings, and securing horses and equipments.

The citizens had been held at bay during the proceedings, which had consumed perhaps three-quarters of an hour. But the city contained about 5,000 inhabitants, and many men began to come into the public square. A number of Federal soldiers appeared among them, and preparations were being made for an attack upon the Confederates, who were now ready to go when a few more horses were equipped.

Suddenly the people began to fire from windows, and three of the Confederates were seriously wounded. A skirmish now ensued, and one citizen was killed. The Confederates dashed their Greek fire against the houses all about on the square, and began their march to escape, with the citizens and a few soldiers, some in buggies and some on horseback, in pursuit. Lieutenant Young took the road to Shelburne, some eight miles distant, and was beyond reach of the pursuers until at Shelburne he reached a bridge over a river, on which a team was found crossing with a load of hay, for which he was obliged to wait. The pursuers approached, when the Confederates halted and opened fire, at the same time halting the team and turning it upon the bridge set fire to the hay, which fired and destroyed the bridge. The pursuers did not again overtake the Confederates. Lieutenant Young and his men, however, pushed forward and reached the border line of Canada about nine o'clock that night. The party at once donned their citizens' clothing and abandoned the St. Albans horses on the highway. They then dispersed and proceeded on foot into Canada.

The next forenoon Lieutenant Young learned that several of his men had been arrested at Phillipsburg. He at once decided that this must necessarily compel him to give himself up to the authorities and make the cause of his men his own, since he was the commander, and holding a commission and the authority for the raid.

Young stopped at a farm-house, and leaving his revolvers in an adjoining room, he sat at the only fire, which was in the kitchen, to get warm. To his surprise, about twenty-five people from St. Albans, in pursuit of his party, learning that there was a stranger in the house, suddenly rushed in and reached Young before he could get to his pistols, which they secured. They promptly seized him and at once proceeded to beat him with the pistols and with swords.

The American party now started with Young to return to St. Albans. They could have killed him, but doubtless deemed it important to deliver him alive in St. Albans for several reasons. They put Young in an open wagon with two men on each side and one in his rear, all in the wagon. The men were excited and carried their pistols cocked, badgering him with threats to shoot, while they denounced him in unmeasured terms. Young, however, continued to protest against their proceedings, insisting that they were in violation of British neutrality, but they said they did not care a d—n for British law or the British nation. The front gate was some two hundred feet from the house. The road which passed in front of the house led from the United States to Phillipsburg. When they reached the gate to pass out, Young suddenly knocked the men from each side with his arms, seized the reins, and quickly turning the horses, drove toward Phillipsburg. But his captors, who were apparently paralyzed for a moment, soon recovered, and pounced upon him with their pistols and swords. In the midst of the mêlée, and fortunately for Young, a British officer happened upon the scene. Young told him of his character—that of a Confederate officer on British soil and entitled to protection, that his captors were Americans who proposed to take him without any authority to the United States in violation of British neutrality and in defiance of British law.

The British officer reasoned with the Americans for a time, who were reluctant to listen to argument or to delay their return to St. Albans. The officer, however, told them that five others of the raiding party had been arrested and were at Phillipsburg, and two at St. Johns, and that all were to be sent to St. Albans the next day. Young's captors then agreed that the officer should take him under their escort to Phillipsburg. Here he found five of his comrades under arrest. But it happened that there was no arrangement for the Americans or any one else to carry the prisoners back to St. Albans.

That night Lieutenant Young and his five men were carried to St. Johns, a distance of about twenty miles, and placed in jail. Here a large garrison of British Regulars was stationed, who manifested the warmest friendship for the prisoners. They went so far as to suggest to Lieutenant Young that he and his men might be rescued. They extended every courtesy, and the citizens were likewise friendly and hospitable to the prisoners. Lieutenant Young and his comrades concluded that it would be unwise now to evade the issue and preferred to await their fate in the courts of Canada, since their extradition had been demanded by the Government of the United States.

Meanwhile, there was unabated excitement in Vermont and consternation among the inhabitants of all the States along the Canadian border.

After a few days Lieutenant Young and his comrades were sent to Montreal under a warrant issued by Judge Charles Coursol, police judge of Montreal. The prisoners were confined in the jail, but received the kindest attention possible from the jailer and his family. Indeed, the jailer set aside his parlors for the accommodation of the prisoners. They were permitted to occupy outside bed-rooms and their meals were served in the jailer's family dining-room. There were no indignities and none of the restrictions incident to imprisonment in a jail.

The large number of Southern people who were sojourning in Montreal vied with each other in kindness to the prisoners. The citizens of the city were equally conspicuous in their manifestations of friendship, sympathy, and courteous attentions.

It was now realized that a great trial and legal battle was inevitable. The friends of Lieutenant Young in Montreal at once united with the Confederate Commissioners in securing the services of all the leading lawyers of this Canadian Province. In view of the universal friendship manifested for the prisoners, and of the indignation aroused by the invasion from St. Albans, by the Americans, the best lawyers were glad to accept retainers, which in any event would enable them to excuse themselves from representing the United States.

Mr. Clay arranged promptly to provide for the proper defense of the prisoners. It was soon developed that the question would be raised by the United States, that Lieutenant Young and his men were not Confederate soldiers, and that their claims to such a character would be denied. Their extradition was demanded for a criminal offense under the laws of Vermont.

The other thirteen men composing Lieutenant Young's command on the expedition to St. Albans were not yet arrested, and there was now very little disposition among the Canadian officials for their apprehension. The kind treatment of the prisoners at Montreal only served to aggravate and intensify the bitter feeling in the United States.

The foregoing account of the noted St. Albans raid was afterward confirmed by Lieutenant Young and a number of his men.

CHAPTER XXVII

Plans for revolution at Chicago and New York City—Attempts to be made to burn Cincinnati, Philadelphia, and Boston—Plans in New York City.

In reviewing the situation it appeared to Colonel Thompson, and to Mr. Clay, who was present when Colonel Martin and I were called in conference, that the all-important field for action must be developed with the cooperation of the "Sons of Liberty." The tangible prospects were best for an uprising at Chicago and New York. The forces of the "Sons of Liberty" were not only organized, but arms had been distributed. It had been deemed surest to rely upon the attempt to organize a Northwestern Confederacy with Chicago as the capital.

In order to promote the movement Captain Hines, Col. St. Leger Grenfel, Colonel Marmaduke, Lieutenant Eastin and all the other available Confederates had been selected to be in Chicago, under command of Captain Hines, and endeavor to carry out plans for the release of the prisoners at Camp Douglas and Rock Island, thus forming the nucleus for an army of Confederates upon which the "Sons of Liberty" were to rally.

The Presidential election which was to be held on the 8th day of November was deemed an opportune time for the blow to be struck at Chicago and in New York. Colonel Thompson advised us that detachments under Captain Churchill in Cincinnati and Dr. Luke Blackburn in Boston would set fire to those cities on election day.

Colonel Thompson referred with confidence to the leadership and management of Mr. Walsh and Mr. Morris in Chicago, and to that of Mr. James A. McMasters, Mr.

Horton, and Fernando Wood in New York City. He confided to Colonel Martin the mission to New York. We were told that about 20,000 men were enlisted in New York under a complete organization; that arms had been provided already for the forces in the city, and we would be expected to take military supervision of the forces at the vital moment. It was proposed by the New York managers to take possession of the city on the afternoon of election day and in order to deter opposition a number of fires were to be started in the city. The United States Sub-Treasury was to be captured and all other property of the Government. And especially we were to release the prisoners at Fort Lafayette and unite them with our forces.

Colonel Thompson told us that he already had an agent, Captain Longmire of Missouri, in New York, who was charged with the details of the preparations for the execution of the plans.

It was deemed especially important that our presence in New York should be known only to a very few persons. And no one in Toronto should know our mission except our friends Godfrey J. Hyams and W. Larry McDonald. He accordingly gave us a letter to Mr. James A. McMasters, the editor and proprietor of the *Freeman's Journal*, which informed Mr. McMasters that Colonel Martin, with me as second in command, had been given authority for all military purposes. Only six others, Capt. Robert Cobb Kennedy of Louisiana, Lieuts. John T. Ashbrook and James T. Harrington of Kentucky, John Price of Maryland, James Chenault of Kentucky, and the other I do not remember, were assigned with us to operate in New York.

During this period Colonel Martin and I had secluded ourselves as much as possible in Toronto in order that we might not attract the special attention of the detectives of the Washington Government. This was also the policy of the other young soldiers who accompanied us on this enterprise.

It was arranged that we should arrive in New York about ten days before the election and become familiar with the streets and localities of the city.

The party of eight members left Toronto and reached New York safely by traveling in pairs, though we all went on the same train by the New York Central Railroad from the Suspension Bridge. Martin and I traveled together and stopped at the St. Denis Hotel, on the northwest corner of Broadway and Eleventh street. We registered under the names of Robert Maxwell and John Williams. Ashbrook and Harrington stopped at the Metropolitan Hotel. I do not now remember the stopping places of the others. However, I considered it safer, after a few days, to separate entirely as to lodging places, and secured a furnished room on the north side of Union Square about the middle of the first block going up Broadway. Martin and I had checks for our trunks, which were still in the baggage-room at the depot. It was Friday when we called on Mr. McMasters at his office and presented our letter of introduction. He received us cordially and said he had a note by mail from Colonel Thompson to the same effect without giving names. We agreed that it would be wise for us and him to meet elsewhere as a rule. His office was considered too public a place for our conferences. He accordingly designated a place for us to go on Saturday and meet himself and Captain Longmire. At this meeting we simply got acquainted, but made an appointment with Longmire at another place for Monday and accepted the invitation of Mr. McMasters to spend Sunday at his residence.

We found Mr. McMasters to be a determined and very able man and a true friend. He was a strong character in all respects. Physically he was of large proportions without much flesh. I would say he was at least 6 feet 3 inches in height, with a large frame, hands and feet. His face was large with a receding but broad forehead. He was bald in front, with brown hair and eagle eyes, and a large rather Roman nose. His voice was strong. Everything about him denoted strength of intellect as well as body.

Our plans were discussed after dinner during the entire afternoon. Mr. McMasters was the practical head of the operations in New York, though in the background and not expected to perform an active part in the proposed uprising. He might be designated chief manager of leaders. He went into details as to the organization, which appeared to be perfect, and we assured him that he could rely upon us for open, bold, and unflinching action when the hour arrived for crucial duty. It was determined that a number of fires should be started in different parts of the city, which would bring the population to the streets and prevent any sort of resistance to our movement. To facilitate this part of the programme he said a supply of Greek fire was being made and Captain Longmire was looking after that arrangement. He wanted the Confederates to put that part of the plan into execution, while the New York commanders of their forces would not only take possession of the city and all the approaches, but furnish the strength to support the military authorities. The city authorities were our friends. In parting, late that afternoon, Mr. McMasters told us he would request Governor Seymour to send a confidential agent down to the city with whom he wished us to confer. It was understood that the Governor would not use the militia to suppress the insurrection in the city but would leave that duty to the authorities at Washington. *Indeed, we were to have the support of the Governor's official neutrality.* We were also told that upon the success of the revolution here a convention of delegates from New York, New Jersey, and the New England States would be held in New York City to form a Confederacy which would cooperate with the Confederate States and Northwestern Confederacy.

Mr. McMasters agreed to send for us when he heard from Albany. On the next Thursday morning a messenger came for us and in the afternoon we went singly to the *Freeman's Journal* office, where we were locked in the private office and introduced to the Governor's private secretary. We were assured that our expectations would be lived up to by the Governor and we could prosecute our plans accordingly.

W. Larry McDonald, who was an intimate counselor of Colonel Thompson at Toronto, had written his brother Henry W. McDonald to assist us in every way. He proposed to secrete our trunks in his wholesale piano store, No. 73 Franklin avenue. We gave him our checks and he had the trunks hauled from the depot. We could go there occasionally to get out articles and to put away others we would not need. Our trunks were there for safety and convenience, as we expected to change our location frequently.

It was a period of enjoyment and recreation in most respects. I made the most of the opportunity and visited all the theaters and points of interest about the city. Among other entertainments I remember especially attending the lecture of Artemus Ward at Wood's Theater on Broadway opposite the St. Nicholas Hotel. Colonel Martin and I went over to Brooklyn one Sunday night and heard the sermon of Henry Ward Beecher. The meetings at Tammany Hall were of particular interest in the closing week of the Presidential campaign. We heard all the celebrities of the Wigwam deliver addresses. But the climax was reached when a monster torchlight procession was formed to march the full length of Broadway, which was reviewed by General George B. McClellan from the balcony of the Fifth Avenue Hotel. Martin and I were on hand early and circulated through the surging politicians who thronged the corridors and upper hall of the hotel. McClellan was the idol of the great assemblages in New York, though the Republican demonstrations in favor of Mr. Lincoln were equally enthusiastic.

After we had surveyed the scene inside of the Fifth Avenue Hotel, Martin and I went into the great crowd which filled Madison Square. Rostrums had been erected for outdoor speakers. Among these James T. Brady had been announced, and we watched for his appearance, when we pushed our way to a position near his stand and listened to his address. He was regarded as the foremost public man in New York who openly criticised the conduct of the war. He used strong language on this occasion.

The procession began to pass about 8.30 o'clock, coming up Broadway, and continued until 1 o'clock in the morning. It was not uncommon to hear hisses and groans for Lincoln from the ranks, and the President was caricatured in many ludicrous and ungainly pictures. Indeed, there was a vicious sentiment voiced all along the line of the procession against the draft and every one connected with the management of the war. The spirit of revolt was manifest and it only needed a start and a leadership.

But, as usual, some few days before the election all the New York papers announced the arrival of 10,000 soldiers and of Maj.-Gen. Benjamin F. Butler, who not only assumed command but issued a proclamation in which it appeared that he proposed to deal with any disorders that might occur to disturb the public peace, and hinted that he had some information of disloyal movements.

Formal notice of arrival of General Butler was given as follows:

NEW YORK, November 4, 1864.

General Orders No. 86.

Maj.-Gen. Benjamin F. Butler having been assigned to duty in this department, will take command of the troops which are arriving and which will be put in service in the State of New York subject to his orders.

By command of Major-General Dix:

CHARLES TEMPLE DIX,
Major and A. A. G.

General Butler first stopped at the Fifth Avenue Hotel, where Colonel Martin was then staying, but moved to the Hoffman House, where he and his staff occupied twelve rooms on the first floor. Of General Butler's arrival the *New York Times* said:

The wisdom of the Government in selecting the man who had scattered the howling rabble of New Orleans like chaff, and reduced that city to order most serene, approved itself to the conscience of every patriot and made Copperheads squirm and writhe in torture.

Malcontents, if such there be, dare not resort to extremes. They will be met at every point. A strong military force is already disposed to nip all disorders in the bud.

There has been widespread and ineffaceable dread that rebel emissaries would seize the exciting time of a general election to put in execution the villainous threats recently made by Richmond papers of laying New York, Buffalo, and other Northern cities in ashes, etc.

The leaders in our conspiracy were at once demoralized by this sudden advent of General Butler and his troops. They felt that he must be aware of their purposes and many of them began to fear arrest, while others were defiant. Among the latter were Mr. Horton of the *Day Book,* Mr. Brooks of the *Express,* and many others. However, Mr. McMasters sent for us and expressed his fears that our plans could not be carried to consummation. He appeared anxious to stem the effects of the arrival of troops but said we could not afford to make a failure. The next day, November 7th, he reported that at a conference of the leaders it was decided to postpone action.

Martin and I could only deal through Mr. McMasters, who was really the head or chief counselor, and we realized that he had agreed with the others that an attempt to seize and hold possession of the city on the day of the election would be a failure. We could do nothing but acquiesce in the views of the New York management. However, we were assured that the delay was only temporary, and it was contended that after the election, if all passed off quietly, then the troops would depart. But to increase the existing fears of our friends, the papers, on the morning before the election and also the next morning, announced the arrest of a number of our friends at Chicago and of a number of the leaders in Chicago of the "Sons of Liberty," who were to cooperate with Hines and his men. It looked as if that expedition had failed already.

Mr. Lincoln was duly elected over McClellan and Andrew Johnson of Tennessee was elected Vice-President.

It was not an unexpected result to us and it served in a measure to increase the popular alarm and opposition to the draft. The manifestation of this feeling had the effect as we thought to continue the Federal garrison in New York. We watched General Butler daily, hoping for his departure, but it began to look as if he and his troops had come to stay.

The next morning after the election we saw from the papers that nothing had occurred in any other city. We presumed that the same difficulties had existed in all the cities. Our New York friends were still unable to agree upon an auspicious day for action.

We did not reproach ourselves, however, as the proposed uprising at Chicago had not materialized. The feints at Boston, Philadelphia, and Cincinnati were likewise not attempted. We had no explanation of all the failures and Mr. McMasters cited those other plans along with ours and justified our failure as being consistent with the others. However, we had told Colonel Thompson he could expect to hear from us in New York, no matter what might be done in the other cities. He seemed to approve our determination and hoped for no more failures, and especially now when our last card was to be played.

But the more we insisted on the attempt in New York the weaker Mr. McMasters became. Captain Longmire was equally anxious with us to make the attempt at all hazards. We tried to get an agreement for Thanksgiving Day, but Butler still occupied the city and our cause had not gained headway in the Confederacy. Finally, after repeated interviews Mr. McMasters decided to withdraw from any further connection with the proposed revolution when it was foredoomed to failure. This left us practically at sea. Captain Longmire at the last moment became discouraged, when we announced our purpose to set the city on fire and give the people a scare if nothing else, and let the Government at Washington understand that burning homes in the South might find a counterpart in the North. Longmire concluded to go out in the country and stay until our sensation was over. He gave me the number of the house in Washington Place where the Greek fire had been made. Also the name and personal description of the old man I would meet when I went for it. I was told all the charges had been paid. On the night before we had determined to strike the blow our party of Confederates met up town and arranged our final plans. The duty of going after the Greek fire was considered rather a dangerous mission under the circumstances, but I was selected to go. I found the place was in a basement on the west side of Washington Place. The heavy-built old man I met wore a long beard all over his face. All I had to do was to tell him that Captain Longmire had sent me for his valise. He handed it over the counter to me without saying a word. I turned and departed with the same silence. The leather valise was about two and a half feet long and heavy. I had to change hands every ten steps to carry it. No carriage was in sight. I had not expected the valise to be so heavy. But I reached the City Hall Square with it safely and boarded a street car which started there for Central Park, going up Bowery street. The car was crowded and I had to put the valise in front of me on the floor in the passway, as the seats ran full length on each side of the car. I soon began to smell a peculiar odor—a little like rotten eggs—and I noticed the passengers were conscious of the same presence. But I sat unconcerned until my getting off place was reached, when I took up the valise and went out. I heard a passenger say as I alighted, "There must be something dead in that valise." When I lugged it into our cottage the boys were waiting and glad of my safe return. I was given the key with the valise and opened it at once with some curiosity to investigate the contents. None of the party knew anything about Greek fire, except that the moment it was exposed to the air it would blaze and burn everything it touched. We found it to be a liquid resembling water. It was put up in four-ounce bottles securely sealed. There were twelve dozen bottles in the valise. We were now ready to create a sensation in New York. It had been agreed that our fires would be started in the hotels, so as to do the greatest damage in the business district on Broadway. The eight members of our party had each taken a room at three or four hotels. In doing this we would buy a black glazed satchel for $1.00 and put an overcoat in it for baggage. The room at each hotel was used enough to show that it was being occupied. In leaving, of course the overcoat would be worn and the satchel left behind empty.

It was agreed that our operations should begin promptly at 8 o'clock p. m., so that the guests of hotels might all escape, as we did not want to destroy any lives.

We separated to meet at the same place the next evening at 6 o'clock, and then, as Captain Kennedy remarked to me, "We'll make a spoon or spoil a horn."

CHAPTER XXVIII

Confederates attempt to burn business section of New York
City—Escape to Canada.

At 6 o'clock promptly on the evening of November 25,
1864, our party met in our cottage headquarters, two failing
to report.

The bottles of Greek fire having been wrapped in paper
were put in our coat pockets. Each man took ten bottles.
It was agreed that after our operations were over we should
secrete ourselves and meet here the next night at 6 o'clock
to compare notes and agree on further plans.

I had rooms at the Astor House, City Hotel, Everett
House, and the United States Hotel. Colonel Martin occu-
pied rooms at the Hoffman, Fifth Avenue, St. Denis, and
two others. Lieutenant Ashbrook was at the St. Nicholas,
La Farge, and several others. Altogether nineteen hotels
were fired, namely: Hoffman House, Fifth Avenue, St.
Denis, St. James, La Farge, St. Nicholas, Metropolitan,
Howard, Tammany, Brandreth's, Gramercy Park, Hanford,
New England, Belmont, Lovejoy's, City Hotel, Astor,
United States, and Everett.

I reached the Astor House at 7.20 o'clock, got my key, and
went to my room in the top story. It was the lower corner
front room on Broadway. After lighting the gas jet I hung
the bedclothes loosely on the headboard and piled the chairs,
drawers of the bureau and washstand on the bed. Then
stuffed some newspapers about among the mass and poured
a bottle of turpentine over it all. I concluded to unlock my
door and fix the key on the outside, as I might have to get
out in a hurry, for I did not know whether the Greek fire
would make a noise or not. I opened a bottle carefully and

ROBERT M. MARTIN
1866

quickly and spilled it on the pile of rubbish. It blazed up instantly and the whole bed seemed to be in flames before I could get out. I locked the door and walked down the hall and stairway to the office, which was fairly crowded with people. I left the key at the office as usual and passed out.

Across at the City Hotel I proceeded in the same manner. Then in going down to the Everett House I looked over at my room in the Astor House. A bright light appeared within but there were no indications below of any alarm. After getting through at the Everett House I started to the United States Hotel, when the fire bells began to ring up town. I got through at the United States Hotel without trouble, but in leaving my key the clerk, I thought, looked at me a little curiously. It occurred to me that it had been discovered that my satchel had no baggage in it and that perhaps the clerk had it in mind to mention the fact.

As I came back to Broadway it seemed that a hundred bells were ringing, great crowds were gathering on the street, and there was general consternation. I concluded to go and see how my fires were doing. There was no panic at the Astor House, but to my surprise a great crowd was pouring out of Barnum's Museum nearly opposite the Astor. It was now a quarter after nine o'clock by the City Hall tower clock. Presently the alarm came from the City Hotel and the Everett. The surging crowds were frantic. But the greatest panic was at Barnum's Museum. People were coming out and down ladders from the second and third floor windows and the manager was crying out for help to get his animals out. It looked like people were getting hurt running over each other in the stampede, and still I could not help some astonishment for I did not suppose there was a fire in the Museum.

In accordance with our plan I went down Broadway and turned across to the North River wharf. The vessels and barges of every description were lying along close together and not more than twenty yards from the street. I picked dark spots to stand in, and jerked a bottle in six different places. They were ablaze before I left. One had struck a barge of baled hay and made a big fire. There were wild scenes here the last time I looked back. I started straight for the City Hall.

There was still a crowd around the Astor House and everywhere, but I edged through and crossed over to the City Hall, where I caught a car just starting up town. I got off on Bowery street opposite the Metropolitan Hotel to go across and see how Ashbrook and Harrington had succeeded. After walking half a square I observed a man walking ahead of me and recognized him. It was Captain Kennedy. I closed up behind him and slapped him on the shoulder. He squatted and began to draw his pistol, but I laughed and he knew me. He laughed and said he ought to shoot me for giving him such a scare.

We soon related to each other our experience. Kennedy said that after he touched off his hotels he concluded to go down to Barnum's Museum and stay until something turned up, but had only been there a few minutes when alarms began to ring all over the city. He decided to go out, and coming down the stairway it happened to be clear at a turn and the idea occurred to him that there would be fun to start a scare. He broke a bottle of Greek fire, he said, on the edge of a step like he would crack an egg. It blazed up and he got out to witness the result. He had been down there in the crowd ever since and the fires at the Astor House and the City Hotel had both been put out. But he had listened to the talk of the people and heard the opinion expressed generally that rebels were in the city to destroy it. He thought our presence must be known. Harrington had broken a bottle in the Metropolitan Theater at 8 o'clock, just after he fired the Metropolitan Hotel adjoining; and Ashbrook had done likewise in Niblo's Garden Theater adjoining the La Farge Hotel.

We went into the crowd on Broadway and stopped at those places to see what had happened. There was the wildest excitement imaginable. There was all sorts of talk

JOHN W. HEADLEY
1865

about hanging the rebels to lamp posts or burning them at the stake. Still we discovered that all was surmise apparently. So far as we could learn the programme had been carried out, but it appeared that all had made a failure. It seemed to us that there was something wrong with our Greek fire.

All had observed that the fires had been put out in all the places as easily as any ordinary fire. We came to the conclusion that Longmire and his manufacturing chemist had put up a job on us after it was found that we could not be dissuaded from our purpose.

Martin and I got together as agreed and found lodging about 2 o'clock. We did not awake until 10 o'clock next day. We went into a restaurant on Broadway near Twelfth street for breakfast. It was crowded, but every one was reading a newspaper. After giving our order we got the *Herald, World, Tribune,* and *Times,* and to our surprise the entire front pages were given up to sensational accounts of the attempt to burn the city. It was plainly pointed out that rebels were at the head of the incendiary work, and quite a list of names was given of parties who had been arrested. All our fictitious names registered at the different hotels were given and interviews with the clerks described us all. The clerk of the United States Hotel especially gave a minute description of my personal appearance, clothing, manners and actions. He said I did not eat a meal at the hotel, though I had been there two days as a guest, and had nothing in my black satchel.

It was stated in the papers that the authorities had a full knowledge of the plot and the ring-leaders would be captured during the day. One paper said the baggage of two of them had been secured, and all avenues of escape being guarded the villains were sure to be caught, the detectives having a full knowledge of the rebels and their haunts.

As soon as we finished breakfast we slipped out and took a car on Bowery street for Central Park. Here we loafed, and read the afternoon papers, which indicated that they had some knowledge of our crowd, although from arrests that had been made we thought the authorities were on a cold trail.

We left the park at 4 o'clock in the afternoon to go down town and get supper and see what appeared in the extra editions which were being issued. As we reached Union Square Martin suggested that he would get out at McDonald's piano store and see about our baggage, while I would go on and order supper at a favorite restaurant on Fourteenth street, by the time he arrived. The car was halted in front of McDonald's; Martin got off and started in —there being two steps to ascend from the pavement to the entrance, which was a vestibule. I noticed Miss Katie McDonald, the daughter of our friend, standing at a front window looking out, and the moment she saw Colonel Martin she shuddered, and putting her hand, palm outward, before her face motioned him away. Martin saw the warning and turned instantly, running to overtake our car. I halted it and he came in, looking pale. He sat down without saying a word but looked back casually.

When we reached the restaurant he told me that he saw a big crowd in McDonald's store, just as Miss McDonald gave him the sign and a look of horror. The last issue of the *Evening Post* gave such particulars as to almost designate our crowd. The account said two had been arrested and the police were close after the others, with every prospect of securing the whole party. It stated that the plot of these rebels had been divulged to the authorities a month before by a man from Canada, but on condition that he was to receive one hundred thousand dollars for his information. The authorities at Washington were willing to pay the price provided the man could prove in any way that his story was true. It appeared so ridiculous that the authorities did not want to part with the money unless they received straight goods. They finally agreed that the rebels should be pointed out to detectives, who would follow us and investigate the case, and, if the story was genuine, the money would be paid. It stated that the detectives had been going with us all over the city and related how we had spent our time. But they had finally abandoned us as a lot of well-behaved young men who seemed to be simply enjoying ourselves, and they had never been able to trace us to any of the places where we would be supposed to go if we had any connection with the New York "Sons of Liberty" who were under surveillance. None of us was known in Canada as having ever been engaged in any raid.

While our betrayer knew the facts he was unable to convince the authorities. It happened that we had never been about any one but McMasters and McDonald, and we did not go to see McMasters but once after the detectives were put on our track; and were in McDonald's store only twice. It appeared that the authorities had only given us up and refused to trade with our betrayer a few days before we started the fires.

Colonel Martin and I decided before leaving the restaurant that we had better meet our companions and arrange a plan to get out of New York and back into Canada. At 6 o'clock we reached our cottage, and soon to our delight the other boys put in an appearance. All had calculated that some of the others had surely been arrested. All approved the suggestion that we had better escape from the city at once if possible. We found that a train left on the New York Central Railroad at 11 o'clock p. m., and that the sleepers were open for passengers at 9 o'clock. After discussing a number of plans it was decided that we would go and get in that sleeper the moment it was opened. As I remember now only two of the party had secured their baggage.

Our first trouble developed when we came to buy tickets. We did not like the idea of approaching the waiting-room. However, we went direct from the cottage to the depot and found that tickets could be bought at 8 o'clock. Two of the party who had boarded on a secluded street and were not well known in Toronto ventured to buy the tickets and succeeded. We slipped into the sleeping-car at 9 o'clock. We believed anyhow that all the policemen could not have a knowledge of us and our greatest fear was from detectives. We retired at once in our berths, but did not undress, and kept a close watch out the windows until the time of departure. When the train backed into the station and back to the sleeper there was a great crowd about the station and a number of men occasionally chatting, that we felt sure were detectives. They scrutinized every passenger that entered the train. We had examined the rear of our car and found a way to get out in case of a fight and a chase.

Colonel Martin had said to me that in case they came on to search for us he would open the ball and we would fight out, with a chance to get mixed in the crowd and escape back into the city. I supposed he had told the others the same plan.

But to our great relief the train pulled out on time. Still, we had a fear that a force might be on board to search the train before we reached any outside stations. However, we lay in waiting for more than an hour, when we felt safe and undressed for much-needed rest and sleep.

We could only get tickets to Albany, which was the destination of this train. The next day was Sunday and no trains ran from Albany to Niagara or Suspension Bridge on Sunday. We arrived at Albany about 6 o'clock Sunday morning and scattered among the hotels, where we spent the day in our rooms. In the evening we took a sleeper on the through train and crossed over the Suspension Bridge into Canada before morning. We arrived at Toronto in the afternoon. That night Colonel Martin and I gave a full account of our operations in New York City to Colonel Jacob Thompson, upon whose orders the enterprise had been undertaken.

It is fair to all concerned to record the fact here that TEN DAYS BEFORE THIS ATTEMPT OF CONFEDERATES TO BURN NEW YORK CITY, GENERAL SHERMAN HAD BURNED THE CITY OF ATLANTA, GEORGIA, AND THE NORTHERN PA-

PERS AND PEOPLE OF THE WAR PARTY WERE
IN GREAT GLEE OVER THE MISERIES OF THE
SOUTHERN PEOPLE. I heard them talk every day in
New York, in restaurants, hotels and on the streets. A fair
expression of the feeling which prevailed is recorded by Gen-
eral Sherman himself. He says:

> About 7 a. m. of November 16th (1864) we rode out of
> Atlanta by the Decatur road, filled by the marching troops and
> wagons of the 14th Corps; and reaching the hill, just outside
> of the old rebel works, we naturally paused to look back upon
> the scenes of our past battles. We stood upon the very ground
> whereon was fought the bloody battle of July 22d, and could
> see the copse of wood where McPherson fell. BEHIND US
> LAY ATLANTA, SMOULDERING AND IN RUINS, the
> black smoke rising high in air, and hanging like a pall over the
> RUINED CITY.
>
>   *   *   *   *   *   *   *
>
> Some band, by accident, struck up the anthem of "John
> Brown's soul goes marching on"; the men caught up the strain,
> and never before or since have I heard the chorus of "GLORY,
> GLORY, HALLELUJAH" DONE WITH MORE SPIRIT,
> OR IN BETTER HARMONY OF TIME AND PLACE.

It was developed that Mr. Godfrey J. Hyams of Little
Rock, Arkansas, was the traitor or spy in our camp. He
was a very smart fellow and had managed to establish the
closest confidential relations with Colonel Thompson. He
had known all the particulars of our mission before we
started to New York.

All could now understand how the other expeditions had
been betrayed. There had always been a mystery about the
betrayal of Captain Cole at Sandusky; and others at Chicago,
Boston and Cincinnati.

We found that Hyams had been mysteriously absent from
Toronto. He returned the day after we arrived, but quickly
discovered that he was getting a cold reception and quietly
left Toronto.

The New York papers continued to report discoveries
and the proceedings of the authorities. Mr. Horton, editor

and proprietor of the *Day Book,* and Mr. Henry W. Mc-Donald were among those arrested. A reward of twenty-five thousand dollars was offered for the incendiaries.

Miss Katie McDonald and a brother of Mr. Horton came over to Toronto at once to solicit financial aid from Colonel Thompson for the defense of McDonald and Horton, but more especially to secure sworn testimony that neither was connected in any way, by knowledge or act, with our attempt to burn New York. Everything was furnished that would help their cases and they were eventually released.

Two days after our arrival in Toronto, Colonel Thompson came to my boarding-house one very cold night in a snow-storm to tell me that a number of detectives from New York had arrived in Toronto and were stopping at the Queen's Hotel. Mr. Horton had recognized several of them and they had casually inquired for Martin and me, Ashbrook and Kennedy, of a gentleman who happened to be our friend. He reported to Colonel Thompson. Colonel Thompson advised that we seclude ourselves as there was danger of a requisition from the Washington authorities for our arrest and extradition.

W. Larry McDonald rented a small cottage in the suburbs of the city and furnished it plainly. I went to stay with him. We were joined by Charles C. Hemming, my young Confederate friend from Jacksonville, Florida, for whom I had formed a strong attachment upon my arrival at Toronto. We did our own house-keeping and cooking, and did not venture to visit the hotels or other public places. All the prominent actors in any previous expedition either secluded themselves in the city or in the country.

Meanwhile, at the suggestion of Colonel Thompson it was deemed advisable that we retain Hon. John McDonald as counsel in the event of a requisition, as he was friendly to our cause and was regarded as a very eminent lawyer. One evening after supper Colonel Martin called for me and we rode in a sleigh to the residence of Mr. McDonald in the suburbs of Toronto. He greeted us cordially and we discussed our case fully until a late hour. The arrangement was made and a retainer fee was paid the following day. But it happened that the time never arrived when his services were required.

CHAPTER XXIX

Northwestern Confederacy vanishes—Plans exposed at Chicago —Arrest of leaders—General report of Thompson upon all operations—Failure conceded—Judge Buckner S. Morris and Col. Vincent Marmaduke acquitted—R. T. Semmes and Charles Walsh sentenced to penitentiary—Col. George St. Leger Grenfel sentenced to be hung.

Colonel Thompson told us the story of the expedition to Chicago under Captain Hines and of the flattering prospects of success until they were betrayed. Not only the release of 8,000 prisoners confined at Camp Douglas, but the successful uprising of the "Sons of Liberty," and the establishment of the Northwestern Confederacy, seemed assured.

Two days before the day of the election the Federal garrison was increased, and the commander being fully advised he proceeded to capture the Confederates at their boarding places. Hines, Eastin and many others escaped. A number of leading commanders of the "Sons of Liberty" at Chicago were arrested and all these parties were now confined in prison.

The report of the Federal commander at Chicago will give a fair account of the situation and of his action in making arrests. It was as follows:

* * * * * * *

HEADQUARTERS POST, CAMP DOUGLAS,
Chicago, Illinois, November 23, 1864.
Brig.-Gen. JAMES B. FRY,
Provost-Marshal-General, Washington, D. C.
GENERAL: About the 1st of November another expedition of like character was organized in Canada, to be commanded by Captain Hines and composed of the same elements as that which had failed at the time of the Chicago convention. It was deter-

mined that the attempt should be made about the period of the
Presidential election, and the night of that day was finally
designated as the time when the plot should be executed.
During the canvass which preceded the election the Sons of
Liberty (a secret organization within and beyond all doubt
unknown to the better portion and majority of the Democratic
party) had caused it to be widely proclaimed and believed that
there was an intention on the part of the Government, and great
danger that such intention would be carried into effect, to interfere by military force at the polls against the Democratic party,
as an excuse under which to arm themselves as individuals, and
had also obtained and concealed at different places in this city,
arms and ammunition for themselves and the rebel prisoners of
war when they should be released. On the evening of the 5th
day of November it was reported that a large number of persons
of suspicious character had arrived in the city from Fayette and
Christian counties, in Illinois, and that more were coming. On
Sunday, the 6th day of November, late in the afternoon, it
became evident that the city was filling up with suspicious
characters, some of whom were escaped prisoners of war and
soldiers of the rebel army; that Captain Hines, Colonel Grenfel,
and Colonel Marmaduke were here to lead; and that Brigadier-
General Walsh, of the Sons of Liberty, had ordered large numbers of the members of that order from southern portions of
Illinois to cooperate with them. Adopting measures which
proved effective to detect the presence and identify the persons
of the officers and leaders and ascertain their plans, it was manifest that they had the means of gathering a force considerably
larger than the little garrison then guarding between 8,000 and
9,000 prisoners of war at Camp Douglas, and that taking advantage of the excitement and the large number of persons who
would ordinarily fill the streets on election night, they intended
to make a night attack on and surprise this camp, release and
arm the prisoners of war, cut the telegraph wires, burn the railroad depots, seize the banks and stores containing arms and
ammunition, take possession of the city, and commence a campaign for the release of other prisoners of war in the States of
Illinois and Indiana, thus organizing an army to effect and give
success to the general uprising so long contemplated by the Sons
of Liberty. The whole number of troops for duty at Camp
Douglas on that day were as follows: Eighth Regiment Veteran
Reserve Corps, Lieut.-Col. Lewis C. Skinner commanding, 273;
Fifteenth Regiment Veteran Reserve Corps, Lieut.-Col. Martin
Flood commanding, 377; total infantry, 650; Twenty-fourth

Ohio Battery, Lieut. James M. Gamble, 146; making a total of 796 to guard 8,352 prisoners of war confined in the garrison square at this camp by a fence constructed of inch boards twelve feet high.

The election was to take place on Tuesday, the 8th, two days thereafter.

By deferring action till the night of Monday, the 7th instant, probably all the officers and leaders and many more of the men and arms of the expedition might have been captured, and more home rebels exposed, but such delay would have protracted the necessary movements and attending excitement into the very day of the Presidential election. The great interests involved would scarcely justify taking the inevitable risks of postponement. Sending a despatch, dated 8.30 p. m., November 6th, by messenger over the railroad, to Brig.-Gen. John Cook, commanding District of Illinois, a copy of which, numbered 1, is annexed to and made a part of this report, the following arrests were made that night: Col. G. St. Leger Grenfel and J. T. Shenks, an escaped prisoner of war, at the Richmond House; Col. Vincent Marmaduke, at the house of Dr. E. W. Edwards, No. 70 Adams street; Brig.-Gen. Charles Walsh, of the Sons of Liberty; Captain Cantrill of Morgan's command, and Charles Travers, rank unknown, probably an officer under an assumed name, at the house of General Walsh; Judge Buckner S. Morris, treasurer of the Sons of Liberty, at his house, No. 6 Washington street; also capturing at the same time, in Walsh's house, about thirty rods from Camp Douglas, arms and ammunition as per annexed schedule, numbered 2. The shotguns were all loaded with cartridges, composed of 9 to 12 largest size buckshot, and capped; the revolvers (Joslyn's patent, 10-inch barrel) also loaded and capped. Reported to Brig.-Gen. John Cook, commanding District of Illinois, and Col. William Hoffman, commissary-general of prisoners, by telegraph despatch, dated Camp Douglas, November 7, at 4 a. m., a copy of which is hereto annexed, numbered 3, and made a part of this report. On the morning of Monday, the 7th instant, Col. John L. Hancock, commanding militia, by order of Governor Yates, reported to me, and Col. R. M. Hough rapidly organized a mounted force, of about 250, which was armed with the revolvers captured from Walsh, reported and was assigned to duty as patrols in the city of Chicago, remaining on duty till the morning of the 9th. Captain Bjerg, military provost-marshal First District of Illinois, the police of the city, and various detachments of the garrison, under different officers, arrested during the day and night of the 7th instant 106 bushwhackers, guerrillas and rebel soldiers, among them many of the notorious Clingman gang of Fayette and Christian counties, in this State, and with their Captain, Sears, and Lieutenant, Garland, all of whom are now in custody at Camp Douglas.

On the 11th of November 47 double-barreled shotguns, 30 Allen's patent breech-loading carbines, and 1 Enfield rifle were seized at Walsh's barn, in city of Chicago. Finding from investigation that the Sons of Liberty in this city continued to meet and plot, on the night of Sunday, the 13th of November, Patrick Dooley, secretary of the Temple in this city, was arrested, and such papers as had not been destroyed, some of them valuable, as showing the intents and purposes of the organization, seized. On the night of Monday, November 14th, the following named persons, members of the Sons of Liberty, were arrested, viz: Obadiah Jackson, grand senior; Charles W. Patten, member of State Council; William Felton, tyler or doorkeeper; James Gearry, a dangerous member; Richard T. Semmes, nephew of Pirate Semmes; Dr. E. W. Edwards, who harbored Colonel Marmaduke; all of whom remain in custody.

On the 15th instant a young Englishman from Canada, under British protection papers, named Mongham, was arrested, who proved to be a messenger between Jacob Thompson, Captain Hines, Brigadier-General Walsh, and the guerrilla, Colonel Jesse, of Kentucky.

An examination of many of the persons so arrested shows, beyond all doubt, that the Sons of Liberty is a treasonable, widely extended, and powerful organization, branching into almost if not all the counties of the State; that it is an organization of two branches, one civil, the other military; the members of the civil being on probation for the military branch; that important secrets in relation to military plans and the location of the depots of arms were carefully guarded from persons of civil membership, though they even well knew that the organization had such depots, and was animated with a spirit of intense hostility to the Government; that many of the leaders must have known of the intended attack on this camp and city; and that some of them have actually been in consultation, face to face, with men who they knew to be rebel officers conspiring to produce a revolution in the Northwest.

A schedule is hereto attached, numbered 4, which is believed to contain the names of some of the leading and most dangerous men belonging to this organization in the several counties in the State of Illinois.

I respectfully recommend that the officers of the rebel army, and as many of the Sons of Liberty and guerrillas above mentioned as the interests of the Government may require, be tried before a military commission and punished.

*   *   *   *   *   *   *

I have the honor to be, General, very respectfully,
Your obedient servant,
B. J. SWEET,
Colonel Eighth Regiment Veteran Reserve Corps, Commanding Post.

Colonel Thompson was at this time greatly discouraged over the prospects for retaliation upon the North or releasing our prisoners of war. Since all the enterprises and expeditions had failed, on account of the treachery of Hyams, or his successful work as a spy in our camp, which had given the United States detectives a familiar knowledge of all the leading Confederates who operated on the border, it seemed impracticable to make other attempts with the same men. He expressed his views freely to those of us who were in his confidence. He now concluded to make a general report of all operations to Mr. Benjamin, Secretary of State of the Confederacy, which follows:

TORONTO, C. W., December 3, 1864.
Hon. J. P. BENJAMIN,
Secretary of State.

SIR: Several times have I attempted to send you communications, but I have no assurance that any one of them has been received. I have relaxed no effort to carry out the objects the Government had in sending me here. I had hoped at different times to have accomplished more, but still I do not think my mission has been altogether fruitless. At all events we have afforded the Northwestern States the amplest opportunity to throw off the galling dynasty at Washington and openly to take ground in favor of States' rights and civil liberty. This fact must satisfy the large class of discontents at home of the readiness and willingness of the Administration to avail itself of every proffered assistance in our great struggle for independence.

On my arrival here I heard that there was such an organization as the order of the "Sons of Liberty" in the Northern States, and my first effort was to learn its strength, its principles, and its objects, and if possible to put myself in communication with its leading spirits. This was effected without much difficulty or delay. I was received among them with cordiality, and the greatest confidence at once extended to me. The number of its members was large, but not so great as Mr. Holt, in his official report, represented it to be. Its object was political. Its principles were that the Government was based on the consent of the parties to it; that the States were the parties and were sovereign; that there was no authority in the General Government to coerce a seceding State. The resolutions of 1798 and 1799 were set forth as presenting the true theory of the Government. Its organization was essentially military. It had its commanders of divisions, of brigades, of regiments, of companies. In the month of June last the universal feeling among its members, leaders and privates, was that it was useless to hold a Presidential election. Lincoln had the power and would certainly re-elect himself, and there was no hope but in force. The belief was entertained and freely expressed that by a bold, vigorous, and concerted movement the great Northwestern States of Illinois, Indiana and Ohio could be seized and held. This being done, the States of Kentucky and Missouri could easily be lifted from their prostrate condition and placed on their feet, and this in sixty days would end the war.

While everything was moving along smoothly to a supposed successful consummation, the first interruption in the calculation was the postponement of the meeting of the Democratic Convention from the 4th of July to the 29th of August, but preparations still went on, and in one of the States the 20th of July was fixed as the day for the movement; but before the day arrived a general council of the order from different States was called, and it was thought the movement on the 20th of July would be premature and the 16th of August was fixed upon for a general uprising. This postponement was insisted on upon the ground that it was necessary to have a series of public meetings to prepare the public mind, and appointments for public peace meetings were made, one at Peoria, one at Springfield, and one at Chicago, on the 16th. The first one was at Peoria, and to make it a success I agreed that so much money as was necessary would be furnished by me. It was held and was a decided success; the vast multitudes who attended seemed to be swayed but by one leading idea—peace. The friends were encouraged and strengthened and seemed anxious for the day when they would do something to hasten them to the great goal of peace. About this time that correspondence between our friends and

Horace Greeley made its appearance. Lincoln's manifesto shocked the country. The belief, in some way, prevailed over the North that the South would agree to a reconstruction, and the politicians, especially the leading ones, conceived the idea that on such an issue Lincoln could be beaten at the ballot-box. At all events, they agreed that the trial of the ballot-box should be made before a resort to force, always a dernier resort. The Springfield meeting came off, but it was apparent that the fire exhibited at Peoria had already diminished. The whole tone of the speakers was that the people must rely upon the ballot-box for redress of grievances. The nerves of the leaders of the order began to relax. About this time a large lot of arms were purchased and sent to Indianapolis, which was discovered, and some of the leading men were charged with the design to arm the members of the order for treasonable purposes. Treachery showed itself at Louisville. Judge Bullitt and Dr. Kalbus were arrested and sent to Memphis. The day on which the great movement was to be made became known to Mr. McDonald, candidate for Governor of Indiana, and believing it would mar his prospects for election unless prevented, he threatened to expose all the parties engaged unless the project was abandoned. Thus the day passed by and nothing was done.

The Chicago convention came, the crowd was immense, the feeling was unanimous for peace. A general impression prevailed that a reconstruction could be had and that it was necessary to so far pander to the military feeling as to take General McClellan to secure a certain success. This nomination, followed as it was by divers disclosures and arrests of persons, prominent members, totally demoralized the "Sons of Liberty." The feeling with the masses is as strong as ever. They are true, brave, and, I believe, willing and ready, but they have no leaders. The vigilance of the Administration, its large detective force, the large bounties paid for treachery and the respectable men who have yielded to the temptation, added to the large military force stationed in those States, make organization and preparation almost an impossibility. A large sum of money has been expended in fostering and furthering these operations and it now seems to have been to little profit. But in reviewing the past I do not see how it could have been avoided, nor has it been spent altogether in vain. The apprehensions of the enemy have caused him to bring back and keep from the field in front at least 60,000 to watch and browbeat the people at home. In this view of the subject the same amount of money has effected so much in no other quarter since the commencement of the war.

In July last Capt. Charles H. Cole, of General Forrest's command, made his escape from prison. He represented to me that he had been appointed a lieutenant in our Navy. I sent him around the Lakes, with instructions to go as a lower-deck passenger, to familiarize himself with all the channels, and different approaches to the several harbors, the strength of each place, the depositories of coal, and especially to learn all that he could about the steamer *Michigan,* and devise some plan for her capture or destruction. This duty he performed very satisfactorily. He was then instructed to return and put himself in communication with the officers of the *Michigan,* and feeling his way, to endeavor to purchase the boat from its officers. For a time he thought he would succeed in this, if he could give the guarantee of payment of the sum stipulated; but by degrees the question was dropped, and he asked permission to organize a force, board and take her. This was given and Acting Master John Y. Beall was sent him to aid in the organization, and in carrying out the enterprise. Their plan was well conceived and held out the promise of success. It had been previously ascertained from escaped prisoners from Johnson's Island that an organization existed among the prisoners of the island for the purpose of surprising the guard and capturing the island. The presence of the steamer *Michigan,* which carried fourteen guns, was the only obstacle.

Secret communications were had by which they were advised that on the night of the 19th of September an attempt to seize the *Michigan* would be made. On that night Captain Cole, who had previously established the friendliest relations with the officers of the steamer, was to have a wine drinking with them on board, and at a given hour Acting Master Beall was to appear, on a boat to be obtained for that purpose, with a sufficient body of Confederate soldiers to board and take the steamer. Should they capture the steamer, a common shot sent through the officers' quarters on Johnson's Island was to signify to the prisoners that the hour for their release had come. Should they take the island, boats were to be improvised and Sandusky was to be attacked. If taken, the prisoners were to be mounted and make for Cleveland, the boats cooperating, and from Cleveland, the prisoners were to make Wheeling and thence to Virginia. The key to the whole movement was the capture of the *Michigan.* On the evening of the 19th, by some treachery, Cole was arrested and the messenger who was to meet Acting Master Beall at Kelley's Island did not reach him. Disappointed, but nothing daunted, Acting Master Beall, having possession of the *Philo Parsons,* passenger steamer from Detroit to Sandusky, went on toward Johnson's Island. Having landed at Middle Bass Island to secure a supply of wood, the steamer *Island Queen,* with a large number of passengers and thirty-two soldiers, came up alongside and lashed herself to the *Parsons.* An attack was at once resolved upon. The passengers and soldiers were soon made prisoners and the boat delivered up to our men. The soldiers were regularly paroled, the passengers were left on the island, having given their promise not to leave for twenty-four hours, and the boat was towed out into the lake and sunk. The *Parsons* was then steered directly for the bay of Sandusky. Here the men, for certain reasons not altogether satisfactory, but possibly fortunately, refused to make the attack on the *Michigan.* Beall returned, landed at Sandwich, C. W., and the men scattered through the country. Most of them have returned to the Confederate States; but a few days since Acting Master Bennett G. Burley was arrested, and the trial is now going on for his delivery under the extradition treaty. If we had Cole's, Beall's, or his own commission I would not fear the result. As it is they will have to prove that they acted under my orders, and that will in all probability secure his release, but it may lead to my expulsion from the Provinces. At least I have it from a reliable source that this last proposition has been pressed upon the Canadian authorities and they have considered it. Should the course of events take this direction, unadvised by you, I shall consider it my duty to remain where I am and abide the issue. I should prefer, if it be possible, to have your views on the subject. Captain Cole is still a prisoner on Johnson's Island.

In obedience to your suggestion, so far as it was practicable, soon after my arrival here, I urged the people in the North to convert their paper money into gold and withdraw it from the market. I am satisfied this policy was adopted and carried into effect to some extent, but how extensively I am unable to state. What effect it had on the gold market it is impossible to estimate, but certain it is that gold continued to appreciate until it went to 290. The high price may have tempted many to change their policy, because afterward gold fell in the market to 150. When it was about 180, and exportation of gold was so small that there appeared to be but little or no demand for it, Mr. John Porterfield, formerly a banker in Nashville, but now a resident of Montreal, was furnished with $100,000, and instructed to proceed to New York to carry out a financial policy, of his own conception, which consisted in the purchase of gold and exporting the same, selling it for sterling bills of exchange, and then converting his exchange into gold. This process involved a certain loss, the cost of transshipment. He was instructed by Mr. Clay and myself to go on with his policy until he had expended $25,000, with which he supposed he would ship directly $5,000,000, and induce others to ship much more, and then, if the effect upon the gold market was not very perceptible, he was to desist and return to Canada and restore the money unexpended. By his last report he had caused the shipment of more than $2,000,000 of gold at an expense of less than $10,000, but it seems that a Mr. Lyons, who had been a former partner of Porterfield, was arrested by General Butler on the ground that he was exporting gold, and although Mr. Lyons had no connection with Porterfield in this transaction, yet he thought it prudent to return to Canada, and while he retains the unexpended balance of the $25,000 to carry out his instructions, he has restored $75,000. I must confess that the first shipment had a marked effect on the market. I am inclined to the opinion that his theory will work great damage and distrust to the Federal finances, if vigorously followed up, and if no untoward circumstances should interfere with the operation.

Soon after I reached Canada a Mr. Minor Major visited me and represented himself as an accredited agent from the Confederate States to destroy steamboats on the Mississippi River, and that his operations were suspended for want of means. I advanced to him $2,000 in Federal currency, and soon afterwards several boats were burned at Saint Louis, involving an immense loss of property to the enemy. He became suspected, as he represented to me, of being the author of this burning, and from that time both he and his men have been hiding and consequently have done nothing.

Money has been advanced to Mr. Churchill, of Cincinnati, TO ORGANIZE A CORPS FOR THE PURPOSE OF INCENDIARISM IN THAT CITY. I consider him a true man, and although as yet he has effected but little, I AM IN CONSTANT EXPECTATION OF HEARING OF EFFECTIVE WORK IN THAT QUARTER.

Previous to the arrival of LIEUTENANT-COLONEL MARTIN AND LIEUTENANT HEADLEY BRINGING AN UNSIGNED NOTE FROM YOU all the different places where our prisoners are confined—Camp Douglas, Rock Island, Camp Morton, Camp Chase, Elmira—had been thoroughly examined, and the conclusion was forced upon us that all efforts to release them without an outside cooperation would bring disaster upon the prisoners and result in no good. All projects of that sort were abandoned, except that at Camp Douglas, where Captain Hines still believed he could effect their release. We yielded to his firmness, zeal, and persistence, and his plans were plausible, but treachery defeated him before his well-laid plans were developed. Having nothing else on hand, Colonel Martin expressed a wish to organize A CORPS TO BURN NEW YORK CITY. HE WAS ALLOWED TO DO SO AND A MOST DARING ATTEMPT HAS BEEN MADE TO FIRE THAT CITY, BUT THEIR RELIANCE ON THE GREEK FIRE HAS PROVED A MISFORTUNE. IT CANNOT BE RELIED ON AS AN AGENT IN SUCH WORK. I have no faith whatever in it, and no attempt shall hereafter be made under my general directions with any such material.

I knew nothing whatever of the raid on St. Albans until after it transpired. Desiring to have a boat on whose captain and crew reliance could be placed, and on board of which arms could be sent to convenient points for arming such vessels as could be seized for operations on the lakes, I aided Dr. James T. Bates, of Kentucky, an old steamboat captain, in the purchase of the steamer *Georgiana*. She had scarcely been transferred when the story went abroad that she had been purchased and armed for the purpose of sinking the *Michigan,* releasing the prisoners on Johnson's Island, and destroying the shipping on the Lakes and the cities on their margin. The wildest consternation prevailed in all the border cities. At Buffalo two tugs had cannon placed on board; four regiments of soldiers were sent there, two of them represented to have been drawn from the Army of Virginia. Bells were rung at Detroit and churches broken up on Sunday. The whole lake shore was a scene of wild excitement. Boats were sent out which boarded the *Georgiana,* and found nothing contraband on board, but still the people were incredulous. The bane and curse of carrying out anything in this country is the surveillance under which we act. Detectives, or those ready to give information, stand on every street corner. Two or three cannot interchange ideas without a reporter.

The Presidential election has so demoralized the leaders of the order of the "Sons of Liberty" that a new organization under new leaders has become an absolute necessity. This is now going forward with great vigor and success. The new order is styled the "Order of the Star." There is a general expectation that there will soon be a new draft, and the members swear resistance to another draft. It is purely military, wholly independent of politics and politicians. It is given out among the members that Stonewall Jackson is the founder of the order, and the name has its significance from the stars on the collars of Southern officers. There is no ground to doubt that the masses to a large extent of the North are brave and true, and believe Lincoln a tyrant and usurper. During my stay in Canada a large amount of property has been destroyed by burning. The information brought me as to the perpetrators is so conflicting and contradictory that I am satisfied that nothing can be certainly known.

Should claims be presented at the War Office for payment for this kind of work, not one dollar should be advanced on any proof adduced until all the parties concerned may have an opportunity for making out and presenting proof. Several parties claim to have done the work at Saint Louis, New Orleans, Louisville, Brooklyn, Philadelphia, and at Cairo.

Within the last few days, Dr. K. I. Stewart, of Virginia, has reached this place, and very mysteriously informs me that he has a plan for the execution of something which has received the sanction of the President. He is in want of money and states to me that you gave him a draft on me for $20,000 in gold, which has been lost on the way. He has sent back to Richmond for a renewal. He has rented a large house and moved his family into it. I cannot doubt his word, but of course I do not feel authorized to advance him money without your authority or that of the President. I have, however, been constrained to advance him $500 in gold, on his written statement that unless the money was in hand the lives and liberties of high Confederate officers would be imperiled.

Owing to the health of Mr. Clay, we separated at Halifax, and since then we have not lived together, though we have been in consulting distance. As the money was all in my name, which I supposed to be controlled by us jointly, and as he desired to have a sum placed in his hands, at all times subject to his personal control, I transferred to him $93,614, for which I hold his receipts, and for which he promises to account to the proper authorities at home. Including the money turned over to Mr. Clay, all of which he has not yet expended, the entire expenditures as yet on all accounts are about $300,000. I still hold three drafts for $100,000 each, which have not been collected.

Should you think it best for me to return I would be glad to know in what way you think I had best return the funds remaining in hand. I INFER FROM YOUR PERSONAL

IN THE NEW YORK *NEWS* THAT IT IS YOUR WISH I SHOULD REMAIN HERE for the present, and I shall obey your orders. Indeed I have so many papers in my possession, which in the hands of the enemy would utterly RUIN and DESTROY very many of the PROMINENT MEN IN THE NORTH, that a due sense of my obligations to them will force on me the extremest caution in my movements.

For the future, discarding all dependence on the organizations in the Northern States, our efforts, in my judgment, should be directed to inducing those who are conscripted in the North, and who utterly refuse to join the army to fight against the Confederate States, to make their way south to join our service. It is believed by many that at least a number sufficient to make up a division may be secured in this way for our service before spring, especially if our army opens up a road to Ohio.   Some are now on their way to Corinth, which at present is the point of rendezvous. *Also to operate on their railroads* and force the enemy to keep up a guard on all their roads, which will require a large standing army at home, and to *burn whenever it is practicable,* and thus make the men of property feel their insecurity and tire them out with the war.   THE ATTEMPT ON NEW YORK HAS PRODUCED A GREAT PANIC, WHICH WILL NOT SUBSIDE AT THEIR BIDDING. This letter, though long, does not, I am aware, report many things of minor importance which have occurred since my sojourn in Canada, but I shall omit them at present.

Very respectfully, your obedient servant,

J. THOMPSON.

The trial and conviction of the Confederates and the leaders of the "Sons of Liberty," who were arrested at Chicago on the 6th of November, 1864, took place before a military commission at Cincinnati, Ohio, under the auspices of General Hooker. The official proceedings were as follows:

General Orders, No. 30.

HEADQUARTERS NORTHERN DEPARTMENT,
Cincinnati, Ohio, April 21, 1865.

I. Before a military commission, which convened at Cincinnati, Ohio, January 11, 1865, pursuant to Special Orders, No. 278, series of 1864, and Nos. 4 and 8, current series, from these headquarters, and of which Col. Charles D. Murray, Eighty-ninth Regiment Indiana Volunteer Infantry, is president, were arraigned and tried:

Charles Walsh, Buckner S. Morris, Vincent Marmaduke, and R. T. Semmes, citizens.

Charge 1. Conspiring, in violation of the laws of war, to release the rebel prisoners of war confined by authority of the United States at Camp Douglas, near Chicago, Ill.

Specification.—In this, that they, the said Charles Walsh, Buckner S. Morris, Vincent Marmaduke, R. T. Semmes, Charles Travis Daniel, George E. Cantrill, G. St. Leger Grenfel, and Benjamin M. Anderson, did unlawfully and secretly conspire and agree among themselves, and with one Captain Hines, so called, alias Doctor Hunter, of the Confederate Army, and others, in violation of the laws of war, to release the rebel prisoners of war, then confined by the authority of the United States at Camp Douglas, near Chicago, Ill., numbering between 8,000 and 9,000 persons, by suddenly attacking said camp on or about the evening of the 8th of November, anno Domini 1864, with a large number of armed men, overpowering the guard and forces then and there stationed on duty, seizing the cannon and arms in the possession of said guard and forces for the purpose of guarding and defending said camp, forcibly opening the gates of said prison camp and removing all obstructions to the successful escape of said prisoners confined within its limits. This, at or near Chicago, in the State of Illinois, within the military lines and the theater of military operations of the Army of the United States, at a period of war and armed rebellion against the authority of the United States, and on or about the 1st day of November, anno Domini 1864.

Charge 2. Conspiring, in violation of the laws of war, to lay waste and destroy the city of Chicago, Ill.

Specification.—In this, that they, the said Charles Walsh, Buckner S. Morris, Vincent Marmaduke, R. T. Semmes, Charles Travis Daniel, George E. Cantrill, G. St. Leger Grenfel, and Benjamin M. Anderson, did unlawfully and secretly conspire and agree among themselves, and with one Captain Hines, so called, alias Doctor Hunter, of the Confederate Army, and others, in violation of the laws of war, to lay waste and destroy, on or about the evening of the 8th of November, anno Domini 1864, the city of Chicago, Ill., by capturing the arsenal in said city, cutting the telegraph wires, burning the railroad depots, taking forcible possession of the banks and public buildings, and leaving the city to be sacked, pillaged, and burned by the rebel prisoners of war confined at Camp Douglas, near Chicago, Ill., which prisoners were to be forcibly released by them on or about the date above mentioned. This, at or near Chicago, in the State of Illinois, within the military lines and the theater of military operations of the Army of the United States, at a period of war and armed rebellion against the authority of the United States, and on or about the 1st day of November, anno Domini 1864.

To which each of the accused pleaded not guilty.

FINDING OF THE COMMISSION.

The commission, after mature deliberation on the evidence adduced, find the accused, Buckner S. Morris, (not guilty.)

And the commission do, therefore, acquit him, the said Buckner S. Morris.

FINDING AND SENTENCE.

The commission, after mature deliberation on the evidence adduced, find the accused, Charles Walsh, (guilty on all charges.)

And the commission do, therefore, sentence him, Charles Walsh, to be imprisoned for the term of five years, at such place as the commanding general may direct, said imprisonment to date from the 7th day of November, 1864.

FINDING AND SENTENCE.

The commission, after mature deliberation on the evidence adduced, find the accused, R. T. Semmes, (guilty on all charges.)

And the commission do, therefore, sentence him, the said R. T. Semmes, to be imprisoned at hard labor at such place as the commanding general may direct for the term of three years.

FINDING OF THE COMMISSION.

The commission, after mature deliberation on the evidence adduced, find the accused, Vincent Marmaduke, (not guilty.)

And the commission do, therefore, acquit him, the said Vincent Marmaduke.

II. The proceedings, findings, and sentences in the foregoing cases of Charles Walsh, Buckner S. Morris, Vincent Marmaduke, and Richard T. Semmes, are approved and confirmed. The penitentiary at Columbus, Ohio, is designated as the place of confinement (at hard labor) of the prisoners Charles Walsh and Richard T. Semmes. The post commandant of Cincinnati, Ohio, is charged with their immediate removal and delivery to the officer in charge of the said penitentiary. The prisoner, Buckner S. Morris, will be released upon taking the oath of allegiance. The prisoner, Vincent Marmaduke, having been acquitted, has been released upon taking the oath of allegiance.

*   *   *   *   *   *   *

O. H. HART,
Lieutenant-Colonel and Assistant Adjutant-General.
By command of Major-General Hooker.

General Court-Martial Orders, No. 250.

WAR DEPARTMENT,
ADJUTANT-GENERAL'S OFFICE,
Washington, May 26, 1865.

*   *   *   *   *   *   *

II. In the case of R. T. Semmes, citizen, sentenced by a military commission "to be imprisoned at hard labor at such place as the commanding general may direct for the term of three years," and now confined in the penitentiary at Columbus, Ohio, as promulgated in General Orders, No. 30, Headquarters Northern Department, Cincinnati, Ohio, April 21, 1865, the sentence is remitted, and he will be released from confinement without delay.

By order of the President of the United States.

E. D. TOWNSEND,
Assistant Adjutant-General.

Col. George St. Leger Grenfel was tried at the same time by the same commission, upon the same charges and specifications, with the following result, to-wit:

SENTENCE.

And the commission does, therefore, sentence him, G. St. Leger Grenfel, citizen, to be hung by the neck until he is dead, at such time and place as the commanding general may direct, two-thirds of the members concurring therein.

II. The proceedings of the commission in the above case were forwarded by the reviewing officer, Major-General Joseph Hooker, for the action of the President of the United States. The following are his orders:

"EXECUTIVE MANSION, July 22, 1865.

"The proceedings and findings in the case of G. St. Leger Grenfel are hereby approved, but, in consideration of the recommendation of members of the court, and of the successful progress of the Government in suppressing the rebellion, and in accordance with the suggestion of the Judge-Advocate-General, the sentence is hereby commuted to imprisonment for life, at hard labor, at the Dry Tortugas, or such other place as the Secretary of War may designate.

"ANDREW JOHNSON,
"President."

III. Maj.-Gen. E. O. C. Ord, U. S. Volunteers, commanding Department of the Ohio, is ordered to send the prisoner, G. St. Leger Grenfel, under charge of a commissioned officer, with a sufficient guard, to the Dry Tortugas, Fla., designated as the place of imprisonment, where he will be delivered to the commanding officer of the post, who is hereby ordered to confine said Grenfel at hard labor during the period designated in his sentence as commuted.

E. D. TOWNSEND,
Assistant Adjutant-General.

By order of the Secretary of War.

WAR DEPARTMENT, BUREAU OF MILITARY JUSTICE,
June 8, 1866.

G. ST. LEGER GRENFEL, Fort Jefferson, Fla.

SIR: Your application for remission of sentence, forwarded by General Hill to the Adjutant-General April 8, has been duly considered by the President in connection with the record of your trial, and I am instructed by him to inform you that it has been decided not to extend Executive clemency to your case.*

Very respectfully, your obedient servant,

J. HOLT,
Judge-Advocate-General.

---

*It appears from the records that Grenfel escaped from Fort Jefferson, Fla., March 7, 1868.

CHAPTER XXX

Expedition to Buffalo and Dunkirk, New York, to rescue Confederate generals on train—Proclamations of General Dix—Efforts to capture the express car—Capture of Captain Beall and George S. Anderson at Suspension Bridge.

There appeared nothing to do now, since all our attempts everywhere had failed. But Colonel Thompson received information from Sandusky, Ohio, that seven of our generals who were in prison at Johnson's Island were to be removed to Fort Lafayette, New York, on the 15th of December. They were Major-Generals Edward Johnson and J. R. Trimble; Brigadier-Generals J. J. Archer, M. Jeff. Thompson, J. R. Jones, W. N. R. Beall, and I. W. Frazier. Colonel Thompson sent for Martin and me on the morning of the 13th. He was anxious that these generals should escape or be released on the train en route. He thought that we, with Captain Beall and a few others, might rescue them if it could be done at all. He said he would not direct us to go unless we had confidence and were willing to undertake the enterprise. We promptly volunteered, and he agreed to get Beall, who was still farther west. He had not been about Toronto. The others selected were Lieut. James T. Harrington, Capt. Robert Cobb Kennedy, Lieut. John T. Ashbrook, Charles C. Hemming of Florida, George S. Anderson of Pittsylvania County, Virginia; W. P. Rutland of Nashville, Tennessee; and Forney Holt of Memphis, Tennessee. Martin, Beall, and Headley made up the party of ten men.

Colonel Thompson directed that after taking the train we should immediately arm the generals and use our judgment after that time, until Captain Beall with a few men should secure all the money in the express safe, when he and Martin would at once give a reasonable amount to each of the generals, and each member of the party, for we might be obliged to scatter in Ohio or New York. It was distinctly understood that nothing should be taken that belonged to passengers, but, if passengers interfered, we would shoot them the same as we would shoot the Federal guards of the prisoners. It was agreed that no human being should have any knowledge whatever of our expedition except the men composing it. All knew that United States detectives were constantly watching our movements.

The men went in pairs to Buffalo on Saturday night the 13th and Sunday the 14th of December. Martin and I went on the same train on Saturday night, getting off at Hamilton, Canada, a little city on Lake Ontario. Here Beall was to join us. He had arrived and retired when we reached the hotel late at night and we did not meet him until the next morning. We spent the day in Beall's room, where our plans were matured to capture the train between Sandusky and Buffalo by surprising the guards and taking their arms. We would then leave the passenger coaches behind on the track between the two stations. After cutting the telegraph wires we would run to Buffalo if near that place, otherwise we would scatter on trains in different directions. We intended to have the generals to change clothing with passengers of the same size and Colonel Martin would pay the difference.

We had never met Beall before, but fell in love with him at once. He was a modest, unassuming gentleman. I soon observed that he did not talk to entertain but was a thinking man and was resourceful and self-possessed. He did not get excited in relating an exciting episode and only smiled at amusing stories when others laughed aloud. And yet he was an interesting companion.

Sunday afternoon, the 14th, we went on, crossed the Suspension Bridge, and made connection for Buffalo. There we stopped at the Genesee House. I saw George Anderson in the office and gave him a sign to follow me outside, which he did, and then up-stairs to our room, where Colonel Martin posted him upon the plans for capturing the train. The other members of our party were also seen and all arrangements were made to leave the next morning for Dunkirk in time to meet the eastbound train from Cleveland on which we expected the generals to come.

The following "Proclamation" appeared among the telegraphic despatches in the newspapers of Buffalo next morning, the 15th:

HEADQUARTERS, DEPARTMENT OF THE EAST,
New York City, December 14th, 1864.
General Orders, No. 97.

Information having been received at these headquarters that the rebel marauders who were guilty of murder and robbery at St. Albans, have been discharged from arrest, and that other enterprises are actually in preparation in Canada, the Commanding-General deems it due to the people of the frontier towns to adopt the most prompt and efficient measures for the security of their lives and property.

ALL MILITARY COMMANDERS ON THE FRONTIER ARE THEREFORE INSTRUCTED IN CASE FURTHER ACTS OF DEPREDATION AND MURDER ARE ATTEMPTED, WHETHER BY MARAUDERS, OR PERSONS ACTING UNDER COMMISSIONS FROM THE REBEL AUTHORITIES AT RICHMOND, TO SHOOT DOWN THE DEPREDATORS IF POSSIBLE WHILE IN THE COMMISSION OF THEIR CRIMES; or if it be necessary with a view to their capture to cross the boundary between the United States and Canada, said commanders are directed to pursue them wherever they may take refuge, and if captured, they are under no circumstances, to be surrendered, but are to be sent to these headquarters for trial and punishment by martial law.

The Major-General commanding this department will not hesitate to exercise to the fullest extent the authority he possesses, under the rules of war exercised by all civilized States, in regard to persons organizing hostile expeditions within neutral territory, and fleeing to it for an asylum after committing acts of depredation within our own; such an exercise of authority having become indispensable to protect our cities and towns from incendiarism, and our people from robbery and murder.

It is earnestly hoped that the inhabitants of our frontier districts will abstain from all acts of retaliation on account of the outrages committed by rebel marauders, and that the proper measures of redress will be left to the action of the public authorities.

By command of Major-General Dix:

D. T. VAN BUREN, C. A. A. G.

It therefore appeared that if any of us were caught we were to be shot down and if we escaped to Canada we would be pursued into that country by troops of the United States and brought back for trial by a court martial.

All were promptly at the depot the next morning, the 15th, and in pairs boarded the train for Dunkirk, New York, on the Lake Shore Railroad. All stopped there except Colonel Martin, who went on to Erie, Pennsylvania. It was understood that he would return on the train which conveyed the Confederate generals, and the rest of us, meanwhile, were to kill time in Dunkirk. It was agreed that Beall and I should make safe inquiries at Dunkirk and learn if possible whether the generals had already passed over the road for the east. Colonel Martin proposed to do the same at Erie and be governed accordingly. It was intended that we should board the train bearing the prisoners and capture it within a short distance of Buffalo, then we would derail the coaches and run the engine and express car within two miles of the city and derail them also. Our party and the generals were then to go into Buffalo and depart on any train west or south for a reasonable distance and go in pairs on their own judgment by the safest route to Canada and report at Toronto to Colonel Thompson.

We went around the depot and watched for Colonel Martin on the arrival of every passenger train going east. He appeared on the arrival of the second train and beckoned us to come aboard. He had learned at Erie that the Confederate generals had not been sent east yet.

It now seemed prudent to secrete our party in Buffalo and watch the incoming trains from Sandusky for the generals and then go on the same train when they left Buffalo. Still, the order of General Dix had put us in greater peril, and it was decided by Martin and Beall that we could not afford to risk ourselves long in one place. It was therefore decided that if the generals did not arrive the next morning we would go out in sleighs and find a level place on the road to halt the next train. We would then mix into the crowd and make inquiries as though we had been driving and had halted on the road to learn their trouble.

If we found the generals on board we would talk with the guards about the mishap just as if we were passengers on the train.

Martin was to give the signal for our attempt on the guards. He intended to get hold of the officer in charge at the beginning and then try to make him surrender the others, while the rest of us would get the drop on the guards at each door. The generals were to be quickly armed, and after changing overcoats with passengers, the engineer would be taken in charge to run into the suburbs of Buffalo, where Martin would get off with the generals and force the engineer to run back into the country. Then after obstructing the road the party would proceed on their judgment to Canada. Meanwhile, the rest of us would hurry back to the city in the sleighs and endeavor to be in time for the Niagara train. If the train should be stopped by an obstruction and get damaged then we intended to secure conveyances for the generals, in the neighborhood, so as to reach Buffalo ahead of the passengers.

We spent the night in Buffalo. Next morning, after it appeared that the generals did not arrive, Martin, Beall, Anderson and myself rode out in a double-seated sleigh about four miles to a place where our road crossed the railroad track. There was no house near by and it was decided that we would come here early that night and halt the train. We would then detach the coaches, carry out our plan of the night before, and after derailing or disabling the engine, get in our sleighs, and reach the city in time to catch the train for Canada. We went back to the city and arranged that two sleighs, containing all our party, would meet in the suburbs at 5 p. m. We reached the appointed place on the road and secreted our conveyances in a wood near by. Colonel Martin concluded to put an iron rail in a fence gap and cover it with snow to stop the train if it did not stop when signaled with a lantern; but before we got ready the train came and went by without any trouble, throwing the iron rail about fifty yards. But it was jarred, and stopped about two hundred yards distant, and one or two men started back with lanterns. We hurried back to the city and took the train for Suspension Bridge, where we were obliged to wait an hour for the train from New York on the Central Railroad.

It had been agreed that on our arrival here we were immediately to walk across the bridge and wait on the Canada side for our train. Martin and I were the first to go. When the train came over and stopped at the station we got on, but could find none of our comrades. We did not understand their failure to come, and got off, thinking this must be the wrong train. Some time after another train came over but still none of our party could be found. We learned from the depot agent that the regular train went by in the first instance and the next train was not due till morning. The night was spent at a hotel. We found none of the men on the morning train and concluded to go on to Hamilton, where Beall had left his baggage. Nothing could be heard of Beall or any of the others in Hamilton. We went on to Toronto and found Ashbrook, Kennedy, Holt and Rutland had arrived. They were on the regular train the night before but we had overlooked them. They said they were worn out and were asleep perhaps when we came in their car.

Colonel Thompson sent a messenger to the Suspension Bridge and Niagara station, New York, to inquire for the missing members of the party.

It was learned in this way that Captain John Yates Beall and George S. Anderson, his companion, had been arrested while asleep, by policemen, in the eating-room where Martin and I had left them when we walked across the bridge.

The last to make his appearance of the others missing was Charles C. Hemming. He found himself pursued before he could cross the bridge, and escaped finally, reaching Fredonia, New York, where he was concealed by a stranger, but a friend, a Miss Mary Cumming.

Strange, but true, Miss Cumming visited Florida, in 1865, and meeting the father of young Hemming, who was a widower, they were married. She was still living, 1901, in Fredonia, New York, at about 80 years of age.

Another proclamation had been issued by General Dix revoking that part of his proclamation of the 14th, which directed the pursuit into Canada. It was as follows:

HEADQUARTERS, DEPARTMENT OF THE EAST,
New York City, December 17th, 1864.
General Orders No. 100.

The President of the United States having disapproved of THAT PORTION OF DEPARTMENT GENERAL ORDER No. 97, current series, which instructs military commanders on the frontier, in certain cases therein specified, TO CROSS THE BOUNDARY LINE BETWEEN THE UNITED STATES AND CANADA, AND DIRECTS PURSUIT INTO NEUTRAL TERRITORY, THE SAID INSTRUCTION IS HEREBY REVOKED.

In case, therefore, of any future marauding expedition into our territory from Canada, military commanders on the frontier will report to these headquarters for orders, BEFORE CROSSING THE BOUNDARY LINE IN PURSUIT OF GUILTY PARTIES.

By command of Major-General Dix:
D. T. VAN BUREN, Col. and A. A. G.
(Official)
CHARLES O. JOBIEL, Major and Aide-de-Camp.

CHAPTER XXXI

Situation in Canada and in the Confederacy—Sherman's march through Georgia and occupation of Savannah.

The ill-fated expedition to Buffalo and Dunkirk ended the active operations against the enemy by the "Raiders from Canada." The most of the Confederates began to depart for the South upon the advice of Colonel Thompson. None of us had ever been paid any wages in Canada. In fact, none were due except in Confederate money when we returned to the Confederacy. Colonel Thompson furnished money for expenses only in Canada and for the journey south.

All the negotiations for peace which had been entered into between Thompson, Clay, Holcomb and Sanders, of the South, and Greeley, Black, and others, for the North, had failed.

All the efforts of Confederates at Chicago, under Hines and Castleman, which promised so much, had failed.

The plan of Cole and Beall to capture the gunboat *Michigan,* which would have given the mastery of the Lakes to the Confederates, had failed.

The mission of the Confederates to New York City under Martin had failed.

The success of either of these undertakings it was believed would have ended the war.

The failures could only be attributed to the treachery of Godfrey J. Hyams who, as all now believed, had furnished full information of the plans, of every movement, to the United States authorities at Washington, or to their chief of detectives in Toronto.

Now many of our best men were in prison. Burley at Toronto. Cole at Sandusky. Young and his comrades at Montreal. Beall and Anderson in New York City.

Grenfel, Shenks, Marmaduke, Cantrill and Travers at Chicago, besides Walsh and Morris of the "Sons of Liberty," at Chicago; and Horton, McDonald, and others in New York.

It appeared that the Confederate Department in Canada was without practical purposes for a longer existence except to wind up its business and the protection of our friends who were in prison. Mr. Clay had been in Toronto a number of times in conference with Colonel Thompson in reference to the defense of our comrades who were in prison and some of them on trial, or awaiting trial, at Montreal.

Lieutenant Young and seven of his comrades had been arrested and arraigned in the Police Court at Montreal, November 7, for trial for extradition, upon the charge of robbery, to the authorities of Vermont, on the requisition of President Lincoln. A delay of thirty days had been granted to enable Young and his men to secure evidence from Richmond that they were Confederate soldiers and acting under orders from the Confederate Government in making the raid on St. Albans. When the case was next called, December 7, the police judge conceded that his court did not have jurisdiction and the prisoners were discharged. But a warrant was issued by the Superior Court for Young and his twenty men. Young and four others had been arrested and were now in prison.

Burley was on trial at Toronto for extradition to the United States on a requisition of President Lincoln.

Lieutenant S. B. Davis of Delaware had volunteered at Richmond to come through to Canada and bring a document from President Davis to Colonel Thompson, in which the President assumed all the responsibility for the expedition of Beall and Burley on Lake Erie, to be used in Burley's trial. Davis also brought a letter from the Secretary of the Navy, as follows:

CONFEDERATE STATES OF AMERICA,
NAVY DEPARTMENT,
Richmond, December 19, 1864.

Hon. J. THOMPSON, Toronto, C. W.

SIR: I have received your letter of the 28th ult., and in compliance with your request I inclose a duplicate of Acting Master Bennett G. Burley's appointment.

He was captured by the enemy in November last, and was confined in Fort Delaware as a prisoner of war. I have learned within a short time that he escaped from that place some time during the summer. The attention of the Federal authorities was called to his capture shortly after it occurred, and were informed, through our Agent of Exchange, that he was an officer in the Navy of the Confederate States.

I have sent through his friends here a duplicate of Acting Master Beall's appointment, which I trust will reach him. He is also an officer of the Navy.

Captain Cole is not an officer of the Navy, and as he is in confinement at Johnson's Island, he had better rely on his commission in the Army, and I have referred your letters to the Secretary of War, requesting him to send a duplicate of his commission, if he held one.

I am, respectfully,
Your obedient servant,
S. R. MALLORY,
Secretary of the Navy.

Lieutenant Davis was a young officer of the highest character in intelligence and daring. I met him several times during the few days he remained in Toronto. Colonel Thompson arranged with him to go through to Richmond and return with the certificates which would be needed in the trial of Lieutenant Young and the other prisoners at Montreal. Mr. Clay had found since the trial of Lieutenant Young began that he might himself be arrested upon a requisition from the United States for having authorized the raid upon St. Albans by Lieutenant Young and receiving the captured money as the agent of the Confederate States. It was deemed best that this proceeding should not occur. The Canadian Government was now in a panic and was willing to extradite Confederates upon a reasonable pretext through fear of the United States. In fact, the Confederates were exposing the Canadians to the bitter enmity of the United States. It was not because of any breach of the treaty but because the people along the border had discovered that the Confederates were in earnest and might do incalculable damage. The United States felt compelled to stop these incursions and the best means conceived was to threaten the Canadians. This was done with success. The Canadian Government not only voted $50,000 to the St. Albans banks, but the Queen's Counsel were chief attorneys for the United States against Lieutenant Young and his comrades. None of us felt comfortable in Canada at this time, although it seemed that a majority of the citizens were enthusiastic friends of the South.

In view of the apparent determination of the Canadian Government to influence the courts to surrender Confederates to the United States it was now Colonel Thompson's determination to stand by them to the bitter end.

While the attorneys of the United States were demanding proof from Richmond that Young and his men were Confederates, every possible effort was made to prevent a messenger from going to Richmond for the very papers that were demanded. Colonel Thompson despatched four different messengers on this errand in the interest of Young and his men. They all volunteered to go on the journey.

The leading Confederates who were at Chicago under Hines, for the operations on the day of the November election, did not return to Toronto. And most of those who had been there had departed for the Confederacy. The few who remained seldom appeared in public places. I still enjoyed life in the secluded cottage with Hemming and McDonald. But of evenings I generally mingled in the throng of skaters on Toronto Bay. This was to me the most delightful recreation in Canada.

The situation in the Confederacy was extremely gloomy. The failure of the campaign of General Hood in Tennessee had destroyed apparently the last hope of that ill-fated department. The army of General Lee was holding Richmond and Petersburg against the double numbers of General Grant's army, but General Hood had left General Sherman in Georgia without opposition. In his masterful position General Sherman threw off his mask and brought the war directly home to the non-combatants, beginning with the women and children of Atlanta.

MORE THAN A MONTH BEFORE LIEUTENANT YOUNG MADE THE RAID ON ST. ALBANS, VERMONT, General Sherman had ordered all the inhabitants to leave Atlanta. His order led to the following correspondence:

ATLANTA, GEORGIA, September 11, 1864.
Major-General W. T. SHERMAN.

SIR: We the undersigned, Mayor and two of the Council for the city of Atlanta, for the time being the only legal organ of the people of the said city, to express their wishes and wants, ask leave most earnestly but respectfully to petition you to reconsider the order requiring them to leave Atlanta.

* * * * * * *

Many poor women are in advanced state of pregnancy, others now having young children, and whose husbands for the greater part are either in the army, prisoners, or dead. Some say: "I have such a one sick at my house; who will wait on them while I am gone?" Others say: "What are we to do? We have no home to go to, and no means to buy, build, or rent any; no parents, relatives or friends, to go to." Another says: "I will take this or that article of property, but such and such things I must leave behind, though I need them much." We reply to them: "General Sherman will carry your property to Rough and Ready, and General Hood will take it thence on." And they will reply to that: "But I want to leave the railroad at such a place, and cannot get conveyances from there on."

We only refer to a few facts, to try to illustrate in part how this measure will operate in practice. As you advanced, the people north of this fell back; and before your arrival here, a large portion of the people had retired south, so that the country south of this is already crowded, and without houses enough to accommodate the people, and we are informed that many are now staying in churches and outbuildings.

This being so, how is it possible for the people still here (mostly women and children) to find any shelter? And how can they live through the winter in the woods—no shelter or subsistence, in the midst of strangers who know them not, and without the power to assist them much, if they were willing to do so?

This is but a feeble picture of the consequences of this measure. You know the woe, the horrors, and the suffering cannot be described by words; imagination can only conceive of it, and we ask you to take these things into consideration.

* * * * * * *

Respectfully submitted,
JAMES M. CALHOUN, Mayor,
E. E. RAWSON, Councilman,
S. C. WELLS, Councilman.

General Sherman replied as follows:

HEADQUARTERS MILITARY DIVISION OF THE MISSISSIPPI,
In the Field, Atlanta, Georgia, September 12, 1864.
JAMES M. CALHOUN, Mayor, E. E. RAWSON and S. C. WELLS,
representing City Council of Atlanta.

GENTLEMEN: I have your letter of the 11th, in the nature of a petition to revoke my orders removing all the inhabitants from Atlanta. I have read it carefully, and GIVE FULL CREDIT TO YOUR STATEMENTS OF THE DIS-TRESS THAT WILL BE OCCASIONED, AND YET SHALL NOT REVOKE MY ORDERS, BECAUSE THEY WERE NOT DESIGNED TO MEET THE HUMANI-TIES OF THE CASE, but to prepare for the future struggle in which millions of good people outside of Atlanta have a deep interest.

* * * * * * *

Now that war comes home to you, you feel very different. You deprecate its horrors, but did not feel them when you sent carloads of soldiers and ammunition, and moulded shells and shot, to carry war into Kentucky and Tennessee, to desolate the homes of hundreds and thousands of good people who only asked to live in peace at their homes, and under the Government of their inheritance. But these comparisons are idle.

* * * * * * *

NOW YOU MUST GO, AND TAKE WITH YOU THE OLD AND FEEBLE, FEED AND NURSE THEM, AND BUILD FOR THEM, IN MORE QUIET PLACES,

PROPER HABITATIONS TO SHIELD THEM AGAINST THE WEATHER UNTIL THE MAD PASSIONS OF MEN COOL DOWN, AND ALLOW THE UNION AND PEACE ONCE MORE TO SETTLE OVER YOUR OLD HOMES AT ATLANTA.

Yours in haste,

W. T. SHERMAN,
Major-General Commanding.

TEN DAYS BEFORE THE CONFEDERATES attempted to fire New York City, General Sherman burned Atlanta and started on his "March through Georgia."

The particulars were published in the newspapers, daily, of this "grand move through Georgia," but it will be fair to General Sherman and his army to let him tell the story of their operations. General Sherman left Atlanta in ruins and began his march on the 16th day of November, 1864, after issuing the following field order to his army.

(Special Field Orders, No. 120.)

HEADQUARTERS MILITARY DIVISION OF THE MISSISSIPPI,
In the Field, Kingston, Georgia, November 9, 1864.

*　*　*　*　*　*　*

The army will forage liberally on the country during the march.

*　*　*　*　*　*　*

TO CORPS COMMANDERS ALONE IS INTRUSTED THE POWER TO DESTROY MILLS, HOUSES, COTTON-GINS, ETC.; and for them this general principle is laid down: In districts and neighborhoods WHERE THE ARMY IS UNMOLESTED, no destruction of such property SHOULD BE PERMITTED; but should GUERRILLAS or BUSHWHACKERS MOLEST OUR MARCH, or SHOULD THE INHABITANTS BURN BRIDGES, OBSTRUCT ROADS, or OTHERWISE MANIFEST LOCAL HOSTILITY, the army commanders SHOULD ORDER AND ENFORCE A DEVASTATION MORE OR LESS RELENTLESS, according to the measure of SUCH HOSTILITY.

6. As for the horses, mules, wagons, etc., belonging to the inhabitants, the cavalry and artillery may appropriate freely

and without limit; discriminating, however, between the rich, who are usually hostile, and the poor and industrious, usually neutral or friendly.

* * * * * * *

By order of Major-General W. T. Sherman:

L. M. DAYTON, Aide-de-Camp.

General Sherman says in his "Memoirs":

McLaws's division was falling back before us, and we occasionally picked up a few of his men as prisoners, who insisted that we would meet with strong opposition at Savannah.

On the 8th, as I rode along, I found the column turned out of the main road, marching through fields. Close by, in the corner of a fence, was a group of men standing around a handsome young officer, whose foot had been blown to pieces by a torpedo planted in the road. He was waiting for a surgeon to amputate his leg, and told me he was riding along with the rest of his brigade-staff of the Seventeenth Corps, when a torpedo trodden on by his horse had exploded, killing the horse and literally blowing off all the flesh from one of his legs. I saw the terrible wound, and made full inquiry into the facts. There had been no RESISTANCE AT THAT POINT, NOTHING TO GIVE WARNING OF DANGER, AND THE REBELS HAD PLANTED EIGHT-INCH SHELLS IN THE ROAD, WITH FRICTION MATCHES TO EXPLODE THEM BY BEING TRODDEN ON. THIS WAS NOT WAR, BUT MURDER, AND IT MADE ME VERY ANGRY. I immediately ordered A LOT OF REBEL PRISONERS TO BE BROUGHT FROM THE PRO-VOST GUARD, ARMED WITH PICKS AND SPADES, AND MADE THEM MARCH IN CLOSE ORDER ALONG THE ROAD, SO AS TO EXPLODE THEIR OWN TORPEDOES, or to discover and dig them up. THEY BEGGED HARD, BUT I REITERATED THE ORDER, AND COULD HARDLY HELP LAUGHING AT THEIR STEPPING SO GINGERLY along the road, where it was supposed SUNKEN TORPEDOES MIGHT EX-PLODE AT EACH STEP, but they found no other torpedoes UNTIL NEAR FORT McALISTER.

At this time the following correspondence took place between General Sherman and General Halleck:

HEADQUARTERS OF THE ARMY,
Washington, December 18, 1864.
Maj.-Gen. W. T. SHERMAN, Savannah (via Hilton Head).

MY DEAR GENERAL: Yours of the 13th, by Major Anderson, is just received. I congratulate you on your splendid success, and shall very soon expect to hear of the crowning work of your campaign—the capture of Savannah. Your march will stand out prominently as the great one of this war. When Savannah falls, THEN FOR ANOTHER WIDE SWATH through the CENTER OF THE CONFEDERACY. BUT I WILL NOT ANTICIPATE. General Grant is expected here this morning, and will probably write you his own views.

*　*　*　*　*　*　*

Should you capture Charleston, I hope by some ACCIDENT the place may be destroyed, and if a little salt should be sown upon its site, it may prevent the growth of future crops of nullification and secession.

Yours truly,
H. W. HALLECK,
Major-General, Chief of Staff.

HEADQUARTERS MILITARY DIVISION OF THE MISSISSIPPI,
In the Field, Savannah, December 24, 1864.
Major-General H. W. HALLECK, Chief-of-Staff, Washington, D. C.

GENERAL: * * * To be sure, Jeff. Davis has his people under pretty good discipline, but I think faith in him is much shaken in Georgia, and BEFORE WE HAVE DONE WITH HER SOUTH CAROLINA WILL NOT BE QUITE SO TEMPESTUOUS.

I WILL BEAR IN MIND your hint as to Charleston, and do not think "SALT" will be necessary. When I move, the Fifteenth Corps will be on the right of the right wing, and their position will naturally bring them into Charleston first; and, if you have MARKED THE HISTORY OF THAT CORPS, you will have remarked that they generally DO THEIR WORK PRETTY WELL. THE TRUTH IS, THE WHOLE ARMY IS BURNING WITH AN INSATIABLE DESIRE TO WREAK VENGEANCE UPON SOUTH CAROLINA. I ALMOST TREMBLE AT HER FATE, BUT FEEL THAT SHE DESERVES ALL THAT SEEMS IN STORE FOR HER. Many and many a person in Georgia asked me why we did not go to South Carolina, and, when I answered that we were en route for that State, the invariable reply was, "Well, if you will make those people feel the utmost severities of war, we will pardon you for your desolation of Georgia."

I LOOK UPON COLUMBIA as quite as bad as Charleston, and I doubt if we will spare the public buildings there as we did at Milledgeville.

W. T. SHERMAN,

Major-General.

General Sherman says further:

The truth is fully given in an original letter of President Lincoln, which I received at Savannah, Georgia, and have at this instant before me, every word of which is in his own familiar handwriting. It is dated—

"WASHINGTON, December 26, 1864.

*   *   *   *   *   *   *

"WHEN YOU WERE ABOUT LEAVING ATLANTA FOR THE ATLANTIC COAST, I was anxious, if not fearful; but, feeling that you were the better judge, and remembering 'nothing risked, nothing gained,' I did not interfere. Now, the undertaking BEING A SUCCESS, THE HONOR IS ALL YOURS; for I believe NONE OF US went further than to ACQUIESCE; and, taking the work of General Thomas into account, as it should be taken, it is indeed a great success. Not only does it afford the obvious and immediate military advantages, but, in showing to the world that your army could be divided, PUTTING THE STRONGER PART TO AN IMPORTANT NEW SERVICE, and yet leaving enough to vanquish the old opposing force of the whole, Hood's army, it brings those who sat in darkness to see a great light. BUT WHAT NEXT? I SUPPOSE IT WILL BE SAFER IF I LEAVE GENERAL GRANT AND YOURSELF TO DECIDE.

"A. LINCOLN."

Apart from the "grand move" of General Sherman there was a reign of terror and scenes of devastation and pillage on a smaller scale in all parts of the Confederacy where Federal troops occupied the country. A few insertions are given that indicate the Federal policy, though hundreds might be quoted. The newspapers were full of accounts of the operations and the people and soldiers of both sections were perfectly familiar with the facts at the time the incidents occurred.

But only the orders and reports of the most prominent officers of the Federal army are given as follows:

HEADQUARTERS IN THE FIELD,
Monocacy, Md., August 5, 1864.

Maj.-Gen. D. HUNTER,
Commanding Department of West Virginia.

GENERAL: Concentrate all your available forces without delay in the vicinity of Harper's Ferry.

*   *   *   *   *   *

In pushing up the Shenandoah Valley, as it is expected you will have to go first or last, it is desirable that NOTHING SHOULD BE LEFT to invite the enemy to return. Take all provisions, forage, and stock wanted for the use of your command; such as cannot be consumed, destroy. It is not desirable that buildings should be destroyed, they should rather be protected, but the people should be informed that so long as any army can subsist among them recurrences of these raids must be expected and we are determined to stop them at all hazards * * * giving regular vouchers for such as may be taken from loyal citizens.

Very respectfully,
U. S. GRANT,
Lieutenant-General.

BERRYVILLE, VA., August 17, 1864.

Lieut.-Gen. U. S. GRANT,
Commanding Armies of the United States:
All despatches have been received.

*   *   *   *   *   *   *

The cavalry engagement in front of Front Royal was splendid; it was on open ground. The saber was freely used by our men.

*   *   *   *   *   *   *

Mosby has annoyed me and captured a few wagons. We hung one and shot six of his men yesterday. I have burned all wheat and hay, and brought off all stock, sheep, cattle, horses, etc., south of Winchester.

P. H. SHERIDAN,
Major-General.

CITY POINT, VA., August 26, 1864,
2.30 P. M.
Major-General SHERIDAN,
Halltown, Va.:

* * * * * * *

Do all the damage to railroads and crops you can. Carry off stock of all descriptions, and negroes, so as to prevent further planting. If the war is to last another year we want the Shenandoah Valley *to remain a barren waste*.

U. S. GRANT,
Lieutenant-General.

CEDAR CREEK, October 11, 1864,
7 P. M.

* * * * * * *

Lieutenant-Colonel Tolles, my Chief Quartermaster and Assistant Surgeon; Emil Ohlenschlauger, Medical Director on my staff, were both mortally wounded by guerrillas to-day on their way to join me from Winchester; they were ambuscaded. Three men were killed and five wounded out of an escort of twenty-four.

The refugees from Early's army, cavalry and infantry, are organizing guerrilla parties and are becoming very formidable and are annoying me very much. I KNOW OF NO WAY TO EXTERMINATE THEM EXCEPT TO BURN OUT THE WHOLE COUNTRY and let the people go north or south. If I attempt to capture them by sending out parties, they escape to the mountains on fleet horses.

P. H. SHERIDAN,
Major-General.

Report of property captured and destroyed, Major-General Sheridan commanding, during the campaign commencing August 10, 1864, and ending November 16, 1864:

Horses	3,772	Wheat (bushels)	435,802
Mules	545	Oats (bushels)	20,000
Flour Mills	71	Corn (bushels)	77,017
Woolen Mill	1	Flour (barrels)	874
Saw Mills	8	Hay (tons)	20,397
Barns	1,200	Fodder (tons)	500
Furnaces	7	Straw (tons)	450
Tanneries	4	Beef Cattle	10,918

Calves	250	Bacon and Hams (lbs.)	12,000
Sheep	12,000	Potatoes (bushels)....	2,500
Swine	15,000		

*   *   *   *   *   *   *

P. H. SHERIDAN,
Major-General U. S. Army, Commanding.

The operations of General Sheridan were the occasion of a letter of thanks as follows:

EXECUTIVE MANSION, Washington, October 22, 1864.
Major-General SHERIDAN:
With great pleasure I tender to you and your brave army, the thanks of the Nation, and my own personal admiration and gratitude, for the *month's operations* in the Shenandoah Valley, and especially for the splendid work of October 19, 1864.
Your obedient servant,
ABRAHAM LINCOLN.

CHAPTER XXXII

Trials of Confederates in progress—Lieut. S. B. Davis captured—Bennett G. Burley ordered to be extradited to United States—Colonel Thompson writes to Confederate minister in England—British Government interferes and saves Burley—Ashbrook and Kennedy depart for the Confederacy—Lieutenant Davis sentenced to be hung—Colonel Thompson appeals to President Lincoln and Secretary of War Stanton on merits of the case—Successful proceedings in behalf of Davis—Capture, trial and execution of Kennedy.

The trial of John Yates Beall was now in progress before a military commission in New York City; also that of Bennett G. Burley before the Recorder at Toronto; and that of Lieutenant Bennett H. Young and others at Montreal.

A sensational despatch was published in the morning papers at Toronto, on the 15th of January, 1865, announcing that Lieut. S. B. Davis, en route from Toronto to Richmond, had been captured at Newark, Ohio. He was searched and his despatches from Colonel Thompson to the authorities at Richmond were found. Under these circumstances Davis confessed that he was an officer in the Confederate Army and explained his presence in Ohio. He was sent to Cincinnati to be tried by court martial.

The trial of Acting Master Bennett G. Burley ended by a decision of the Recorder, at Toronto, that while Burley was a Confederate officer and that the Confederate Government assumed all responsibility, yet that Burley was guilty of unlawful warfare on Lake Erie. It was therefore ordered by the Recorder that Burley should be surrendered to the authorities of the United States. An appeal was taken to the Supreme Court of Canada, which sustained the Recorder, but meanwhile Colonel Thompson had written the following letter to the Confederate Minister in England:

TORONTO, CANADA WEST,
January 21, 1865.
Hon. JAMES M. MASON, Minister C. S. A., London.

SIR: Inclosed I send you copies of the evidence in the case of Acting Master Bennett G. Burley, and the judgment of the Recorder of this city as committing magistrate. I think you will agree with me that in this case not only is a great outrage about to be perpetrated on a citizen, but a great wrong is to be done and an insult offered to the Confederate States. You will observe that in the United States Burley is charged with piracy; in the proceedings in Canada he is charged with robbery. Burley is admitted on all hands to have been a belligerent, and he was engaged in a warlike expedition under the order of the Confederate Government. While the Recorder admits him to have acted in this character, yet while so acting he did an act not considered by the Recorder justified by the usages and practices of war. I wish to call the attention of the proper authorities of England to this case, and, if possible, induce them to instruct the Governor-General of Canada, by whom alone Burley can be extradited, to withhold this warrant of extradition. You will perceive by the manifesto of the President "that the Government of the Confederate States of America assumes the responsibility of answering for the acts and conduct of any of its officers engaged in said expedition, and especially of the said Bennett G. Burley." In the event of a refusal to interfere and release the said Burley, I hope you will protest in the name of the Confederate States against his extradition. If you will refer to the history of the extradition treaty, you will observe that President Tyler expressly excludes from its application all such cases as the present. (See message of 1842, communicating treaty to the Senate.) The parties deny having violated the neutrality laws of Great Britain, and are perfectly willing to be tried on such a charge, and abide the issue. Let me hear from you as soon as possible. Mr. Cameron, our counsel in the case, believes the matter of extradition can be put off until the Imperial Government shall have an opportunity to be heard from.

I am, with great respect,
Your obedient servant,
J. THOMPSON,
Commissioner C. S. A.

While Mr. Mason had not been received officially as the Confederate Minister, yet his representations and presentation of the record of the trial resulted in an order from the

British Government to the Governor-General of Canada to hold up the delivery of Bennett G. Burley to the United States. After an investigation by the British authorities, Burley was set free in Canada.

It seemed almost impossible now for a Confederate to leave Canada for the South without being followed by detectives, as Davis had been; but Lieut. John T. Ashbrook and Capt. Robert Cobb Kennedy, the last of our friends to go, concluded to attempt the journey to the Confederacy. They bade us good-by and left on the Grand Trunk Railway, going west to Lake St. Clair, and crossed over to St. Clair station in Michigan, where they connected with a train going southward and west of Detroit. They started on the trip through Michigan in the early part of the night. The weather was extremely cold and a deep snow covered the ground. In entering the coach Kennedy and Ashbrook were unable to find seats together. Kennedy took the first vacant seat on entering the car while Ashbrook went on and finally found one near the front end of the car and next to the window. They had traveled for about an hour when Ashbrook looking back observed two men enter the rear door and go straight to Kennedy. Without saying a word they seized him by each arm and made him a prisoner, as Ashbrook could see. There was some confusion among the passengers in adjacent seats though none got up. Kennedy submitted without a struggle. There was nothing else to do. Ashbrook could not afford to await events. The two men had pistols drawn. One of them looked forward a moment as if to locate him. He decided not to wait for any one to come in at his end of the car. It did not appear that he could successfully go to the rescue of Kennedy; and the question was as to how he could escape without risking an exit out of the front door, where he might expect to meet opposition from that direction. He raised his window-sash, put one leg out, ducked his head and out he went in the darkness. Although the train was flying fortune favored Ashbrook. He fell upon the side of an embankment in the snow and rolled down into a ditch. When he got up he found that he had not sustained any injury whatever. He had alighted on his side as he aimed to do. The train sped away leaving him in the darkness, but he was greatly relieved to escape alive and sound. Still he must immediately find a highway where his tracks would be erased before morning or before pursuers would find his trail. He succeeded, before walking far, in reaching a farm-house, and early next morning was conveyed across the country to a station on another railroad, where he caught a train and reached Cincinnati in safety. Here he found friends and readily made his way across Kentucky to the Confederacy.

The two men who arrested Kennedy were United States detectives who had gone all the way from Toronto with Ashbrook and Kennedy. And except for the hasty exit of Ashbrook his arrest would have followed in a few minutes by others from a forward coach who had been telegraphed to come on board in Michigan.

Meanwhile, Lieutenant Davis was tried by court martial at Cincinnati, declared to be guilty as a spy, and was ordered to be hung on the 17th day of February, at Johnson's Island.

Colonel Thompson addressed a letter to President Lincoln in behalf of Lieutenant Davis as follows:

TORONTO, CANADA, February 2, 1865.

To His Excellency, A. LINCOLN, President of the United States.

SIR: The telegraph announces that Lieut. S. B. Davis, identified at Newark, Ohio, confessed, on his arrest, to being the bearer of important despatches from Richmond to Canada, has been sentenced to be hung at Johnson's Island on the 17th of February. Another paper states that Lieutenant Davis has been condemned as a spy. This young man's life is in your hands, and I hope you will allow me to discharge a duty I owe to you, to myself, to Lieutenant Davis, to justice, and to humanity, to demonstrate fully the facts in the case, so far as they are known to me, on honor.

Lieutenant Davis is a citizen of the State of Delaware, and has been for some time an officer in the Confederate service.

No braver or truer soldier can be found in either army. He is a gentleman of education, true in all his transactions, and beloved and respected by all who know him. In the trial of Acting Master Bennett G. Burley, a case for extradition, the Recorder at Toronto has postponed the investigation for thirty days to enable the accused to obtain certain documentary evidence deemed important to his defense, from Richmond. The Government at Richmond was duly informed of this. Mr. Burley's counsel deemed these documents essential, and Lieutenant Davis volunteered to bring them to Canada. As he was pressed for time, he came direct through the United States and reached here in six days, which was regarded a most expeditious trip. It was impossible for him on this trip to have acted the spy in any sense of that term. He remained here but three days in all. Lieutenant Davis was directed to return by the most certain route to Richmond, with all possible despatch, in order that the authorities might furnish the documents asked for by the counsel of the accused. The whole object and aim of his coming here was to obtain the proofs deemed necessary to secure the administering of justice to his former companion in arms. As I received the despatches he brought and wrote those he carried, I know every word in them, and as every word related to the case then undergoing judicial investigation, there could have been no objection to your reading them; hence I know that, however much you may desire to crush out the Confederate States Government, it must be repugnant to your sense of right and justice and humanity to pursue individuals with unnecessary harshness. When Lieutenant Davis was arrested he was on the very route he had advised me he would take in order to avoid all contact with the military authorities. He was expecting to gain no information with respect to the movements of your armies, nor do I believe he sought to do so. As a private citizen speaking to one clothed with authority, I ask you to spare this young man's life, not from any favor to me, but for the sake of justice, humanity, and all the conditions which control intercourse between hostile people. You have a right to retain him as a prisoner of war, but I declare on honor he is not a spy.

Very respectfully yours,

(Signed.)   JACOB THOMPSON.

He also wrote a similar letter to Hon. E. M. Stanton, Secretary of War of the United States. The letter to Stanton contained some reference to the past. Thompson and Stanton had served together in the Cabinet of President James Buchanan. Davis was saved and finally set at liberty.

Captain Kennedy was forwarded to New York City, where he was imprisoned in Fort Lafayette. His trial by military commission was promptly held. I am unable to present the names or testimony of the witnesses but give the result as follows:

HEADQUARTERS DEPARTMENT OF THE EAST,
New York City, March 20, 1865.

General Orders No. 24.

I. Before a military commission, which convened at Fort Lafayette, New York Harbor, and at New York City, by virtue of Special Orders, No. 14, current series, from these headquarters, of January 17, 1865, and of which Brig.-Gen. Fitz-Henry Warren, U. S. Volunteers, is president, was arraigned and tried:

ROBERT C. KENNEDY.

Charge 1. Acting as a spy.

Specification 1.—In this, that Robert C. Kennedy, a captain in the military service of the insurgent States, was found acting as a spy in the city of New York, in the State of New York, on or about the 1st day of November, 1864.

Specification 2.—In this, that Robert C. Kennedy, a captain in the military service of the insurgent States, was found acting as a spy in the city of Detroit, in the State of Michigan, on or about the 29th day of December, 1864.

Charge 2. Violation of the laws of war.

Specification.—In this, that Robert C. Kennedy, a captain in the military service of the insurgent States, undertook to carry on irregular and unlawful warfare in the city and State of New York, and in the execution of said undertaking attempted to burn and destroy said city of New York by setting fire thereto. All this in said city of New York on or about the 25th day of November, 1864.

To which charges and specifications the accused pleaded not guilty.

The verdict was guilty on all the charges.

SENTENCE.

And thereupon the commission sentence him, said Robert C. Kennedy, captain in the military service of the insurgent States, to be hanged by the neck until dead, at such time and place as the general in command of the department may direct, two-thirds of the members concurring therein.

II. The major-general commanding approves the proceedings, finding, and sentence of the court. It is shown by the testimony:

1. That the accused has been an officer in the service of the insurgent States since August, 1861.

2. That he was in the city of New York in disguise, and under a false name, in the month of November, several weeks immediately preceding the attempt to set the city on fire.

3. That he was here for a purpose which he refused to disclose, and that he returned hastily by night to Canada.

4. That he stated in the presence of several persons that he set fire to Barnum's Museum and to one of the "down-town" hotels.

5. That he was arrested at Detroit in disguise, armed with a revolver, traveling under a false name, and with a passport representing himself to be a loyal citizen.

On proof of these facts he was convicted of acting as a spy and carrying on irregular and illegal warfare. The person who testified to his confession of having set on fire Barnum's Museum and one of the hotels in the lower part of the city was not under duress or an accomplice, was a reluctant witness, and could have had no motive to make a false statement. He is corroborated by other testimony.

The attempt to set fire to the city of New York is one of the greatest atrocities of the age. There is nothing in the annals of barbarism which evinces greater vindictiveness. It was not a mere attempt to destroy the city, but to set fire to crowded hotels and places of public resort, in order to secure the greatest possible destruction of human life. The evidence shows that Barnum's Museum and ten hotels were fired on the evening of the 25th of November, the fires in most of them breaking out in quick succession, and indicating not only deliberate and complex design and concert on the part of the incendiaries, but a cool calculation to create so many conflagrations at the same time as to baffle the efforts of the fire department to extinguish them. In all the buildings fired, not only non-combatant men, but women and children, were congregated in great numbers, and nothing but the most diabolical spirit of revenge could have impelled the incendiaries to act so revoltingly.

The participation of the accused in this inhuman enterprise is a crime, which follows him, and his liability to answer for it is not to be cast off by withdrawing for a time from the jurisdiction within which it was committed. He has not only been guilty of carrying on irregular warfare, in violation of the usages of civilized States in the conduct of war, but he has, by outraging every principle of humanity, incurred the highest penalty known to the law.

His escape to Canada was followed in a few days by his return to the United States, again in disguise, with a new name, and personating a loyal citizen, while holding a commission in the service of the insurgents, thus furnishing the highest *prima facie* evidence that he was acting as a spy. No rebutting evidence was produced on the trial, although it continued twenty-three days, of which fifteen were given to the accused, by adjournments, to procure testimony and prepare his defense. Two papers were read as a part of his address to the court—one a pledge given to the transportation agent in Canada to return with all due diligence "to the Confederacy," and the other a certificate made by him that he was a citizen of the State of Louisiana, with a request that he might be provided with means to return "to the Confederacy." Admitting their genuineness, they do not repel the presumption raised by the circumstances attending his arrest—the disguise and the false pretenses with which he was found within our lines. His flight to Canada was not a return within the lines of his own army. If he had found his way back to the insurgent States and had been subsequently captured in battle he could not have been convicted under the first specification of the first charge. But neither of these facts exist to remove or terminate his liability to conviction under that specification.

Whatever question may exist as to the effect of his return to Canada after having lurked as a spy, as charged in the first specification, no such question can arise as to his guilt as a spy, as charged in the second specification, which sets forth an offense entirely distinct from the first, of which he has been convicted on full proof.

The major-general commanding considers his duty as clear in this case as that of Beall. The lives, the property, the domestic security of non-combatant citizens must be protected against all invasion not in strict accordance with the laws and usages of civilized States in the conduct of war. Crimes which outrage and shock the moral sense by their atrocity must not only be punished and the perpetrators deprived of the power of repeating them, but the sternest condemnation of the law must be presented to others to deter them from the commission of similar enormities.

Robert C. Kennedy will be hanged by the neck till he is dead at Fort Lafayette, New York Harbor, on Saturday, the 25th day of March, instant, between the hours of 12 noon and 2 in the afternoon.

The commanding officer of Fort Lafayette is charged with the execution of this order.

By command of Major-General Dix:

D. T. Van Buren,
Colonel and Assistant Adjutant-General.

It appears that Captain Kennedy made a confession on the early morning of the day of his execution which is reported by the Federal authorities as follows:

Fort Lafayette, March 25, 1865.—6 a. m.
Major-General Dix,
Headquarters Department of the East, New York.

Sir: I have the honor to report that last night, about half after 10 o'clock, I visited Kennedy, taking with me Mr. Howard, of the *New York Times.* After some conversation relative to the matter for which he has been sentenced, he made the following confession. He requested that I would make no use of his confession to his detriment, in case a respite or reprieve should be received.

* * * * * * *

I have the honor to remain, respectfully,
Your obedient servant,
Martin Burke,
Lieutenant-Colonel, Commanding.

"Confession of Robert C. Kennedy.

"After my escape from Johnson's Island I went to Canada, where I met a number of Confederates. They asked me if I was willing to go on an expedition. I replied, 'Yes, if it is in the service of my country.' They said, 'It's all right,' but gave no intimation of its nature, nor did I ask for any. I was then sent to New York, where I stayed some time. There were eight men in our party, of whom two fled to Canada. After we had been in New York three weeks we were told that the object of the expedition was to retaliate on the North for the atrocities in the Shenandoah Valley. It was designed to set fire to the city on the night of the Presidential election, but the phosphorus was not ready and it was put off until the 25th of November. I was stopping at the Belmont House, but moved into Prince street. I set fire to four places—Barnum's Museum, Lovejoy's Hotel, Tammany Hotel, and the New England House. The others only started fires in the house where each was lodging and then ran off. Had they all done as I did we would have had thirty-two fires and played a huge joke on the fire department. I know that I am to be hung for setting fire to Barnum's Museum, but that was only a joke. I had no idea of doing it. I had been drinking and went in there with a friend, and just to scare the people, I emptied a bottle of phosphorus on the floor. We knew it wouldn't set fire to the wood, for we had tried it before, and at one time concluded to give the whole thing up.

"There was no fiendishness about it. After setting fire to my four places I walked the streets all night and went to the Exchange Hotel early in the morning. We all met there that morning and the next night. My friend and I had rooms there, but we sat in the office nearly all the time reading the papers, while we were watched by the detectives, of whom the hotel was full. I expected to die then, and if I had it would have been all right; but now it seems rather hard. I escaped to Canada, and was glad enough when I crossed the bridge in safety.

"I desired, however, to return to my command, and started with my friend for the Confederacy via Detroit. Just before entering the city he received an intimation that the detectives were on the lookout for us, and, giving me a signal, he jumped from the cars. I didn't notice the signal, but kept on and was arrested in the depot.

"I wish to say that killing women and children was the last thing thought of. We wanted to let the people of the North understand that there are two sides to this war, and that they can't be rolling in wealth and comfort while we at the South are bearing all the hardships and privations.

"In retaliation for Sheridan's atrocities in the Shenandoah Valley we desired to destroy property, not the lives of women and children, although that would of course have followed in its train.

"Done in the presence of Lieutenant-Colonel Burke."

Under date of March 25, 1865, Lieut.-Col. Martin Burke reported to Gen. John A. Dix the execution of Kennedy.

Captain Robert Cobb Kennedy was related to the Cobb family of Georgia. His home was in Louisiana. I supposed him to be at the time of his death about 26 years old. He possessed all the attributes of a gentleman, and was sincere, true, intelligent, and absolutely fearless.

CHAPTER XXXIII

Operations of General Sherman in South Carolina, and General
Hunter in Virginia—General Early retaliates in Pennsylvania.

In the mean time, General Sherman had begun his march
into South Carolina, having started from Savannah on the
19th of January. It was uncertain at first whether he would
go through the center or not. We all believed he would go
direct to Charleston.

General Sherman says:

I determined to go in person to Pocotaligo, and there act as
though we were bound for Charleston. On the 24th of January
I started from Beaufort with part of my staff, leaving the rest
to follow at leisure, rode across the island to a pontoon-bridge
that spanned the channel between it and the mainland, and
thence rode by Garden's Corners to a plantation not far from
Pocotaligo, occupied by General Blair. There we found a
house, with a majestic avenue of live-oaks, whose limbs had
been cut away by the troops for firewood, and desolation marked
one of those splendid South Carolina estates where the proprie-
tors formerly had dispensed a hospitality that distinguished the
old regime of that proud State. I slept on the floor of the house,
but the night was so bitter cold that I got up by the fire several
times, and when it burned low I rekindled it with an old mantel-
clock and the wreck of a bedstead which stood in a corner of the
room—the only act of vandalism that I recall done by myself
personally during the war.

* * * * * * *

We therefore rested quietly about Pocotaligo, collecting stores
and making final preparations until the 1st of February.

* * * * * * *

Across the Congaree River lay the city of Columbia, in plain,
easy view. I could see the unfinished State-House, and the
ruins of the railroad depot, which were still smouldering.
Occasionally a few citizens or cavalry could be seen running

across the streets, and quite a number of negroes were seemingly busy in carrying off bags of grain or meal, which were piled up near the burned depot.

Captain De Gres had a section of his twenty-pound Parrott guns unlimbered, firing into the town. I asked him what he was firing for; he said he could see some rebel cavalry occasionally at the intersection of the streets, and he had an idea that there was a large force of infantry concealed on the opposite bank, lying low, in case we should attempt to cross over directly into the town. I instructed him not to fire any more into the town, but consented to his bursting a few shells near the depot, to scare away the negroes who were appropriating the bags of corn and meal which we wanted, also to fire three shots at the unoccupied State-House. I stood by and saw these fired, and then all firing ceased. Although this matter of firing into Columbia has been the subject of much abuse and investigation, I have yet to hear of any single person having been killed in Columbia by our cannon.

In this connection it may not be amiss to make a correction and insert an account of one casualty which doubtless escaped the attention of General Sherman during his sojourn in Columbia. It is as follows:

*The Executive Mansion of the State of South Carolina, situated at Columbia, is a quaint structure of stone. The old house is spacious and well built, and has many noble chambers, among them a banquet hall and a great reception or ball-room. It has been the scene of many important political, and of some splendid social gatherings. It has also been the scene of one tragedy which occurred during the latter part of the war, when the Northern forces across the Congaree River were shelling Columbia. This tragedy was the marriage of Anne Pickens, the daughter of Governor Francis W. Pickens, to Lieutenant Le Rochelle, and the death of the bride which followed immediately after the ceremony.

On the afternoon preceding the evening of the marriage, the Northern army began shelling Columbia, but preparations for the wedding continued. Finally the guests were all assembled and the mansion was ablaze with light, fragrant with flowers and joyous with music, although the occasional dull whirr of a

_____

*Ladies' Home Journal, October, 1900, by Mrs. Thaddeus Horton.

cannon ball kept the company aware that danger was not far off. The clergyman stood beneath the chandelier and in the white robe of his office. The groom in his regimentals, and the bride, tall and stately, fair and lovely in her snowy bridal gown, walked into the crowded chamber and paused before him.

The clergyman was proceeding with the solemn ceremony, and had just joined the right hands of the happy pair when, suddenly, there was an awful crash, and a ball from the enemy's cannon penetrated the mansion and burst in the middle of the marriage chamber, scattering its death-dealing missiles in every direction. There were screams and heartrending groans; mirrors crashed; the house shook; women fainted; and walls rocked to and fro.

When the first confusion was over it was discovered that in all the crowd only one person was injured, and that was the bride herself. She lay partly on the floor and partly in her lover's arms, crushed and bleeding, pale but very beautiful, her bridal gown drenched with warm blood, and a great cut in her breast. Laying her on a lounge the frantic bridegroom besought her by every term of tenderness and endearment to allow the ceremony to proceed, to which she weakly gave consent, and lying like a crushed flower, no less white than the camelias of her bridal bouquet, her breath coming in sharp gasps, and the blood flowing from this great, angry wound, she murmured "yes" to the clergyman, and received her husband's first kiss. A moment more and all was over.

Annie Pickens Le Rochelle was laid to rest under the magnolias, and the heartbroken bridegroom, reckless with despair, returned to his regiment.

General Sherman continued:

I sat with General Howard on a log, watching the men lay this bridge; and about 9 or 10 a. m., a messenger came from Colonel Stone on the other side, saying that the Mayor of Columbia had come out of the city to surrender the place, and asking for orders. I simply remarked to General Howard that he had his orders, to let Colonel Stone go on into the city, and that we would follow as soon as the bridge was ready.

* * * * * * *

Having walked over much of the suburbs of Columbia in the afternoon, and being tired, I lay down on a bed in Blanton Duncan's house to rest. Soon after dark I became conscious that a bright light was shining on the walls; and calling some one of my staff (Major Nichols, I think) to inquire the cause, he said there seemed to be a house on fire down about the market house. The same high wind still prevailed, and, FEARING THE CONSEQUENCES, I bade him go in person to see if the PROVOST-GUARD WAS DOING ITS DUTY. * * * Fortunately, about 3 or 4 a. m., the wind moderated, and gradually the fire was got under control; but it had burned out the very heart of the city, embracing several churches, the old State-House, and the school or asylum of that very Sister of Charity who had appealed for my personal protection. Nickerson's Hotel, in which several of my staff were quartered, was burned down, but the houses occupied by myself, Generals Howard and Logan, were not burned at all. Many of the people thought that this fire was deliberately planned and executed. This is not true.

* * * * * * *

Having utterly ruined Columbia, the right wing began its march northward, toward Winnsboro, on the 20th, which we reached on the 21st, and found General Slocum, with the left wing, who had come by way of Alston.

* * * * * * *

General Sherman, for ten years after the war, left those who idolized his character to believe and circulate the accusation that General Wade Hampton had set fire to Columbia or had it done when his last troops evacuated the city, but now General Sherman says:

IN MY OFFICIAL REPORT OF THIS CONFLAGRA-
TION, I DISTINCTLY CHARGED IT TO GEN. WADE
HAMPTON, AND CONFESS I DID SO POINTEDLY,
TO SHAKE THE FAITH OF HIS PEOPLE IN HIM, ETC.

Major-General Henry W. Slocum, commanding a corps of Sherman's army on the "grand move," was a witness of the burning of Columbia. He says:

During the night of February 17th the greater portion of the city of Columbia was burned. The lurid flames could easily be seen from my camp, many miles distant. Nearly all the public buildings, several churches, an orphan asylum, and many of the residences were destroyed. The city was filled with helpless women and children and invalids, many of whom were rendered houseless and homeless in a single night. No sadder scene was presented during the war. The suffering of so many helpless and innocent persons could not but move the hardest heart. The question as to who was immediately responsible for this disaster has given rise to some controversy. I do not believe that General Sherman countenanced or was in any degree responsible for it. I believe the immediate cause of the disaster was a free use of whisky (which was supplied to the soldiers by citizens with great liberality). A drunken soldier with a musket in one hand and a match in the other is not a pleasant visitor to have about the house on a dark, windy night.

General Sherman in an effort to defeat the payment of a claim for damages by writing a letter to the United States Senate, in April, 1866, charged the burning of Columbia upon the citizens and General Wade Hampton. Here is General Hampton's exposure nine years before the confession of General Sherman:

WILD WOODS, MISSISSIPPI, April 21, 1866.
To Hon. REVERDY JOHNSON, United States Senate.
    SIR: A few days ago I saw in the published proceedings of Congress that a petition from Benjamin Kawles, of Columbia, South Carolina, asking for compensation for the destruction of his house by the Federal army, in February, 1865, had been presented to the Senate, accompanied by a letter from Major-General Sherman. In this letter General Sherman uses the following language: "The citizens of Columbia set fire to thousands of bales of cotton rolled out into the streets, and which were burning before we entered Columbia; I, myself, was in the city as early as nine o'clock, and I saw these fires, and knew that efforts were made to extinguish them, but a high and strong wind prevented. I gave no orders for the burning of your city, but, on the contrary, the conflagration resulted from the great imprudence of cutting the cotton bales, whereby the contents were spread to the wind, so that it became an impossibility to arrest the fire. I saw in your Columbia newspaper the printed order of Gen. Wade Hampton, that on the approach of the Yankee army all the cotton should thus be burned, and, from what I saw myself, I have no hesitation in saying that he was the cause of the destruction of your city."

* * * * * * *

I deny, emphatically, that any cotton was fired in Columbia by my order. I deny that citizens "set fire to thousands of bales rolled out into streets." I deny that any cotton was on fire when the Federal troops entered the city. I most respectfully ask of Congress to appoint a committee, charged with the duty of ascertaining and reporting all the facts connected with the destruction of Columbia, and thus fixing upon the proper author of that enormous crime the infamy he richly deserves. I am willing to submit the case to any honest tribunal. Before any such I pledge myself to prove that I gave a positive order, by direction of General Beauregard, that no cotton should be fired; that not one bale was on fire when General Sherman's troops took possession of the city; that he promised protection to the city, and that, in spite of his solemn promise, he burned the city to the ground, deliberately, systematically, and atrociously. * * * Trusting that you will pardon me for troubling you, I am, very respectfully,

Your obedient servant,
WADE HAMPTON.

It will now not be unfair to submit the story of the warfare carried on by the Federals in the Southern States, which was perfectly familiar, at all periods, to the soldiers of the South and to the Confederate Government. The people of the North who applauded the war upon the South derived their chief comfort from the miseries of its inhabitants.

Alexander H. Stephens says:

I refer not only to the general sacking of private houses—the pillaging of money, plate, jewels, and works of art, paintings, pictures, private manuscripts and family relics; but I allude, besides these things, especially to the hostile acts directly against property of all kinds, as well as outrages upon non-combatants— to the laying waste of whole sections of country; the attempted annihilation of all the necessaries of life; to the wanton killing, in many instances, of farm stock and domestic animals; the burning of mills, factories and barns, with their contents of grain and forage, not sparing orchards or growing crops, or the implements of husbandry; the mutilation of county and municipal records of great value; the extraordinary efforts made to stir up servile insurrections, involving the widespread slaughter of women and children; the impious profanation of temples of worship, and even the brutish desecration of the sanctuaries of the dead.

*　*　*　*　*　*　*

On June 19, 1864, Major-General Hunter began his retreat from before Lynchburg down the Shenandoah Valley. Lieutenant-General Early, who followed in pursuit, thus describes the destruction he witnessed along the route:

Houses had been burned, and helpless women and children left without shelter. The country had been stripped of provisions, and many families left without a morsel to eat. Furniture and bedding had been cut to pieces, and old men and women and children robbed of all the clothing they had, except that on their backs. Ladies' trunks had been rifled, and their dresses torn to pieces in mere wantonness. Even the negro girls had lost their little finery. At Lexington he had burned the military institute with all its contents, including its library and scientific apparatus. Washington College had been plundered, and the statue of Washington stolen. The residence of ex-Governor Letcher at that place had been burned by orders, and but a few minutes given Mrs. Letcher and her family to leave the house. In the county a most excellent Christian gentleman, a Mr. Creigh, had been hung, because, on a former occasion, he had killed a straggling and marauding Federal soldier while in the act of insulting and outraging the ladies of his family.

*　*　*　*　*　*　*

While at Martinsburg it was ascertained beyond all doubt that Hunter had been again indulging in his favorite mode of warfare, and that, after his return to the Valley, while we were near Washington, among other outrages, the private residences of Mr. Andrew Hunter, a member of the Virginia Senate, Mr. Alexander R. Boteler, an ex-member of the Confederate Congress, as well as of the United States Congress, and Edmund I. Lee, a distant relative of General Lee, all in Jefferson County, with their contents, had been burned by his orders, only time enough being given for the ladies to get out of the house. A number of towns in the South, as well as private country-houses, had been burned by Federal troops, and the accounts had been heralded forth in some of the Northern papers in terms of exultation, and gloated over by their readers, while they were received with apathy by others. I now came to the conclusion that we had stood this mode of warfare long enough, and that it was time to open the eyes of the people of the North to its enormity by an example in the way of retaliation. I did not select the cases mentioned as having more merit or greater claims for retaliation than others, but because they had occurred within the limits of the country covered by my command, and were brought more immediately to my attention.

The town of Chambersburg was selected as the one on which retaliation should be made, and McCausland was ordered to proceed with his brigade and that of Johnson's and a battery of artillery to that place, and demand of the municipal authorities the sum of one hundred thousand dollars in gold, or five hundred thousand dollars in United States currency, as a compensation for the destruction of the houses named and their contents; and in default of payment to lay the town in ashes, in retaliation for the burning of those houses and others in Virginia, as well as for the towns which had been burned in other Southern States. A written demand to that effect was also sent to the municipal authorities, and they were informed what would be the result of a failure or a refusal to comply with it. I desired to give the people of Chambersburg an opportunity of saving their town, by making compensation for part of the injury done, and hoped that the payment of such a sum would have the desired effect, and open the eyes of people of other towns at the North to the necessity of urging upon their Government the adoption of a different policy.

On July 30th McCausland reached Chambersburg, and made the demand as directed, reading to such of the authorities as presented themselves the paper sent by me. The demand was not complied with, the people stating that they were not afraid of having their town burned, and that a Federal force was approaching. The policy pursued by our army on former occasions had been so lenient that they did not suppose the threat was in earnest at this time, and they hoped for speedy relief. McCausland, however, proceeded to carry out his orders, and the greater part of the town was laid in ashes. He then moved in the direction of Cumberland, but found it defended by a strong force. He then withdrew and crossed the Potomac, near the mouth of the South Branch, capturing the garrison and partly destroying the railroad bridge. Averill pursued from Chambersburg, and surprised and routed Johnson's brigade, and caused a loss of four pieces of artillery and about three hundred prisoners from the whole command.

CHAPTER XXXIV

Trial of John Yates Beall by military commission—Character as a Confederate officer established—His acts authorized and approved by the Confederate Government—Arguments of counsel.

The imprisonment of Captain Beall and George S. Anderson at Fort Lafayette, New York, was in separate cells. Beall was manacled with irons. Anderson, it appears, agreed upon terms with the Federal military authorities under which he was to appear as a witness against Beall and himself to be set free. The fact that Beall and Anderson were serving under Colonel Martin and were escaping to Canada from the Buffalo-Dunkirk expedition was then disclosed by Anderson. Through this witness, of course, the name, Confederate character of Beall, and the purposes of the expedition were given to the authorities so far as Anderson had knowledge. A military commission was then ordered by General John A. Dix, for the trial of Captain Beall, as follows:

General Orders No. 14.

HEADQUARTERS DEPARTMENT OF THE EAST,
New York City, January 17th, 1865.

* * * * * * *

6. A military commission, to consist of the following named officers, will assemble at Fort Lafayette, N. Y. H., at 11 a. m., on Friday, January 20th, 1865, or as soon thereafter as practicable, for the trial of such cases as may be brought before it, by orders from these headquarters, to sit without regard to hours, and to hold its sessions in New York City, if the convenience require it; four members to constitute a quorum, for the transaction of business.

DETAIL FOR THE COURT.

Brig.-Gen. Fitz Henry Warren, U. S. V.; Brig.-Gen. W. H. Morris, U. S. V.; Col. M. S. Howe, Third U. S. Cavalry; Col. H. Day, U. S. A.; Brev. Lieut.-Col. R. F. O'Bierne, Fourteenth U. S. Infantry; Major G. W. Wallace, Sixth U. S. Infantry. Major John A. Bolles, A. D. C., is appointed Judge-Advocate.

By command of Major-General Dix:

D. T. VAN BUREN,
Assistant Adjutant-General.

The official record of the trial shows that the first session of the military commission was held on the 17th day of January, 1865. A postponement was granted to allow Beall to procure counsel and the trial began on the 1st day of February. Hon. James T. Brady of New York appeared as the attorney of Captain Beall. The charges and specifications against Captain Beall were as follows:

Charge 1. Violation of the laws of war.

Specification 1. In this that John Y. Beall, a citizen of the insurgent State of Virginia, did on or about the 19th day of September, 1864, at or near Kelley's Island, in the State of Ohio, without lawful authority, and by force of arms, seize and capture the steamboat *Philo Parsons*.

Specification 2. In this that John Y. Beall, a citizen of the insurgent State of Virginia, did on or about the 19th day of September, 1864, at or near Middle Bass Island, in the State of Ohio, without lawful authority, and by force of arms, seize, capture and sink the steamboat *Island Queen*.

Specification 3. In this that John Y. Beall, a citizen of the insurgent State of Virginia, was found acting as a spy at or near Kelley's Island, in the State of Ohio, on or about the 19th day of September, 1864.

Specification 4. In this that John Y. Beall, a citizen of the insurgent State of Virginia, was found acting as a spy on or about the 19th day of September, 1864, at or near Middle Bass Island, in the State of Ohio.

Specification 5. In this that John Y. Beall, a citizen of the insurgent State of Virginia, was found acting as a spy on or about the 16th day of December, 1864, at or near Suspension Bridge in the State of New York.

Specification 6. In this that John Y. Beall, a citizen of the insurgent State of Virginia, being without lawful authority, and for unlawful purposes, in the State of New York, did in the said State of New York undertake to carry on irregular and unlawful warfare as a guerrilla; and in the execution of said undertaking, attempted to destroy the lives and property of the peaceable and unoffending inhabitants of said State, and of persons therein traveling, by throwing a train of cars and the passengers in said cars from the railroad track, on the railroad between Dunkirk and Buffalo, by placing obstructions across said track; all this in said State of New York, and on or about the 15th day of December, 1864, at or near Buffalo.

Charge 2. Acting as a spy.

Specification 1. In this that John Y. Beall, a citizen of the insurgent State of Virginia, was found acting as a spy in the State of Ohio, at or near Kelley's Island, on or about the 19th day of September, 1864.

Specification 2. In this that John Y. Beall, a citizen of the insurgent State of Virginia, was found acting as a spy in the State of Ohio, on or about the 19th day of September, 1864, at or near Middle Bass Island.

Specification 3. In this that John Y. Beall, a citizen of the insurgent State of Virginia, was found acting as a spy in the State of New York, at or near Suspension Bridge, on or about the 16th day of December, 1864.

JOHN A. BOLLES, Major and A. D. C.,
Judge-Advocate.

The fact that a trial was in progress, and in fact the arrest of Captain Beall and Anderson, was not published in any of the Northern newspapers. The Confederate authorities in Richmond, therefore, were kept in ignorance of the whole proceeding; otherwise, the treatment of Beall as a prisoner of war would have been demanded and enforced by threats of retaliation, as was done in the case of the privateers who were condemned to be hung at Philadelphia, in 1861, and Beall would have been saved.

The prosecution introduced David H. Thomas, a police officer of Niagara, New York, who testified that he and another police officer, named Saule, arrested Beall and Anderson, in the depot of the New York Central Railroad

Company, at Niagara City, on the 16th day of December, 1864, at about 9 or 10 o'clock at night. He said Beall and Anderson were sitting on a settee; that he seized Beall and Saule took Anderson while both were asleep.

W. O. Ashley, the clerk who commanded the *Philo Parsons* on Lake Erie, recognized Beall and testified to the capture of his boat in Ohio waters, and that he delivered the boat's books, papers, and money ($100) over to Beall and Burley; that they took no personal property from him or others. He said his vessel was captured within six miles of Johnson's Island. I quote a short extract from the testimony of the only passenger introduced by the prosecution, as follows:

The Judge-Advocate then called William Weston, a witness for the prosecution.

Q. Have you ever seen the accused, Captain Beall, before?
A. Yes, sir.
Q. When for the first time, and where?
A. The first time I saw him was on board the *Philo Parsons,* on the 19th of September last.
Q. State what you saw him do, and what you heard him say?
A. After the capture of the boat, and we got a little excited, he came forward and told us what they were going to do with us, and the boat; I was a passenger on board; he said they were not going *to hurt or harm any of us,* and that they would land us as soon as they saw fit. He also stated that he was an escaped prisoner from Johnson's Island, and that they had taken the boat for the purpose of capturing the United States vessel *Michigan.* He said they were going to liberate the prisoners on Johnson's Island, and were going to destroy the commerce on the Lakes; that is all I recollect he said.
Q. Did you ever see what was done with any of the freight on board the *Philo Parsons* after the boat was seized?
A. I did not see them do anything with the freight, only they threw out one of my boxes, that I got afterwards on the beach, that was pitched out; that was after they landed us on the island; they pitched one of my boxes into the water.   * * *

The prosecution introduced George S. Anderson, the comrade of Beall, who detailed the story of the expedition to

Buffalo and Dunkirk. There are quite a number of errors in his statements but they are not of particular interest.

There was no defense for Captain Beall except that his warfare was authorized by the Confederate Government. It should be said here that Captain Beall was not a spy because he was not within the lines of an army or a camp of the enemy, and was not seeking information. He was not a guerrilla because he was acting by authority. He was a Confederate "raider" upon the enemy's country.

It would be fair perhaps to note that Captain Beall was tried in the same manner that Generals Paine, Burbridge, and Burnside tried all Confederate officers and soldiers who were captured in the rear or north of the Federal armies. These were denounced and condemned as spies and guerrillas, and seldom had any means of making a defense, or of calling upon their Government for relief. General Sheridan generally executed Mosby's men as soon as captured. And this was the proceeding of the others in most cases.

An affidavit of Colonel Robert M. Martin, made at Toronto and showing the authority and orders for the Buffalo-Dunkirk expedition, was produced and offered but was not allowed in evidence by the military commission. Mr. Brady, however, introduced as evidence Exhibits E and F. The latter had been brought from Richmond by Lieutenant S. B. Davis for the defense of Bennett G. Burley in Canada. It was equally applicable in Beall's case as he was the commander of the expedition. The exhibits marked A, B, and C are letters that Beall wrote in his cell, before he had secured counsel, which the authorities failed to forward, and he was thereby deprived of timely assistance from his Government.

Exhibit E.

Confederate States of America, Navy Department,
Richmond, March 5th, 1863.

Sir: You are hereby informed that the President has appointed you an Acting Master in the Navy of the Confederate States. You are requested to signify your acceptance or nonacceptance of this appointment; and should you accept, you will sign before a magistrate the oath of office herewith, and forward the same, with your letter of acceptance, to this Department.

Registered No.........................

The lowest number takes rank.

(Signed.)   S. R. MALLORY,
                            Secretary of the Navy.

Acting Master JOHN Y. BEALL, of Virginia, C. S. N.,
    Richmond, Va.

(Indorsed.)

CONFEDERATE STATES OF AMERICA, NAVY DEPARTMENT,
            Richmond, 23d December, 1864.

I certify that the reverse of this page presents a true copy of the warrant granted to John Y. Beall, as an Acting Master in the Navy of the Confederate States, from the records of this Department.

In testimony whereof I have herewith set my hand and affixed the seal of this Department, on the day and year above written.

(Signed.)   S. R. MALLORY,
                            Secretary of the Navy.

EXHIBIT F.

By authority—Confederate States of America.

Whereas, It has been made known to me that Bennett G. Burley, an Acting Master in the Navy of the Confederate States, is now under arrest in one of the British North American Provinces, on an application made by the Government of the United States for the delivery to that Government of the said Bennett G. Burley, under the treaty known as the Extradition Treaty, now in force between the United States and Great Britain; and whereas it has been represented to me that the said demand for the extradition of said Bennett G. Burley is based on a charge that the said Burley is a fugitive from justice, accused of having committed the crimes of robbery and piracy in the jurisdiction of the United States; and whereas, it has further been made known to me that the accusations and charges made against the said Bennett G. Burley are based solely on the acts and conduct of said Burley, in an enterprise made or attempted in the month of September last, 1864, for the capture of the steamer *Michigan*, an armed vessel of the United States, navigating the lakes on the boundary line between the United States and the said British North American Provinces, and for the release of numerous citizens of the Confederate States, held as prisoners of war by the United States at a certain island called Johnson's Island; and whereas, the said enterprise or expedition for the capture of the said armed steamer *Michigan,* and for the release of the said prisoners on Johnson's Island, was a proper and legitimate belligerent operation, undertaken during the pending public war, between the two Confederacies, known respectively as the Confederate States of America and the United States of America, which operation was ordered, directed, and sustained by the authority of the Government of the Confederate States, and confided to its commissioned officers for execution, among which officers is the said Bennett G. Burley.

Now, therefore, I, Jefferson Davis, President of the Confederate States of America, do hereby declare and make known to all whom it may concern, that the expedition aforesaid, undertaken in the month of September last, for the capture of the armed steamer *Michigan,* a vessel of war of the United States, and for the release of the prisoners of war, citizens of the Confederate States of America, held captive by the United States of America at Johnson's Island, was a belligerent expedition ordered and undertaken under the authority of the Confederate States of America, against the United States of America, and that the Government of the Confederate States of America assumes the responsibility for answering for the acts and conduct of any of its officers engaged in said expedition, and especially of the said Bennett G. Burley, an Acting Master of the Confederate States Navy.

And I do further make known to all whom it may concern, that in the orders and instructions given to the officers engaged in said expedition, they were specially directed and enjoined to "abstain from violating any of the laws and regulations of the Canadian and British authorities in relation to neutrality," and that the combination necessary to effect the purpose of said expedition "must be made by Confederate soldiers and such assistance as they might (you may) draw from the enemy's country."

In testimony whereof I have signed this manifesto, and directed the same to be sealed with the seal of the Department of State of the Confederate States of America, and to be made public.

Done at the city of Richmond, on the 24th day of December, 1864.

JEFFERSON DAVIS.

By the President,
    J. P. BENJAMIN, Secretary of State.

Exhibits A, B, and C, were submitted as showing Beall's views of the charges against him, and his reliance upon his authority as a Confederate officer. He had really committed no act except upon Lake Erie.

EXHIBIT A.

(One U. S. stamp enclosed.)

FORT LAFAYETTE, N. Y., January 22d, 1865.

Mr. D. B. LUCAS,
    173 Main St., Richmond, Va.

DEAR DAN: I have taken up board and lodging at this famous establishment. I was captured in December last, and spent Xmas in the Metropolitan Hd. Qrs. Police Station. I am now being tried for irregular warfare, by a Military Commission, a species of court.

The acts are said to have been committed on Lake Erie and the Canada frontier. You know that I am not a "guerrilla" or "spy."

I desire that you get the necessary evidence that I am in the Confederate service, regularly, and forward it to me at once. I shall write to Colonels Boteler and Holliday in regard to this matter. I must have this evidence. As the Commission so far have acted fairly, I am confident of acquittal. Has Will been exchanged? I saw that Steadman had been killed in Kentucky. Alas! how they fall. Please let my family know if possible of my whereabouts. Where is my Georgia friend? Have you heard anything from her since I left? May God bless her. I should like so much to hear from her, from home, Will, and yourself. Be so kind, therefore, as to attend at once to this business for me. Remember me to any and all of my friends that you may see.

Send me some stamps for my correspondence.

Hoping to hear from you soon,
    I remain your friend,
        J. Y. BEALL, C. S. N.

If Mr. Lucas is not in Richmond, will Mr. Hunter attend to this at once?

EXHIBIT B.

(I enclose a U. S. stamp.)

FORT LAFAYETTE, N. Y., January 22d, 1865.
Col. A. R. BOTELER,
Richmond, Va.

DEAR SIR: I am on trial before a Military Commission for irregular warfare, as a "guerrilla" and "spy." The acts are said to have been committed on Lake Erie and at Suspension Bridge, in September and December last.

As I cannot in person procure any papers from Richmond, I have to rely on my friends, and therefore I request you to procure evidence of my being regularly in service, and forward such evidence at once to me. I have also written to Messrs. Hunter and Lucas. Please call on them in regard to this, and also Mr. Henderson if necessary.

Very truly, your friend,
J. Y. BEALL, C. S. N.

EXHIBIT C.

FORT LAFAYETTE, N. Y., January 22d, 1865.
Col. JACOB THOMPSON,
Toronto, C. W.

SIR: I was captured in December, and am on trial before a Military Commission for irregular warfare, as a "guerrilla" and "spy." The acts are said to have been committed on Lake Erie and at Suspension Bridge, N. Y., in September and December last.

I desire to procure from my Government and its authorities evidence of my being regularly in service, and of having been acting under and by authority. Please secure and forward me, as soon as possible, certificates or other evidence confirming this fact.

The Commission so far have evidenced a disposition to treat me fairly and equitably. With the evidence you can send, together with that I have a right to expect from Richmond and elsewhere, I am confident of an acquittal.

Please attend at once to this, acknowledging at any rate the receipt of this letter.

Very respectfully,
J. Y. BEALL.

James T. Brady, Esq., counsel for Captain Beall, now
addressed the commission at length in defense of the prisoner. It would be interesting matter, perhaps, to present
the entire address, but for all practical purposes his remarks
upon one or two points only are deemed sufficient and extracts are given as follows:

* * * * * * *

But I had supposed the WORD "LINES" had some reference in general parlance to a CAMP. You may make a city a
camp or an entire district, but I don't know that you can make
a WHOLE COUNTRY A CAMP. I don't know whether
Cæsar, Hannibal, or Alexander, in any of their extensive
marches, could have established as their camps the whole
country through which they went. I don't suppose that General
Sherman could claim the whole State of Georgia as his camp.
All this may be of very little consideration to you, because you
know so much more about it than I; but I respectfully submit
that the word "lines" must mean some imaginary or prescribed
territory relating to, and directly affected by the government of
the army as such; and in that sense I don't see how Beall was
within our lines in a military sense, because he happened to be
in the State of Ohio taking passage in a steamboat, or up at
Niagara in the State of New York; the State of New York
never for one moment being subject to any kind of military
occupation. I don't see how the State of Ohio or the State of
New York could be within our lines. But that proposition I
submit to your intelligence and judgment.

* * * * * * *

Now, on this subject we find that the accused did not come
here as a spy, nor for any such purpose. He came on one
occasion, if you believe the testimony in this case, to assist in a
demonstration for the relief of the prisoners on Johnson's
Island; a specific purpose of war if he acted in a military
capacity. And in the other case, he was in the State of New
York engaged in the capture of a railroad train, so as to get
possession of the mails and money in the express safe; and
coming for either of those purposes, he did not come to lurk
or make himself a spy in any way.

* * * * * * *

He was acting under a commission; he was in the service
of the rebel Government; he was engaged in carrying on warfare; he was not endeavoring to perpetrate any offense against

society. And if he were not acting under a commission or with authority, but was acting upon his own responsibility and from the wicked intent of his own heart for motives of personal malice or gain, he is not amenable to this tribunal, but must answer to the ordinary courts of the State within which the crime was committed.

* * * * * * *

The soldiers who surround Captain Beall on his way to this court, and unknown to their superior officer, when the opportunity presents itself, murmur out in his hearing words that would denote that he was contemplated by them as a murderer, an outcast, and a villain, have not brought themselves to understand, to contemplate the dreadful fact, that war is nothing but legalized deception, and fraud, and murder. If I slay my fellow-being upon a provocation or insult—if he should assail the reputation of my mother, or offer insult to my sister in my presence, and in a moment of passion I slay him, by the law of the land I am guilty of murder, although the circumstances might recommend me to the clemency of the court. And yet, if in obedience to the call of my country I do that against the phalanx of men who have done me no personal wrong, do not I always gain my military triumph by the massacre of those innocent men? If you march your battalions against the conscripted armies of the South, who suffer but the innocent? While the guilty leaders—the wicked men who set this rebellion on foot, have thus far escaped, and seem destined to escape, whatever may be the issue of the war. Soldiers like you are not to be horrified by the fact that men engaged in a warfare, who treat you, and consider you to be their enemies, take possession of your steamboats, or obstruct railroads, or endeavor to throw railroad trains off the track. * * * But has it not been a customary thing in this war, in all these expeditions called raids, for leaders to earn brilliant reputations by, among other things, tearing up rails, removing them, intercepting and stopping railroad cars, without reference to the question of who happened to be in them? Would a general officer, or any one in command, who sought to interrupt the communication by rail between two of the enemy's posts, let a train pass through or stop it? If he seeks to stop it he must apply to it the means necessary to accomplish it. Before the days of railroads, when soldiers were transported by the means of animals attached to some kind of conveyance, did a general engage in warfare who wanted to stop the soldiers, whether they were in stage-coaches (if soldiers ever traveled in that manner) or

in caravans, ever stop to see how many innocent people would
suffer by assailing them with weapons of destruction? Certainly not. It is death, desolation, mutilation, and massacre,
that you are permitted to accomplish in war. And you look
at it not through the medium of philanthropy, not through the
Divine precept that tells you to love your neighbor as yourself, but through the melancholy necessity that characterizes
the awful nature of war. You must change your whole intellect and moral nature to look at it as it is, the *ultima ratio regum*
—the last necessity of kings. This being so, legalized war
justifying every method, every horrible resource of interrupting
communication, where do you draw the line of distinction
between the act of one you call a guerrilla and the act of one
you call a raider, like Grierson? Where do you make the
distinction between the march of Major-General Sherman
through the enemy's country, carrying ravage and desolation
everywhere, destroying the most peaceable and lawful industry,
mills and machinery, and everything of that nature—where do
you draw the line between his march through Georgia and an
expedition of twenty men acting under commission who get into
any of the States we claim to be in the Union, and commit
depredations there? And what difference does it make if they
act under commission, if they kill the innocent or the guilty?
There are no distinctions of that kind in war. You kill your
enemy; you put him *hors de combat* in any way, with some few
qualifications that civilization has introduced. You may say that
it is not allowed to use poisoned weapons, and yet we use Greek
fire. You may not poison wells, but you may destroy your
enemy's property. * * * At the outbreak of this war the
Savannah privateers were captured; they were held and tried as
pirates. I was one of the counsel for the accused. The jury
in the city of New York disagreed. In Philadelphia they
convicted some of them; and as the honorable members of
this court remember, the Confederate Government proposed
retaliation, and took an equal number of our men, their lot
being determined by chance, and secured them, to be executed
in case death were visited upon any of the privateers; and one
of the men who was so held was Major Cogswell, who has
just left this room; and for the first time in my life I had an
involuntary client; because the life of my friend Cogswell was
dependent upon the result. Very soon, however, the Government set that idea aside and gave up the notion that privateers
were pirates.

*   *   *   *   *   *   *

We see that there may be transactions which do not seem at the first blush to belong to those of war; and yet on a closer examination of them they prove to come within that description. I refer you to General Halleck's book, at page 306, and I beg your attention to this, as I know you will give it:

"Partisans and guerrilla troops are bands of men self-organized and self-controlled, who carry on war against the public enemy, without being under the direct authority of the State. They have no commissions or enlistments, nor are they enrolled as any part of the military force of the State; and the State is, therefore, only indirectly responsible for their acts. * * * If authorized and employed by the State, they become a portion of its troops, and the State is as much responsible for their acts as for the acts of any other part of its army. They are no longer partisans and guerrillas in the proper sense of those terms, for they are no longer self-controlled, but carry on hostilities under the direction and authority of the State. * * * It will, however, readily be admitted, that the hostile acts of individuals, or of bands of men, without the authority or sanction of their own Government, are not legitimate acts of war, and, therefore, are punishable according to the nature or character of the offense committed."

If that be so, you cannot convict any man as a guerrilla who holds a commission in the service of the Confederate Government, and perpetrates any act of war in that capacity. He is not self-organized with his command, nor self-controlled. He is acting under authority of our foe, and he is regarded as under so much protection as belongs to the laws of war.

*	*	*	*	*	*	*

You will find that in this case Captain Beall was acting as an officer of the Confederate Government, either in command himself of Confederate soldiers or under the command of some Confederate officer, as in the attempt on the railroad where Colonel Martin of the Confederate service was in command. Commissioned officers of the Confederate Government engaged in depredations for the purposes of war within our territory, are not guerrillas within this definition of General Halleck, or any definition recognized in any book that I have had occasion to refer to. So far as that definition and the like is concerned, that it is ratified by this Government, is shown from this proclamation of Jefferson Davis, referred to in specific terms showing that it was done by the authority of the Government. * * *

A guerrilla must be a marauder, self-controlled, not acting by the authority of his government, without a commission—a mere self-willed and self-moving depredator. The question is, whether there is any proof of any such character in regard to Captain Beall. As to the transaction on Lake Erie, I accept all the proof which has been given by the Government. It was an expedition to take possession of that steamboat, at a distance of some six miles from Johnson's Island, TO RUN DOWN THE UNITED STATES ARMED STEAMER *MICHIGAN,* then lying at about the distance of a mile from Johnson's Island, and thus give the prisoners on Johnson's Island an opportunity to escape.

*   *   *   *   *   *   *

That was the purpose of the armed expedition of Confederate soldiers or officers, to take possession of, or capture the *Michigan,* and thus aid to release the prisoners on Johnson's Island. That I call a military expedition; and that I call an expedition which being carried on by men under commission from the Confederate Government, is legalized warfare and not the conduct of guerrillas.

*   *   *   *   *   *   *

I think we have two distinct questions here, and only two: Is the accused proved to be a spy? What proof is there for the purpose of establishing these charges? In the one case we say he was shown to be within our lines, if within our lines at all, not for the purpose of acting as a spy, but for other developed and proved objects inconsistent with his being a spy. In the other case it appears that he was not a guerrilla because he was a commissioned officer in the Confederate service, acting under the authority of that Government during the war, in connection with other military men, for an act of war. If so, then he is not amenable to this jurisdiction. If I were before a tribunal who had not been accustomed to look at war with its grim visage, with the eye of educated intelligence, I should apprehend that the natural detestation of violence and bloodshed and wrong would pursue this man. But however wrong the South may be—however dismal its records may remain in the contemplation of those who have the ideas of patriotism that reside in our minds—yet not one of you, gentlemen, would even be willing to acknowledge to any foreigner, hating our institutions, that you did not still cling to the South in this struggle, wrong and dreadful as it has been, and award them attributes of intelligence and courage never before perhaps equaled, and certainly never surpassed, in the annals of the human race.

Bad as their act may be in our contemplation, have you any doubt that in the conscience of that man, in the judgment of his mother, in the lessons he received from his father, he has what we may think the misfortune of believing himself right?

* * * * * * *

I leave his fate in your hands. I have endeavored to avoid any attempt to address to you anything but what becomes the sober reason of intelligent men. * * * This is a thing to reason upon. You will view it through the medium of reason with which the Almighty has endowed you.

* * * * * * *

Judge-Advocate-General John A. Bolles then followed in a lengthy address to the commission, and it would likewise be interesting if given in full, but the extracts quoted will convey a fair idea of the claims of the prosecution. He said:

Two papers have been put in evidence by the accused, without objection on my part,—his letter of appointment as master's mate in the rebel Navy, and the "manifesto" of Mr. Davis in regard to Burley and the Lake Erie expedition. I was willing to admit that Beall was a rebel officer, and that all he did was authorized by Mr. Davis; because, in my view of the case, all that was done by the accused, being in the violation of the law of war, no commission, command, or manifesto could justify his acts. A soldier is bound to obey the lawful commands of his superior officer. Our 9th article of war punishes him for disobedience to such commands, but none other. His superior cannot require or compel any soldier to act as a spy, or as an assassin. If, then, such unlawful command be given and obeyed, its only effect is to prove that both he who gave and he who obeyed the command are criminals, and deserve to be gibbeted together. When did a spy ever seek to justify himself by pleading the command of his general? How can the manifesto of the arch-rebel screen any of his subordinates who has trampled under foot that law of war—for war hath its laws no less than peace—which is binding upon all alike, from the rebel President to the rebel raider?

* * * * * * *

And now, Mr. President, I come to the final inquiry in this most interesting and important trial. What are the facts proved by the evidence under the 1st, 2nd, and 6th specifications of Charge 1st?

I submit to the court that we have proved:

1st. That the accused was and is a rebel officer.

2nd. That he was within our lines in disguise.

3rd. That he, at Kelley's Island, in Ohio, in September last, with the help of other rebel officers and soldiers in disguise, seized the American private steamboat *Philo Parsons*.

4th. That he stole the money and destroyed the freight on board of her.

5th. That in September, at Middle Bass Island, in Ohio, he, still in disguise, and with the same friends in disguise, seized in like manner another steamboat, the *Island Queen,* and scuttled and sunk her.

6th. That in December he came from Canada to Buffalo, in New York, in disguise, and with other disguised rebel officers and soldiers attempted unsuccessfully to throw a railroad train from the track.

7th. That he went back to Canada, and again returned in the same treacherous manner as before, and repeated his infamous attempt upon a night train from Dunkirk, and was caught as he fled from the scene of his unenviable exploits.

*   *   *   *   *   *   *

It is important that you and I, sir, and our wives and children—that all of our fellow-citizens, may feel, when they enter a railroad car within the loyal States, that they are safe from all perils but those of ordinary travel; and that if any party of rebel soldiers in disguise, enemies of the Republic and friends of the Confederacy, attempt to place obstructions on the track, and throw off the train, they will be punished with the most exemplary speed, certainty, and severity. Enormities like this cannot be justified or screened from legal vengeance by the plea or proof of a military commission, command, or ratification, no matter how exalted may be the rank of the commander; since the law of war, which forbids and punishes the crime, is obligatory upon all.

*   *   *   *   *   *   *

The piracy of the lake, and the outrage on the railroad, were parts of that system of irregular warfare, UNDER THE FEAR OF WHICH NO MAN, WOMAN OR CHILD CAN SLEEP WITH ANY FEELING OF SECURITY IN OUR

MIDST. Such atrocities are attempts, on the part of the rebel officers and soldiers who engage in and countenance them, TO BRING BACK WAR TO ITS OLD CONDITION OF BARBARISM—TO IMITATE THE STEALTHY CRUELTY OF THE NORTH AMERICAN SAVAGE, WHO CREEPS UNDER COVER OF MIDNIGHT UPON HIS UNSUSPECTING VICTIM, AND SMITES HIM TO DEATH ERE THE SOUND OF APPROACHING FOOT-STEPS HAS ROUSED THAT VICTIM FROM SLUM-BER. With the accused this savage purpose takes form in the robbery of steamboats and the destruction of railroad trains and travelers. In other hands, it manifests itself in midnight attempts to burn great cities. There is nothing of Christian civilization, nothing of regular warfare, nothing of a high, noble, bold, manly, chivalrous character about it. It is an outbreak of passions so bad and violent that they have overcome all the native elements of manliness, and have led men, of whom four years ago to have suspected such things possible would have been a calumny and a crime, to indulge in atrocities from month to month and year to year, SUCH AS HAVE NOT STAINED THE PAGES OF WARFARE FOR TWO HUNDRED YEARS. And you sit here today, AS THE REPRESENTA-TIVES OF RECOGNIZED LAW AND HONORABLE WARFARE, TO SEE THAT SUCH OUTRAGES, when they are clearly and distinctly brought home to the guilty party by the evidence adduced upon the trial, shall not escape unpunished.

CHAPTER XXXV

Efforts of the friends of Beall, with President Lincoln, for his pardon—Beall hung on Governor's Island—Buried in Greenwood Cemetery, Brooklyn.

The commission on February 8th, 1865, found Captain Beall guilty on every count in the charges, announcing their verdict as follows:

And the commission do therefore sentence him, the said John Y. Beall, to be hanged by the neck until dead, at such time and place as the General in command of the Department may direct, two-thirds of the members concurring therein.

An extract from the order of General Dix, approving the verdict of the commission, is as follows:

General Orders, No. 14.

HEADQUARTERS DEPARTMENT OF THE EAST,
New York City, Feb. 14th, 1865.

I. Before a Military Commission which convened at Fort Lafayette, New York Harbor, by virtue of Special Orders No. 14, current series from these headquarters, of January 17, 1865, and of which Brigadier-General Fitz Henry Warren, United States Volunteers, is President, was arraigned and tried John Y. Beall.

* * * * * * *

"After eight hours, he and his associates, arming themselves with revolvers and hand-axes, brought surreptitiously on board, rose on the crew, took possession of the steamer, threw overboard part of the freight, and robbed the clerk of the money in his charge, putting all on board under duress. Later in the evening he and his party took possession of another unarmed steamer (the *Island Queen*), scuttled her, and set her adrift on the lake. These transactions occurred within the jurisdiction of the State of Ohio, on the 19th day of September, 1864.

On the 16th day of December, 1864, the accused was arrested near the Suspension Bridge, over the Niagara River, within the State of New York. The testimony shows that he and two officers of the insurgent States, Colonel Martin and Lieutenant Headley, with two other Confederates, had made an unsuccessful attempt, under the direction of the first-named officer, to throw the passenger train coming from the West to Buffalo off the railroad track, for the purpose of robbing the express company. It is further shown that this was the third attempt in which the accused was concerned to accomplish the same object; that between two of the attempts the party, including the accused, went to Canada and returned, and that they were on their way back to Canada when he was arrested. In these transactions, as in that on Lake Erie, the accused, though holding a commission from the insurgent authorities at Richmond, was in disguise, procuring information, with the intention of using it, as he subsequently did, to inflict injury upon unarmed citizens of the United States and their private property.   *

* *   In these attempts three officers holding commissions in the military service of the insurgent States were concerned. The accused is shown by the testimony to be a man of education and refinement, and it is difficult to account for his agency in transactions so abhorrent to the moral sense, and so inconsistent with all the rules of honorable warfare.

The accused, in justification of the transaction on Lake Erie, produced the manifesto of Jefferson Davis, assuming the responsibility of the act, and declaring that it was done by his authority. It is hardly necessary to say that no such assumption can sanction an act not warranted by the laws of civilized warfare.   * * *   War, under its mildest aspects, is the heaviest calamity that can befall our race; and he who, in a spirit of revenge, or with lawless violence, transcends the limits to which it is restricted by the common behest of all Christian communities, should receive the punishment which the common voice has declared to be due to the crime. The Major-General commanding feels that a want of firmness and inflexibility, on his part, in executing the sentence of death in such a case, would be an offense against the outraged civilization and humanity of the age.

It is hereby ordered that the accused, John Y. Beall, be hanged by the neck till he is dead, on Governor's Island, on Saturday, the 18th of February, inst., between the hours 12 and 2 in the afternoon.

The commanding officer at Fort Columbus is charged with the execution of this order.

By command of Major-General Dix:

D. T. VAN BUREN, Col. A. A. G.

The date of Captain Beall's execution was postponed from the 18th of February until the 24th. His fate being fixed for the 24th of February, Captain Beall wrote his brother, who was a private in the Stonewall Brigade, as follows:

FORT LAFAYETTE, Feb. 14th, 1865.

DEAR WILL: Ere this reaches you, you will most probably have heard of my death through the newspapers; that I was tried by a military commission, and hung by the enemy; and hung, I assert, unjustly. It is both useless and wrong to repine over the past. Hanging, it was asserted, was ignominious; but crime only can make dishonor. "Vengeance is mine, saith the Lord, and I will repay"; therefore do not show unkindness to the prisoners—they are helpless.

Remember me kindly to my friends. Say to them, I am not aware of committing any crime against society. I die for my country. No thirst for blood or lucre animated me in my course; for I had refused, when solicited, to engage in enterprises which I deemed destructive, but illegitimate; and but a few months ago I had but to have spoken, and I would have been red with blood, and rich with the plunder of the foe. But my hands are clear of blood, unless it be spilt in conflict; and not a cent enriches my pocket.

Should you be spared through this strife, stay with mother, and be a comfort to her old age. Endure the hardships of the campaign like a man. In my trunk and box you can get plenty of clothes. Give my love to mother, the girls too. May God bless you all now and evermore, is my prayer and wish for you.

JOHN Y. BEALL.

His faithful friend—his "biographer"—now entered earnestly and untiringly upon the task of saving Beall, by an appeal to President Lincoln, upon the merits of the case, alleging that Beall was not a spy but honestly endeavoring, without motives, to serve the cause of his country.

J. A. L. McClure retained the professional services of Andrew Ridgely, of Baltimore. McClure received a letter from Beall as follows:

FORT LAFAYETTE, 14th Feb., 1865.

Mr. JAMES A. L. McCLURE, Baltimore, Md.

DEAR SIR: Last evening I was informed of the finding and sentence of the Commission in my case. Captain Wright Rives, of General Dix's staff, promised to procure you a copy of the record of the trial.

I am solicitous for you, who represent my friends, to have one, and to attach this statement to it: Some of the evidence is true, SOME FALSE. I am not a spy nor a guerrilla. The execution of the sentence will be murder. And at a convenient season, to forward that record, and my statement to my friends.

I wish you to find out the amount of the expenses of the trial, and forward it to me at once, so that I can give a check for the amount.

Captain Wright Rives assured me that my friends could have my body. For my family's sake, please get my body from Fort Columbus after the execution, and have it plainly buried, not to be removed to my native State till this unhappy war is over, and my friends can bury as prudence and their wishes may dictate.

Let me again thank you for your kindness, and believe me to be now, as in days of yore, your attached friend,

JOHN Y. BEALL.

His "biographer" says:

On Thursday morning Mr. McClure received a letter from John in which he announced his conviction and sentence. This letter was answered by telegraph through Captain Rives.

He instantly thought that nothing could give to the President a clearer idea of the polished character, and manly tone that John possessed, than the simple reading of this letter—and I went at once to Washington to have it presented through Mr. Ridgely. Mr. Ridgely, however, had returned to Baltimore before I reached Washington, so that I was obliged also to return the same night. We had immediately an interview with him, to ascertain the result of his visit, and efforts. He brought no encouragement. Friends at Washington had interested themselves, and had appealed to the President even before Mr. Ridgely's arrival; and in his interview with that gentleman, he was positive in his determination not to interpose against the order, and judgment of General Dix, with whom, without the active interference of the President, the case entirely rested.

*   *   *   *   *   *   *

Among those who persistently labored with the President in behalf of Captain Beall were the following:

Francis L. Wheatley, John S. Gittings and his wife, and many ladies of Baltimore and Washington; Mr. Hendricks of Missouri, Rev. Dr. Bullock of Baltimore, Hon. Montgomery Blair, ex-Senator O. H. Browning of Illinois, Hon. Robert Mallory of Kentucky, besides a petition signed by ninety-one members of Congress.

Continuing, his "biographer" says:

Mr. Brady, in company with Mr. Francis Blair and Mr. Stabler of Montgomery County, personal friends of the President, and Mr. Wheatley, called upon Mr. Lincoln at an early hour on Friday morning. There had already been two companies of gentlemen to see him on the same mission; whether they procured an interview or not I cannot say, but Mr. Brady and the gentlemen with him were informed by the President's private secretary, that the case of Captain Beall "was closed," and that he could not be seen any further in reference to it.

Mr. McClure, in company with Mrs. Basil B. Gordon, reached New York from Baltimore, on Friday morning. Mrs. Gordon, at a very early hour, had an interview with General Dix, and appealed to him in John's behalf, in the most earnest manner.

It will thus be seen that no stone was left unturned to obtain a reprieve, and to the extent of a short respite these efforts were successful; during this respite every legitimate means was resorted to to influence the President or General Dix, either of whom had the power to interpose between the sentence and its victim, but all intercessions were in vain. For days before the execution the President closed the doors of the Executive palace against all suppliants, male or female, and his ears against all appeals, whether with the tongue of men or of angels, in behalf of his unfortunate prisoner. From the first Mr. Lincoln had responded to all applications for his interposition, "General Dix may dispose of the case as he pleases—I will not interfere." General Dix, on his part, replied, "All now rests with the President—as far as my action is concerned there is not a gleam of hope." Thus they stood as the pillars of the gallows, on which Beall's fate was suspended, and between them he died. The credit, if any, in resisting all appeals for mercy, belongs jointly, in whole or in part, to both; and in the same manner, the infamy, if such attach to the execution, pertains in the same undivided, indivisible estate to both. There was one expedient which might have proved successful had it been adopted; that was to have purchased the more influential of the Republican journals of New York over in favor of mercy. There was one influence to which President Lincoln never failed to yield when strongly directed against him—THE VOICE OF HIS PARTY; this he did upon principle, as the head of a popular government. It was in response to such partisan appeals that Fish, ex-provost marshal of Baltimore, who on conviction of open and shameless bribery, and peculation, was sentenced to the penitentiary, obtained pardon; WHILE GENERAL PAINE, FOUND GUILTY BEFORE A MILITARY TRI-BUNAL OF OUTRAGING ALL THE PROPRIETIES OF WAR UPON THE PERSONS AND PROPERTY OF WOMEN, CHILDREN, AND OTHER DEFENSELESS NON-COMBATANTS, SUCCEEDED BY SIMILAR MEANS IN PROPITIATING EXECUTIVE CLEMENCY. Unfortunately neither Beall nor his friends belonged to the Republican party; hence the doors of mercy were closed against him.

At some period during the respite granted, Mrs. Beall having come on from Virginia, HAD AN OPPORTUNITY OF VISITING HER SON.

* * * * * * *

The character of this interview, which took place in the presence of officers, was naturally affecting, though both exhibiting that degree of composed fortitude which might have been expected by those acquainted with their characters. The son derived from it great comfort, for, said he, "I saw the moment she entered the cell that she could bear it, and that it made no difference to her whether I died upon the scaffold, or fell upon the field." He gave her no ground to indulge the hope of final pardon for himself. "No," said he, "they are thirsting for my blood!" And thus parted mother and son to meet again only in that realm where the changed and spotless are clothed in the transcendent beauty of immortal and incorruptible spirits.

* * * * * * *

The Rev. Joshua Van Dyke (of Brooklyn) visited him on the day before his execution, and writes: "I found him to be all you had described him, and much more. He was confined in a narrow and gloomy cell, with a lamp burning at midday; but he received me with as much ease as if he were in his own parlor, and his conversation revealed at every turn the gentleman, the scholar, and the Christian. There was no bravado, no strained heroism, no excitement in his words or manner, but a quiet trust in God, and a composure in view of death, such as I have read of, but never beheld to the same degree before. He introduced the subject of his approaching end himself, saying that while he did not pretend to be indifferent to life, the mode in which he was to leave it had no terrors or ignominy for him; he could go to heaven, through the grace of Christ, as well from the gallows as from the battlefield, or his own bed; he died in defense of what he believed to be right; and so far as the particular things for which he was to be executed were concerned, he had no confession to make or repentance to exercise. He did not use one bitter or angry expression toward his enemies, but calmly declared his conviction that he was to be executed contrary to the laws of civilized warfare. He accepted his doom as the will of God. * * * I left his cell, saying to myself, 'The chamber where the good man views his fate is privileged above the common walks of life!'"

*   *   *   *   *   *   *

At a little past one o'clock (February 24th, 1865) the cortege passed out of the stern, arched sallyport of Fort Columbus. * * *

The band struck up the death-march, and the solemn procession moved forward.

Beall caught the step of the regulars, and moved with them; he was a soldier, and knew how to keep step even to music of his own death-dirge. But his step was lighter than that of the heavy soldiers; it was as light, as free, as tameless as Tell's in the mountains of Switzerland; as proud and firm as McGregor's on the skirts of Ben Lomond. Here was no malefactor at all. Here was a groom leaping to the bridal-chamber; or a conqueror passing under the triumphal arch of an ovation!

Suddenly, upon a little eminence overlooking the spot and instrument of execution, the procession calls a halt. What does it mean? The victim's face is turned full upon the gallows, and upon the rough pine coffin at its foot. "Oh! this, this is cruel, and cowardly!" exclaims one of his two faithful friends who are following afar off. Beall might avert his face, but he is a soldier, and will not do it. For nine solid minutes by the watch is he kept face to face with the gallows, tête-à-tête with his own coffin.

*   *   *   *   *   *   *

The eager multitude who, to the number of from three hundred and fifty to five hundred, had assembled to witness the execution, are appalled at this delay. But now Beall no longer regards it; he does not see the crowd around him; once or twice he has smiled at their eager curiosity; now he no longer sees them at all. He asks the direction of Fort Lafayette, remarks that he has many kind friends there; he looks smilingly over the gibbet across the waters of the Bay to the hills of Staten Island, and the mountains of New Jersey beyond, thence to the soft blue sky on which they are projected, and finally, up to the glorious God of day himself; then he exclaims—"How beautiful the sun is! I look upon it for the last time!" * * *

Again the march is resumed, and the victim passes in the hollow-square around the scaffold. Before stepping upon it he turns with a smile to Dr. Weston, and remarks, "As some author has said, we may be as near God on the scaffold as elsewhere."

* * * * * * *

Mounting to the platform, the prisoner takes his seat upon the chair immediately under the fatal rope. The adjutant of the post (Lieutenant Keiser of the Second U. S. Infantry) commences to read the charges, specifications, and the orders of General Dix for his execution. Beall, little dreaming of the test to which he is to be subjected, rises respectfully when the reading is commenced; but finding that, instead of the last, and briefest order for his execution, the whole prolix, and unmilitary, and unsoldierly pronunciamento of General Dix is to be gone through with,—he deliberately draws up a chair with his foot, and resumes his seat. When he hears himself designated as a citizen of the "insurgent State of Virginia" his smile grows intensely sad and significant; he sees now the men before him no longer as his own murderers only, but as the executioners of a sovereign State—his own beloved Virginia, and he smiles not in derision, but in protest and remonstrance. Again when they denounce his heroic attempt to rescue from a vault the souls of three thousand fellow-soldiers, "piracy," he smiles; but when they accuse him of an attempt as a "guerrilla" to "destroy the lives and property of peaceable, and unoffending inhabitants of said State" (New York), he ceases to smile, and mournfully shakes his head in denial. But finally, when the adjutant reaches the concluding passages of the order of General Dix * * * Beall laughs outright; it is at this point that the reporters declare that the "prisoner seems to be reminded of some amusing incident in his military experience." The reporters do not understand the joke; the truth is, Beall hears this homily upon the proprieties of war COMING FROM A FEDERAL OFFICER; HE hears it, whose home is in the VALLEY OF THE SHENANDOAH! There rises up before him his own homestead, its desolated fields, its level forests, the ash heaps which now mark the positions of its once beautiful, and cottage-like out-houses; and the thousand other vestiges of rural beauty despoiled by the brutality of the Federal soldiers, in its unrestrained career of pillage, plunder, wholesale robbery, and wanton destruction. He hears the protests of his helpless mother, and her appeals for protection heeded only by the God of the widow and fatherless. He remembers the deep burning insults which Federal officers have heaped, in their language, upon his own sisters. He hears in the hypocritical cant of General Dix that officer's own self-condemnation; and knows that every breath which the commanding general draws is in default of the penalty which he himself attaches to the violation of the laws of civilized warfare. He hears a sermon on the "rules which govern sovereign States in the conduct of hostilities with each other," by the man who, through his unlicensed, ill-disciplined, unrestrained, and unpunished soldiery, laid in ashes William and Mary College, an institution whose associations were hallowed by the literary nurture of the fathers of the Republic, and whose vulnerable walls were whitened by the frosts of a century. A general who, after an arduous campaign, succeeded in capturing a lunatic asylum, and who is said to have tendered to its patients the oath of loyalty to the United States, and who is known to have treated its refractory and unfortunate inmates with cruelty and inhumanity.   *   *   *

Even the executioner himself grows impatient, and cannot endure this ordeal. "Cut it short, cut it short!" cries he; "the Captain wishes to be swung off quick!" The crowd murmurs, and the reporters call his eagerness to perform his office, "brutality"; they mistake, he means it in mercy and kindness; he is protesting against brutality.

*   *   *   *   *   *   *

His (Beall's) manner has been throughout one of respectful attention; but when he mounts the scaffold, and sits down under the fatal coil, he turns his back upon the adjutant while he is reading, and faces in the opposite direction. This attitude he does not change. What does he mean? His face is turned upon his own beloved South! Far over waters, mountains, valleys, and intervening hills, through the deep azure sky, travel his thoughts to the land of tobacco and cotton, of orange and palmetto, of moss and magnolia, of chivalrous deeds, and political ideas which, rightly understood, gather in their scope the eternal years of God's own truth, and for which no man should hesitate to die! As the martyr sets his face toward Jerusalem, or the Mussulman toward the shrine of Mecca, so this hero, dying for the faith of his fathers, turns his face upon the South. Thus he faces when the last duty save one of the executioner is performed; and while standing thus, the provost-marshal asks him whether he has anything to say. Turning upon the officer of the day, he speaks in a calm, firm voice:

"I protest against the execution of this sentence. It is a murder! I die in the service and defense of my country! I have nothing more to say."

A moment afterwards a sword-flash is seen behind him, which is the signal to the executioner, and the soul of the hero springs upward with his body.

Thus died in the thirty-first year of his age, on the scaffold, John Yates Beall. Shameless women, who had long lost the sense of an emotion, save the curiosity which brought them to the island on this occasion, were now awed by the grandeur of this death; rough "machines" (regulars), rebuked this title by the tribute of a silent tear; while Federal officers, some of whom would have given a right arm to have saved this heroic life, were not ashamed to weep freely, tears both of pity and admiration.

His body, when dead, was given to his two faithful friends whose devotion had halted at no sacrifice in their efforts to save him while living, and they laid it privately to rest in Greenwood Cemetery, near New York City. Dr. Weston read the burial service of the Episcopal Church, and poured over the dead hero the full-tide flood of inspiration which flowed from the lips of Paul as he described the victorious, stingless, and eternal triumph of those who "die in the hope of a resurrection."

At this moment, on Fern Hill, in Greenwood, a plain marble slab is to be seen inscribed—"John Y. Beall, died February 24th, 1865," marking a green turf COVERED DAILY BY THE HANDS OF STRANGERS WITH FRESH, BLOOMING FLOWERS.

The summary hanging of Captain Beall for the crime of capturing a vessel on Lake Erie with the view of releasing prisoners on Johnson's Island, and for the crime of an attempt to capture a railroad train for the purpose of releasing Confederate generals, and securing the safe of the express company for the use of the Confederate Commissioners in Canada in defraying the expenses of war, was heard of at Richmond. The interest of the Confederate Government in the matter may be inferred from the following official proceedings:

RICHMOND VA., March 14, 1865.

THE HOUSE OF REPRESENTATIVES:

In response to your resolution of the 2d instant I herewith transmit for your information communications from the Secretary of the Navy and the Commissioner for the Exchange of Prisoners relative to the trial and execution of John Y. Beall, acting master of the C. S. Navy, by the authorities of the United States. JEFF'N DAVIS.

(Enclosure No. 1.)

CONFEDERATE STATES OF AMERICA, NAVY DEPARTMENT,
Richmond, March 4, 1865.

THE PRESIDENT.

SIR: I have the honor to state in response to the following resolution of the House of Representatives, referred by you to this Department—

"Resolved, That the President be respectfully requested to communicate to this House any information he may have in regard to the execution of John Y. Beall, of Jefferson County, Va., by the authorities of the Federal Government; and whether any and what action has been taken by this Government on the subject."

—that the only information I have with regard to the execution of John Y. Beall is derived from the Federal newspapers, whose accounts of the event were copied by the Richmond papers of the 27th ultimo.

Triplicate copies of Mr. Beall's appointment as an acting master in the Navy were furnished to the Department of State, upon the request of the Secretary of State, so soon as his arrest was known here, and another copy was sent by me to the Hon. Jacob Thompson in Canada.

The printed slip herewith, from the Federal newspapers, purporting to give the details of the arrest, trial, and conviction of Mr. Beall, is enclosed for further information.

I am, respectfully, your obedient servant,

S. R. MALLORY,
Secretary of the Navy.

(Sub-enclosure.)

Arrest.

(From a Northern newspaper.)

Beall was arrested through information received on the Canadian border by John S. Young, chief of the Metropolitan Detective Police. Mr. Young also received at the same time information concerning one of the principal witnesses against the pirate, and the party being brought to New York, fully identified Beall by picking him out of a crowd in one of the rooms at police headquarters. The recognition by this witness was complete, he having instantly stepped up to Beall and called him by name, much to the discomfiture of the rebel captain.

(Enclosure No. 3.)

RICHMOND, March 11, 1865.

HIS EXCELLENCY THE PRESIDENT.

SIR: In the matter of the accompanying resolution of the House of Representatives I have the honor to submit the following report:

The case of Acting Master John Y. Beall was never brought to the attention of the office by any communication, verbal or written, prior to his execution. The proceedings of the military commission which tried him were not published in the Northern papers until the 15th of February. The day for his execution had been fixed for the 18th of the same month, as if for the purpose of making any efforts in his behalf by his Government impossible. He was reprieved from the 18th to the 24th, though it seems to have been quietly, if not secretly, done. For some days after the 24th it was not known here whether or not he had been executed. On the 27th of February I received a letter from him, of which the following is a copy, which was forwarded by order of General Dix after the unfortunate man had been put to death:

"FORT COLUMBUS, February 21, 1865.

"Col. R. OULD, Commissioner of Exchange, Richmond, Va.

"SIR: The proceedings of a military commission in my case published in the New York papers of the 15th instant made you and my Government aware of my sentence and doom. A reprieve, on account of some informality, from the 18th to the 24th, was granted. The authorities are possessed of the facts in my case. They know that I acted under orders. I appeal to my Government to use its utmost efforts to protect me, and if unable to prevent my murder, to vindicate my reputation. I can only declare that I was no 'spy' or 'guerrilla,' and am a true Confederate.

"Respectfully,
"JOHN Y. BEALL,
"Acting Master, C. S. Navy."

The cruelty of the enemy was so swift that no sufficient time intervened between a knowledge of the facts and the execution to enable any proceedings to be taken.

Respectfully, your obedient servant,
R. OULD,
Agent of Exchange.

CHAPTER XXXVI

Trial of Lieutenant Young and his men at Montreal—Complete vindication.

The expedition under command of Lieut. Bennett H. Young upon St. Albans had continued to excite universal interest on account of the panic it had created in the United States along the borders and likewise among the authorities of Canada.

Lieutenant Young and some of his comrades were in prison at 'Montreal, for whom the sympathies of the people of Canada were cordial and unabated during the impending trial for extradition. The trial of these Confederates had now become the most celebrated which occurred during the Civil War, for the reason that it was forcing an issue between England and the United States.

Immediately after the raid the grand jury at St. Albans had indicted Bennett H. Young, Squire Turner Teavis, Alamanda Pope Bruce, Marcus Spurr, Charles Moore Swager, Joseph McGorty, William H. Hutchinson, George Scott, Caleb Mc-Dowell Wallace, James Alexander Doty, Samuel Simpson Gregg, Dudley Moore, Samuel Eugene Lackey, and Thomas Bronsdon Collins, for robbery and arson, and the President of the United States demanded their extradition upon the charge of a felony under the Ashburton Treaty. This was the plan for bringing Young and his men into the United States, when of course the military authorities could at once take them into custody and execute them as spies or guerrillas. The demand for extradition could not be made upon the ground that Young and his men were Confederates who were guilty of conducting illegitimate warfare. It was therefore contended at the trial, by the Attorney-General of Canada and the counsel employed by the United States, that the prisoners were guilty of robbery and arson, and their character as Confederates and the orders of the Confederate Government for raids upon the United States territory were disputed and ignored. Every effort was made to prevent the prisoners from furnishing the evidence from Richmond to prove their identity and the authority for this or any other raid in Northern territory.

The prisoners were arrested by a magistrate of Stanbridge, accompanied by United States detectives and one or more citizens of St. Albans, who could identify the raiders. Lieutenant Young surrendered voluntarily in order to stand trial and share the fate of his men.

The prisoners were arraigned in the Police Court at Montreal, Canada, November 7th, 1864, when the proceedings began by the testimony of the arresting officers and others.

The charges having been read to the prisoners the court then said:

Having heard the evidence, do you wish to say anything in answer to the charge? You are not obliged to say anything, unless you desire to do so; but whatever you say will be taken down in writing, and may be given in evidence against you at your trial.

Whereupon the said Bennett H. Young saith as follows: "I am a native of Kentucky, and a citizen of the Confederate States, to which I owe allegiance. I am a commissioned officer in the Army of the Confederate States, with which the United States are now at war. I owe no allegiance to the United States. I herewith produce my commission as first lieutenant in the Confederate States Army, and the instructions I received at the time that commission was conferred upon me; reserving the right to put in evidence further instructions I have received at such time and in such manner as my counsel shall advise. Whatever was done at St. Albans was done by the authority and order of the Confederate Government. I have not violated the neutrality laws of either Canada or Great Britain. Those who were with me at St. Albans were all officers or enlisted soldiers of the Confederate Army, and were then under my command. They were such before the 19th of October last, and their term of enlistment has not yet expired. Several of them were prisoners of war, taken in battle by the Federal forces, and retained as such, from which imprisonment they escaped. The expedition was not set on foot or projected in Canada. The course I intended to pursue in Vermont, and which I was able to carry out but partially, was to retaliate in some measure for the barbarous atrocities of Grant, Butler, Sherman, Hunter, Milroy, Sheridan, Grierson, and other Yankee officers, except that I would scorn to harm women and children under any provocation, or unarmed, defenseless, and unresisting citizens, even Yankees, or to plunder for my own benefit. I am not prepared for the full defense of myself and my command without communication with my Government at Richmond, and inasmuch as such communication is interdicted by the Yankee Government, by land and by sea, I do not think I can be ready for such full defense under thirty days, during which time I hope to be able to obtain material important testimony without the consent of said Yankee Government, from Richmond."

And further the examinant saith not, and hath signed, the foregoing having previously been read in his presence.

(Signed.)   "BENNETT H. YOUNG."

The statement of Captain Collins fairly represents the responses of all the prisoners:

Whereupon the said Thomas Bronsdon Collins saith as follows: "I am a native of Kentucky and a commissioned officer of the Army of the Confederate States at war with the so-called United States. I served under the command of General John Morgan, and became separated from it at the battle of Cynthiana, Kentucky. Having eluded the Yankees, I joined Lieutenant Young afterwards at Chicago, knowing it to be my duty to my government as well as to myself never to desert its cause. I owe no allegiance to the so-called United States, but am a foreigner and public enemy to the Yankee Government. The Yankees dragged my father from his peaceful fireside and family circle, and imprisoned him in Camp Chase, where his sufferings impaired his health and mind, and my grandfather has been banished by brute Burbridge. They have stolen negroes and forced them into their armies, leaving their women and children to starve and die. They have pillaged and burned private dwellings, banks, villages and depopulated whole districts, boasting of their inhuman acts as deeds of heroism and exhibiting their plunder in Northern cities as trophies of Federal victories. I have violated no laws of Canada or Great Britain. Whatever I may have done at St. Albans, I did as a Confederate officer acting under Lieutenant Young. When I left St. Albans, I came to Canada solely for protection. I entered a hotel at Stanbridge unarmed and alone, and was arrested and handcuffed by a Canadian magistrate (Whitman) assisted by Yankees. He had no warrant for my arrest, nor had any sworn complaint been made to him against me. About $9,300 was taken from me when arrested, part Confederate booty lawfully captured and held by me as such, and part of my own private funds. I ask the restoration of the money taken from me and my discharge as demanded by the rules of international law. The treaty under which my extradition is claimed applies to robbers, murderers, thieves, and forgers. I am neither, but a soldier serving my country in a war commenced and waged against us by a barbarous foe in violation of their own Constitution, in disregard of all the rules of warfare as interpreted by civilized nations and Christian people, and against Yankees too wise to expose themselves to danger, while they can buy mercenaries and steal negroes to fight their battles for them, who whilst prating of neutrality seduce your own people along the border to violate the proclamation of your august Sovereign by joining their armies, and leave them when captured by us to languish as prisoners in a climate unwholesome to them. If I aided in the sack of the St. Albans banks, it was because they were public institutions, and because I knew the pocket-nerve of the Yankees to be the most sensitive, that they would suffer most by its being rudely touched. I cared nothing for the booty, except to injure the enemies of my country. Federal soldiers are bought up at $1,000 a head, and the capture of $200,000 is equivalent to the destruction of 200 of said soldiers. I therefore thought the expedition 'would pay.' I 'guess' it did in view of the fact also, that they have wisely sent several thousand soldiers from the 'bloody front' to protect exposed points in the rear. For the part I took I am ready to abide the consequences, knowing that if I am extradited to the Yankee butchers, my Government can avenge if not protect its soldiers."

And further the examinant saith not, and hath signed, the foregoing having been previously read in his presence.

(Signed.)   "THOMAS BRONSDON COLLINS."

It will be observed that the prisoners relied upon the fact that they were Confederate soldiers and possessed authority for the raid upon St. Albans.

The prosecution claimed that the written authority of Lieutenant Young did not bear the seal of the Confederacy and other requisites which could only be certified at Richmond.

After the adjournment in November had been granted the cases were again called for trial on the 13th of December, 1864. The question was now raised and fully argued by Mr. Kerr, of counsel for the prisoners, of the jurisdiction of this court. There was a colloquy and discussion over the point. At the afternoon session, the Police Judge, Charles J. Coursol, J. S. P., rendered a lengthy decision in which he conceded his lack of jurisdiction under the law and the prisoners were discharged.

The authorities at St. Albans had issued warrants for thirteen of the raiders whose names had been obtained. The names of the remainder of the party were never learned by the authorities of St. Albans or the United States. They were John D. McInnis, William T. Tevis, Charles H. Higby, Lewis Price, Daniel Mock Butterworth of Alabama, and John E. Moss. Eight of the number, for whom a requisition had been issued, namely, Alexander Pope Bruce, George Scott, Caleb McDowell Wallace, James Alexander Doty, Joseph McGorty, Dudley Moore, Samuel Eugene Lackey, and Thomas Bronsdon Collins, managed to elude the officers in Canada and were never again apprehended.

Immediately after the discharge of the prisoners by Judge Coursol, Mr. Justice Smith issued a warrant for the re-arrest of the prisoners, similar to those under which they had been previously in custody. On this warrant, five out of the thirteen, namely, Lieut. Bennett H. Young, W. H. Hutchinson, Squire Turner Teavis, Charles Moore Swager, and Marcus Spurr, were again arrested, near Quebec, on the 20th day of December, 1864, and brought to Montreal for examination in the Superior Court.

A question of jurisdiction was now raised by Mr. Kerr on behalf of the prisoners. This was argued and considered from day to day until the court on January 10th, 1865, over-ruled the point.

A motion was now made for a delay of thirty days to enable messengers to return who had been sent through the United States to Richmond, in order to obtain certified copies of Lieutenant Young's commission and orders from the Confederate Government, and of the records showing the other prisoners to be Confederate soldiers. The adjournment for thirty days was finally agreed to by the attorneys on both sides.

J. G. K. Houghton, an eminent attorney of Montreal, on behalf of the prisoners, had gone to Washington and applied to Secretary of State Seward and President Lincoln for a pass through the lines, but both had refused. Mr. Seward's response was as follows:

DEPARTMENT OF STATE, WASHINGTON,
January 30, 1865.

J. G. K. Houghton, Esq., advocate and attorney for the prisoners whose extradition in the matter of the St. Albans murders and robberies has been demanded, is informed that the Government of the United States can hold no communication or correspondence with him on that subject. The prisoners, if they submit themselves to the authority of the United States, need no foreign mediation. So long as they remain under the protection of a foreign government, and a demand upon that government for their delivery to the United States is pending, communications concerning them can be received only from that foreign government through the customary channels of national intercourse.

A copy of the papers submitted by Mr. Houghton has been taken, and the originals are herewith remitted to him, and he is expected to leave the United States without crossing the military lines, or attempting to enter the scene of insurrection, or to communicate with the insurgents.

(Signed.)   WILLIAM H. SEWARD.

These facts were alleged by Young and his men as grounds for a further delay of thirty days. But the court decided to proceed with the trial, leaving the Confederates in a helpless plight.

The prosecution having introduced their witnesses to prove that the prisoners were of the party who made the attack upon St. Albans, the testimony was now taken in behalf of the prisoners. The counsel for the defense then filed paper "P," as evidence of the Confederate character of Lieutenant Young, etc. A number of witnesses testified in behalf of the prisoners, and just before the trial ended Rev. S. F. Cameron arrived safely from Richmond, bringing the certified documents bearing the great seal of the Confederacy.

Mrs. ————,* a widow only 24 years old, employed by the Confederate Government for secret service in the Northern States, had come to Montreal and called on the prisoners at the jail. She volunteered for the journey to Richmond. After leaving the railroad in Maryland she walked much of the way through the country occupied by the enemy in Virginia. She departed from Richmond with the necessary certified papers, well concealed, one day before Rev. Mr. Cameron arrived there. These two messengers, traveling by different routes, reached Montreal on the same day. She declined to accept from Col. Jacob Thompson any compensation whatever for her services or expenses. This devotee of the South was a Kentucky lady. About 1867 she visited Frankfort when the legislature was in session. During a recess of fifteen minutes taken in her honor she was the recipient of an ovation, being presented by Hon. Thomas T. Coger, of Jessamine County, the home of Lieut. Bennett H. Young.

---

*The prisoners never met this lady before or after her visits to the jail at Montreal. One of the survivors secured her photograph at the jail, but after forty years her name is forgotten.

In memory of her heroic interest when the lives of the Confederate prisoners were hanging by a thread all the tribute that can be paid on their behalf is cheerfully recorded.   —AUTHOR.

Young Confederate Widow who was a messenger for the
St. Alban's Raiders in getting the proper papers
from the Confederate Government

Paper P.
Mem. for Lieut. Bennett Young, C. S. A.

Your report of your doings, under your instructions of 16th June last from the Secretary of War, covering the list of twenty Confederate soldiers who are escaped prisoners, collected and enrolled by you under those instructions, is received.

Your suggestion for a raid upon accessible towns in Vermont, commencing with St. Albans, is approved, and you are authorized and required to act in conformity with that suggestion.

October 6, 1864.   C. C. CLAY, Jun.,
                                    Commissioner, C. S. A.

Stephen F. Cameron's deposition follows:

I am a citizen of Maryland. I have been in the Confederate service as a chaplain, from the beginning of the war to the present time. I was in Richmond on the 1st February instant.

[The counsel for the defense produced muster-roll of Company A, Eighth Kentucky Cavalry, containing the name of Marcus Spurr; copy of muster-roll of Lagrange Light Guard of Georgia, containing the name of William Hutchinson Huntley; copy of muster-roll of Company B, Colonel Chenault's Kentucky Cavalry, containing the name Squire Teavis; a copy of muster-roll of Company H, Second Kentucky Infantry, containing the name of Charles M. Swager; also copies of two letters of instructions addressed to Lieut. Bennett H. Young, dated June 16th, 1864, and purporting to be signed by James A. Seddon, Secretary of War.]   *   *   *

Being shown and having the said papers—I say that I received them from Secretary Benjamin, Secretary of State of the Confederate States. He affixed his signature to them in my presence. I did not part with them until I handed them to the Honorable Mr. Abbott yesterday. The seal was affixed at that time—that is, the great seal of the Confederate States was affixed to them when he signed them; and he called my attention to the seal. This was in the office of the Secretary of State. I volunteered to go for the papers for the prisoners.

I carried a missive from Colonel Thompson, who arranged with me about going, and supplied the funds. I called upon Mr. Benjamin about an hour after my arrival in Richmond, and he informed me that the papers had been sent by another messenger on the day before. He said that the papers had been sent, that everything had been sent, necessary to establish their belligerent character, and that they acted under orders. The following day I called on the President, by appointment, and asked, that to insure the safe delivery of the papers, I might be entrusted with a duplicate as a second messenger. He readily acquiesced, and expressed great anxiety that they should be so placed as to escape detection, suggesting that the paper containing the great seal should be photographed upon tissue paper, so as to take up less space. Mr. Benjamin being present, explained that the muster-roll would take so much space, that the size of the great seal would be of no consequence. He stated that he had sent the orders under which the young men had acted, previous to their making the raid. He thought that these papers would be fully sufficient to justify their doings, and that they would have full justice done them he had no doubt. The President stated that the prisoners' orders under which they acted having been sent, constituted superior testimony to any subsequent ratification. He expressed some surprise as to the result of Burley's case. I explained to him that in that case the judge was only a police magistrate, accustomed to deal only with petty larcenies, but that in this case it was before a Superior Court judge who would appreciate questions of international law. He stated as his reason for not issuing his order in this case, that his general order in the Burley case had been disregarded, and he seemed piqued and indignant at that fact. I told him that if the Confederate States had been as near neighbors as the Federal States, there would have been, probably, a different result. I looked at the papers in the Department of State, to see that the names were affixed; they are precisely in the same condition now as when I received them; I made no request for any particular papers; I merely presented the message with which I was entrusted; I never read the letter with which I was entrusted, and do not know its contents, except that I understood that it was a letter of introduction, and contained the names of the prisoners.

[The counsel for the United States, objecting to the whole of this evidence as illegal and incompetent, decline to cross-examine this witness.]

(Signed.) S. F. Cameron.

Lewis Sanders testified:

I know Lieut. Bennett H. Young, one of the prisoners; I know the Hon. Clement C. Clay, Jun.; I was present at several conversations between said Mr. Clay and said Lieut. Bennett

Rev. Stephen F. Cameron

H. Young, between the 29th of August and the 9th of September last. I heard conversations between them about the attack on St. Albans, which was subsequently made on the 19th of October. The purport of these conversations was that Young was to burn the town if possible, and sack the banks. I am aware that Mr. Clay furnished Young with money to cover his expenses at the said raid. Mr. Clay sent me a cheque for $400 or upwards for Mr. Young, toward the expenses of the said expedition. I gave him the said cheque, and he got the money on it at Montreal; this was about two weeks before the raid. I had no personal knowledge that he got the money, but I presume he did, as there were funds to meet it.

* * * * * * *

The attorneys in the case delivered elaborate speeches, which would be of special interest except for their length.

Mr. Abbott, in defense of the prisoners, in the course of his speech took occasion to describe a Federal raid in comparison with the St. Albans raid:

* * * * * * *

The sacking and burning of Darien, Georgia, gives us an excellent practical exemplification of the doctrine of the Federal States as to what constitutes an act of war. And it forms the best possible commentary on the scorn, the indignation, and the horror which the learned counsel have been at such pains to express, at the comparatively insignificant injuries inflicted by the prisoners upon the town of St. Albans. I say that I can find the record in this book (War Record, No. 42) of a thousand times worse acts than the St. Albans raid, committed in a thousand instances in the South, by Federal troops, since this war began.

At the close of the speeches by counsel the court rendered a lengthy decision in which the case was discussed in all its phases.

Lieutenant Young and the other prisoners were discharged by the court upon the ground that they were Confederate soldiers and duly authorized by their Government to engage in expeditions against the United States. An extract from his decision is given as follows:

Acts of war by the law of nations, are just such acts as the belligerents choose to commit within the territories of each other. These acts are done upon the responsibility of the nation, and the soldiers committing them can in no way be held punishable for them. They may be what is termed unlawful acts of war, and violations of the law of nations, but I, as a judge in a neutral country, cannot sit in judgment upon them. Being committed within the territory of the belligerent, there is no violation of our law; nor can the belligerent invoke their unlawfulness before me. By the international code, reciprocity is acknowledged by all authors to be one of the obligations of belligerents, and one of the tests of the lawfulness of their acts as against each other. Whatever, then, is done by one nation to the other, within belligerent territory in carrying on the war, must necessarily be permitted to the other. As a matter of fact, raids of this description have been constantly permitted and justified by and on behalf of the United States. On what principle then can they be denied to the so-called Confederate States? However, as far as regards the violence or unlawfulness of these acts, as a neutral I have no authority to decide. It is for the belligerents themselves to deal with these questions; and WHERE AUTHORITY, EITHER EXPRESSED OR IMPLIED, IS GIVEN BY ONE BELLIGERENT TO DO.THE ACT IT IS AN ACT OF WAR FOR WHICH ALONE THE BELLIGERENT IS RESPONSIBLE.

It is now of special interest to state that the questions involved in this trial had been formulated and submitted to the Government of Great Britain. The decision of the Queen's Counsel, Sir Hugh Cairns and Mr. Francis Reilly, in England, was not received until after the trial was ended, but completely exonerated the Confederate soldiers who composed the expedition against St. Albans.

At the conclusion of the trial of Lieutenant Young and his comrades, W. H. Hutchinson, S. T. Teavis, C. M. Swager, and Marcus Spurr, the Attorney-General of Canada held them upon a warrant from Toronto, which charged a violation of the neutrality laws of Canada. The penalty for this offense if convicted was imprisonment for several years and a fine of ten thousand dollars. The Confederates were accordingly carried to Toronto in the custody of a large force of policemen, where they were placed in jail.

The prisoners received the same ovation from Southern refugees and Canadian friends at Toronto as in Montreal. The jailer extended every possible courtesy and accommodation for the comfort of the prisoners.

After a delay of some weeks the prisoners secured an examining trial. There was no evidence whatever against Hutchinson, Teavis, Swager and Spurr, and they were discharged. The only testimony against Lieutenant Young was that of Godfrey J. Hyams, the confidant of Colonel Thompson, who had deserted to the enemy. Hyams testified that Young had told him of the force which was being organized in Canada for the St. Albans raid. But the character of this man had become notorious in Toronto and his unsupported testimony was not even now relied on by the Canadian Government. Young was allowed to execute bond for $10,000 and was released. Canadian sympathizers promptly furnished the bond. Young continued to appear and demand trial for months, when, finally, the Government finding that no case could be made against him, a *nolle prosequi* was entered and this noted prisoner departed in peace.

CHAPTER XXXVII

Arrangements to leave Canada for Richmond—Plan for the
next campaign—Last ditch in the Northern States—Colonel
Thompson remains in Canada to assist in the trials of Confederates.

The events which had transpired since the departure of
Hon. C. C. Clay, Jr., from Canada in December had thrown
the entire responsibility of all our affairs upon Colonel
Thompson and he had devoted himself to the interests of
the Confederates whose lives were at stake.

Martin and I had remained in Toronto at Colonel Thompson's request and much of our time had been occupied in conference with him, not only with reference to current troubles
in Canada but also concerning the situation in the Confederacy and in the Northern States. We had discussed all possible chances for the success of the South, making estimates
of our military strength and its distribution. It had been
evident for weeks that General Sherman would be practically unopposed on his march northward from Savannah,
and then would come the end. The South was exhausted,
not only in soldiers but in supplies, and without a radical
change of base we all felt that the war was over with the
opening of good weather in the spring when armies could
move. It could not be continued long with Richmond cut
off from the States southward.

It was finally agreed that Martin and I should go through
to Richmond and submit a plan in which Colonel Thompson
had equal confidence with ourselves. It had been his judgment at all times that the Confederacy could get support in
the North if our armies could advance and remain there, but
the "Sons of Liberty" could not be expected to rally upon an

army of invasion that could be readily driven back. General Lee had been met promptly by superior numbers in Maryland and Pennsylvania, and Generals Bragg and Smith, even in Kentucky, had only made a circuit apparently to obtain recruits.

The plan was about as follows: We should go to General Breckinridge, who was now Secretary of War, and first enlist him in the enterprise if possible. Martin had been a scout for Breckinridge at Shiloh and knew him well. If Breckinridge agreed we would go with him to the President and submit what seemed to be a practical movement.

It should be first stated that at this time Thomas's army was at Nashville with the advance as far south as Florence, Alabama, and Chattanooga; Sherman at Columbia, South Carolina; Grant in front of Petersburg, and some 30,000 or 40,000 troops under different commanders in the Shenandoah Valley and West Virginia.

The Federal armies were in fact far to the south on the west of the mountains and likewise along the Atlantic.

The forces opposing Sherman were north of his position. It was proposed that this force with all the others being organized by Beauregard, in North Carolina, should be combined with Lee's army, which would suddenly evacuate Richmond and Petersburg. All these troops it was calculated would aggregate 90,000 to 100,000 men of all arms, including all in North Carolina and Virginia. They could all concentrate between Richmond and Lynchburg and march direct to Staunton and on to Pennsylvania, leaving the South abandoned. Then threaten Washington and Philadelphia until confronted by Grant. Meanwhile, the cavalry should gather up all the horses in the country and mount the infantry, until eventually the entire army would be mounted, and then instead of taking any risks in front of Washington and Philadelphia, fall back and capture Pittsburg and locate with the seat of government at Wheeling, some forty miles west but still in the South. The army could then face east and guard the line from the Ohio River to Lake Erie, a distance of about one hundred miles.

With the railroads in Pennsylvania torn up and bridges destroyed, Grant and Sherman would require some time to meet the new condition of affairs. They would have to march from the east. The mountains of West Virginia and the Ohio River were a safeguard on the south and Lake Erie on the north of Pittsburg. Thomas would be obliged to find a new base if he kept his army in Tennessee.

Meanwhile, Lee and Johnston would have time to equip their armies and obtain ample supplies in the enemy's country and would sever the West from the East.

It seemed that Lee and Johnston would have as little trouble in making this movement as Sherman had in marching from Atlanta to Savannah. And that a column of 10,000 cavalry under A. P. Hill could have ridden around in New York, creating considerable alarm in New York City, while 10,000 under Longstreet might have marched west through Ohio, Indiana, and Illinois, threatening Cincinnati and taking Indianapolis.

While this was going on there would be a cry in the North for help or peace, perhaps both.

The President and Cabinet, being at the temporary seat of government, could direct affairs from Wheeling. It could be proclaimed that this army would hold this position until threatened, when it would retire in marching columns and be governed by circumstances and the orders of the Government in the conduct of the war. Meanwhile, fragments could follow from the South, coming up through the mountains.

The army it was believed could not be captured after it was mounted. Ohio, Indiana, Illinois, Michigan, and Pennsylvania could subsist the troops without serious inconvenience.

The organized and armed forces of the "Sons of Liberty" could now get help to rendezvous at Chicago or Indianapolis.

It was not believed that Grant alone would undertake to march from Richmond and follow in pursuit of such an army. The best that Grant and Sherman could do would be to come up the Atlantic on transports to Washington, Philadelphia, and New York. And this would require enough time to enable Lee and Johnston to establish the new base.

At all events, this army could fall back westward, gathering strength on the march and creating consternation all over the North. It did not appear that Grant, Sherman, and Thomas would have any chance to prevent the movement in the beginning or the subsequent operations.

Of course this change of base would leave the South absolutely at the mercy of the enemy, but the Northern people and their property would be equally in the power of the Confederates, who would be unopposed in marching west on horseback.

Colonel Thompson was fearful that President Davis would want to hold Richmond until it would be too late. He appeared to be informed to the extent that in case of emergency Lee's army would be directed south through western North Carolina and then toward Alabama. It was his opinion that if the proposed change of base should be approved it ought to be attempted not later than the 1st of May.

I got the impression from Colonel Thompson that Mr. Clay had expected to communicate with Richmond and propose the movement, but we had never heard anything on the subject since his departure. We believed Breckinridge would favor the plan for the reason that it would free Kentucky from occupation by the enemy, for if Thomas faced north he would probably go farther west and be reinforced on the river by the army at New Orleans and troops along the Mississippi. This would enable us to gather strength from Kentucky and the South. And Dick Taylor and Forrest by uniting with Kirby Smith would make another army of 60,000 to march west of the Mississippi

River to be mounted in Iowa. It could then march eastward in support of Lee and Johnston and Beauregard. This would still leave over 100,000 troops scattered over the South, who could be gotten North and mounted.

None of us could see the propriety of making the last ditch in the impoverished South when the gates to the North and then to the West stood wide open. We felt certain that the South could afford to have the seat of war transferred to the North, where we could win or lose at the expense of the enemy.

Colonel Thompson estimated that our troops in the Northern prisons numbered over 80,000 men and that more than half of them were at Camp Chase, Camp Morton, Camp Douglas, Springfield, and Rock Island. They could not be moved east, and likewise those at Johnson's Island. If possible these would be released promptly and added to the army.

But we all believed if Lee and Beauregard united their forces and escaped from Grant the movement was certain of success. And that with this army mounted the prospects for the desolation of the North would be so apparent that peace would be made without further bloodshed or ruin.

After the 1st of May it was not believed that gunboats could ascend to Pittsburg, and if they did they would hardly expose it to destruction. However, we did not make calculations beyond the escape of 100,000 men from Grant before Sherman arrived in Lee's rear. Still, we thought the largest number it was possible to concentrate had better take that route by the 1st of May. All the remainder of the programme could well be left to the authorities and commanders.

The proposed movement had been discussed until we were now enthusiastic on the subject. Colonel Thompson had been hoping for some tidings from Mr. Clay or some notice of his arrival in the Confederacy, in which event we would remain in Canada with Colonel Thompson, and await developments. The arrival of Sherman at Columbia, where he had halted at this time, February 1st, indicated that perhaps he would now turn upon Charleston and remain to desolate the entire State of South Carolina, with the purpose of drawing forces away from Lee and other parts of Virginia.

It was yet midwinter, and the armies were in winter quarters, but it was deemed best for us to make our way through the United States and submit the question at Richmond. Sherman had spent over two months marching through Georgia, and in Savannah, and we believed he would spend at least three months in South Carolina and North Carolina to starve Lee's army, while Grant would keep it employed in holding Petersburg and Richmond. Therefore, the North was the easiest place to reach and the best place to go. We thought it would relieve the South.

To us it appeared that nothing could be lost and everything might be gained by the movement. There was one other objection that we all feared might be raised at Richmond. President Davis had not been friendly to the cavalry forces during the war, and might take a stand against venturing north with the idea of mounting the army, preferring to consolidate the remaining strength and fight through toward the west, whenever Richmond must be abandoned.

In the event of the occupation of Pennsylvania and Ohio by the Confederate army of cavalry, the holders of government bonds and of large amounts of greenbacks, we thought, would clamor for peace in order to save their profits on the war.

If necessary the Federal prisoners in the South might be paroled and allowed to go home.

We learned afterwards that Mr. Clay did reach the Confederacy, and it is possible that the Northern movement may have been suggested by him to President Davis and the Secretary of War, but, if so, it must have been considered with disfavor, as no mention is made of it by Mr. Davis.

President Davis says:

> In the early part of March, as well as my memory can fix the date, General Lee held with me a long and free conference. He stated that the circumstances had forced on him the conclusion that the evacuation of Petersburg was but a question of time. * * * There naturally followed the consideration of the line of retreat. A considerable time before this General Hood had sent me a paper, presenting his views and conclusions that, if it became necessary for the Army of Northern Virginia to retreat, it should move toward Middle Tennessee. The paper was forwarded to General Lee and returned by him with an unfavorable criticism, and the conclusion that, if we had to retreat, it should. be in a southwardly direction toward the country from which we were drawing supplies, and from which a large portion of our forces had been derived. In this conversation the same general view was more specifically stated, and made to apply to the then condition of affairs. The programme was to retire to Danville, at which place supplies should be collected and a junction made with the troops under General J. E. Johnston, the combined force to be hurled upon Sherman in North Carolina, with the hope of defeating him before Grant could come to his relief. Then the more southern States, freed from pressure and encouraged by his success, it was expected, would send large reinforcements to the army, and Grant, drawn far from his base of supplies into the midst of a hostile population, it was hoped, might yet be defeated, and Virginia be delivered from the invader. Efforts were energetically continued to collect supplies in depots where they would be available, and, in furtherance of the suggestion of General Lee as to the necessary improvement in the condition of his horses, the Quartermaster-General was instructed to furnish larger rations of corn to the quartermaster at Petersburg.

*   *   *   *   *   *   *

It appears from the plans of President Davis that a retreat to Middle Tennessee was not approved by General Lee, and that the route due south from Danville was adopted.

It had occurred to us that the Confederate troops would be in far better spirits on horseback in the North, where supplies were abundant, than struggling in hunger and in rags through the summer months in the sultry South, among the famine-stricken families and ruined homes of the soldiers, with scenes of desolation yet to follow the paths of the invading armies of the enemy.

CHAPTER XXXVIII

The trouble of reaching Richmond—Situation in Kentucky, West Virginia, and Tennessee.

It was now a serious undertaking not only to get safely out of Canada but to pass through the United States and reach the lines of the Confederacy in Virginia.

We must either go through the department of Burbridge in Kentucky, striking the trail for Pound Gap about Mt. Sterling, or through the West Virginia mountains, an equally dangerous route that would be new to us.

At Toronto we were fully advised of local conditions in all the border States, including Tennessee. We finally concluded to venture through Kentucky. Two cases in Kentucky and two in Tennessee will fairly show the situation:

RICHMOND, January 12, 1865.
Lieut.-Col. JOHN E. MULFORD, Assistant Agent of Exchange.
SIR: Reliable information has been furnished to the Confederate authorities that Col. J. D. Morris and Major T. Steele, of the Confederate Army, are confined in the jail at Lexington, Ky., and are heavily ironed. It is further represented that they are to be tried as spies. Colonel Morris and Major Steele were acting under orders from the War Department at Richmond at the time of their capture. They had been ordered to go into Kentucky for the purpose of recruiting their regiments and bringing out soldiers belonging to the Confederate Army.

I now notify you and the Federal authorities through you that Col. W. R. Hartshorne, One Hundred and Ninetieth Pennsylvania Regiment, and Maj. E. S. Horton, Fifty-eighth Massachusetts Regiment, have been selected for treatment similar to that received by Colonel Morris and Major Steele. Whatever punishment is suffered by the latter will be visited upon the two named Federal officers.

Respectfully, your obedient servant,
R. OULD,
Agent of Exchange.

OFFICE COMMISSARY-GENERAL OF PRISONERS,
Washington, D. C., January 21, 1865.
Bvt. Maj.-Gen. S. G. BURBRIDGE,
Commanding District of Kentucky, Lexington, Ky.
GENERAL: I am authorized to request that Col. J. D. Morris and Major T. Steele, of the rebel army, who are said to be confined in the jail at Lexington, Ky., and in irons, be immediately released and forwarded under proper guard to Lieut.-Col. John E. Mulford, agent for exchange of prisoners, Fort Monroe, Va. Please report action taken.
I am, General, very respectfully,
Your obedient servant,
H. W. WESSELLS,
Brig.-Gen., U. S. Vols., Inspector and Com.-Gen. of Prisoners.

When Colonel Morris arrived at Richmond he reported as follows:

RICHMOND, March 13, 1865.
TO THE HONORABLE COMMITTEE OF THE CONFEDERATE SENATE.
SIRS: During a short conference held on yesterday, at the suggestion of Colonel Ould, between the Honorable Senator Watson, a member of your committee, and myself, the statements which I then made respecting my own treatment and that of other prisoners confined by the Federal authorities at Lexington, Ky., during the past fall and winter, were regarded by Mr. Watson of much importance.

 * * * * * * *

For certain purposes which it would be irrelevant to state here, with a commission of C. S. colonel in my pocket. I went into Kentucky about the middle of October last. I was accompanied by Col. R. J. Breckinridge and Major Steele. Upon reaching the interior, after passing over a country almost ruined by the marauding parties of both armies, by extraordinary exertions and precautions, we reached the hills of Owen County, on the Kentucky River, all safe.

 * * * * * * *

Colonel Morris, after a graphic account of his concealment, encounters with Federal scouting parties, and capture, continues as follows:

At Lexington we were carried to the office of the provost-marshal, who, after insulting and using the most abusive language to us all, had us committed to the prison. The prison was an old warehouse, in a long room in which were about 120 men of all descriptions—Yankee deserters, men belonging to General Grant's army who had been sent through the lines by the Confederate Government and captured in Kentucky, men who belonged to the guerrilla bands who infest the State, bounty jumpers, disaffected citizens, and Confederate soldiers.

* * * * * * *

The executions under the bloody order of General Burbridge commenced about this time. One day immediately after my arrival the provost-marshal, Lieutenant Vance, came into the room, and looking over the men picked out fifteen. They were carried down-stairs. In a short time five of them returned. They had drawn lots for their lives and escaped; the other ten were taken out and shot. The day after six others were carried out and executed. Three men who were brought in and belonged to Jessee's command, within four hours after their arrival were carried from the prison and hung, and this went on until twenty-eight of our number, almost invariably Confederate soldiers, had fallen victims to this unheard-of barbarity. You may imagine—I cannot describe—the horror and dread which spread among the prisoners at witnessing these scenes. These men were not tried before a military commission or court martial. They were simply selected by the provost-martial, as it seemed to me, without any reference to the guilt or innocence of the parties, just as a butcher would go into a slaughter pen and select at his will the beeves or the sheep or the hogs which he might wish to destroy. The thing was very horrible. About one-half of the men in the prison were in irons, some of them with handcuffs on their wrists, others with balls and chains on their limbs; many of them chained together two and two.

* * * * * * *

In the late part of January I was taken ill. I suffered greatly for several days. The doctor, who was kind, on the fourth day after my attack pronounced my disease smallpox or varioloid and decided to send me to the pest-house. A horse-cart was driven to the door of the prison and I was placed in it with a poor negro from another prison, and, with the wind blowing fiercely and the snow falling fast, we were carried to a house some three miles in the country, which was used as a hospital for smallpox patients of all kinds. My courage had been tried upon many a battlefield—I have confronted death in a thousand shapes—but never was it so severely tried as when I was conducted into the small room where I was to be treated for this loathsome disease. There were seven patients already in the room, several of them in the last stages of the disease, all of them horribly swollen and wretchedly offensive. My clothes, everything belonging to me except the chains upon my limbs, were taken from me and carried away. I was dressed in some old Federal traps and placed upon a straw mattress on a little iron bedstead. The same evening one of the men in my room died; he was taken out at once to be buried, and I was immediately transferred to his place. There was a large negro on one side of me dreadfully ill, and beyond conception offensive. Next morning another man died. This poor fellow was from my prison, and like me had fetters upon his limbs. After his death men came in, knocked the chains from the stiffening corpse, and he was carried off. Immediately I was changed to his place. Next day another man, one of the negroes, died, and they were about to move me again, but I protested and they desisted. My attack was a slight one, and in ten days I was back in my prison quarters. Here, after remaining some time longer, it was announced to me that I was to be sent on for special exchange. My irons were taken off and I was placed upon the cars and sent to Louisville and thence to Fort Monroe.

Such is an imperfect narrative of my capture and confinement.

Very respectfully,
J. D. MORRIS,
Colonel, C. S. Army.

City of Richmond, Va., *to-wit:*

Col. J. D. Morris, C. S. Army, being by the undersigned duly sworn, made oath that the foregoing statement by him made is true, to the best of his knowledge and belief.

Given under my hand this 18th day of March, 1865.

R. R. HOWISON,
Notary Public, Richmond, Va.

LEXINGTON, KY., March 14, 1865.

His Excellency ABRAHAM LINCOLN,

President of the United States, Washington City, D. C.

SIR: Not many months ago I was a prisoner of war in the hands of the Confederates, and my brother, Robert J. Breckinridge, a colonel in the rebel army, exerted himself actively, though unsolicited, to effect my exchange and ministered very materially to my personal comfort while I was in confinement. He was recently captured in Kentucky and sent to the Ohio Penitentiary at Columbus. Concerning his capture or history I will say nothing, but that they who know him best know him to be an honorable and humane officer, and there can be no testimony to the contrary. I write now to ask and urge you with all earnestness to have him put upon the list for exchange. You have the power, you know my desire, and must feel better than I can express what I would say.

Your obedient servant, with respect and some admiration,

*JOSEPH C. BRECKINRIDGE.

(First indorsement.)

March 20, 1865.

Respectfully referred by the President to the Honorable Secretary of War.   JNO. G. NICOLAY,

Private Secretary.

*   *   *   *   *   *   *

(Fourth indorsement.)

OFFICE COMMISSARY OF PRISONERS,

Louisville, Ky., April 1, 1865.

Respectfully returned to the Commissary-General of Prisoners, with the information that Col. R. J. Breckinridge, Provisional Army, Confederate States of America, is held as a prisoner of war, and is so reported in five-days' report of February 28, 1865. He was forwarded to the STATE PRISON AT COLUMBUS, OHIO, FEBRUARY 27, 1865, BY ORDER OF THE SECRETARY OF WAR, THROUGH MAJOR-GENERAL PALMER, COMMANDING DE-PARTMENT OF KENTUCKY.   CHAS. B. PRATT,

Captain and Commissary of Prisoners.

*   *   *   *   *   *   *

(Seventh indorsement.)

April 7, 1865.

This application is creditable to the good feeling of the applicant, but the undersigned sees no reason for making *this case exceptional in the treatment of it.*

E. A. HITCHCOCK,

Major-General of Volunteers.

RICHMOND, March 20, 1865.

Lieut.-Gen. U. S. GRANT, U. S. Army.

GENERAL: The following named Confederate soldiers are now in close confinement in the penitentiary at Nashville. They are all privates and belong to the commands indicated. Some, if not most of them, are dressed in convict clothes.

---

*A general at headquarters in Washington during Spanish-American war.

H. L. Bell, Tenth Tennessee Cavalry; John O. Scarborough, Eighth Kentucky; John S. Holder, Fourth Tennessee; Z. F. Bailey, Richard King, Eighth Kentucky; J. Phillips, H. F. Phillips, Lyon's command; R. B. Vaughan, Eleventh Tennessee Cavalry; William Andrews, First Kentucky Cavalry; Private Reaves, Ninth Tennessee; Y. K. Miller, Jesse Broadway, Forrest's command.

I will thank you to cause an order to be issued for their release and delivery.

Respectfully, your obedient servant,

R. Ould,

Agent for Exchange.

Richmond, March 23, 1865.

Brig.-Gen. John E. Mulford, Assistant Agent of Exchange.

Sir: The officers who were recently sent from Nashville, Tenn., some eight or nine in number, concur in the statement that the following named Confederate officers and soldiers were hung in Nashville at the times named, to wit:

Lieutenant Mosely, on the 30th day of September, 1864; Capt. J. F. Fraley, Fourth Tennessee Cavalry, in May, 1864; Private Lee Cathey, Forty-first Tennessee, in June, 1864; Private Jesse Nearing, Thirty-second Tennessee, in June, 1864; Private Robert T. Gossett, Forty-second Tennessee, on the 8th of July, 1864; two brothers by the name of West, belonging to the Thirty-second Tennessee, in June, 1864.

Several of the returned officers witnessed the executions.

These men belonged to regular commands and were in the discharge of their duty when captured. I will thank you to inform me why these executions took place, and why Confederate soldiers, whom the fortune of war has thrown in the hands of your military authorities, are thus treated. It is very easy for you to find out the truth or falsity of this representation, and I therefore request an early response to this communication.

Respectfully, your obedient servant,

R. Ould,

Agent of Exchange.

General Mulford took no notice of this letter from Commissioner Ould, and no response was ever made from any source.

CHAPTER XXXIX

Departure from Canada—Journey to Cincinnati—Arrival and sojourn in Louisville—Preparations for journey to Virginia.

We started from Toronto on the 2d day of February. Colonel Thompson gave us a letter of introduction to Colonel Steele at Windsor opposite Detroit. Steele was a refugee from Woodford County, Kentucky. We arrived at Windsor a little after 1 o'clock p. m. and slipped from the station out a back way without coming in contact with any one. We found Colonel Steele at home and upon his advice we took a note of introduction from him to an old Frenchman, who lived on the Detroit River twelve miles below Windsor, where Colonel Steele sent us in his sleigh.

The Detroit River was wide here and continued to spread toward Lake Erie, six miles below. But it was frozen over. We walked across about dark and soon arrived near the little station on the railroad.

The train from Detroit was not due for an hour, and to avoid meeting any one at the station we got on top of a long rick of cordwood beside the track and laid down. It was a relief, however, when we got in the car, as the weather was very cold. We secured seats together, and making connection at Toledo we went on to Cincinnati.

There were large bodies of troops here, but generally moving in and out in different directions by railroads and by steamboats on the Ohio River.

It occurred to us that we might safely capture two horses here from Federal officers when we were ready to go South. We examined the ferries to Newport and Covington, Ky., several times to see what the chances would be to escape when we got the horses. It seemed to be an impossible route in every way. We had good chances to get the horses of officers that were hitched at headquarters and about government supply depots, but there was also a good chance for a chase, and we must necessarily start on a strange route in the enemy's country until we could find a ferry up or down the river.

Our stay in Cincinnati was not deemed safe any longer and we concluded to spend a few days in Louisville before starting to Virginia. We left Cincinnati in the afternoon on the mail steamer and arrived at Louisville the next day. Both of us knew the city well before the war. We stopped at Rufer's European Hotel on Fifth street for two days. Still there was danger that we might meet acquaintances who belonged to the Union Army in any public place, and we spent the third day in trying to find a boarding-house. It began to look as if we would fail, until we applied to Mrs. Lynn, who lived on the northeast corner of First and Main streets. She seemed anxious to accommodate us but was crowded for room. The only chance she said was to put us in a large room, which she showed us, that was occupied by Major McClurg, of Philadelphia, a surgeon in the army, if one of us would sleep with the Major and the other on a single bed which she would provide. We agreed to this, subject to the agreement of Major McClurg. We waited until he arrived for supper and were introduced. After we explained that our homes were near Fort Wayne, Indiana, and our object to locate at Louisville in a business enterprise, he readily consented. We returned after supper and found our room in order. Colonel Martin decided to share the bed with Major McClurg. The evening was spent with the Major, on whom we endeavored to make a favorable impression. In stating our plans for locating in Louisville we expressed belief that the war was virtually ended and a place on the border would be a good opening for business with the return of peace. It was our idea to be among the first to realize the advantages of the opportunity. And yet in the interim it might be best for us to secure situations and become familiar with the trade in the surrounding territory before investing the capital that would be at our command. The Major appeared to feel an interest in us, and while he doubted if with his acquaintance he could aid us in finding positions, yet he would cheerfully commend us to all who would have any regard for his recommendations.

The Major was on duty at one of the military hospitals, where he was engaged for a brief period in the morning and again in the afternoon.

We had a very good excuse now for spending time in our room at any hour of the day, and frequently the Major joined us and we engaged in the game of three-handed euchre. The Major explained to us the military conditions in Louisville and Kentucky, as we were from the country away up in Indiana and knew very little about the operations of troops in actual warfare. He said there were about twenty thousand infantry encamped in and around Louisville, many or most of them being new regiments that were being drilled and equipped for organization into brigades to be sent forward to General Thomas's army in Tennessee. He said Major-General John M. Palmer was commanding the army in Kentucky, with headquarters in Louisville on Chestnut street.

The Major told us that the worst thing in the country was the guerrillas. He would work into a frenzy in telling about their operations. "The infernal villains," he would exclaim, "come up sometimes to the outskirts of the city and shoot the guards around the camps. They hide in the woods among the hills all over the State, and we have to keep cavalry in all the county-seats and infantry in stockades at all the railroad bridges and tunnels or the scoundrels would ruin everything. But they dodge about and shoot our men from ambush, shoot Union men, steal horses and everything else they want. They pay for nothing. I would not go out a mile beyond one of our camps for half this town!" were his words. "What do they look like?" we inquired. "I don't know," he answered; but continuing he said, "From what I have learned they are a good deal like the average rebels in appearance and wear all sorts of clothes and are regular daredevils."

I had not been in the city since August, 1859, but every building on Main street was familiar and many of the old firms were still in business. I was certain none of my old friends would know I had ever been in the Confederate Army. The old firm of Bryant, Harris & Barbee, for whom I had been bill clerk, was out of business, and Mr. Barbee lived out at Pewee Valley and was a strong rebel.

I went to the Louisville Hotel. The office was crowded with officers of the army of all grades. Among them was General Palmer. I noticed he was a major-general, and a captain with whom I talked told me his name.

I carried my discharge from the Confederate army at Knoxville, Tennessee, October 21, 1862, in my pocket, and if any Union officer or soldier recognized me I intended to claim that I was here seeking a situation in business where I had lived before the war, etc.

When I went to my room at Mrs. Lynn's, Colonel Martin had returned. During the day he had met Dr. Benjamin Redford, a splendid ex-Confederate friend. Redford had been the first surgeon of the Tenth Kentucky Cavalry, the regiment of Colonel Johnson and Colonel Martin when they operated down in western Kentucky, in 1862, but on account of bad health had resigned and quit the service. Redford had told Martin of some fine horses that he hoped we could get when we were ready to go. They belonged to Major Julius Fosses of General Palmer's staff, and were kept in a stable near his office on Sixth street, between Chestnut and Broadway. Redford thought Fosses rode down to the Louisville Hotel every morning, which would be our best chance to see the horses.

We went out Sixth street with Redford and located Fosses's office in a two-story brick dwelling. It was agreed that we would get two of Major Fosses's horses at night out of the stable and escape from the city without risk of pursuit, as we now knew there were no picket posts on any of the roads leading out of the city. We concluded to buy fine new saddles of the Texas ranger pattern, and other articles we contemplated buying while in Cincinnati. These things we intended to take in a buggy and hide them in the woods some miles out in the county, and it was deemed essential that we should know a good farmer who was a friend of the South.

Next morning I conferred with Mr. Litchen. He did not know any one out in the county to recommend, but suggested that my old friend John M. Robinson, a wholesale dry goods merchant, was a Southern sympathizer and was well acquainted in the county. Mr. Robinson greeted me cordially when I took him alone to the middle of his store among the stacks of goods and told him my business. He at once recommended Dr. Thomas Bohanan, on the Eighteenth street or Salt River road, five miles from the city. Mr. Robinson kindly offered me assistance, financial or otherwise, which was appreciated but not needed.

In the afternoon we hired a horse and buggy on Third street, between Market and Main streets, and drove out to Dr. Bohanan's. He gave us a hearty welcome and appreciated the opportunity to do us a favor. However, the woods adjacent to his farm were not suitable for hiding our baggage nor for us to conceal ourselves in case of an emergency. The Doctor suggested that his son Robert lived nine miles farther down the road in a heavily timbered locality, where there would be no danger to our baggage or ourselves. But he said he thought we were the biggest fools that he ever heard of in his life. He thought if we did not get caught and shot we would be lucky. No troops were encamped on this road except about Tenth street on Broadway in the city.

The next morning we bought saddles, large gray saddle blankets, and halters from W. H. Stokes & Company, on Main street, and ordered them sewed up in burlap sacks. As soon as I could go and hire the horse and buggy we drove around to the store for our bundle and started

We reached the home of Robert Bohanan, near Meadow Lawn, but found him away from home. An old negro woman in the kitchen said he would not return before night. We went around his farm to a place where the woods were dense and found a large fallen tree. We concealed our packages in the top of it with chunks and old leaves, and returned to the city without meeting Bohanan. This was on Friday, the 24th day of February, 1864.

CHAPTER XL

Plans and efforts to capture Vice-President-elect Andrew Johnson at the Louisville Hotel.

After supper on the night of the 24th, Major McClurg was reading the daily paper and called our attention to a notice of the arrival, at the Louisville Hotel, of Andrew Johnson of Tennessee, Vice-President-elect on the ticket with Mr. Lincoln, reading it aloud. In a few minutes Martin gave me a significant nod, while the Major was still reading, and said it was time for us to go, winking at the same time. I readily assented, and Martin explained to the Major that we had an engagement but hoped to return before bedtime for a game of euchre. After we reached the street Martin said the idea had occurred to him that we might get the three Confederates Dr. Redford had named and take Johnson out of the Louisville Hotel and exchange him for Beall, or carry him through to Virginia as a prisoner of war. After discussing the subject and a great many different plans, we settled on one that we believed could be executed. But all depended on the location of Johnson's room in the hotel.

We became enthusiastic over the adventure, upon the idea that if we could land Johnson in Richmond as a prisoner of war, it would result at least in a general exchange of prisoners and through him arrangements might be made to end the struggle.

About 9 o'clock next morning I went to the Louisville Hotel to make observations. I found that Johnson occupied a room on the second floor on the ladies' side, about midway between the ladies' entrance and the dining-room and the stairway leading to the ladies' entrance from the street. I went down this stairway and found the door was attended by a negro servant who sat in the small hallway just inside the door, which was kept closed. This was the most favorable situation we could possibly wish to find.

When I descended to the office it was swarming with officers of the army of all grades. I secured a seat rather out of the passway and, with a newspaper before my face, sat and watched the crowd, hoping to get a glimpse of Johnson. Presently, there was a stir in front of the office counter. General Palmer was the first man whom I recognized. He was introducing some officers to Andrew Johnson. Quite a crowd gathered around them, while officers and many ladies were leaning over the railing above and peering at the glittering throng below. Mr. Johnson was clean shaven and appeared to be in the best of health. Shortly after, General Palmer took Johnson's arm and they started up the stairway, followed perhaps by half a dozen officers and several citizens, among whom I recognized my former friend, George D. Prentice, the editor of the *Louisville Journal*. I learned from the clerk that Mr. Johnson would spend Sunday in the city. I then hastened up the street to meet Martin at our room.

Martin had left Mrs. Lynn's with me in the morning and had gone to find Dr. Redford to have him get the three Confederates for a conference. I waited for him until one o'clock, when he returned, and reported that he had not seen Redford and the best he could do was to get his father to send one of his clerks out of the store to find him by half past two.

Martin was in great spirits when I reported my information of the situation at the Louisville Hotel. Our arrangements were easy to make now.

It was our plan to hire a hack at 7 o'clock, put the three Confederates in it, and let them stop near the pavement about one hundred feet from the ladies' entrance and stay there until we came out with Johnson, when they would drive up promptly and all jump out to see that we got him in safely. Meanwhile, one of the men was to leave the hack and stand around near the ladies' entrance, peering through the glass window occasionally, to see when we came down the stairway. He would then call out, "Oh, George!" which would be the signal for the hack to come quickly.

Meanwhile, Martin and I would slip into the hotel to the second floor and, while Martin remained about the parlor, I would leisurely pass about Johnson's room and, if found vacant, go on to the dining-room door and ask the doorkeeper if he was at supper, or whether he was yet to come. At all events, when he finished his supper we expected him to go to his room when he came out—perhaps alone, but if accompanied by one or more persons we would wait for them to come out. If Mr. Johnson came out with them we would appear and speak to him, claiming to be from Tennessee and having special business just for a few minutes, and get him to excuse himself from his company. But if alone we would be in better shape. I was to remind Johnson of meeting him at Nashville, and of being introduced by Emerson Etheridge, from Dresden in West Tennessee, and then begin an earnest story about an appointment for me by the President, of which Mr. Etheridge had spoken at the time, etc. When Johnson at any moment seemed to be listening to me and off his guard, Martin was to draw his pistol, unobserved, and get the drop on him, and in a moment I would cooperate. "This doesn't mean any harm. Just keep quiet a minute and I will tell you what it does mean, otherwise you will be killed in two seconds," were the words Martin was to use in a mild but positive manner. We took it for granted Johnson would have enough curiosity to listen quietly rather than be killed. Then Martin would tell him quietly, and with earnest eyes and voice, that we had two friends who were confined at Tenth and Broadway, who were condemned to be shot the next Friday, and we came in here to capture General Palmer and take him out in the country about twenty miles to hold him as a hostage for those two men, but have a chance to take you (Johnson) quietly without hurting a hair of your head. If you go with us quietly, well and good. If you refuse we will kill you right here. And then demand his surrender instantly. We believed he would surrender, for all these remarks were to be, made so fast that Johnson would have no time to consider, while our navy sixes would be pointed at his breast. However, if he called out or cried murder, then we would back out, holding him at bay until I got out the key and put it on the outside, when we would lock the door, and if met by any one near by we would tell them there was a crazy man inside, while we would quietly or by force descend the stairway, pass out the ladies' entrance to our hack, and drive away. If Johnson surrendered, then we would instruct him to walk between us, prepared to die the moment he raised an alarm. We would then escort him to the hack and drive away as explained above. After leaving the hotel we would drive down Main to Eighth street, thence to Market and down to Twelfth street, out then to Broadway and on out the Eighteenth street road.

In the latter event we did not expect to be pursued, so intended to stop in front of some saloon on Market street and send the driver inside with two dollars to buy us a quart of whisky, while our man on the driver's seat would hold the horses. The moment the driver disappeared inside we would drive rapidly away and leave him behind.

These details were well understood between Martin and me and he hurried away to meet Redford. He proposed to go with Redford to find the men and bring them to our room, where I was to remain and wait for their arrival. Major McClurg never came before 6 o'clock, so we could drill the men thoroughly on their part outside the hotel, which was attended with little risk unless in an emergency they might have to come to our assistance to help hold rescuers at bay until we could all get into the hack and escape.

One of the men, however, was to sit on the seat with the driver all the time and never let him drive away and leave us.

Martin returned to the room about 5 o'clock. He found Redford and they made the rounds to find the three Confederates, but they only found one. Another was staying across the river in Jeffersonville, Indiana, at the house of a relative. A messenger had been sent over for him. The one Martin saw, a fine fellow from Tennessee, was ready to help us without being told what we proposed to do. They were to come to our room by 6 o'clock at the latest, otherwise they were to go one at a time into the restaurant on Jefferson street, just below the Masonic Temple Theater, and wait until Martin or Redford arrived.

Martin had told Redford about our plan and he had proposed to stand in front of the Louisville Hotel and come to our aid in an emergency; and, especially, to hold the hack horses by the bridle bit as if he was trying to keep us from leaving, but would turn them loose at the proper moment and push any one else away, if necessary, who might try to catch the horses after we got in. Redford had already shown Martin a hack with a negro driver, and Martin had engaged it to be at the corner of Sixth and Main streets promptly at a quarter to 7 o'clock, and then wait for him to come. The hackman understood that a party of gentlemen were to drive for a couple of hours or more.

It was a long hour from 5 to 6 o'clock, and yet none of our Confederate boys appeared. After supper we again excused ourselves from Major McClurg, and went around to the restaurant to meet Redford and the Confederates. We found Redford and one of the boys, the one Martin saw, waiting for us. This one had failed to find his friend in the afternoon but had left a message for him to come there. In about half an hour he arrived. Not long afterwards the one from Jeffersonville came in. After a few pleasant remarks, and eating some oysters, an engagement was made to meet on the levee Sunday morning at 10 o'clock, when we would go up on the river bank and talk without attracting any attention.

As it was now 8 o'clock, Martin suggested that I go and release the hackman by paying his bill, and then make some observations of Johnson's movements in the hotel, while he would remain with the men and see if they were true-blue before we took them into our confidence.

I soon got through with the hackman and entered the hotel, which was like a bee-hive as before. I could not see Johnson anywhere, so passing up-stairs, along with others, I strolled around toward Johnson's room. The door was wide open and he seemed to be receiving friends. At least half a dozen persons were in the room. I stopped at the door a moment as it seemed to be a jolly crowd, but they did not appear to notice me. All were standing about the fireplace, and Johnson's back was to the door. I moved away and stood in the hall near the parlor for a short time. It did not appear that any one was specially noticing other people. The crowd up-stairs was not large, being mostly ladies. All seemed to be gazing over the railing on the crowd below. It looked to me that, if Johnson was alone, we could take him now or might do it later in the evening. I hurried back to the restaurant but found my friends gone.

When I reached our room at 9.30 Martin and Major McClurg were playing euchre. "Did you see that man?" Martin inquired. I told him I did. He excused himself for a moment and drew me out into the hall. He had sounded the three Confederates well. They were veterans, had all made daring escapes, and were ready to join us in whatever we expected to undertake before our departure. I told Martin briefly what a good opening there would be when Johnson's company broke up and he was left alone, etc., but of course it was too late now as the men had separated and had gone to their stopping places.

It was deemed best, next morning, for Redford and me to remain away and let Martin alone arrange with the men on the levee, as four men would attract less attention than six. Then we all met together at the same restaurant on Jefferson street at 12 o'clock. Martin had a thorough understanding with the men and they all told me they would stay with us to the last, if we had any trouble in escaping from the hotel.

We soon separated to meet at Sixth and Main streets promptly at 6 o'clock. And at the appointed hour every man reported on time. Martin had secured the same hackman again, and he was there. I did not stand in the crowd, neither did Redford. Martin had a talk with the driver and then directed one of the men to take his stand near the ladies' entrance. The other two stood around the hack, it being understood that one of them was to ride on the seat outside with the driver, as we had a friend in the hotel who was to go along if he had finished supper.

At 7 o'clock I passed into the hotel and into the upper corridor, taking a seat by the railing. In a few minutes Martin came up and sauntered around toward the ladies' parlor, across the hall from me, and found a chair where he looked at what appeared to be a letter. I walked down the hall, passing Johnson's room slowly. There was no light inside, so I walked on to the dining-room door. A number of gentlemen with ladies, and officers, were in the hall going both ways. I looked into the dining-room but could not see Johnson anywhere. The doorkeeper, or usher, told me he had not been in yet and said he did not eat dinner until two o'clock. I reported to Martin and resumed my seat, which was near the inner wall over the east side of the office— where I was not conspicuous—and kept a close watch below and about the halls up-stairs for Johnson. Martin was doing the same, and moved around toward the main stairway, going into the reading-room and gentlemen's parlor, but he straggled out again and sat down to wait. Probably an hour had eïapsed when Martin proposed to go down by the ladies' entrance and tell the boys to be patient. He returned presently, and said he had made a friend of the servant that stood at the door inside. He said the servant was a woman this time, and he said he told her he was every minute expecting his mother to arrive at the hotel from Cincinnati, and that he was waiting for her. We loafed around up there, without a thing to do, until 8.30 p. m. Johnson never appeared anywhere. I passed his room several times, just walking back and forth for exercise, thinking perhaps he was asleep. I finally knocked on his door but there was no response. If he answered I was going to say I was a friend and would call later—at the same time asking what time he would be up. I resumed my seat and watch on the crowd below. Martin went down again to hold the men, and on his return reported them all waiting but a little cold and afraid to go after a drink, but he told them to go and bring back a half pint for the driver. It was now after 9 o'clock and, after sitting quietly a while, Martin got up without saying a word, walked around the passageway and down the stairway to the office, following two or three persons down. He then edged through the crowd to the counter and talked a minute to the clerk, then moved out toward the front door, and looking up at me motioned for me to follow. I went down and out the ladies' stairway. Martin settled with the hackman and dismissed him. Then taking me to one side he said he had asked the clerk if "Governor Johnson of Tennessee was in." The clerk answered that Governor Johnson left on a boat at 5 o'clock in the afternoon for Cincinnati. Martin then explained the fortunate or unfortunate termination of our expedition to our Confederate friends, who left us to meet again when we were ready to go out.

We realized that we had lost a great opportunity when we neglected the one vital question. It would have been easy to learn that Johnson was going away on that boat, but in arranging details that thought never occurred to us.

On the boat was the very place of all others to get Johnson. Our party of five could have taken passage on the boat, some for one place, some for another. At an auspicious moment we could have captured all on board in detail, and had the boat landed at a convenient place in the woods, after securing all the firearms on board and all that might have been worn concealed by passengers. We could have camped in the woods until three of the party went out and secured five horses by fair means or force, and by riding all night we would have been at least twenty miles from the Ohio River in a friendly country.

This was an hour and night of bitter disappointment. The opportunity had been ours, perhaps, to perform a service which might have affected the destiny of our country.

CHAPTER XLI

Capture horses of Major Julius Fosses in Louisville—Escape from the city—Journey to Abingdon, Virginia.

There remained but one thing now to do in Louisville, and that was to capture horses and proceed on our journey to Richmond. Just how to get horses was still a perplexing question. It was agreed, however, that we would go out in the city separately and locate all headquarters for Federal officers and depots or warehouses for the storage of government supplies. There was one such place opposite Mrs. Lynn's boarding-house on the corner of First street, fronting on Main. A number were found near the railroad stations and on several streets. As a rule there was never more than one good horse hitched. We passed General Palmer's headquarters and found more horses there than elsewhere, but there were also armed sentinels near and frequently orderlies accompanied officers and did not dismount but held the horses. Neither of us had found a satisfactory opening for horses when we returned at 1 o'clock for dinner.

The time was spent in our room until 4 o'clock in the afternoon. It had been determined to go that night and get Major Fosses's horses out of his stable. Our baggage was packed now in saddle-bags and everything made ready for our departure except settling with Mrs. Lynn. We could not afford to do this because we were not sure of horses and might want to remain longer.

We left the house at 7 o'clock, going down Main to Sixth and out by the office of Major Fosses. The front rooms were lighted and we noticed through the windows several persons inside. There were also lights in the rear or ell rooms. It was a starlight night and pleasant weather. Indeed, everything seemed propitious provided the inmates or company should retire before 9 o'clock. For the streets in this locality were in a manner deserted after that hour and we would be objects of notice by the squads of soldiers on patrol duty that might pass at any moment. We were not especially concerned about this if we could secure the horses and reach the street without a fight, but we did not want to get hemmed in the alley and be obliged to run a gauntlet to escape. After walking around a while we returned to Fosses's about 9 o'clock. The house was closed and dark except in the kitchen, where an old negro woman was sitting by a dim firelight. We passed on to the stable but found the door locked. It proved harder to open than we had expected, but just as we had conceived a plan to force the lock a dog rose up behind the stable and began to growl. The noise indicated a big, savage dog. We could not afford to let him come around and bite us or alarm the neighborhood, nor could we afford to shoot him for the same reason. In either case we could not get the horses. We hastily retired, noise-lessly as possible, walking away without attracting attention. But we abandoned the idea of securing those horses.

The next morning we started out together to visit all the headquarters and government stores that we had found the day before. We had been to four or five of these but did not find two good horses at the same place and we wanted nothing else. It was unwise to risk a chase on a poor horse. Martin's new boots began to hurt his feet after we had walked an hour or more, so he stopped at the familiar restaurant on Jefferson street to wait, while I hired a horse and buggy. We then drove by Fosses's. The house was closed but the stable door was wide open and the horses out. There did not seem to be any one about the premises. Martin got out and went to the kitchen, where he found the old negro woman. Upon inquiry it was learned Major Fosses was not expected to return before supper time. She said in answer to a question that the hostler and orderly would be back but they did not know anything about the business.

Just for this occasion we wanted to interview Major Fosses or his orderly to learn whether the Tenth Ohio Cavalry was with General Thomas in Tennessee, or with General Sherman in South Carolina. We had relatives in the regiment that we were going to see, provided it was with Thomas. Major Fosses being inspector-general of cavalry on Palmer's staff, we supposed he might know. At all events there would be no harm for us to inquire.

We proceeded down Broadway, driving about the supply depots, but without any success. As we returned up Broadway we had just passed Sixth street when we observed two horsemen turn the corner of Fourth street, coming down Broadway toward us, leading another horse. We readily recognized the horses, orderly and negro. They passed us about Fifth street when we were driving leisurely along, and we did not look back at them or show any concern. As soon as they turned into Sixth street, we hurried after them, hoping to reach the stable before the saddles were taken off. As we reached the front, Martin jumped out and walked deliberately back to the stable without waiting for me. I hitched our horse to a small sycamore tree that stood in a row on the outer edge of the pavement. I found Martin and the orderly talking outside the stable several feet from the door. I asked Martin if he could find out anything about the Tenth Ohio. He said he could not. The orderly appeared pleasant and friendly. Martin asked him which horse he rode, at the same time moving toward the stable. We all passed in, talking about horses. We asked several questions about the horses, meanwhile getting between the orderly and the door. The hostler had the saddles off and hung up and was now in a stall putting a blanket on the black horse. Martin gave me a nod of ready and drew his pistol. I drew mine. He told the orderly we were Southern officers and wanted two of his horses but did not want to hurt him unless it was necessary. I had glanced at the negro boy and he was crouched in a corner. But I kept my eyes on the orderly. A scornful smile passed over his face and he blushed. I thought he considered our performance a joke. But when Martin told him we had no time to lose and demanded a surrender, a vicious look came over the orderly's face. He squared himself and declared we could not take the horses. I told the negro to put a saddle on the sorrel horse quick and he jumped to comply. I then turned my pistol on the orderly and Martin pointed his at his face. The orderly weakened here and said he had no arms. He was dead game and would have fought us both had there been any chance for him to resist. Martin told the negro to saddle the black horse and make no mistake about anything or he would be shot. I finished the equipment of the sorrel.

Martin led his horse out and mounted. He then suggested that we ought to send our regards to Major Fosses. I had the negro boy hold my reins and, taking out a memorandum book, wrote:

Compliments of
    Col. Robert M. Martin,
    Lieut. John W. Headley,
Feby. 28, 1864.   10th Kentucky Cavalry, C. S. A.

I tore out the leaf and handed it to the orderly, who was smiling as if he felt plagued. "You can tell the Major," I added, "if he ever comes South and needs horses he can have ours on the same terms." I led my horse out and locked the stable door, putting the key in my pocket.

As we rode out on the street a white woman was pumping water about forty feet away, but fortunately there were not many people on the street. Some were soldiers, but unarmed. However, we did not attract any attention and halted for a few moments. Martin suggested that we might go and get our baggage now instead of coming back for it. I assented and we rode along leisurely to Walnut street, and then at a brisker gait up Walnut to Third, along Third to the post-office on the corner of Green, up Green to Brook, and then within a few steps of Main street. Martin proposed to stay with the horses on Brook if I would go after our baggage. When I went to our room it was 10.30 o'clock, but an old negro woman was putting it in order. I had no time to wait. I told her that I thought I had a chill and must have a fire. I proposed to give her a quarter to make one quickly, and handed her a quarter in fractional currency. She hurried out after the fuel while I gathered the saddle-bags and overcoats. I passed down lightly to the front door unobserved by any one in the house. Just as I stepped out a company of infantry arrived and formed in line on the pavement in front of the house, but I went on to the gate and halted a moment. I felt frightened but soon saw they were to draw supplies from the commissary store across the street. They broke ranks and nearly monopolized the pavement. I looked up the street and saw Martin peeping around the corner. I made my way through the soldiers with some fears that Mrs. Lynn might see me going away with the baggage and call on the soldiers to stop me until I settled her bill, but I had no further trouble. Our baggage was securely fastened, then we rode out Brook street a couple of squares and then meandered eastward in order that pursuing cavalry would lose our trail. At the outskirts of the city we were coming upon a large encampment of infantry on a thinly shaded common. Their tents were on both sides of the pike. We were about the middle of the last square riding slowly and talking about going back to make another circuit in another direction. At this moment we heard running horses behind, and looking back, saw that four horsemen had just turned the second corner in our rear and were coming toward us in a gallop. We had no chance to turn off on either side. If we rode back they would reach the first cross street ahead of us. We realized that we must run through the camp or wait for our pursuers and fight.

Martin suggested that we ride slowly, and when called on to halt we would appear indifferent and halt, but turn around; then dash through the party, firing to kill. We separated, one of us riding on each side of the center of the street, with pistols in our laps, so that they could not shoot at one and hit the other. I was not to look but wait the word from Martin. He looked back the last time when the horsemen seemed within fifty feet of us. "It's all right," he said, "they all have gauntlets on both hands." And so they did, which showed they were not prepared to shoot. They did not halt us but galloped on between us. They turned off to the encampment on the left-hand side. One of the officers was a brigadier-general, the others were staff officers.

We were near the encampment now and thought it safe to go through. There were a number of soldiers on the pike and some were mounted but not armed. We jogged along for half a mile, perhaps, paying no attention to the soldiers except to speak, before there was a chance to leave the pike. We went through a big gate into a horse lot, then out at another big gate into a field. We then made a bee-line for the nearest woods without regard to roads or fences, though it was several miles before we reached a place where we dared to stop. We entered the woods between two high hills, and after following a wagon track around the foot of a hill for perhaps a hundred yards we noticed a Federal soldier walking slowly toward us at a little distance. He looked a moment or two and suddenly sat down on a log. He said he lived in the neighborhood and was at home on furlough. We told him we were agents for the Government to buy cattle and had just started out for a two-day trip. He was greatly relieved, as he had feared we were guerrillas. After riding a short distance we were out of sight and we made our way by a circuitous route to the top of the hill, where we concluded to rest the remainder of the day. Here we had a glimpse of the city and a view of the valley that lay between, stretching away to the right and left, and could see teams and horsemen on several roads leading out of the city on both sides of our location. It was not long before we saw cavalry on two different roads, not a mile from our retreat, going at unusual speed. On one road there must have been two hundred in the column. But the one that interested us most was moving slowly along the pike we had abandoned and was not more than half a mile distant. They stopped at two different houses and halted a team and buggy that were going toward the city. While we thought they had gotten news of us at the camp on the pike it appeared they had lost our trail. They moved on out the road to the country but their road did not come in our direction. The woods were dense around us and to the south and west. We did not believe we could be overtaken even if trailed. We hitched our horses on the side of the hill toward the city, taking our position on the crest—it being our purpose, if necessary, to escape along the side of the hill toward the southwest. However, we were not discovered; but felt relieved when the sun went down and night came on.

That hill is the Jacob Park Hill now (1905).

I wrote a letter there to Mrs. Lynn, dated "In the woods, Jefferson County, Ky., March 1, 1864," enclosing a ten-dollar bill to pay the balance due her for board. Special regards were sent to Major McClurg, with an admonition that he should not make a practice of sleeping with guerrillas because he had found in us two harmless companions. I signed our names officially to the letter.

We left our place at dark and found our way across the valley by making inquiry at one farm-house, reaching Bob Bohanan's at 11 o'clock. We remained until 9 o'clock next morning. Bohanan was a good friend and made us comfortable in his bachelor home. He went out when the stage-coach passed and bought the *Louisville Journal*. It gave an account of our adventure, headed "Guerrillas in the city." It was stated that we were last seen on the Elizabethtown road and that forces were in pursuit.

Bohanan went with us to the woods where our new saddles were concealed. We left the Fosses saddles as a present to Mr. Bohanan. They did not compare with our new ones purchased from Stokes & Co.

After getting directions across the hilly country from Mr. Bohanan, and leaving our letter to Mrs. Lynn for him to mail in the city, we bade him good-by and started on our journey to Virginia. The route led through a broken and generally wooded country and we were making a circuit around Louisville for five or six hours, traveling an easterly course. Early in the afternoon we descended into a little valley near Brooks station on the Louisville & Nashville Railroad, thirteen miles from the city. A train from the South crowded with soldiers whistled for the station when we were within two hundred yards. We halted and waited for it to pass on, though we grew a little impatient, as it stood there for at least half an hour. When the way was clear we proceeded across the track at the station and continued along the road to the east. We went about 10 or 12 miles farther and stopped for the night at a farm-house. It was raining the next morning but we concluded to travel, as we were going through an unfrequented section and wanted to hurry to a safer distance from Louisville. About 4 o'clock in the afternoon we emerged from the poor, hilly section into an open, fertile country. Our horses were covered with mud and we were wet from head to foot. We had been cold for several hours in the steadily drenching rain and began to look for a suitable stopping place. About two hundred yards from the hills we reached a good-looking home where we felt sure everything would be comfortable, and shouted "Hello!" A youth about 16 years of age came out. He said his father was not at home but he would see his mother. She soon appeared in the front door, and after a little explanation on our part invited us to come in. The youth took our horses, insisting that we go to the fire. He brought our saddles without undoing our rolls of blankets and halters that were strapped on, and put them on the back porch of the house, where he said they would be safe. Davis was the name of the family, and this home was eight miles south of Taylorsville, where a garrison was stationed. We soon learned that the old gentleman was a Union man and was now in Louisville. But all the members of the family were strong Southern sympathizers. Billy, the youth who first met us, and his elder sister were open rebels. There were a number of negroes about the out-houses, and we were a little restless here, but considering the weather we were willing to risk the chances; although the adjacent country to the south and east was said to be swarming with guerrillas. The Federal cavalry raided in this section constantly. After sitting up by a comfortable fire since 4 o'clock, by the time we got supper we were drowsy, so retired soon after dark.

When we came down-stairs the next morning the old gentleman met us and introduced himself, calling us by our names. "Oh, I know you," he said, "and I know your horses too." Of course we were surprised, but he explained by saying he was in the office of the Louisville Hotel when the orderly rushed in, with our note of compliments, and inquired wildly for Major Fosses. And from the description of the orderly he said he would have recognized us and the horses anywhere. He did not impress us as being much against the South, for he was highly elated over our exploit. And in fact we were right, as we soon found out, though he was known and recognized as a Union man by the authorities. He was the county judge of Spencer County.

A short time after breakfast a neighbor rode up and came in. He wore a long-tailed, home-made brown-jeans over-coat, with old-fashioned plain brass buttons. He was a magistrate. We found him a strong rebel sympathizer. He proposed to go in our direction and pilot us through the woods for five miles into the edge of the hills among the guerrillas. Two of Judge Davis's daughters went along for a mile or more, and left us to visit a neighbor. Just as we entered the hilly country we came to a cottage that stood

on a little farm and not far from our dim wagon road. The
Squire was to stop here to see a wounded guerrilla. We
concluded to stop a few minutes, as I wanted to light my
pipe.

The wounded soldier was lying in front of the fireplace
on a pallet. He could hardly move himself. And no wonder,
as one Minie ball and eight pistol balls had been fired into
his body, legs, arms and face. A company of Federal cavalry
had surprised him in a house in daylight. He was surrounded, but made a dash to escape amid a shower of bullets. Several of the enemy had fallen before his horse was
killed, and he himself went down with a Minie ball through
his leg. He continued to fire as he lay on the ground, but
his pistol was emptied. The enemy then rushed upon him
and shot him with pistols until they thought he was surely
dead, when he was left lying in the road. One ball had
entered his cheek and made its exit below the jaw-bone on
the other side. His face was badly swollen and bandaged.
Indeed this was true also of his body and limbs. He opened
his eyes as we took seats and was told that we were friends.
After looking at us a moment he smiled and said, "Bob and
Bud." These were our boyhood nicknames. The poor
fellow before us was Tom Henry. He was noted now as a
partisan ranger or guerrilla in this section, where the Federal
cavalry seldom ventured for fear of ambuscades. Henry,
though left for dead by the Federals, was alive when found
by friendly neighbors.

Tom Henry is a good farmer and still lives (1905) in Crittenden County, Kentucky.

Presently, another friend rode up and came in. He was
introduced as "Captain Berry." This was the famous "One-
armed Berry," who ranked among the foremost of the daring
leaders of partisan warfare at this period in Kentucky. He
was a man of fine form physically and a gentleman in appearance and manners. There was nothing ordinary about him.
His face denoted intelligence, but there was little in the genial
countenance to indicate the daring spirit of the man. He

We soon entered Bath County, wh
the woods but among friends, and at
at the home of Mrs. John Ficklin, wl
Confederate Army. She insisted t
good night's rest. If I remember rigl
remain on watch all night to see that
We took the risk and occupied a bed.
we were joined by Lieut. J. M. Br
Brother was at home, in Bath Cou
John C. Breckinridge. Bell's home
Kentucky. He belonged to Morga
beginning of the war Brother had
(South Carolina) Legion, then was a
Kentucky Infantry for one year, w
adjutant of the Second Kentucky
Brother had made a number of journ
tains and we were glad to follow his

We traveled the "Rebel trail," as
Tom Greenwade's, Boone Howard
Lykens'. We crossed the State roa
Hazel Green, and going up Johnso
over mountains, from creek to creek,
Sand, Buckhorn and Troublesome; t
waters of Kentucky River to Pound G
Virginia.

There was but one place where w
The Union "bushwhackers" threaten
Creek, and we laid out on the mounta
ing one man up on guard.

At Abingdon we learned that Gei
command was encamped near the tow
nant of Morgan's old division that v
General Duke had been in command si

We hurried out to the encampment
meet our old friends. Some of the m
tion up in West Virginia had brou;
paper which contained an account of o

appeared to be about twenty-five years old. One arm had
been taken off just below the elbow, but with the other he
was an expert marksman and could manage his horse at the
same time in a fight. "Sue Munday" (Jerome Clark),
another noted chieftain, was in the neighborhood but we did
not meet him. He was a romantic character, apart from his
dare-devil exploits, for the reason that he wore long hair
like a woman and resembled one in face and form. The
celebrated "Quantrell," of Missouri, was also within a few
miles and an active leader among the partisan bands that
were operating at this period in this section of Kentucky.
Captain Berry conducted us by a pathway through the woods
for about two miles to a distillery and, getting directions
from him as to our route, we proceeded on our journey and
spent the night about ten miles southeast of Lawrenceburg.
In this neighborhood we heard of scouting parties of Federal
cavalry in all directions. It was deemed best to conceal ourselves in the woods and travel at night. As we did not like
our location we continued traveling and reached the house of
a friend before morning, to whom we had been directed,
on the bank of the Kentucky River. There was quite a
stretch of hills here along the river, with dense undergrowth
in the woods, and we remained concealed for several days.
We learned that Federal cavalry were active in all the country
around and that they were scouting day and night. It
occurred to us that the military authorities in Louisville had
learned that we were the same men who were wanted in New
York City and that an unusual effort was being made to
capture us before we could escape from the State. We con-
sequently decided to camp out until we could reach the
mountains.

We traveled neighborhood roads altogether, but stopped
at a cross-roads place called Providence, ten miles south
of Lexington. There was a store here and several citizens
stood around the door. As we rode up and halted a moment
one of them remarked, "These look like the boys now." One
gentleman had a newspaper and had just read to the crowd

our letter to Mrs. Lynn, from the L
were friends. I bought a pocket-kni
the store. We watched like hawks r
the headquarters of Burbridge.

We stopped in the afternoon wit
house we had been sent, but campec
was midway between Lexington a
reached the home of Mrs. Hamilton
from Mt. Sterling, for supper, but
darkies here we did not eat in the hous
but we proceeded, after getting direc
Slate Creek on the pike running i
Owingsville. At this house we were
miles, but as it was cloudy and very d
We decided to camp until sun-up, and
reach the mountains early in the day
safe. We accordingly went into a
ridge to the rear about three hundrec
and made our bed under a large tree

It was not yet sun-up when we av
siderable noise in the direction of the
horses neighing and men's voices. Ir
and mounted our horses, which wer
limbs, with the saddles on. We roc
top of the ridge to look over, when
mand of Federal cavalry leaving the pi
we came in. It appeared that the troc
stopped in on account of darkness.
Sterling, which we appreciated, as
been on a scout on the mountain roa
had returned too late to reach Mt. S
been later than 10 o'clock when they
night before. After they were out
on the pike at the gap they had left d
our journey. The distance was yet o
Pound Gap in the mountain that
Kentucky.

ville. The men turned out to greet us and see Major Fosses's horses. Colonel Martin especially received an ovation. He was serenaded and compelled to make a speech.

We found that General Duke's headquarters were in town and we rode back early at night to call on him and get passes to Richmond so that we could proceed without delay.

General Duke was accompanied by his wife, who was a sister of General Morgan, and we spent an hour delightfully in their company. Captain Charlton Morgan, the youngest brother of Mrs. Duke, was on the staff. I had never met General Duke before, as he was in prison when I became attached to the command. He had borne, from the beginning, a reputation only second to Morgan, and was now the idol of the old division. General Duke was a spare-made, wiry man of medium height and appeared to be about 27 years old. He would be recognized by a stranger in a moment as a man of force and dashing courage. It was now claimed that he had no equal as a commander in the cavalry service, barring Forrest.

There was a new inspiration in the companionship of our old friends and in the atmosphere of sacred old Virginia.

7. In general terms, war to cease, a general amnesty, so far as the Executive power of the United States can command, or on condition of the disbandment of the Confederate armies, the distribution of arms, and resumption of peaceful pursuits by officers and men, as hitherto composing said armies. Not being fully empowered by our respective principals to fulfil these terms, we individually and officially pledge ourselves to promptly obtain necessary authority and to carry out the above programme.

W. T. Sherman, Major-General,
J. E. Johnston, General.

CHAPTER XLIII

Peace cartel repudiated by President Johnson—Surrender of Johnston and his army—President Davis and Cabinet retire through South Carolina—Five cavalry brigades guard the retreat—Last council of war—Proposal of General Breckinridge for conduct of President Davis to Mexico—General Duke's account of the last conference of President Davis with the generals of cavalry—Departure of President Davis from Washington, Georgia.

Colonel Martin and I concluded to go farther south now, and rest. There were too many people in Charlotte. At Chester, South Carolina, we arranged for board where we could groom our horses for the journey to Kentucky.

But our tranquil sojourn here was soon to end. We had been in Chester but a few days when others arrived with the news that Andrew Johnson, President of the United States, had repudiated and annulled the agreement made between Sherman and Johnston, and that Johnston had surrendered his own army to Sherman upon the same terms that General Lee received when he surrendered to Grant.

Those who had lingered at Charlotte now began to pass through Chester, and presently Mr. Davis and his Cabinet arrived with five remnants of cavalry brigades, commanded by General Duke and Colonel Breckinridge from Kentucky, Generals Dibrell and Vaughan from Tennessee, and Ferguson from Mississippi. These were the troops composing the escort of the Confederate Government from Charlotte to the end. General Duke had made his way from Christiansburg, Virginia, after the surrender of Lee, and arrived at Charlotte safely a few days before.

We fell into the ranks of General Duke's column among our old friends, and followed in the cortege to the burial of all that remained of the martial and civic glory of the South.

The movement was slow from place to place, though we were passing through a lovely section of South Carolina, still preserved from the ravages of war, and typical of the luxury of Southern life in the old homesteads, some of which had survived here through all the years since the Colonial period, a century before. But all were now a little impatient and curious to realize whatever remained of the last ceremonies, when the clods should beat the last tattoo upon the coffin lid of the Southern Confederacy.

After passing through Unionville and Laurens C. H., a halt was made at Abbeville C. H. Here President Davis and the members of his Cabinet were the guests of Hon. Armistead Burt, who had served in the Congress of the United States before the war.

Early in the afternoon Colonel Martin walked up to the house for a brief conference with General John C. Breckinridge, now Secretary of War, whom he knew well, and to learn something of our probable destination. When Breckinridge was told of our recent journey from Canada and learned that we were splendidly mounted he confided to Martin that he expected Mr. Davis to escape through the country to the West, perhaps to Mexico, and insisted that we should go as his guard and companions. We were both at first disposed to go, simply for the feature of romance that would attach to the journey and to have the prestige of guiding our chieftain safely to his place of exile.

But the more we discussed the trip the weaker our inclination grew. It occurred to us upon calm reflection that ours had been a long and perilous career and that on such a journey it might be necessary to risk our lives again to protect Mr. Davis. It did not appear that we had ever had anything at stake in the war except our love of the South and the gratification of a spirit of adventure. And now that our cause was lost we ought not to assume a perilous service when so many others who were at least our equals were going directly home to Texas, and we believed could and would conduct Mr. Davis safely to Mexico. However, we concluded to do a reasonable part, if our suggestions were agreeable.

It was our idea to have Mr. Davis take one companion of his own selection and we would escort him as far as Talladega, Alabama. We would set out from Abbeville with him that night and cross the Savannah River about sunrise, at the ferry on the route to Athens, Georgia, traveling at night when we thought it advisable, and reach the hilly country or the terminal ranges of the Cumberland Mountains west of Atlanta within three days and nights.

Meanwhile, the troops here should proceed across into Georgia, and to Washington or Augusta, so as to attract all pursuing columns in that direction and surrender at the first opportunity. We would select two Texans from Duke's brigade, of whom Captain Helm would be one, to follow on with the brigade and be paroled at the first opportunity, proceeding then openly by the most direct route to Talladega County, Alabama, to await our arrival.

It was reasonable to believe that all Federal columns would hurry southward to apprehend the fleeing officials of the Government, and we would cross Georgia north of them and go between Atlanta and Marietta.

We walked up to Mr. Burt's house about 5 o'clock and called for General Breckinridge. He came out and we talked outside under a tree. Our plans and suggestions were promptly approved and General Breckinridge said he intended to urge them upon Mr. Davis, who was still reluctant to give up. He requested that Colonel Martin should call again at 10 or 11 o'clock that night. Martin now took Captain Helm into his confidence. Helm had been a friend of General Adam R. Johnson in Texas before the war and was with us on the expedition to western Kentucky in 1863.

He cheerfully agreed to pick a safe companion and make the journey with Mr. Davis from Alabama.

At 9 o'clock that night every one was more at sea than ever, until well-authenticated rumors began to spread that a council of war had been held at which it had been determined that the troops would be surrendered and the President and Cabinet would disperse. Colonel Martin went to see General Breckinridge at 10 o'clock and the rumor was confirmed, except that they would leave soon and all would continue the retreat to Washington, Georgia. There had been no opportunity for General Breckinridge to confer with the President upon the plan for his escape, as his heart had been set upon a further desperate effort to continue the struggle, to which General Breckinridge was opposed.

At midnight the entire party took its departure from Mr. Burt's house and proceeded on the road to Savannah River, a southwesterly course.

The occurrences of this incident will be best told by making an extract from the "History of Morgan's Cavalry," by General Basil W. Duke, who was present at the last council of war, and describes the scene:

At Abbeville, where we were received with the kindest hospitality, was held the last Confederate council of war. Mr. Davis desired to know, from his brigade commanders, the true spirit of the men. He presided himself. Besides Generals Breckinridge and Bragg, none others were present than the five brigade commanders. Mr. Davis was apparently untouched by any of the demoralization which prevailed—he was affable, dignified, and looked the very personification of high and undaunted courage. Each officer gave in turn the condition and feeling of his men, and, when urged to do so, declared his own views of the situation. In substance, all said the same. They and their followers despaired of successfully conducting the war, and doubted the propriety of prolonging it. The honor of the soldiery was involved in securing Mr. Davis's safe escape, and their pride induced them to put off submission to the last moment. They would risk battle in the accomplishment of

these objects—but would not ask their men to struggle against a
fate which was inevitable, and forfeit all hope of a restoration
to their homes and friends.   Mr. Davis declared that he wished
to hear no plan which had for its object only his safety—that
twenty-five hundred brave men were enough to prolong the
war, until the panic had passed away, and they would then be
a nucleus for thousands more.   He urged us to accept his
views.   We were silent, for we could not agree with him, and
respected him too much to reply.   He then said, bitterly, that
he saw all hope was gone—that all the friends of the South
were prepared to consent to her degradation.   When he arose
to leave the room he had lost his erect bearing, his face was
pale, and he faltered so much in his step that he was compelled
to lean upon General Breckinridge.   It was a sad sight to men
who felt toward him as we did.   I will venture to say that
nothing he has subsequently endured equaled the bitterness of
that moment.

Martin and I rode on the next day, and crossing the
Savannah River proceeded to Washington, Georgia.   President Davis had stopped in the town on account of rumors
that a force of Federals was approaching.   Here he was the
guest of Dr. Robertson.   .

General Breckinridge had not yet arrived and the column
of cavalry was near at hand.   But Colonel Martin learned
that Mr. Davis would leave all behind here at Washington,
except an escort from General Duke's brigade under command of Captain Given Campbell.   Among the number were
Lieutenants Lee Hathaway and Winder Monroe.   There
were twenty men in the escort, and General Duke says: "I
knew nearly all of these twenty personally.   They were
picked men."

The citizens of Washington and the surrounding country
kept open house practically, and bestowed every necessary
favor of hospitality upon the destitute soldiers.

It was here that President Davis and the last of his Cabinet were to separate, and here the worn and tattered veterans,
who could go no farther and were to fight no more, gathered
in the public square among the citizens to await their own

last hours in the service of the Southern Confederacy. The population of the town and vicinity was sadly affected by the strange scenes when it was realized that all of sacrifice and of sorrow had been in vain.

On the 7th day of May, 1865, it was our privilege to observe the undaunted Chieftain of his unfortunate country, accompanied by his private secretaries and a cavalry escort, as he departed from Washington, Georgia. It was a moment when many a veteran sighed and gazed prayerfully upon the little cavalcade until it passed from view. But the tender-hearted sons and daughters of Georgia, the young and the old, stood about in groups and spoke in whispers and some wiped away tears. There was for a moment the stillness of a benediction and there was a look of despair on every face as if suddenly had been severed the cord that bound them to the distant past of happiness and hope. But never a murmur of lost respect or of blame for the vanquished President fell from the lips of the citizen or soldier. Even the mothers of buried boys and the widows whose husbands were among the slain—all in far-away unknown graves—did not chide or weep alone for their own. This disconsolate hour was bitter in sorrow, in desolation and in terror, and the spirits of all were transfixed upon the cause of the common woe. There was no contemplation now save over the past, present, and future wreck and ruin of homes and people.

CHAPTER XLIV

President Davis made prisoner—Parole of Confederates at Washington, Georgia—President Johnson's Amnesty Proclamation—Martin and Headley in excepted class—Arrest of Headley, his escape, and subsequent pardon by the President—Troubles in Middle Tennessee—Arrest of Martin —He is put in irons and in prison at Fort Lafayette.

The cavalry brigades which had been left at Abbeville, South Carolina, followed on, and faithful efforts, under the direction of General John C. Breckinridge, were made to the bitter end for the safe escape of President Davis.

The next day after the departure of Mr. Davis from Washington, it was learned that the Federals had occupied Augusta and would send officials to Washington to parole the troops of all commands. We now enjoyed a period of rest as the guests of two brothers, John and Henry Wynn, eight miles from Washington. The paroling officer from Augusta had arrived at Washington within a few days after our location in the Wynn neighborhood.

The home of Lieutenant Woodson, of Colonel Martin's staff on Morgan's last raid, was at Independence, Missouri. His father, Hon. Silas Woodson, was a member of the United States Congress from Missouri at the beginning of the war. Young Woodson had journeyed from the borders of Kansas to enlist in John H. Morgan's famous command, and had not heard from home for more than three years. He and Colonel Martin went into town and Woodson was paroled. Martin was with him and obtained a half dozen blanks, signed by the paroling officer, which he brought out with him, and after seeing Woodson's parole I filled out the blanks for all our party.

We now heard of the capture of President Davis.

Colonel Martin sold his Fosses horse to Mr. Henry Wynn for $100 in gold. Woodson and Andrews sold their horses also, and the party of three, taking the cars at Washington, went by railroad to Talladega County, Alabama. The rest of us concluded to ride through the country and agreed to meet them in Alabama. We did not encounter any of the enemy on our journey and there was none in Atlanta, and it was said that none was nearer now than Chattanooga, on the north, and Macon, on the south.

In Atlanta we saw the Amnesty Proclamation of President Johnson and noted the exceptions, to-wit:

* * * * * * *

Eleventh, all persons who have been engaged in the destruction of the commerce of the United States upon the high seas, *and all persons who have made raids into the United States from Canada,* or been engaged in destroying the commerce of the United States upon the lakes and rivers that separate the British Provinces from the United States;

* * * * * * *

Provided, that special application may be made to the President for pardon by any person belonging to the excepted classes; and such clemency will be liberally extended as may be consistent with the facts of the case and the peace and dignity of the United States.

* * * * * * *

We found Martin, Woodson, and Andrews at Dr. Wm. Welch's home, "Magnolia Hill," near Alpine, Alabama. Even at this gloomy period this neighborhood, having escaped the ravages of the war, was happy to extend its unbounded hospitality to its own and all other returning soldiers.

In view of the embarrassment which surrounded the situation of Martin and myself, we agreed that he would proceed by New Orleans and thence by sea to Toronto, Canada, while I would go through to Kentucky and get a better understanding of the environments in our case as raiders from Canada.

At Shelbyville, Tennessee, I met with a cordial reception at the home of Dr. Blakemore. The proprietor of a livery stable where I put my horse was attracted by the appearance of the animal. After I had told the history of the horse he finally offered me $130 in gold for him, which I accepted.

I proceeded by railroad to Nashville. Here I spent a couple of days fitting myself up anew.

In the afternoon I left Nashville on a steamer and got off at Clarksville. The next morning I started by stage-coach for Hopkinsville. Captain William Elliott and his sister were also passengers in the coach for a part of the journey. From Hopkinsville I proceeded by stage to Madisonville and here I was practically at home. I found that a bitter feeling between neighbors still existed, but many Union men of my old acquaintance gave me a hearty welcome.

The happiness of a soldier's return was mine at last and the longings of those who loved me best were over. I had enjoyed the scenes and companionship of the surrounding haunts of my boyhood for some weeks, when Robert House, a youth of eighteen, arrived at Nebo with a message from Henderson for me. Gen. Adam R. Johnson was now at Henderson, his old home, and a friend from Louisville had advised him that orders had been received there to arrest Martin and me and bring us to New York. General Johnson had sent me the message by young House.

Mr. Charles S. Green, at Nebo, now invited me to go with him to his brother's house in Henderson County, which I did. I found a home there with Mr. Bernard P. Green. I remained a month. While at this home, near Corydon, I wrote an application to the President of the United States for a pardon. I frankly stated in the application that I had been one of the raiders from Canada and had endeavored to serve the cause of the South in every capacity. But that none of the expeditions from Canada had been a success.

I wrote a letter to my old friend John Barbee, at Louisville, and enclosed the application to the President. I suggested to Mr. Barbee that perhaps his influence would secure the intercession of George D. Prentice. In due time Mr. Barbee responded from his home at Pewee Valley, that he found Mr. Prentice willing to aid me, and that Prentice had mailed my application with his own personal letter to William H. Seward, Secretary of State.

I returned home in August, but visited around in the neighborhood so as to avoid arrest until I could hear from Washington City on the subject of a pardon.

One morning I went up to Nebo and in a little while rode down to Providence. I then went on home. I found quite a crowd of neighbors here in the orchard, who were engaged with a steam thrasher in thrashing my father's crop of wheat. Of this crowd some were Union men and some were Southern sympathizers, but all were my friends. The weather was hot and I strolled out to the orchard in my shirt-sleeves. I had hardly finished a greeting to all, and some of them I had not seen since the war began, when Phil, my darky friend, told me that the Yankees were up at Mr. Sandy Johnson's. I got a glimpse of them, the distance being only three hundred yards, and started at full speed around the dwelling to a cornfield of some thirty acres bounded on the outside by woods. I soon reached the woods, having followed a cross-fence on the grass so as to leave no tracks. I climbed a medium-sized sugar tree, with dense foliage. From a position near its top I had a view of our house, the orchard, and Mr. Johnson's house. I saw the Federals ride along the public road in front of the house and pass out of sight on the road to Burnett's bridge. I then went around to the left to Johnson's house and made inquiries. The Federals had asked for water and the distance to some place across Clear Creek. I then walked along the lane to my father's place, climbing over his fence. I had not gone more than fifty yards inside before I was halted. There were four of the Federals. They had made a circuit in the woods and returned to a point from which they could see me if I came in sight.

They dismounted, and approaching me said I was a prisoner. I agreed to it cheerfully. I knew them all—Harrison Gill, George Peyton, William Peyton, and Daniel Matthews. They shook hands and seemed glad to see me. I invited them cordially to walk on to the orchard with me, saying I would be ready to go with them in a few minutes. They were kindly greeted by all present and it was getting to be a pleasant occasion. At this time I observed my uncle, Captain Headley, coming to the dwelling from the barnyard. He had survived the war and lived four miles from our home. He came on through the yard to the orchard. The soldiers greeted him kindly, but I could see that he did not enjoy the situation. William Peyton was the pilot of the Federal company that captured my uncle at Dixon, in 1863, and wanted to shoot him after he became a prisoner. Still, Peyton was a jovial sort of man and felt generous now since it appeared that he was to march me away a captive to Madisonville. He told me that I was arrested on orders from Bowling Green. These Federal soldiers all lived near Rose Creek, only two miles from Nebo, and I had known them well before the war.

I then, in a familiar way, called Harrison Gill to come with me as a guard to the house to get my clothes, and we would start. He assented and the others remained with the crowd. I explained to my distressed mother, in Gill's presence, that I thought I would only have to go to Madisonville and would return within a day or two. She set to work packing my garments, etc., in a pair of saddle-bags in her bed-room.

The house had two rooms in front with a large hall between. A stairway ran up in the hall and my room was up-stairs. One of the lower rooms was my mother's. I told Gill to stand in the hall while I went up for my baggage. When I reached my room and got my pistol my first impulse was to go down and get the drop on Gill and disarm him. But I thought it would end in a general fight, which I preferred to avoid in the presence of my mother and the children, if I could escape otherwise. I concluded to hide my pistol and try another plan. I went down in a jolly mood, passed Gill in the hall, and stepped into my mother's room, giving her some collars, etc., to put in my baggage. Gill was standing at the hall door and I asked him what kind of smoking-tobacco he had. I didn't fancy his chewing twist and went to the mantel and began to fill my pipe. I was so friendly with Gill that he began to look as if he was sorry to take me. He began to walk slowly back and forth from the front to the rear door of the hall. Mrs. Gore, a neighbor, was sitting in the dining-room, in the ell part of the house, and I called to her to please have a coal of fire sent me from the kitchen to light my pipe.

While I was waiting I observed that the sash was hoisted in a window near the fireplace and a solid curtain hung down over it full length. Just as Gill passed the hall door going to the rear I stepped to the window, lifted the curtain, put one foot out and went through, letting the curtain drop behind me. I sprang over the yard fence into the barnyard, and screened by a rail fence for some eighty yards it was only a minute or two until I was in the cornfield. I heard no noise behind and stopped behind the fence to look back. I heard Gill shouting to his comrades on the other side of the house. I now followed the cross-fence on the grass as I had done in the forenoon. I climbed the same sugar tree and had a plain view of the scene in the orchard. I observed the soldiers going in and around the house, but it appeared they had not discovered my trail. I got down and proceeded through the woods across Wier's Creek flats toward Providence and safely reached the house of my friend Daniel Head, Jr.

I decided to go to Tennessee. I traveled the old trail at night to the home of Mr. Ellis Suttle near Murfreesboro. Before my departure, Miss Mary Overall arrived, en route to Triune, her home, from a visit to relatives on the other side of Murfreesboro. She related to me many stories of the conduct of the Federals about Triune and in this section. One of General Joel A. Battle's daughters, Miss Fannie, on account of aid and hospitality to Confederates, had been arrested and after an imprisonment at Nashville had been forwarded under guard by way of Washington City to Grant's army in Virginia and then banished through the lines of the Confederates to Richmond.

Mrs. Cherry, the widow near whose home I had camped when General Morgan sent me to the vicinity of Nashville in the spring of 1864, had also been in trouble the past winter. Her son, Buck Cherry, who was a Confederate and had operated with Dee Jobe, Frank Battle, and others against the Federals, was at home one winter night when the Federal cavalry surrounded the house at midnight. By a rush he escaped. The Federals then set fire to the house and burned it to the ground with all else of any value. Mrs. Cherry was put on a horse and carried off, reaching Franklin the next morning, where she was put in prison. She was afterwards sent to Nashville and imprisoned in a room at the penitentiary. It was a bitter cold night but the buildings made a good fire for Mrs. Cherry's five children, who huddled around it until some of the neighbors ventured to the scene and made provision for their comfort.

Some weeks afterward the trouble began to spread in that locality. It happened that Mr. Trammell, a Confederate soldier going south, found himself among the enemy's cavalry near Wartrace and was killed. General Milroy, in reading the letters he carried, came upon one from Miss Overall signed "Mollie." Mrs. Dollie Battle, the young widow of General Battle's son who had been killed at Shiloh, and Miss Sallie Battle immediately rode on horseback to Wartrace, a distance of forty-five miles, to endeavor to recover the body of Trammell and have him decently buried. General Milroy at once accused them of writing the letter signed "Mollie," and of sending the horse, Selam, to Van Houton. They were promptly arrested and imprisoned in a room of the residence. Day after day they were brought out to Milroy's headquarters and confronted with the accusation, but they persistently denied the charge, and persistently refused to tell that Miss Overall was the authoress. Mrs. Battle was a native of Chillicothe, Ohio, and three of her brothers were in the Federal Army. But she had become intensely Southern and had refused to meet a brother while in prison at Nashville.

It happened that Lieutenant Sheets, of Chillicothe, was stationed at Murfreesboro. He had been a friend of Mrs. Battle before her marriage, just prior to the war. The imprisonment of the ladies became notorious, and Lieutenant Sheets heard if it. Through his superior officers he managed to have the prisoners sent to Nashville. Miss Overall had heard of the trouble and wrote General Rousseau, at Nashville, the facts. Rousseau thought the matter should be dropped, but forwarded the papers to General Thomas at Chattanooga. General Thomas ordered the arrest of Miss Overall. A detachment of cavalry was then sent to Triune to bring her to Nashville. She was accompanied by her sister, Sophia, who proposed to share the prison fate of her sister.

Captain Goodwin, the provost-marshal, who had not been courteous before, now told them that Miss Overall would occupy the room with the Battle girls. This was satisfactory and she was sent in an ambulance under guard to the penitentiary. It turned out, however, that Captain Goodwin sent along a note to Colonel Barrett, who commanded at the penitentiary, instructing him to put Miss Overall in the room with Mrs. Cherry and not allow her to see the Battles.

The next day Mrs. Cherry was taken to headquarters for trial and was set at liberty. This left Miss Overall alone, but Colonel Barrett told her then that he would stretch his orders from Captain Goodwin and allow her to come out in the hall upon her promise not to speak to the Battle girls.

After Miss Overall had been confined here for about two weeks, her uncle, Mr. Ned Jordan, a banker of Murfreesboro and a Union man, came to Nashville and secured her release.

Adjutant-General J. G. Parkhurst of Detroit, Michigan, went out to the prison in a carriage to bring Miss Overall to headquarters, but she declined his kindness and rode alone in the ambulance under guard of the soldiers. She was required to take the oath of allegiance, however, to which she had no serious objection now. It was the 1st of May, 1865, and the war was over. Mrs. Battle and Miss Battle were kept in prison for two weeks afterward, when they were released without any trial.

There were many similar proceedings all over the South. Still, these faithful people loved their own country and its defenders. They could not help or suppress the sentiment for either and suffered in consequence according to the nature of the Federal commander.

General Rousseau did not favor the policy of persecution, and except for his lenient disposition the citizens of Nashville and the surrounding country would, at that period, have been subjected to a much harsher fate.

The conduct of General E. A. Paine, at Gallatin, had been merciless toward both sexes, old and young. Before the war ended he was arraigned for trial by a military court and found guilty, but was rescued by a pardon from President Lincoln.

But the most aggravating conduct of the Federals, toward the miserable people of this and all other sections of the South, was the employment of the slaves as soldiers and sending them around, under Northern officers, in their old neighborhoods to taunt, pillage, and burn out the families that had raised them. These licensed detachments would take possession of a house and drive the family out with pompous airs and then smash and pillage till satisfied, when the torch would be applied and everything reduced to ashes. The jolly soldiers would then march away singing "John Brown's body lies moldering," etc., and other favorite songs.

The darkies were organized in large numbers at Nashville, and after the retreat of Hood in December were sent all over the Murfreesboro country to take and destroy the remnants that might still be left among the people. Several of these crowds had been caught that had committed depredations and were loaded with plunder.

The Federal authorities report an instance, but it will be observed that they carefully omit the business in which the detachments were engaged. Lieutenant Fitch, an *acting assistant quartermaster,* with some colored infantry, had business out in the country, fourteen miles southeast of Murfreesboro, when a party of Forrest's men caught him, two other white officers, and thirteen colored men. They seemed to have been detailed to go with him, as he appears to be in doubt as to the command to which they belonged. It also appears that some of the same class in another crowd were caught, who belonged to General Steadman's command, at Murfreesboro. It will be remembered that General Steadman commenced burning farm-houses, barns, etc., in this country in 1863. But I will let Lieutenant Fitch tell his story:

NASHVILLE, TENN., January 3, 1865.
Maj. WILLIAM INNES,
Assistant Commissioner, Organizing U. S. Colored Troops.
MAJOR: The following report of my capture and subsequent attempted murder is respectfully submitted for your information:

I was captured on the 20th of December, FOURTEEN MILES IN A SOUTHEASTERLY DIRECTION FROM MURFREESBORO, in company with two other officers, Lieut. D. G. Cooke, Twelfth U. S. Colored Infantry, and Capt. Charles G. Penfield, Forty-fourth U. S. Colored Infantry, by a company of scouts belonging to Forrest's command, numbering thirty-six men, commanded by Captain Harvey. As soon as captured we were robbed of everything of any value, even to clothing. We were kept under guard for three days with some other prisoners (private soldiers of General Steadman's division, *who were captured near Murfreesboro*) until we reached a small town called Lewisburg, some eighteen miles south of Duck River. There the officers were sent under a guard of four men to report, as I supposed, to General Forrest's headquarters. The guard told (me) that was their destination. They took us along the pike road leading from Lewisburg to Mooresville, about four miles, and then left the road and turned to the right for the purpose, as they said, of stopping at a neighboring house for the night.

After leaving the road about half a mile, as we were walking along through a wooded ravine, the man in advance of us halted, partially turned his horse, and as I came up, drew his revolver and fired at me without a word. The ball entered my right ear just above the center, passed through and lodged in the bone back of the ear. It knocked me senseless for a few moments. I soon recovered, however, but lay perfectly quiet, knowing that my only hope lay in leading them to believe they had killed me. Presently I heard two carbine shots, and then all was still. After about fifteen minutes I staggered to my feet and attempted to get away, but found I could not walk. About that time a colored boy came along and helped me to a house near by. He told me that the other two officers were dead, having been shot through the head. That evening their bodies were brought to the house where I lay. Next morning they were decently buried on the premises of Col. John C. Hill, near by.

The shooting occurred on the 22d, and on the 23d, about midday, one of Forrest's men came to the house where I was lying and inquired for me; said that he came to kill me. The man of the house said that it was entirely unnecessary, as I was so severely wounded that I would die anyway, and he expected I would not live over an hour. He then went away, saying that if I was not dead by morning I would be killed. After he left I was moved by the neighbors to another house, and was moved nearly every night from one house to another until the 27th, when I was relieved by a party of troops sent from Columbia and brought within the Federal lines.

The privates were sent off on a road leading to the right of the one we took; about in the direction of Columbia, I should judge. I cannot but think they were killed, as about that time our forces occupied Columbia, the rebel army having retreated. There were twelve privates, belonging, I think, to Cruft's brigade.

Very respectfully, your obedient servant,

GEO. W. FITCH,

First Lieutenant, Twelfth U. S. Colored Infty., and A. A. Q. M.

I went down to Nashville in October to make some purchases, and stopped at the Commercial Hotel. After taking a seat in the dining-room, I had just finished giving my order for dinner, when looking around I observed Colonel Martin following a waiter to another table.

Martin had gone from New Orleans to Cuba and thence to Canada by sea, after leaving me at Alpine, Alabama, in June. He found nothing to do as an exile in Canada and had passed through the United States to Washington, Georgia, and had been sojourning at the country home of Mr. Henry Wynn for two weeks. He was now en route to his home in Kentucky.

When I had given Martin a full understanding of the situation in Kentucky we agreed that we had no prospect for peace at home. We finally concluded, in view of the summary hanging of people in different sections and the prospective execution of Mr. Davis and Mr. Clay, that we would go up in the Northwest on the border and engage in some employment under assumed names.

Martin had left Gen. John C. Breckinridge at Toronto, teaching a class in law, and among his pupils were Captain Hines, Lieutenants Young and Eastin.

It was agreed that I should go back to Mr. Suttle's for my horse and ride through to Kentucky, while Martin would proceed by Bowling Green and thence down Green River on a boat to Paradise, near his father's home. Martin expected to get some money at home, as his exchequer was about exhausted. We agreed to meet at the house of Dr. William Jenkins, near Slaughtersville in Webster County, Kentucky, on a stated night, and if either should be delayed the other would wait.

I hurried through to my father's house, arriving after dark, and felt safe at least for a night. The moment our greeting was over my mother rushed to her bureau and back with a large envelope. It contained my pardon from President Johnson.

Two days afterward Captain Temp. Martin, ex-Union soldier, arrived from Muhlenburg County to tell me that his brother got home safely but the house was surrounded that night and Colonel Bob was carried off a prisoner to Louisville. He had been recognized at Bowling Green and a detail had followed to make his arrest.

I, being free, was disposed to identify myself with his friends to assist him in his troubles. Captain Martin returned home and friends were sent to Louisville who might have influence with the authorities and look after the comfort of Colonel Martin. But it was found that Colonel Martin had been put in irons at Louisville; and it was also learned that he had been arrested on orders from New York.

Gen. Walter C. Whittaker, an ex-Union officer of Louisville, had been engaged as one of the attorneys to defend Martin.

It was now about the middle of November, 1865.

CHAPTER XLV

Robert M. Martin pardoned—Many sentences remitted—Parole of C. C. Clay, Jr.—Jefferson Davis delivered to United States Court at Richmond—Released on bail-bond—Ovation to Mr. Davis in the South—*Nolle prosequi* entered—Finally settles in Mississippi to spend his last years—Visit to birthplace in Kentucky—Subsequent lives of Confederate officers who served in Canada.

The public sentiment of the North now became aroused against the further prosecutions of individuals, and President Johnson proceeded gradually to discharge large numbers not yet tried, and many noted prisoners who had been confined at hard labor in penitentiaries. Among the prisoners who were in irons or close confinement and awaiting trial was Colonel Robert M. Martin, at Fort Lafayette. The President granted him an unconditional pardon, which was issued in the summer of 1866, after a wretched confinement of about seven months.

Many orders were issued of this class, to-wit:

WAR DEPARTMENT, ADJUTANT-GENERAL'S OFFICE,
Washington, March 10, 1866.
General Court-Martial Orders, No. 71.

In the case of Robert M. Harrover, citizen, sentenced by a military commission "to be shot to death by musketry, at such time and place as the Secretary of War may direct, two-thirds of the commission concurring therein," which sentence was commuted "to confinement at hard labor in the penitentiary for ten years," as promulgated in General Court-Martial Orders, No. 314, War Department, Adjutant-General's Office, October 3, 1864, the sentence is hereby remitted, and he will be paroled, as recommended by Lieutenant-General Grant, upon taking the oath of allegiance.

By order of the President of the United States:
E. D. TOWNSEND,
Assistant Adjutant-General.

EXECUTIVE OFFICE,
Washington, D. C., February 26, 1866.—12 m.

ALEXANDER H. STEPHENS, Crawfordville, Ga.:

Your letter of the 5th instant just received. The parole heretofore granted you is hereby amended so as to permit you to visit Washington, D. C., and such other places in the United States as your business may render necessary, subject to the conditions imposed in said parole.

ANDREW JOHNSON,
President of the United States.

The trial of prominent citizens of the North who were in sympathy with the South may be understood from the following cases, to-wit:

HEADQUARTERS DISTRICT OF INDIANA,
Indianapolis, Ind., May 31, 1865.

General Orders, No. 37.

The execution of General Orders, No 27, dated Headquarters District of Indiana, Indianapolis, May 9, 1865, having been suspended by the following telegram, dated Washington, May 16, 1865, to-wit:

"WASHINGTON, May 16, 1865.

"Brevet Major-General HOVEY:

"I have commuted the sentence of death of Horsey to imprisonment at hard labor for life. You will suspend the execution of Milligan and Bowles until Friday, June 2.

"A. JOHNSON,
"President."

Said order is, in accordance with said telegraphic order, so modified as to be:

William A. Bowles, citizen of the State of Indiana, will be hanged by the neck until he be dead, on Friday, the 2d day of June, 1865, between the hours of 12 o'clock m. and 3 o'clock p. m., on the parade grounds between Camp Morton and Burnside Barracks, near the city of Indianapolis, Ind. Bvt. Brig.-Gen. Ambrose A. Stevens, commanding Camp Morton and Burnside Barracks, is charged with the execution of this order, and will make report thereof to the commanding general.

Lambdin P. Milligan, citizen of the State of Indiana, will be hanged by the neck until he be dead, on Friday, the 2d day of

June, 1865, between the hours of 12 o'clock m. and 3 o'clock p. m., on the parade grounds between Camp Morton and Burnside Barracks, near the city of Indianapolis, Ind. Bvt. Brig.-Gen. Ambrose A. Stevens, commanding Camp Morton and Burnside Barracks, is charged with the execution of this order, and will make report thereof to the commanding general.

Stephen Horsey, citizen of the State of Indiana, will be confined at hard labor during the term of his natural life, and the penitentiary at Columbus, Ohio, is designated as the place of his confinement. He will be sent under guard to said penitentiary with a copy of this order, together with a copy of General Orders, No. 27, current series, from these headquarters, of which this order is a modification. Lieutenant-Colonel John H. Gardner, Seventeenth Regiment Veteran Reserve Corps, commanding post, Indianapolis, Ind., will cause the order in this case to be executed.

By command of Bvt. Maj.-Gen. Alvin P. Hovey:

J. W. WALKER,
Major and Assistant Adjutant-General.

HEADQUARTERS DISTRICT OF INDIANA,
Indianapolis, Ind., June 2, 1865.
General Orders, No. 38.

The sentence of general court martial, as promulgated in General Orders, No. 27, dated Headquarters District of Indiana, Indianapolis, May 9, 1865, and the commutation thereof, as promulgated in General Orders, No. 37, dated Headquarters District of Indiana, Indianapolis, Ind., May 31, 1865, having been further commuted, by telegram, of which the following is an extract, to-wit:

"WASHINGTON, May 30, 1865—9.30 p. m.
"Major-General HOVEY:

"The President of the United States orders that the sentence of death, heretofore passed against Horsey, Bowles, and Milligan, be commuted to imprisonment of each at hard labor in the penitentiary during his life. The penitentiary at Columbus, Ohio, is designated as the place of imprisonment. * * *

"E. M. STANTON,
"Secretary of War."

Now, therefore, in accordance with said telegram, William A. Bowles, Lambdin P. Milligan, and Stephen Horsey, citizens of the State of Indiana, will be confined at hard labor during

the terms of their and each of their natural lives, at the penitentiary at Columbus, Ohio. The prisoners will be sent under guard to said penitentiary with a copy of this order, together with said General Orders, Nos. 27 and 37, current series, from these headquarters. Lieut.-Col. John H. Gardner, Seventeenth Regiment Veteran Reserve Corps, commanding post, Indianapolis, Ind., will cause this sentence to be executed.
By command of Bvt. Maj.-Gen. Alvin P. Hovey:

J. W. WALKER,
Major and Assistant Adjutant-General.

(Enclosure.)

OFFICE OHIO PENITENTIARY,
Columbus, Ohio, June 2, 1865.
Received of Lieut.-Col. John H. Gardner, commanding post, Indianapolis, Ind., the following named prisoners, with copies of General Orders, No. 27, No. 37, and No. 38, to-wit:
William A. Bowles, Lambdin P. Milligan, and Stephen Horsey (three).

JOHN A. PRENTICE,
Warden.

A $2.00 case in Maryland is an instance of the proceedings against citizens for giving "aid and comfort" to Confederates:

WAR DEPARTMENT, ADJUTANT-GENERAL'S OFFICE,
Washington, June 1, 1865.
General Court-Martial Orders, No. 260.
I. Before a general court martial which convened at Washington, D. C., May 2, 1865, pursuant to Special Orders, No. 196, dated War Department, Adjutant-General's Office, Washington, May 1, 1865, and of which Maj.-Gen. J. G. Foster, U. S. Volunteers, is president, was arraigned and tried—
Benjamin G. Harris, citizen.
Charge: Violation of the 56th Article of War.
Specification 1. In this, that Benjamin G. Harris, a citizen of Maryland, and a member of the Congress of the United States, did relieve, with money, to-wit, the sum of $2.00, the public enemy, to-wit, Sergt. Richard Chapman and Private William Read, of Company K, Thirty-second Regiment Virginia Infantry, soldiers of the Army of the so-called Con-

federate States of America, then in rebellion against and at war with the United States, he, the said Harris, then and there well knowing said Chapman and Read to be soldiers of said Army, and treating and offering to relieve them as such, and at the same time advising and inciting them to continue in said Army and to make war against the United States, and emphatically declaring his sympathy with the enemy and his opposition to the Government of the United States in its efforts to suppress the rebellion. This at or near Leonardtown, Saint Mary's County, Md., on or about April 26, 1865.

Specification 2. In this, that Benjamin G. Harris, a citizen of Maryland and a member of the Congress of the United States, did knowingly harbor and protect the public enemy, to-wit, Sergt. Richard Chapman and Private William Read, of Company K, Thirty-second Regiment Virginia Infantry, soldiers of the Army of the so-called Confederate States of America, then in rebellion against and at war with the United States, by procuring them to be lodged and fed in a private house, and furnishing them with money therefor, he, the said Harris, then and there well knowing said Chapman and Read to be soldiers of said Army, and treating them, and offering and giving them money as such, and at the same time advising and inciting them to continue in said Army and to make war against the United States, and emphatically declaring his sympathy with the enemy and his opposition to the Government of the United States in its efforts to suppress the rebellion. This at or near Leonardtown, Saint Mary's County, Md., on or about April 26, 1865.

To which charge and specification the accused, Benjamin G. Harris, citizen, pleaded not guilty.

FINDING.

The court, having maturely considered the evidence adduced, finds the accused, Benjamin G. Harris, citizen, as follows:

Of the first specification, guilty.

Of the second specification, guilty, except as to the words, 'and fed in a private house.'

Of the charge, guilty.

SENTENCE.

And the court does therefore sentence him, Benjamin G. Harris, citizen, to be forever disqualified from holding any office or place of honor, trust, or profit under the United States, and to be imprisoned for three years in the penitentiary at Albany, N. Y., or at such other penitentiary as the Secretary of War may designate.

II. The record in the foregoing case of Benjamin G. Harris, citizen, was transmitted to the Secretary of War, and by him submitted to the President of the United States. The following are the orders of the President in the case:

"EXECUTIVE OFFICE, May 31, 1865.

"In the within case of Benjamin G. Harris the findings and sentence of the court are hereby approved and confirmed. Additional evidence and affidavits, however, bearing upon this case and favorable to the accused having been presented to and considered by me since the sentence aforesaid, I deem it proper to direct that the sentence in the case of said Harris be remitted and that he be released from imprisonment.

"ANDREW JOHNSON."

III. In accordance with the foregoing order Benjamin G. Harris, citizen, will be immediately released from imprisonment.

By order of the President of the United States:

E. D. TOWNSEND,
Assistant Adjutant-General.

WAR DEPARTMENT, ADJUTANT-GENERAL'S OFFICE,
Washington, April 10, 1866.

Warden of Ohio State Penitentiary, Columbus, Ohio:

You will please discharge from custody William A. Bowles, Lambdin P. Milligan, and Stephen Horsey, confined in the Columbus Penitentiary for life, under orders of the President, dated May 30, 1865, the President having remitted further execution of the sentence.

By order of the President of the United States:

E. D. TOWNSEND,
Assistant Adjutant-General.

WAR DEPARTMENT, ADJUTANT-GENERAL'S OFFICE,
Washington, D. C., April 17, 1866.

General Court-Martial Orders, No. 104.

Frank B. Gurley, citizen, sentenced by a military commission "to be hanged by the neck until he is dead, at such time and place as the general commanding may order, two-thirds of the members of the commission concurring in said sentence," as promulgated in General Court-Martial Orders, No. 505, War Department, Adjutant-General's Office, September 6,

CHARLES C. HEMMING
1902

1865, upon the recommendation of Lieutenant-General Grant, is hereby released from confinement and will be placed upon his parole as a prisoner of war duly exchanged.

E. D. TOWNSEND,
Assistant Adjutant-General.

Meanwhile, the Confederates and persons sentenced by military commissions had been released from the Northern prisons and a large number of pardons had been granted by the President as shown by the following correspondence:

EXECUTIVE MANSION,
Washington, D. C., June 5, 1866.
Hon. EDWIN M. STANTON, Secretary of War.

SIR: The President directs me to request that you will cause to be prepared, for his information, statements showing—

First. The number of prisoners of war discharged since the 15th day of April, 1865; and

Second. The number of persons who, having been sentenced by military commission or court martial, have been pardoned since the 15th day of April, 1865.

I have the honor to be, very respectfully,
Your obedient servant,
WM. G. MOORE,
Assistant Adjutant-General.

WAR DEPARTMENT,
Washington City, June 15, 1866.
The President of the United States.

MR. PRESIDENT: In compliance with your instructions of the 5th instant I have the honor to make the following statements:

"The number of prisoners of war discharged since the 15th day of April, 1865," is 5,501 officers, 53,679 enlisted men, and 1,220 citizens, and "the number of persons who, having been sentenced by military commission or court martial, have been pardoned since the 15th day of April, 1865," is 1,953.

Very respectfully, your obedient servant,
EDWIN M. STANTON,
Secretary of War.

C. C. Clay, Jr., was released from prison upon the following order, to-wit:

War Department, Adjutant-General's Office,
Washington, April 17, 1866.—4.45 p. m.
Maj.-Gen. N. A. Miles, Commanding, etc., Fort Monroe, Va.:
Clement C. Clay, Jr., is hereby released from confinement and permitted to return to and remain in the State of Alabama and to visit such other places in the United States as his personal business may render absolutely necessary upon the following conditions, viz: That he takes the oath of allegiance to the United States and gives his parole of honor to conduct himself as a loyal citizen of the same, and to report himself in person at any time and place to answer any charges that may hereafter be preferred against him by the United States.
By order of the President of the United States:

E. D. Townsend,
Assistant Adjutant-General.

Finally the following writ was issued and served upon the President and General Burton:

May 1, 1867.
The President of the United States to Brig.-Gen. Henry S. Burton, and to any other person or persons having the custody of Jefferson Davis, greeting:
We command you that you have the body of Jefferson Davis, by you imprisoned and detained, as it is said, together with the cause of such imprisonment and detention, by whatsoever name the said Jefferson Davis may be called or charged, before our Circuit Court of the United States for the District of Virginia at the next term thereof, at Richmond, in the said district, on the second Monday of May, 1867, at the opening of the court on that day, to do and receive what shall then and there be considered concerning the said Jefferson Davis.
Witnesses Salmon P. Chase, our Chief Justice of our Supreme Court of the United States, this the first day of May, in the year of one thousand eight hundred and sixty-seven.
(Seal.)   W. H. Barry,
Clerk of the Circuit Court of the
United States for the District
of Virginia.

A true copy:
W. A. Duncan,
Deputy Marshal.

Allowed May 1, 1867.

John Underwood,
District Judge.

CAPTAIN THOMAS H. HINES
1884

The following order was issued in response:

WAR DEPARTMENT, ADJUTANT-GENERAL'S OFFICE,
Washington, May 8, 1867.

Bvt. Brig.-Gen. H. S. BURTON, U. S. Army, or Commanding
Officer, Fort Monroe, Old Point Comfort, Va.

SIR: The President of the United States directs that you
surrender Jefferson Davis, now held in confinement under
military authority at Fort Monroe, to the United States marshal
or his deputies, upon any process which may issue from the
Federal court in the State of Virginia.

You will report the action taken by you under this order,
and forward a copy of any process which may be served upon
you to this office.

By order of the President:

E. D. TOWNSEND,
Assistant Adjutant-General.

Mr. Davis was delivered into the custody of the United
States Court at Richmond, Virginia, on the 13th day of May,
1867, when he executed a bond for $100,000 for his appear-
ance when wanted and was then released. His bondsmen
were Cornelius Vanderbilt, Gerritt Smith, and Horace
Greeley, all of New York.

The people of Richmond at once received Mr. Davis with
the heartiest ovation and all the kindness that it was possible
to bestow. The gates were wide open, in his own loved
South, to the manly sufferer now returning from his lonely
dungeon home.

In December, 1868, a *nolle prosequi* was entered in the
case and Jefferson Davis, at 59 years of age, was again at
personal liberty to resume his walk of life among his fellow-
men. The proud spirit of this heroic character had not been
broken by the days and years of torture nor by the taunts and
gibes of merciless foes.

It was a day of joy in which every Southern bosom
swelled with veneration and love that knew no bounds. The
gifted and chivalrous Chieftain survived for many years an
honored and unpretentious example of exemplary citizen-

ship. His last years were devoted to historic work and a tranquil home life at a beautiful retreat that fronted the Gulf of Mexico on the shore of Mississippi.

The honorable life of Jefferson Davis at this period served to inspire the vanquished people of the South with a spirit of proud submission to a woeful fate which they were powerless to avert and were doomed to suffer in sack-cloth and ashes.

Upon all occasions of fellowship and reunion, among the surviving Confederates in all parts of the South, Jefferson Davis and his wife and children were honored guests, and everywhere the wildest enthusiasm greeted their presence. In his last years he made a visit to his birthplace in Todd County, Kentucky. There were continued ovations along the route of his journey from Mississippi, at all the stations, and wherever the people could get a glimpse of his form they crowded forward to shake his hand and to shout a welcome and a "God bless you."

Mr. Davis died at New Orleans in 1889.

The character of the young Confederate officers and soldiers who operated from Canada may be estimated by their subsequent lives. I never met many of them after our separation in Canada. But I can report as to the four who were specially detailed by the Confederate Government, namely, Capt. Thomas H. Hines, Lieut. Bennett H. Young, Lieut.-Col. Robert M. Martin, and Lieut. John W. Headley, and of several others from Kentucky and some who were my friends in Toronto.

Capt. Thomas H. Hines became Chief Justice of Kentucky, and represented the capital, Frankfort, in the Constitutional Convention of 1890-1. He died in 1897, having ranked among the foremost lawyers of Kentucky.

Lieut. Bennett H. Young for a number of years was engaged in the railroad business. He was president of the Monon Route, a railroad from Louisville to Chicago; was president of the Louisville Southern Railroad Company, and

Colonel Bennett H. Young
1906

of the Kentucky and Indiana Bridge Company, which were constructed under his immediate management. He was a member from Louisville of the Constitutional Convention of 1890-1; is president of the Louisville Free Public Library, President of Board at the Confederate Home, and Major-General commanding the Confederate Veterans of Kentucky. Lieutenant Young has been promoted, like all the rest since the war, and is known far and near as Col. Bennett H. Young. Colonel Young is an attorney at law and enjoys wide fame as a popular orator. His home is at Louisville, Kentucky, 1906.

Col. Robert M. Martin, after his release from prison, in 1866, settled at Evansville, Indiana, and engaged in the tobacco warehouse business. In 1874 he removed to New York City. For fourteen years he was manager of tobacco inspections for David Dowes & Co., in their Brooklyn warehouses. He located at Louisville, Kentucky, in 1887, engaging in the tobacco brokerage business. In the fall of 1900, his old wound in the lung having produced frequent hemorrhages, his health gave way. He bade me good-by in October, 1900, upon his departure for New York, where he hoped some specialist might prolong his life, but he died on the 9th day of January, 1901. He was 61 years of age. The South did not have a better soldier in the ranks of its armies, and his friends never had a truer friend. In all the years of our companionship a harsh word never passed between us. Col. Robert M. Martin is buried in Greenwood Cemetery, New York City.

John W. Headley lives at Louisville, Kentucky. He has followed a business career, living since the war, two years at Nebo, Hopkins County, Kentucky; sixteen years at Evansville, Indiana, and twenty years at Louisville, Kentucky. During the latter period was Secretary of State of Kentucky, from September 1, 1891, to January 1, 1896.

I never met Captain Charles H. Cole and have not heard of him since his release from captivity.

Bennett G. Burley, the companion of John Yates Beall, returned to Scotland, his native land, after the war was over. In 1887 Lieut. Bennett H. Young was in England and met Burley in London. He was at that time a member of the British Parliament from Glasgow, Scotland.

Capt. John B. Castleman is a member of the firm of Barbee & Castleman, which has represented the Royal Insurance Company of Liverpool, for all the Southern States since the war. He was colonel of the Louisville Legion for many years, and twice Adjutant-General of Kentucky. Colonel Castleman commanded the Louisville Legion in the Spanish-American war, serving on the expedition of General Nelson A. Miles in Porto Rico. On his return from Porto Rico, Colonel Castleman was commissioned a brigadier-general by President McKinley. General Castleman has been president of the Board of Park Commissioners of Louisville since the creation of the board. Resides at Louisville, 1906.

Lieutenant George B. Eastin served as judge of the Court of Appeals of Kentucky, from the Louisville district. During a tour of Europe for his health, accompanied by his wife, he died in Italy. His remains were brought home and are buried in Cave Hill Cemetery, at Louisville.

Lieutenant James T. Harrington was an attorney of the Southern Pacific Railroad, and resided at Los Angeles, California, in 1896.

Lieutenant John T. Ashbrook resided at Cynthiana, Kentucky, 1905. 'He has followed a business career, principally insurance, and was for years adjuster for the Underwriters' Association for Kentucky and Tennessee.

W. Larry McDonald resided after the war in New York City, where he died some years ago.

Charles C. Hemming, the youngest of our party in Toronto, only 18 years old, resides at Colorado Springs, Colorado. He is vice-president of the El Paso National Bank of that city. A few years ago Hemming erected at his

JOHN B. CASTLEMAN
1898

own personal expense a Confederate monument at Jacksonville, Florida, which is regarded as one of the handsomest in the South.

Dr. Luke P. Blackburn located at Louisville, and was Governor of Kentucky from 1879 to 1883. He died a few years afterwards, leaving a name that is honored by Kentuckians.

William W. Cleary, secretary of the Confederate Commission in Canada, located at Covington, Kentucky, after the President's proclamation of general amnesty, and attained a notable eminence in the practice of law. He died in 1897.

Hon. Clement C. Clay, Jr., after his release from Fortress Monroe, where he was so long incarcerated with Mr. Davis, returned to his old home at Huntsville, Alabama. This distinguished United States Senator from Alabama at the beginning of the war, was endeared to the people of his native State and of the South, by reason of the prolonged and ignoble treatment which he had suffered, during the period when Judge-Advocate-General Joseph Holt was engaged with a corps of perjured and suborned witnesses for his conviction and execution at the hands of a military commission. Mr. Clay was among the foremost public men of the South.

Colonel Jacob Thompson, a typical Southern gentleman of the old school, settled at Memphis, Tennessee, after the war ended. Having served in the Cabinet of President Buchanan, and in the Congress of the United States from Mississippi, he now retired from public life. He was possessed of an ample private fortune, after losing hundreds of slaves and other property at Oxford, Mississippi. He spent his last years in comfort, and with the highest esteem of his fellow-citizens of Mississippi and Tennessee. Colonel Thompson was one of the closest personal friends of Jefferson Davis, and one of his ablest and most trusted friends during the war.

CHAPTER XLVI

The truth—The premises—Summary of conduct of the war—
Impartial testimony and views of Federal commanders—
Confederate success in battle—Troops engaged—Cause and
result of the war.

The war between the North and the South was deplorable
in all its consequences. There is no consolation in recalling
its darker phases and yet the truth of history may be due to
the dead, the living and the unborn, as a lesson and an
example in determining hereafter the price of peace and the
pretexts for war.

It has been my purpose to be faithful and conscientious in
presenting the truth as it appears from experience, observation, and from the official record of the events and the conduct of the war. But in order to anticipate to some extent
the deductions that reveal themselves in the narrative itself,
a summary may be made as collateral evidence.

It should not be a question of who was right or who was
wrong. The question should be, what occurred during the
war and what was the result?

The premises are that the Southern States seceded from
the Union and formed a new government called the Confederate States of America. The United States Government
treated this action as rebellion and the war followed. It
appears that about one-half of the Northern people were in
favor of the war to preserve the Union, *including those who
favored the war solely for the abolition of slavery, for hum-
bling the Southern people and for the founding of a nation—
a supreme government.* The latter class were in control,
and relying on the military power which was *readily ob-*

tained upon the idea of preserving the Union, they established a military espionage and authority over the North, and *inaugurated a war of conquest against the South.* This policy was announced by the proclamation of General John C. Fremont, in 1861, from his headquarters at St. Louis. Mr. Lincoln objected to the proclamation *upon the ground only that* it would injure their prospects in Kentucky and would provoke retaliation.

Every Federal commander after that time, it appears, was either retired or else, in greater or less degree, pursued the policy marked out by General Fremont, and no evidence is found in the official records that Mr. Lincoln ever again objected to any conduct of generals or armies; but on the contrary it appears that he either authorized or acquiesced in all that was ever done by either until it was apparent that the war was over, when he was ready and determined to extend such terms as would be honorable to the South.

After three years of desolating hostilities and failure to overcome the South in battle and by warfare on non-combatants, General Kilpatrick and Colonel Dahlgren were sent from Washington with orders to sack and burn Richmond, and to kill President Davis and his Cabinet. This occurred March 1st, 1864, at which time the Confederate authorities seem in no way to have attempted to retaliate upon the Northern people for the policy of devastation and the impoverishment of non-combatants in the captured territory of the Southern States. The inhabitants of Atlanta had been banished and the city appropriated by General Sherman before Captain Beall with twenty Confederate soldiers took possession of two steamers on Lake Erie for use in an effort to release the Confederate prisoners on Johnson's Island, for which Beall was hung, he having been captured at another period in the United States. And this was before twenty Confederates had frightened the inhabitants of St. Albans, Vermont, besides taking $200,000 from their banks. Atlanta was burned and General Sherman's order, No. 120, had been issued before the attempt was made by Confederate soldiers to burn New York City, for which Captain Kennedy was hung, he having been apprehended afterward in passing through the United States. The Shenandoah Valley of Virginia had been made a barren waste before General Early sent Colonel McCausland to burn Chambersburg, Pennsylvania. This appears to be the extent of all the retaliation that was ever inflicted by Confederates upon the Northern people, except the burning of steamboats at St. Louis and Louisville by Confederates under Capt. John B. Castleman.

The unsupported statements, which I have made as to the conduct of the war, would not be fair, and therefore I have relied upon the official records and the testimony of the foremost commanders of the Federal armies.

The Federal and Confederate official reports of all the important engagements of the war have been published by the War Department and in many histories of the conflict, and therefore but little account of battles has been attempted in this work.

A sufficient reference to the battles, the character of soldiers and forces engaged is found in the summaries of the result by Generals Don Carlos Buell and Ulysses S. Grant, the commanders at Pittsburg Landing, which are submitted.

General Don Carlos Buell says:

A philosophical study of our civil conflict must recognize that influences of some sort operated fundamentally for the side of the Confederacy in every prominent event of the war, and nowhere with less effect than in the Tennessee and Kentucky campaign. They were involved in the fact that it required enormous sacrifices for 24,000,000 of people to defeat the political scheme of 8,000,000; 2,000,000 of soldiers to subdue 800,000 soldiers; and, descending to details, a naval fleet and 15,000 troops to advance against a weak fort, manned by less than 100 men, at Fort Henry; 35,000 with naval co-operation to overcome 12,000 at Donelson; 60,000 to secure a victory over 40,000 at Pittsburg Landing; 120,000 to enforce the retreat of 65,000 entrenched, after a month of fighting and maneuvering, at Corinth; 100,000 repelled by 80,000 in the first Peninsular campaign against Richmond; 70,000, with a powerful naval force to inspire the campaign, which lasted nine months, against 40,000 at Vicksburg; 90,000 to barely withstand the assault of 70,000 at Gettysburg; 115,000 sustaining a frightful repulse from 60,000 at Fredericksburg; 100,000 attacked and defeated by 50,000 at Chancellorsville; 85,000 held in check two days by 40,000 at Antietam; 43,000 retaining the field uncertainly against 38,000 at Stone River; 70,000 defeated at Chickamauga, and beleaguered by 70,000 at Chattanooga; 80,000 merely to break the investing line of 45,000 at Chattanooga; 100,000 to press back 50,000, increased at last to 70,000, from Chattanooga to Atlanta, a distance of 120 miles, and then let go—an operation which is commemorated at festive reunions by the standing toast of "one hundred days under fire"; 50,000 to defeat the investing line of 30,000 at Nashville; and finally 120,000 to overcome 60,000 with exhaustion after a struggle of a year in Virginia. The rule which this summary establishes will determine absolutely the relative merit of the different achievements, but is not to be ignored in a judgment upon particular events.

* * * * * * *

The habits of the Southern people facilitated the formation of cavalry corps which were comparatively efficient even without instruction; and accordingly we see Stuart, and John Morgan, and Forrest riding with impunity around the Union armies, and destroying or harassing their communications.

* * * * * * *

At Cold Harbor, the Northern troops, who had proven their indomitable qualities by losses nearly equal to the whole force of their opponents, when ordered to another sacrifice, even under such a soldier as Hancock, answered the demand as one man, with a silent and stolid inertia; at Gettysburg, Pickett, when waiting for the signal which Longstreet dreaded to repeat, for the hopeless but immortal charge against Cemetery Hill, saluted and said, as he turned to his ready column: "I shall move forward, sir!"

General Grant in his Memoirs says:

After the fall of Petersburg, and when the armies of the Potomac and the James were in motion to head off Lee's army, the *morale* of the National troops had greatly improved. There was no more straggling, no more rear-guards. The men *who in former times had been falling back,* were now, as I have already stated, striving to get to the front.

* * * * * * *

In the North the press was free up to the point of open treason. The citizen could entertain his views and express them. Troops were necessary in the Northern States to prevent prisoners from the Southern army being released by outside force, armed and set at large to destroy by fire our Northern cities. * * * The copperhead disreputable portion of the press magnified rebel successes, and belittled those of the Union Army. It was, with a large following, an auxiliary to the Confederate Army. The North would have been much stronger with a hundred thousand of these men in the Confederate ranks and the rest of their kind thoroughly subdued, as the Union sentiment was in the South, than we were as the battle was fought.

As I have said, the whole South was a military camp. * * * The cause was popular, and was enthusiastically supported by the young men. * * * It would have been an offense, directly after the war, and perhaps it would be now, to ask any able-bodied man in the South, who was between the ages of fourteen and sixty at any time during the war, whether he had been in the Confederate Army. He would assert that he had, or account for his absence from the ranks. Under such circumstances it is hard to conceive how the North showed such a superiority of force in every battle fought. I know they did not.

* * * * * * *

I commanded the whole of the mighty host engaged on the victorious side. I was, no matter whether deservedly so or not, a representative of that side of the controversy.

General Grant says again in his Memoirs:

During 1862 and '3, John H. Morgan, a partisan officer, of no military education, but possessed of courage and endurance, operated in the rear of the Army of the Ohio in Kentucky and Tennessee. He had no base of supplies to protect, but was at home wherever he went. The army operating against the South, on the contrary, had to protect its lines of communication with the North, from which all supplies had to come to the front. Every foot of the road had to be guarded by troops stationed at convenient distances apart. These guards could not render assistance beyond the points where stationed. Morgan was foot-loose and could operate where his information—always correct—led him to believe he could do the greatest damage. During the time he was operating in this way he killed, wounded, and captured several times the number he ever had under his command at any one time. He destroyed many millions of property in addition. Places he did not attack had to be guarded as if threatened by him. Forrest, an abler soldier, operated farther west, and held from the National front quite as many men as could be spared for offensive operations. It is safe to say that more than half the National army was engaged in guarding lines of supplies, or were on leave, sick in hospital or on detail which prevented their bearing arms. Then, again, large forces were employed where no Confederate army confronted them. I deem it safe to say that there were no large engagements where the National numbers compensated for the advantage of position and entrenchment occupied by the enemy.

*   *   *   *   *   *   *

The cause of the war seems to be stated in a few lines fairly and candidly by General Grant, and that question is not considered in this work. He says:

The cause of the great War of the Rebellion against the United States will have to be attributed to slavery. For some years before the war began it was a trite saying among some politicians that "A State half slave and half free cannot exist." All must become slave or all free, or the State will go down. I took no part myself in any such view of the case at the time, but since the war is over, reviewing the whole question, I have come to the conclusion that the saying is quite true.

*   *   *   *   *   *   *

He (Stanton) was an able constitutional lawyer and jurist; but the Constitution was not an impediment to him while the war lasted. In this latter particular I entirely agree with the view he evidently held. The Constitution was not framed with a view to any such rebellion as that of 1861-5. While it did not authorize rebellion it made no provision against it. * * * The Constitution was therefore in abeyance for the time being, so far as it in any way affected the progress and termination of the war.

The enlistments in the Northern armies as reported by the Secretary of War were as follows:

NORTHERN STATES AND TERRITORIES.		SOUTHERN STATES.	
California	15,725	Alabama	2,576
Colorado	4,903	Arkansas	8,289
Connecticut	51,937	Delaware	11,236
Dakota	206	District of Columbia	11,912
Illinois	255,057	Florida	1,290
Indiana	193,748	Georgia	
Iowa	75,797	Kentucky	51,743
Kansas	18,069	Louisiana	5,224
Maine	64,973	Maryland	33,995
Massachusetts	122,781	Mississippi	545
Michigan	85,479	Missouri	100,616
Minnesota	23,913	New Mexico	6,561
Nebraska	3,157	North Carolina	3,156
Nevada	1,080	Tennessee	31,092
New Hampshire	32,930	Texas	1,965
New Jersey	67,500	Virginia	
New York	409,561	West Virginia	31,872
Ohio	304,814		
Oregon	1,810		
Pennsylvania	315,017		
Rhode Island	19,251		
Vermont	32,549		
Washington	964		
Wisconsin	91,029		
Total	2,199,081	Total	295,511

Total in Northern States	2,199,081
Total in Southern States	295,511
	2,494,592
Sailors and marines	101,207
Colored troops	178,975
Grand aggregate	2,774,774

Of the 2,199,081 white enlisted men from the Northern States it is fair, perhaps, to assume that less than half were volunteers. The Secretary of War reported on November 15, 1865, that 800,963 volunteers had been mustered out of the service. This number, perhaps, included colored troops. The Secretary of War reported on November 22, 1865, that Confederate soldiers had been surrendered and released on parole, as follows:

Army of Northern Virginia, commanded by Gen. R.
E. Lee.. 27,805
Army of Tennessee and others, commanded by Gen.
Joseph E. Johnston............................. 31,243
Gen. Jeff. Thompson's Army of Missouri............ 7,978
Miscellaneous paroles, Department of Virginia......... 9,072
Paroled at Cumberland, Maryland, and other stations.. 9,377
Paroled by Gen. Edward M. McCook in Alabama and
Florida 6,428
Army of the Department of Alabama, Gen. Richard
Taylor 42,293
Army of the Trans-Mississippi Department, Gen. E.
Kirby Smith.................................... 17,686
Paroled in the Department of Washington.......... 3,390
Paroled in Virginia, Tennessee, Alabama, Louisiana,
and Texas...................................... 13,922
Surrendered at Nashville and Chattanooga, Tennessee, 5,029

174,223

The following table, made from official returns, shows
the whole number of men enrolled (present and absent) in
the active armies of the Confederacy:

	Jan. 1, 1862.	Jan. 1, 1863.	Jan. 1, 1864.	Jan. 1, 1865.
Army of Northern Virginia......	84,225	144,605	92,050	155,772
Dep't of Richmond	....	7,820	8,494	16,601
Dep't of Norfolk	16,825	....	....	......
Dep't of the Peninsula..........	20,138	....	....	......
Dep't of Fredericksburg	10,645	....	....	......
Dep't of North Carolina........	13,656	40,821	9,876	5,187
Dep't of Miss. and E. La.......	4,390	73,114	46,906	32,148
Dep't of South Carolina and Ga..	40,955	27,052	65,005	53,014
Dep't of Pensacola	18,214	....	....	......
Dep't of New Orleans..........	10,318	....	....	......
Dep't of the Gulf..............	....	10,489	17,241	12,820
Western Department............	24,784	....	....	......
Army of Tennessee	....	82,799	88,457	86,995
Dep't of Kentucky	39,565	....	....	......
Dep't of East Tenn............	....	18,768	52,821	......
Dep't of Northwest	4,296	....	....	......
Dep't of Western Virginia......	....	10,116	18,642	7,138
Trans-Mississippi Department....	30,000	50,000	73,289	*70,000
Aggregate	318,011	465,584	472,781	439,675

*Estimated.

Very few, if any, of the local land forces, and none of the naval, are included in the tabular exhibit. If we take the 472,000 men in service at the beginning of 1864, and add thereto at least 250,000 deaths occurring prior to that date, it gives over 700,000.

CHAPTER XLVII

Conduct of Southern authorities and soldiers.

Among the results of the war was the overthrow, ruin and humiliation of the people of the South. Their property to the amount of two billions of dollars in negroes had been sacrificed. Untold millions of property of every description had been appropriated or destroyed. Barns, mills, homes, towns, and cities had been sacked and burned to ashes. The sufferings of women and children and of the aged cannot be told. They wandered, penniless and aimless, seeking subsistence, and shelter from the storms of all seasons and the winds of winter.

And now the surviving soldiers of the prisons and the armies, many of them tramping for weeks, reached at last the hills or the valleys where their homes had been in years gone by. But all was changed. Little was left of the remembered scene save ground and streams and sky. It will never be known how many returning war-worn boys have exclaimed like Thaddeus of Warsaw, "Oh, God! give me a shelter for my mother." The brave beaten soldiers could only sigh while the women and children wept for joy. But alas! how many of the host of the land would never come home? Many a mother and many a wife was looking and hoping for years for a soldier that never returned. Some were in the soldiers' sepulchre where they fell, with the sod thrown over the grave; some in a lonely spot of the woodland or field and some far away in the prison grounds of the clime of ice and snow; some under the willows of family graveyards and some in cemeteries the whole country over.

It was deemed a privilege to be alive in that ill-fated land. But in this hour of defeat and desolation there was little of reproof or of blame. It was a time of prayer with some and

of heart-crying with all. There was one consolation, however, in the Southern breast. The warfare of the South
had been honorable. It had been heroic. The Confederacy,
young in years and full of hope, had perished from the earth,
a star of Bethlehem in its day but a phantom now.

The archives of the Confederacy have been published and
there is not an order or a letter inconsistent with the character
of a chivalrous spirit. Every Confederate general and his
children may feel secure that the record is to his credit and
his honor. A number of the Confederate generals, notably
Robert E. Lee and Thomas J. Jackson, attained to world-
wide renown as among the greatest generals of any period
in the world's history and

> "Great not like Cæsar stained with blood,
> But only great as *they were* good."

But in all the list there does not appear to have been a
Butler, or Sherman, or Grant, or Milroy, or Paine, or Bur-
bridge, or Sheridan, or Merritt, or Hunter, or McNeil, or
Pope, or Stanley, or Grierson, or Wilson. There was not a
Howard or a Fifteenth Army Corps in the history of the
Confederacy; nor a Burnside, an Edwin M. Stanton, an H.
W. Halleck, a John A. Dix, and certainly not a Joseph Holt.
It is the fault of the official record if the facts of history are
not as they ought to be.

The authorities of the Confederate States appear, by the
record, to have exhausted all possible efforts for humane
and honorable warfare, and at no time to have manifested
any other disposition. President Davis to General Lee, of
General Pope's orders in 1862, said:

We find ourselves driven by our enemies in their steady
progress toward a practice which we abhor, and which we are
vainly struggling to avoid. Some of the military authorities
of the United States seem to suppose that better success will
attend a savage war in which no quarter is to be given and no
sex is to be spared than has hitherto been secured by such
hostilities as are alone recognized to be lawful by civilized men
in modern times.

For the present, we renounce our right of retaliation on the innocent, and shall continue to treat the private enlisted soldiers of General Pope's army as prisoners of war; but if, after notice to the Government at Washington of our confining repressive measures to the punishment only of commissioned officers, who are willing participants in these crimes, these savage practices are continued, we shall reluctantly be forced to the last resort of accepting the war on the terms chosen by our foes, until the outraged voice of a common humanity forces a respect for the recognized rules of war.

* * * * * * *

You are therefore instructed to communicate to the commander-in-chief of the armies of the United States the contents of this letter.

In a message to Congress on August 15, 1862, President Davis said:

* * ' * * * * *

Rapine and wanton destruction of private property, war upon non-combatants, murder of captives, bloody threats to avenge the death of an invading soldiery by the slaughter of unarmed citizens, orders of banishment against peaceful farmers engaged in the cultivation of the soil, are some of the means used by our ruthless invaders to enforce the submission of a free people to a foreign sway. Confiscation bills, of a character so atrocious as to insure, if executed, the utter ruin of the entire population of these States, are passed by their Congress and approved by their Executive.

* * * * * * *

Again, to Congress, in January, 1863, he said:

It is my painful duty again to inform you of the renewed examples of every conceivable atrocity committed by the armed forces of the United States at different points within the Confederacy, and which must stamp indelible infamy, not only on the perpetrators, but on their superiors, who, having the power to check these outrages on humanity, numerous and well authenticated as they have been, have not yet in a single instance, of which I am aware, inflicted punishment on the wrong-doers. Since my last communication to you, one General McNeil murdered seven prisoners of war in cold blood, and the demand for his punishment remains unsatisfied.

The Government of the United States, after promising examination and explanation in relation to the charges made against Gen. B. F. Butler, has, by its subsequent silence, after repeated efforts on my part to obtain some answer on the subject, not only admitted his guilt, but sanctioned it by acquiescence.   *   *   *   Recently I have received apparently authentic intelligence of another general by the name of Milroy, who has issued orders in West Virginia for the payment of money to him by the inhabitants, accompanied by the most savage threats of shooting every recusant, besides burning his house, and threatening similar atrocities against any of our citizens who shall fail to betray their country by giving him prompt notice of the approach of any of our forces. And this subject has also been submitted to the superior military authorities of the United States, with but faint hope that they will evince any disapprobation of the act.

*   *   *   *   *   *   *

In occupying Maryland General Lee issued a proclamation, which is somewhat in contrast with the proclamation of General Fremont in Missouri, in 1861:

HEADQUARTERS ARMY OF NORTHERN VIRGINIA,
        Near Fredericktown, September 8th, 1862.
To the People of Maryland:

*   *   *   *   *   *   *

Under the pretense of supporting the Constitution, but in violation of its most valuable provisions, your citizens have been arrested and imprisoned upon no charge, and contrary to all forms of law.   The faithful and manly protest against this outrage, made by the venerable and illustrious Marylander, to whom, in better days, no citizen appealed for right in vain, was treated with scorn and contempt.   The government of your chief city has been usurped by armed strangers; your Legislature has been dissolved by the unlawful arrest of its members; freedom of the press and of speech have been suppressed; words have been declared offenses by an arbitrary decree of the Federal Executive, and citizens ordered to be tried by a military commission for what they may dare to speak.

Believing that the people of Maryland possessed a spirit too lofty to submit to such a government, the people of the South have long wished to aid you in throwing off this foreign yoke, to enable you again to enjoy the inalienable rights of freemen, and restore independence and sovereignty to your State.

In obedience to this wish, our army has come among you, and is prepared to assist you with the power of its arms, in regaining the rights of which you have been despoiled. * * * No restraint upon your free will is intended—no intimidation will be allowed. We know no enemies among you, and *will protect all, of every opinion.* * * *

R. E. LEE,
General Commanding.

General Lee issued an order, in which he said:

HEADQUARTERS ARMY NORTHERN VIRGINIA,
Chambersburg, Pa., June 27, 1863.
General Orders, No. 73.
* * * * * * *

The General Commanding considers that no greater disgrace could befall the army, and through it, our whole people, than the perpetration of the barbarous outrages upon the innocent and defenseless, and the wanton destruction of private property, that have marked the course of the enemy in our own country. Such proceedings not only disgrace the perpetrators, and all connected with them, but are subversive of the discipline and efficiency of the army, and destructive of the ends of our present movements. It must be remembered that we make war only upon armed men, and that we cannot take vengeance for the wrongs our people have suffered, without lowering ourselves in the eyes of all those whose abhorrence has been excited by the atrocities of our enemy, and offending against Him to whom vengeance belongeth, without whose favor and support our efforts must all prove in vain.

The Commanding General, therefore, earnestly exhorts the troops to abstain, with most scrupulous care, from unnecessary or wanton injury to private property; and he enjoins upon all officers to arrest and bring to summary punishment all who shall in any way offend against the orders on this subject.

R. E. LEE,
General.

General Lee issued an address to his army, after Gettysburg, as follows:

HEADQUARTERS ARMY NORTHERN VIRGINIA,
(Hagerstown), July 11, 1863.
* * * * * * *

Once more you are called upon to meet the enemy from whom you have torn so many fields; names that will never die. Once more the eyes of your countrymen are turned upon you, and again do wives and sisters, fathers and mothers, and helpless children lean for defense on your strong arms and brave hearts. Let every soldier remember that on his courage and fidelity, depends all that makes life worth having, the freedom of his country, the honor of his people, and the security of his home. * * *

R. E. LEE,
General Commanding.

General Lee issued another address, as follows:

HEADQUARTERS ARMY NORTHERN VIRGINIA,
November 26, 1863.

The enemy is again advancing upon our Capital, and the country once more looks to this army for its protection. Under the blessings of God your valor has repelled every previous attempt, and invoking the continuance of His favor, we cheerfully commit to Him the issue of the coming conflict.

A cruel enemy seeks to reduce our fathers and our mothers, our wives, and our children, to abject slavery; to strip them of their property and drive them from their homes. Upon you these helpless ones rely to avert these terrible calamities, and secure to them the blessing of liberty and safety. Your past history gives them the assurance that their trust will not be in vain. Let every man remember that all he holds dear depends upon the faithful discharge of his duty, and resolve to fight and, if need be, to die, in defense of a cause so sacred and worthy the name won by this army on so many bloody fields.

R. E. LEE,
General.

Again the cause of the South is stated:

HEADQUARTERS ARMY OF NORTHERN VIRGINIA,
January 22, 1864.

General Orders, No. 7.

The Commanding General considers it due to the army to state that temporary reduction of rations has been caused by circumstances beyond the control of those charged with its support. Its welfare and comfort are the objects of his constant and earnest solicitude, and no effort has been spared to provide for its wants. It is hoped that the exertions now being made will render the necessity of short duration: but the history of the army has shown that the country can require no sacrifice too great for its patriotic devotion.

Soldiers! *you tread, with no unequal steps, the road by which your fathers marched through suffering, privation, and blood to independence!*

Continue to emulate in the future, as you have in the past, their patient endurance of hardships, their high resolve to be free, which no trial could shake, no bribe seduce, no danger appall: and be assured that the just God, who crowned their efforts with success, will, in His own good time, send down His blessing upon yours.

(Signed.) R. E. LEE,
General.

* * * * * * *

The record of General Lee appears to be the record of all the Confederate commanders. The survivors, and the descendants of all who suffered and died in vain for the South, need never hang their heads, or whisper to mankind, the true story of the battles, or of the Confederate record of humanity and honor in the conduct of the conflict for Southern independence.

The following lines were written by Philip Stanhope Wormsley, of Oxford University, England, in the dedication of his translation of Homer's Iliad to Gen. Robert E. Lee, "The most stainless of earthly commanders, and, except in fortune, the greatest."

> The grand old bard that never dies,
>   Receive him in our English tongue;
> I send thee, but with weeping eyes,
>   The story that he sung.
>
> Thy Troy is fallen, thy dear land
>   Is marred beneath the spoiler's heel;
> I cannot trust my trembling hand
>   To write the things I feel.
>
> Ah, realm of tombs! but let her bear
>   This blazon to the end of time.
> No nation rose so white and fair,
>   None fell so pure of crime.

The widow's moan, the orphan's wail
   Come round thee—but in truth be strong—
Eternal right, though all else fail,
   Can never be made wrong.

An angel's heart, an angel's mouth,
   Not Homer's, could alone for me
Hymn well the great Confederate South,
   Virginia first and Lee.